PREVENTING
DEADLY CONFLICT

Final Report

With Executive Summary

**CARNEGIE COMMISSION ON
PREVENTING DEADLY CONFLICT**

CARNEGIE CORPORATION OF NEW YORK

DECEMBER 1997

Suggested citation:
Carnegie Commission on Preventing Deadly Conflict, *Preventing Deadly Conflict: Final Report*
(Washington, DC: Carnegie Commission on Preventing Deadly Conflict, 1997).

On the World Wide Web: www.ccpdc.org
The Commission's Web site offers the full text of the final report and other Commission publications.
For ordering information, please consult the Web site.

Printed on acid-free paper.

ISBN: 1-8850-3901-8

Library of Congress Cataloging-in-Publication Data
Carnegie Commission on Preventing Deadly Conflict.
    Preventing deadly conflict: final report/Carnegie Commission on Preventing Deadly Conflict.
    p.   cm.
    Includes bibliographical references and index.
    ISBN 1-885039-01-9 (pbk.: alk. paper)
    1. Conflict management.   2. War.   I. Title.
JZ5595.C37 1998   98-29056
327.1'7--dc21   CIP

DEDICATION

His colleagues on the Carnegie Commission on Preventing Deadly Conflict join in dedication of this report to Cyrus R. Vance. He has devoted his life to preventing, alleviating, and resolving deadly conflict. His integrity, ingenuity, and compassion over many decades have provided inspiration to us and to our fundamental mission.

CONTENTS

FIGURES

TABLES

BOXES

PREFACE

It has been our privilege to lead a unique effort over the past three years, one that has been rooted in the spirit of Andrew Carnegie's quest for peace in the early part of the twentieth century. Carnegie, an authentic pioneer in both industry and philanthropy, searched for and sought to establish conditions and institutions conducive to durable peace. For this purpose he created four foundations, three peace palaces, and made many proposals for arbitration of international disputes, courts of various kinds—including the World Court—and an international police force. He provided ideas, buildings, and money for social action to overcome the perennial scourge of war. It was in this spirit that the Board of Trustees of Carnegie Corporation of New York created the Carnegie Commission on Preventing Deadly Conflict in 1994.

The Commission—16 international leaders and scholars with long experience and path-breaking accomplishments in conflict prevention and conflict resolution—deliberately sought a worldwide, long-term view and faced many fundamental issues of human conflict in all their complexity. The Commission sponsored research by leading scholars and policymakers and is disseminating the products of this work in a series of reports, background papers, and books. This final report will be disseminated throughout the world as a stimulus to preventive policies and actions at the highest levels of governments and international organizations.

We have worked closely as cochairs with Executive Director Jane Holl and her dedicated staff, who managed an enormous number of projects and meetings. The Commission also has a distinguished international Advisory Council of 42 eminent practitioners and scholars who have contributed their thoughtful advice. Altogether, the contributions of Commissioners, staff, and advisors have been immense, and we will continue to draw on these resources in the two years of follow-up to the Commission's work.

It is particularly interesting and relevant that many Commissioners have tried to help resolve very bitter conflicts, often at a late stage. We challenged ourselves in this enterprise to ask what might have been done at an early stage to avert mass violence and achieve a just outcome. These are very hard problems. If it were otherwise, prevention would have gained ascendancy long ago.

Prevention is based on long-range foresight, anticipation, and action. In this effort, the Commission used the best available knowledge to discern the major risk factors that increase the likelihood of mass violence. We then examined what steps might be taken to counteract or avoid the risk factors, especially through changes in the behavior of leaders and their constituencies. We focused attention on the pivotal institutions that can shape and support constructive behavior while avoiding the risk factors and dangerous directions. Thus, in seeking to prevent the deadly conflicts leading to mass violence, we explored ways in which governments, intergovernmental organizations, and the institutions of civil society could help to build favorable conditions in which different human groups can learn to live together amicably. The application of such prevention concepts in the public health sphere is familiar, for example, in the provision of immunizations through the combined efforts of institutions of scientific research, health care, and education. We have found a similar view of the prevention process useful in this arena of international conflict. The Commission had a vision of a worldwide system of conflict prevention.

Peace and equitable development will require not only effective institutions, but also greater understanding and respect for differences within and across national boundaries. We humans do not have the luxury any longer of indulging our prejudices and ethnocentrism. They are anachronisms of our ancient past. The worldwide historical record is full of hateful and destructive behavior based on religious, racial, political, ideological, and other distinctions—holy wars of one sort or another. Will such behavior in the next century be expressed with weapons of mass destruction? If we cannot learn to accommodate each other respectfully in the twenty-first century, we could destroy each other at such a rate that humanity will have little to cherish.

The human species has a virtuoso capacity for making harsh distinctions between groups and for justifying violence on whatever scale the technology of the time permits. It is disturbing that fanatical behavior has a way of recurring dangerously across time and locations. Such behavior is old, but what is historically new and very threatening is the

destructive power of our weaponry and its ongoing worldwide proliferation. Also new is the technology that permits rapid, vivid, widely broadcast justification for violence. This combination is what will make the world of the next century so dangerous. In such a world, human conflict is a subject that deserves the most careful and searching inquiry. It is a subject *par excellence* for fresh thinking and public understanding.

All these considerations are made more complex by the rapid and drastic world transformation in which we are living as the twentieth century draws to a close. The power of technological advance and global economic integration to change social conditions is a critical issue for the conflict agenda. The economic and social changes fostered by global technological developments in information and telecommunication—combined with parallel developments in research and development on space, energy, materials, and biotechnology—are likely to be profound and pervasive.

Historically, technological advances have resulted in social and economic transformations on a vast scale. This is especially likely when fundamental new technologies are unfolding across the entire frontier of scientific and engineering research and are rapidly disseminated throughout the world. The impact over the long term has been positive. Along the way, there have been massive dislocations. In this context, it is worth recalling the severe disruptions of the industrial revolution; they had much to do with the emergence of Communism and fascism, especially the Nazi catastrophe.

The contemporary world transformation, with all its intense pressures and unforeseen consequences, tends to pull people toward strongly supportive groups. These groups, in turn, particularly with charismatic, inflammatory leadership, may easily become harsh, separatist, and depreciatory toward others. A deadly combination of severe social stress and distinctively hateful, fanatical leadership can produce mass killing, even genocide. Such conditions occur again and again. The seductive justifications for hideous atrocities can be provided to fill in the murderous blanks, as they were by Hitler, Stalin, and Pol Pot. Indeed, they can be spread more efficiently and vividly than ever before by advanced telecommunications. Such intergroup tensions may readily be exacerbated by deteriorating economic conditions, erosion of social norms, or mass migration. Hateful attitudes may be directed either toward outsiders or minorities in one's own country—or both.

Now there are great new worldwide opportunities and profound stresses that will affect human development in ways hard to foresee. Surely there is no basis for complacency. The frustrations and uncertainties in a complex, rapidly changing world can trigger scapegoating of highly visible groups—e.g., minorities, immigrants, or government officials—who then become targets of irrational, hateful, or extremist responses. These challenges have serious implications for societies throughout the world. It is crucial to seek factual and analytical bases for policies and practices that could help us to cope with such problems and take advantage of the immense, emerging opportunities in an equitable way.

In view of these momentous developments, the recent rash of "internal" wars and genocides, and the wide scope of our mandate, the Commission has developed a comprehensive approach to preventing deadly conflict. In our view, prevention consists not only of avoiding escalation in a crisis, but also of creating a durable basis for peaceful alternatives. In the long run, we can be most successful in preventing ethnic, religious, and international wars by going beyond ways to avert immediate confrontation between hostile groups to promote democracy, market economies, and the creation of civil institutions that protect human rights. Effective preventive strategies rest on three orientations: early responses to signs of trouble; a comprehensive, forward-looking approach to counteract the risk factors that trigger violent conflict; and an extended effort to resolve the underlying causes of violence. All of these are considered in the Commission's work.

The recommendations of this report are addressed to leaders and governments as well as many elements of the international community, among them the democracies, the United Nations, regional organizations, the business community, the global scientific community, educational and religious institutions, the media, and nongovernmental organizations. Only with the active participation of all these groups can we move toward the vision of an international system for preventing deadly conflict. What we seek is a way of thinking that becomes pervasive in many institutions and in public understanding.

As we examined the relevant institutions, we found them all to be modest in preventive achievements and not strongly oriented to this great mission. Indeed, several have at times done more harm than good in cultivating hatred and inciting violence. Yet the people of the world cannot let that record stand. The stakes are simply becoming too high, the dangers in the next century too great. So we have sought ways to strengthen each actor for prevention, to find good examples (even if rare), and to identify the best practices through which their potential could be fulfilled.

Clearly, the world was unprepared for the genocidal slaughters of Bosnia and Rwanda. After the unparalleled horrors of the first half of the twentieth century, and the unprecedented risks of nuclear annihilation during the Cold War, it was reasonable to assume (wishfully) that mass killing would go away by the close of the century. Policymakers of good will and human decency were confounded and often paralyzed by the rush of murderous events in the 1990s. Deep perplexity led to hesitation. The Commission recognizes the dilemma of policymakers and seeks ways to facilitate their tasks in the future. It is not in the interests of nations, large or small, to neglect the emergence of genocide. Such events are not merely unfortunate, in the distant past, or far away. They have immediate, powerful ramifications for all of humanity.

We have come to the conclusion that the prevention of deadly conflict is, over the long term, too hard—intellectually, technically, and politically—to be the responsibility of any single institution or government, no matter how powerful. Strengths must be pooled, burdens shared, and labor divided among actors. This is a practical necessity. We have tried to clarify the tasks and strategies, the tools available, and the opportunities for various actors: who can do what to make a truly civilized world.

In the course of our work, we have considered very hard problems from many perspectives, trying to put old issues in the radically new context of the twenty-first century. These issues span geopolitics, cultural (and even civilizational) differences, terrorism, historic problems of aggression, the behavior of strong powers and the perspective of small countries, special responsibilities of the democracies, the unfulfilled potential of the powerful media and business communities, the shared vulnerability of all humanity, the risks of preventive efforts and the costs of failing to prevent violence, the ubiquitous significance of leadership, individual and group rights, paths to equitable development, and the necessity to build a worldwide culture of prevention that will shape decent human relations at every level.

To be sure, we could not possibly cover all the topics of importance for the great problems addressed in this report. Some of these topics are considered in greater depth in the Commission's collateral publications. We emphasize the significance of these publications, prepared by world leaders and distinguished scholars. They are listed in appendix 4. Others are noted in our extensive references, identifying excellent resource material on a wide range of relevant subjects. Moreover, in the international meetings to be sponsored by the Commission and Carnegie Corporation in the years ahead, we hope to stimulate better ideas by moving this subject higher on the world's agenda.

Given the complexity and sensitivity of the issues addressed in the wide span of the Commission's work, it is inevitable that we encountered differences of opinion. We brought many fields, nations, and kinds of experiences to the endeavor. To a remarkable extent, these differences were reconciled in the course of our work—partly by a relentless effort to get the facts straight, partly by a premium on objective analysis, partly by an open-minded desire to learn from each other and from the world's experience, and partly by a respectful attitude toward the importance and difficulty of our task.

Still, not every Commissioner has equal enthusiasm for every finding and recommendation stated in this report. Certain topics were treated more lightly or more heavily than some would have wished. Yet the convergence has indeed been powerful; the differences are overwhelmed by our fundamental agreement. Indeed, there is a sense in which we were all guided by a commitment to our shared humanity in the face of almost infinite human diversity. It is the future of our shared humanity that impels us to undertake this difficult mission.

To diminish the likelihood of violence, it is important to identify elements of government, social structure, institutions, leadership, and public attitudes that can be used to enhance orientations of caring, concern, social responsibility, and mutual aid within and between groups. Such ends are facilitated by crosscutting relations that bring members of different groups together under favorable conditions on a regular basis, whether within or across national boundaries. It is important that groups develop positive reciprocity in their relationships, that there be perceived elements of mutual benefit from their interaction. Our various reports delineate ways in which such improvements can occur.

For better or worse, this Commission is distinctive in several ways. Its approach to prevention was broad, encompassing political, economic, military, social, and psychological considerations. It used a public health model, with emphasis on primary prevention; its wide-ranging delineation of strategies and tactics of prevention included operational prevention dealing with incipient crises as well as structural prevention dealing with long-term, under-lying factors conducive to peace and equitable development (linking security, well-being, and justice). It emphasized the potential of institutions of civil society for these missions—in addition to governments and intergovernmental organizations. It took a long-term and world-wide view of emerging problems and unprecedented opportunities.

People of humane and democratic inclination will need sustained cooperation throughout the world to build systems that will work. Useful models exist, ideas are emerging, analysis is proceeding, and the current turmoil could provide a constructive stimulus for practical arrangements that help us learn to live together at last.

As our children and their children learn about the horrifying mass violence through the ages—at its worst in the twentieth century—we hope to be able to say that at the beginning of the third millennium, the communities of the world planted seeds of cooperation and reconciliation that grew into a system in which mass violence became diminishingly rare. Perhaps this Commission can envision, however dimly, such a precious legacy for future generations.

DAVID A. HAMBURG
CYRUS R. VANCE
Cochairs

EXECUTIVE
SUMMARY

Three inescapable observations form the foundation of this report. First, deadly conflict is not inevitable. Violence on the scale of what we have seen in Bosnia, Rwanda, Somalia, and elsewhere does not emerge inexorably from human interaction. Second, the need to prevent deadly conflict is increasingly urgent. The rapid compression of the world through breathtaking population growth, technological advancement, and economic interdependence, combined with the readily available supply of deadly weapons and easily transmitted contagion of hatred and incitement to violence, make it essential and urgent to find ways to prevent disputes from turning massively violent. Third, preventing deadly conflict is possible. The problem is not that we do not know about incipient and large-scale violence; it is that we often do not act. Examples from "hot spots" around the world illustrate that the potential for violence can be defused through the early, skillful, and integrated application of political, diplomatic, economic, and military measures.

The Carnegie Commission on Preventing Deadly Conflict does not believe in the unavoidable clash of civilizations or in an inevitably violent future. War and mass violence usually result from deliberate political decisions, and the Commission believes that these decisions can be affected so that mass violence does not result.

To undertake effective preventive action, the Commission believes that we must develop an international commitment to the concept of prevention, a habit of preventive investment, more effective regimes for controlling destructive weaponry, and a working portfolio of legal standards that rest on a normative consensus regarding the responsibilities of governments to each other and to their peoples. Responsible leaders, key intergovernmental and nongovernmental institutions, and civil society can do far better in preventing deadly conflict than the record of this century and the current epidemic of violence suggest.

THE NATURE OF THE PROBLEM

Violent conflict has often resulted from the traditional preoccupation of states to defend, maintain, or extend interests and power. A number of dangerous situations today can be understood in these terms. Yet, one of the most remarkable aspects of the post–Cold War world is that wars within states vastly outnumber wars between states. These internal conflicts commonly are fought with conventional weapons and rely on strategies of ethnic expulsion and annihilation. More civilians are killed than soldiers (by one estimate at the rate of about nine to one), and belligerents use strategies and tactics that deliberately target women, children, the poor, and the weak.

Many factors and conditions make societies prone to warfare: weak, corrupt, or collapsed states; illegitimate or repressive regimes; acute discrimination against ethnic or other social groups; poorly managed religious, cultural, or ethnic differences; politically active religious communities that promote hostile and divisive messages; political and economic legacies of colonialism or the Cold War; sudden economic and political shifts; widespread illiteracy, disease, and disability; lack of resources such as water and arable land; large stores of weapons and ammunition; and threatening regional relationships. When long-standing grievances are exploited by political demagogues, the scene is set for violence.

The Commission's work has identified three broad aims of preventive action:

- **First, prevent the emergence of violent conflict.** This is done by creating capable states with representative governance based on the rule of law, with widely available economic opportunity, social safety nets, protection of fundamental human rights, and robust civil societies. The aim is to prevent dangerous circumstances from developing and coalescing through efforts to establish these more desirable circumstances. A network of interlocking international regimes underwritten by the rule of law provides a supporting environment for this purpose. This approach is comparable to primary prevention in public health—and has been the Commission's main emphasis.

- **Second, prevent ongoing conflicts from spreading.** This is done by creating political, economic, and, if necessary, military barriers to limit the spread of conflict within

and between states. Firebreaks may be created through well-designed assertive efforts to deny belligerents the ability to resupply arms, ammunition, and hard currency, combined with humanitarian operations that provide relief for innocent victims.

- **Third, prevent the reemergence of violence.** This is done through the creation of a safe and secure environment in the aftermath of conflict and the achievement of a peace settlement. This environment can be established through the rapid introduction of security forces to separate enemies, oversee disarmament plans, and provide a stabilizing presence. Simultaneous, immediate steps will also be necessary to restore legitimate political authority, to install functioning police, judicial, and penal systems, and to integrate external and internal efforts to restore essential services and restart normal economic activity.

Effective preventive strategies rest on three principles: early reaction to signs of trouble; a comprehensive, balanced approach to alleviate the pressures, or risk factors, that trigger violent conflict; and an extended effort to resolve the underlying root causes of violence.

- **Early reaction to signs of trouble.** Early action requires early detection and skilled analysis of developing trends. In addition, leaders and governments will need to formulate clear statements of interest, develop measured, pragmatic courses of action to respond to the warning signs, and provide support for locally sustainable solutions. Normally, early reaction will also require broad political consultations to gain the confidence of the parties to the dispute and to establish a common framework for preventive engagement. And this demands that governments develop a flexible repertoire of political, economic, and military measures—and options for their use—to stop dangerous trends.

- **A comprehensive, balanced approach to alleviate the pressures that trigger violent conflict.** Large-scale crises strain the capacity of any single government or international organization. This strain becomes particularly unbearable when, as is often the case in intrastate disputes, a government is itself party to a worsening conflict. Outside help is often necessary to deal with building crises within and between states. An effective response usually requires a range of political, economic, social, and military measures and the deliberate coordination of those measures.

- **An extended effort to resolve the underlying root causes of violence.** Discrimination and deprivation combine in deadly fashion, particularly when deliberately and systematically imposed. To address the root causes of violence, leaders and governments must ensure fundamental security, well-being, and justice for all citizens. Such a structural approach to prevention not only makes people better off, it inhibits the tendency to use violence to settle differences.

Strategies for prevention fall into two broad categories: operational prevention (measures applicable in the face of immediate crisis) and structural prevention (measures to ensure that crises do not arise in the first place or, if

they do, that they do not recur). The report develops these approaches and suggests how governments, international organizations, and the various institutions of civil society might implement them.

OPERATIONAL PREVENTION: Strategies in the Face of Crisis

When violence appears imminent, the responsibility for operational prevention falls mainly on those closest to an unfolding crisis. But since the parties in a crisis often cannot find nonviolent solutions on their own, the help of outsiders is necessary in many instances. It is of vital importance, however, that the economic, military, or diplomatic actions and policies of outsiders not exacerbate dangerous situations. Even well-intentioned efforts, if not carefully planned, can make matters worse.

Operational prevention relies on early engagement to help create conditions in which responsible leaders can resolve the problems giving rise to the crisis. Four key elements increase prospects for success:

- A lead player—an international organization, country, or even prominent individual around which or whom preventive efforts can mobilize

- A coherent political–military approach to the engagement designed to arrest the violence, address the humanitarian needs of the situation, and integrate all political and military aspects of the problem

- Adequate resources to support the preventive engagement

- A plan for the restoration of host country authority (particularly applicable to intrastate conflict)

These elements provide a framework for applying various preventive political, economic, social, and military measures. These steps may not be sufficient in themselves to forestall violence indefinitely, but they can help open up the political space and time necessary for those closest to the conflict to pursue other means to resolve the dispute. The following discussion explores this framework and many of the measures the Commission believes can be used to prevent the emergence of mass violence.

Leadership

Effective leadership derives from a special relationship or capacity that makes an organization, government, agency, or prominent individual the logical focal point for rallying the help of the international community. For example, U.S. leadership in the Gulf War, supported strongly by the UN, was critical in maintaining unity within a diverse coalition of nations; and in the early 1990s, the UN led an ambitious international peace initiative in Cambodia. In most cases, the active support of the members of the UN Security Council—especially the permanent members—is important to success.

A Comprehensive Political–Military Response

Preventive responses must seek not only to reduce the potential for violence but also to create the basic conditions to encourage moderation and make responsible political control possible. This means that in the acute phase of a crisis, assertive efforts may be necessary to deny belligerents weapons and ammunition. These military steps may need to be complemented by economic steps to deny access to the hard currency to procure weapons and pay combatants (steps that themselves demand that outsiders refrain from providing weapons, funds, and other resources to factions in conflict). In addition, humanitarian assistance will usually be needed to help noncombatant victims of the crisis, and such assistance must be carried on in close coordination with the other political, military, and economic efforts under way. This last point bears emphasis: the crisis response must integrate the humanitarian, economic, political, and military elements if it is to have increased prospects for success.

Moreover, an integrated response should bring together the efforts of governments, international organizations, nongovernmental organizations (NGOs), and private relief agencies. It should also coordinate the efforts of outside parties with those of the local responsible leadership.

Resources

As a crisis escalates, and even as efforts begin to help defuse its effects, political rhetoric to mobilize preventive efforts often outpaces the flow of resources, which consists of cash and contributions "in kind" by governments, the International Committee of the Red Cross, and global NGOs, such as CARE and Oxfam. Significant resources also come from many smaller humanitarian organizations, such as Médecins Sans Frontières, and other private sector agencies. While these nongovernmental and private sector organizations may not play leading roles in either mobilizing the international response to a crisis or in developing the general plan of engagement, their services and resources are vital to the larger effort and should be systematically integrated into the overall approach.

Transition to Host Nation Control

The international response to a potentially explosive intrastate situation, from its outset, must plan for the full restoration of authority and responsibility to the leaders of the country in crisis. The participation of community and national leaders in all aspects of the international response helps allay fears regarding the motives of outside parties, and a plan to restore local authority also reassures outsiders that their job will come to an end. While many governments may be willing to help in a crisis, few if any are willing to stay indefinitely—competing domestic demands and other international concerns drastically restrict even a willing government's ability to engage in a costly international effort over the long term. The Commission believes that the primary responsibility to avoid the reemergence of violence once peace has been achieved belongs to the people and their legitimate leaders; they must resume complete responsibility for their own affairs at the earliest opportunity.

Measures to avoid imminent violence fall into four broad groups:

- Early warning and early response

- Preventive diplomacy

- Economic measures, such as sanctions and inducements

- The use of force

Early Warning and Early Response

The capacity to anticipate and analyze possible conflicts is a prerequisite for prudent decision making and effective action. Indicators of imminent violence include widespread human rights abuses, increasingly brutal political oppression, inflammatory use of the media, the accumulation of arms, and sometimes a rash of organized killings. This was certainly true of the violence in Rwanda and Bosnia in the first half of the 1990s.

Yet even practical early warning will not ensure successful preventive action unless there is a fundamental change of attitude by governments and international organizations. A systematic and practical early warning system should be combined with constantly updated contingency plans for preventive action. This would be a radical advance on the present system where, when a trigger event sets off an explosion of violence, it is usually too difficult, too costly, and too late for a rapid and effective response. Thus, in addition to the relatively easy identification of major hot spots and checklists of problem conditions, policymakers also need specific knowledge of the major elements of destabilization and the way in which they are likely to coalesce to precipitate an outbreak of violence.

During the early stages of a crisis, policymakers should not only be attentive to how circumstances could worsen, but they should also be alert for opportunities to make constructive use of local issues and processes that could help avoid violence. And they should exercise great care as to whom they support and how that support is offered.

States, international organizations, nongovernmental organizations, business enterprises, religious leaders, scientific groups, and the media all have, in their different ways, a capacity for early warning. NGOs, for example, are often the first to be aware of, and to act in, crisis areas, and they have a wealth of information regarding the conditions and grievances that give rise to violence. (Indeed, the disruption of normal NGO operations is itself an early warning signal that conditions are deteriorating dangerously, a signal that governments often miss.) For example, in Rwanda, the human rights NGO Africa Watch warned in 1993 that Hutu extremists had compiled lists of individuals to be targeted for retribution—individuals who the next year were among the first victims.

But there are problems involved when humanitarian and other nongovernmental and private sector groups take on an increased information and early warning role. The information these groups provide is not always accurate or balanced. Many conflicts today occur in relatively remote regions where accurate information about the competing sides and their partisans is hard to obtain, which makes it difficult to form a valid picture of the overall situation. Moreover, humanitarian organizations, business enterprises, and religious institutions that operate regularly within or near crisis areas develop their own agendas that often do not conform to those of governments, the parties to the dispute, or outsiders. Thus, what might appear to one group as an unambiguous opportunity for action may be seen as the opposite by another.

Governments and international organizations are ultimately best suited to alert the broader international community to a coming crisis and to assess the validity of the information available from other sources. But they seldom do so; there are no mechanisms in place for governments or the decision-making bodies of the major regional organizations to acquire systematically the information that international and national NGOs, religious leaders and institutions, the business community, or other elements of civil society have accumulated from years of involvement. There are signs that this may be changing, however. In a major report on UN reform issued in July 1997, UN Secretary-General Kofi Annan recognized the importance of NGOs and other elements of civil society and acknowledged the essential contribution they make to UN operations.

In sum, it is difficult for major governments to claim that they did not know that violence on the scale of a Rwanda or Bosnia could happen. Similarly, it is implausible for such governments, especially of the larger, more powerful, and wealthy states, to claim that nothing could be done to avert such crises. Increasingly, they are being held accountable not only for "What did they know and when did they know it?" but also for "What could they have done and when should they have done it?"

To repeat, to prevent deadly conflict, the problem is less one of early warning than of early action. As a first step, diplomatic engagement can help overcome this problem.

Preventive Diplomacy

When crisis threatens, traditional diplomacy continues, but more urgent efforts are also made—through unilateral and multilateral channels—to pressure, cajole, arbitrate, mediate, or lend "good offices" to encourage dialogue and facilitate a nonviolent resolution of the crisis. Diplomacy and politics need to find ways to cope with grievous circumstances occurring anywhere in the world, not only because these circumstances are tragic in themselves, but also because they have an increasing capacity to harm others. The efforts needed today are therefore tied, perhaps as never before, to a complex web of economic and social relationships that span the globe.

In deteriorating circumstances a number of steps may help manage the crisis and prevent the emergence of violence. First, states should resist the traditional urge to suspend diplomatic relations as a substitute for action and instead maintain open, high-fidelity lines of communication with leaders and groups in crisis. Second, governments and international organizations must express in a clear and compelling way the interests in jeopardy. This step is particularly important should more assertive steps to deal with the crisis become necessary later.

Third, the crisis should immediately be put on the agenda of the UN Security Council or of the relevant international organization, or both, early enough to permit preventive action. At the same time, a means should be established to track developments in the crisis, to provide regular updates, and to include a mechanism to incorporate information from NGOs and other nongovernmental actors to support high-level deliberations on unfolding events.

Fourth, and notwithstanding the foregoing imperative to broaden the multilateral context of an unfolding crisis, governments should be attentive to opportunities to support quiet diplomacy and dialogue with and between moderate leaders in the crisis. Special envoys and representatives of key states or regional organizations or on behalf of the UN have time and again demonstrated their value, particularly in the early stages of a crisis.

Diplomatic and political strategies to avert a looming crisis demand creative ways of defusing tensions and facilitating mutual accommodation among potential belligerents. Such strategies can include a serious discussion of peaceful border adjustments or revisions, new constitutional arrangements, forms of regional or cultural autonomy, or even, in unusual circumstances, partition. Potential solutions may lie in various forms of power sharing to help assure groups that their interests are not at the mercy of the whim of the majority.

Official diplomacy can be greatly strengthened by private sector activity. Long used in international negotiations by leaders to take informal soundings of adversaries' intentions, so-called Track Two diplomacy is increasingly the strategy of choice for dealing with problems beyond the reach of official efforts. Some governments have found NGOs very useful in brokering political agreements and supplementing governmental roles. In recent years, many groups in the United States and Europe, such as The Carter Center's International Negotiation Network, the Conflict Management Group, the Institute for Multi-Track Diplomacy, International Alert, the International Crisis Group, the Project on Ethnic Relations, and Search for Common Ground, have developed models for multitrack diplomacy and conflict resolution. These organizations have played active roles in building relationships between conflicting parties and with interested governments, offering training in diplomacy and conflict resolution, and providing good offices to parties that are committed to the peaceful resolution of conflict.

Economic Measures

In circumstances of incipient conflict, a number of economic measures are at the disposal of states and international organizations in a position to influence potential belligerents to avoid violence. Sanctions, of course, are one such tool. But beyond sanctions, inducements, economic conditionality, and the dispute resolution mechanisms of international trade and other economic organizations may also prove useful.

Sanctions

Sanctions can play an important role in support of preventive diplomacy, notwithstanding the fact that practical questions remain about governments' abilities to use sanctions effectively. Sanctions serve three broad policy functions for governments: to signal international concern to the offending state (and, by example, to others), to punish a state's bad behavior, and to serve as a precursor to stronger actions, including, if necessary, the use of force.

Sanctions should be part of a broader influence strategy that puts maximum political and economic pressure as precisely as possible on the offending parties—preferably ruling parties or specific leaders rather than whole populations. States that impose sanctions should also take steps, in accordance with the UN Charter, to reduce unwanted or undesirable side effects and minimize the privation and suffering of innocent civilians and the economic losses often suffered by neighboring countries.

Sanctions regimes that are focused on commodities exclusively must be swiftly and comprehensively imposed to be most effective. Graduated, piecemeal approaches are unlikely to work. Sanctions regimes should be supported, where necessary, with the forceful measures suitable to ensure compliance and demonstrate resolve. Diplomatic and other political communications should be clear on the behavior necessary for sanctions to be lifted and, where possible, accompanied by an incentive package.

"Targeted" sanctions offer a way to focus the penalty more directly on those most responsible for the crisis. Such targeted sanctions include freezing leaders' personal assets or denying them access to hard currency. For this purpose, financial information can be shared among cooperating nations to identify and restrict the cash flows of leaders who threaten to use violence.

Inducements

Inducements could have greater preventive potential if they were better understood. Essentially, the inducement process involves the granting of a political or economic benefit in exchange for a specified policy adjustment. Inducement policies strive to make cooperation and conciliation more appealing than aggression and hostility. Examples of inducements include favorable trade terms, tariff reductions, direct purchases, subsidies for exports or imports, economic and military aid, favorable taxation, access to advanced technology, military cooperation, and the many benefits that accrue to members in good standing in international organizations. Policymakers often juggle a variety of political, military, and economic elements in a package of inducements.

Inducements are especially influential when used against the backdrop of sanctions—where benefits of cooperation can be weighed against stark punishments for pursuing violence.

Conditionality

One particularly potent tool for effective preventive action may be conditionality, the forging of links between responsible, nonviolent behavior and the promise of greater reward through growing integration into the community of market democracies. Increasingly, through their bilateral programs and through pressure on the international financial institutions, states are attaching good governance conditions to the development assistance provided to emerging economies. Associating assistance with responsible governance in this way may give the international community a powerful source of leverage with those who persistently use violent means to pursue their aims. States that attach these kinds of conditions to their aid are not themselves above scrutiny, however. The potential leverage of conditionality is diminished when donor states demand higher standards of behavior than they themselves are prepared to observe.

Economic Dispute Resolution Mechanisms

Every major international trade organization has mechanisms to help broker disputes that may arise among members, and members commit themselves to pursue their grievances through these organizational processes and to be bound by their findings. The dispute resolution mechanism of the World Trade Organization (WTO) is typical: following the identification of a grievance, a panel of experts may be assembled to rule on the merits of the case. If found in violation, an offending party is required to bring its policies or practices into compliance within a reasonable period of time or face a damage judgment. If corrective action is not taken, the aggrieved party may retaliate by raising duties. Decisions may be appealed, and uncorrected behavior can lead to more serious measures such as sanctions or expulsion from the organization.

These mechanisms are designed to work between governments, of course, and may be less suitable for brokering internal eco-

nomic disputes, and governments do not appear uniformly eager to invite outside engagement on such matters. Nevertheless, some similar mechanisms may be adaptable for use by governments in internal affairs, and they remain in any case important tools to help manage disputes between states. Given the great significance of economic issues in an increasingly interdependent world, the lessons learned from these mechanisms for nonviolent dispute resolution deserve closer attention.

Forceful Measures

At first sight, contemplation of the threat or use of forceful measures might seem at odds with the Commission's focus on the prevention of deadly conflict. But situations will continue to arise where diplomatic responses, even supplemented by strong economic measures, are simply insufficient to prevent the outbreak or recurrence of major violence. The question arises as to when, where, and how individual nations, and global and regional organizations, should be willing to apply forceful measures to curb incipient violence and stop potentially much greater destruction of life and property. The Commission believes that there are three broad principles that should govern any such decision:

- First, any threat or use of force must be governed by universally accepted principles, as the UN Charter requires. Decisions to use force must not be arbitrary, or operate as the coercive and selectively used weapon of the strong against the weak.

- Second, the threat or use of force should not be regarded only as a last resort in desperate circumstances. Governments must be attentive to opportunities when clear demonstrations of resolve and determination can establish clear limits to unacceptable behavior.

- Third, states—particularly the major powers—must accept that the threat or use of force, if it does become necessary, must be part of an integrated, usually multilateral strategy, and used in conjunction with political and economic instruments. One way to achieve these aims is to institutionalize the emerging view that when employing force for preventive purposes, states should only do so with a UN Security Council resolution specifying a clear mandate and detailing the arrangements under which force will be used and the units that will be involved in the action.

The Commission does not mean to suggest that there are no circumstances under which the unilateral use of force might be contemplated. Indeed, the Charter authorizes unilateral force in certain circumstances. For the kinds of preventive action contemplated here, however, a multilateral response should be the norm, as envisaged in the UN Charter, and a norm that should apply to large as well as small states.

There are three distinct kinds of operations where the use of force and forces—that is, military or police personnel—may have an important role in preventing the outbreak or recurrence of violent conflict: postconflict peacekeeping, preventive deployments, and "fire brigade" deployments. Only the third of these involves personnel on the ground having the mandate or capacity to apply forceful measures (other than in self-defense)—but the credibility of all three as preventive strategies depends on the perception that if peace breaks down, forceful measures to restore it may well be forthcoming.

Peacekeeping and Maintaining Civil Order

In the aftermath of cease-fires and more substantial peace settlements, traditional, lightly armed peacekeeping missions can help monitor and restrain tense situations. These operations have been most effective when deployed in very specific circumstances where the parties to a conflict are separated along clearly demarcated boundaries and when they agree to a cease-fire and the presence of the outside forces. Such deployments could also be applied as a valuable means of improving security for UN humanitarian enterprises, especially refugee camps. These missions serve several purposes, including to signal the interest and engagement of the international community, to observe and monitor relations between antagonistic parties, and to act as a deterrent against renewed fighting.

Experience in a number of UN missions—Bosnia, Cambodia, Haiti, Rwanda, Somalia, Western Sahara, and elsewhere—suggests the particular need to plan carefully and execute responsibly peacekeeping deployments, as well as law-and-order operations designed to establish and maintain legitimate civil control. An international policing force can monitor situations of potential unrest, establish a presence through patrols and precincts to help keep tensions in check, retrain or replace problematic elements within the host country's own police force, and restrain gang or other organized criminal activities until local authorities can resume complete control. Strengthening local policing capacities through international, regional, or ad hoc arrangements may reduce the necessity for military interventions. Technological innovations that permit law enforcement and military forces to use less-than-lethal means for keeping order may increase the effectiveness of their operations.

Policing cannot by itself ensure civil control. Good police practices are not a substitute for political systems providing alternative outlets for grievances. Success depends on the degree to which policing practices are supported (and regulated) by legitimate governmental, judicial, and penal systems underwritten by the rule of law.

"Thin Blue Line" Preventive Deployments

Until recently, peacekeeping operations—both traditional and expanded—were only used in the aftermath of conflict to help reconcile the parties and to prevent the recurrence of fighting. A new concept has now emerged with the deployment in late 1992 of a small force of troops and civilian monitors to the Former Yugoslav Republic of Macedonia, with the objective, so far successful, of preventing the spread of hostilities from other areas of the former Yugoslavia. The essence of the strategy is a preventive military rather than diplomatic response involving the positioning of troops and related personnel on one or both sides of a border between parties in dispute.

The success to date of the deployment in Macedonia may suggest that this measure could prove a particularly effective preventive device. One potential disadvantage, as the experience in Cyprus illustrates, is that sometimes the international community must be prepared to stay for an extended, perhaps even indefinite, period of time.

"Fire Brigade" Deployments

Much debate has swirled around the idea of establishing a rapid reaction capability within the UN or through other regional arrangements to give the international community a means to respond quickly to an emerging crisis. Many political difficulties attach to such a capability, however, and governments have in large measure proved unwilling to take the steps necessary to establish such a force.

The Commission supports the establishment of a rapid reaction force of some 5,000 to 10,000 troops, the core of which would be contributed by members of the Security Council. The force would also need a robust planning staff, a standing operational headquarters, training facilities, and compatible equipment. The Commission offers two arguments for such a capability: First, the record of international crises points out the need in certain cases to respond rapidly and, if necessary, with force; and second, the operational integrity of such a force requires that it not be assembled in pieces or in haste. A standing force may well be a necessity for effective prevention.

Currently, the UN Security Council is ill-equipped to implement quick decisions to establish a military presence on the ground in a crisis. The political machinery and the logistical and financial structure necessary to make things happen within days do not exist. Transportation, communications, and supply functions are contracted out through a competitive, laborious, and time-consuming system. Crisis military staffing is ad hoc and drawn from standing organizations within the UN. This lack of capacity creates genuine operational hazards. The existence of a standing rapid reaction capability would help ensure that these problems are solved.

The Security Council should immediately establish a working group to develop the operational requirements for such a capability and make recommendations for a Council decision regarding the guidelines for raising and funding such a force. The force would be under the authority of the Security Council and its deployment subject to a veto by any of the permanent members.

In the end, of course, the use of such a capability may mean that other efforts to forestall violence have not been effective. The foregoing discussion has illuminated measures that can help defuse a crisis that has reached an acute phase. But the question remains: What can be done to prevent crises from getting to that point to begin with? In other words, what conditions inhibit the rise of violence and how can these conditions be established and maintained?

STRUCTURAL PREVENTION: Strategies To Address the Root Causes Of Deadly Conflict

Structural prevention—or peace building—comprises strategies such as putting in place international legal systems, dispute resolution mechanisms, and cooperative arrangements; meeting people's basic economic, social, cultural, and humanitarian needs; and rebuilding societies that have been shattered by war or other major crises.

This report argues that whatever model of self-government societies ultimately choose, and whatever path they follow to that end, they must meet the three core needs of security, well-being, and justice and thereby give people a stake in nonviolent efforts to improve their lives. Meeting these needs not only enables people to live better lives, it also reduces the potential for deadly conflict.

Security

People cannot thrive in an environment where they believe their survival to be in jeopardy. Indeed, many violent conflicts have been waged by people trying to establish and maintain a safe living space. There are three main sources of insecurity today: the threat posed by nuclear and other weapons of mass destruction; the possibility of conventional confrontation between militaries; and sources of internal violence, such as terrorism, organized crime, insurgency, and repressive regimes.

Nuclear Weapons

The retention of nuclear weapons by any state stimulates other states and nonstate actors to acquire them. Thus, the only durably safe course is to work toward elimination of such weapons within a reasonable time frame, and for this purpose to be achieved, stringent conditions have to be set to make this feasible with security for all. These conditions must include rigorous safeguards against any nuclear weapons falling into the hands of dictatorial and fanatical leaders. Within this context, steps that should be taken promptly in this direction include developing credible mechanisms and practices:

- To account for nuclear weapons and materials

- To monitor their whereabouts and operational condition

- To ensure the safe management and reduction of nuclear arsenals

Since nuclear arms are the deadliest of weapons, they create an especially critical problem of prevention. The Commission believes that preventive efforts against violence with conventional weapons or other weapons of mass destruction would be strongly reinforced if fuller efforts were made to control the nuclear danger. For example, the world would be a safer place, and the risks of deadly conflict would be reduced, if nuclear weapons were not actively deployed. Much of the deterrent effect of these weapons can be sustained without having active forces poised for massive attack at every moment. The dramatic transformation required to remove all nuclear weapons from active deployment is feasible in technical terms, but substantial changes in political attitudes and managerial practices would be necessary as well.

The Commission endorses the ultimate objective of elimination long embodied in the Non-Proliferation Treaty (NPT) and recently elaborated in separate reports issued by the Canberra Commission on the Elimination of Nuclear Weapons and by the U.S. National Academy of Sciences. Precisely because of its importance, we wish to emphasize the conditions that would have to be achieved to make elimination a responsible and realistic aspiration.

In a comprehensive framework to achieve that objective, the foremost requirement would be an international accounting system that tracks the exact number of fabricated weapons and the exact amounts of the fissionable materials that provide their explosive power. For technical as well as political reasons, it will inevitably require a considerable amount of time to develop an accounting system that could support a general agreement to eliminate active nuclear weapons deployments. The requisite accuracy is not likely to be achieved until such a system has been in operation over a substantial period of time. The Commission strongly recommends that efforts be initiated immediately to create such a system as a priority for the prevention of deadly conflict.

Concurrently, governments should eliminate the practice of alert procedures (i.e., relying on continuously available weapons) and set an immediate goal to remove all weapons from active deployment—that is, to dismantle them to the point that to use them would require reconstruction. In addition, the major nuclear states should reverse their commitment to massive targeting and establish a presumption of limited use. Finally, as this process proceeds, multilateral arrangements will need to be made to ensure stability and the maintenance of peace and security in a world without nuclear weapons.

In several regions of the world today, volatile circumstances involve neighbors, one or more of which may possess nuclear weapons. These circumstances give added impetus to developing improved methods of accounting for and safeguarding nuclear weapons and materials. The aim must be to move the specter of nuclear weapons far to the background of any conventional confrontation. For this to happen, the nuclear states must demonstrate that they take seriously Article VI of the NPT, which calls for signatories to make good faith progress toward complete disarmament under strict and effective international control.

Biological and Chemical Weapons

Although there have been numerous protocols, conventions, and agreements on the control and elimination of biological and chemical weapons, progress has been slowed by a lack of binding treaties with provisions for implementation, inspection, and enforcement. Regarding biological weapons, it is impossible to control completely or deny access to materials and information. But it may be possible to gain greater control through mechanisms to monitor the possession of and the construction of facilities for the most dangerous pathogens. A registry could be established in which governments and other users would register strains under their control and detail the purposes of experimentation. Registrants would be required to publish the results of their experiments. This registry would seek to reinforce the practice of systematic transparency and create a legal and professional expectation that those working with these strains would be under an obligation to reveal themselves. In addition, the professional community of researchers and scientists must engage in expanded and extensive collaboration in this field and establish a close connection to the public health community.

The Commission believes that governments should seek a more effective categorical prohibition against the development and use of chemical weapons. The international community needs systematic monitoring of chemical compounds and the size of stockpiles to ensure transparency and to guard against misuse.

If progress on these fronts is to be made, complex disagreements within both the international community and individual states must be addressed. While there remains a critical need for continued progress, the gains that have been made in the control of nuclear weapons have created important expectations of transparency, accountability, and reciprocity, and may help improve the control of biological and chemical weapons.

Conventional Weapons

As detailed in the report, violent conflict today is fought with conventional weapons. The Commission recognizes that all states have the right to maintain adequate defense structures for their security and that achieving global agreement on the control of conventional weapons will be difficult. Nevertheless, progress should be possible to control the flow of arms around the world. The global arms trade is dominated by the five permanent members of the UN Security Council and Germany. Jointly, they account for 80–90 percent of such activity. To date, few efforts to control the flows of conventional weapons have been undertaken, and the trade in small arms and ammunition—which account for the majority of deaths in today's conflicts—remains largely unregulated. One effort in the right direction is the international movement to institute a worldwide ban on the production, stockpiling, distribution, and use of land mines. The Commission strongly endorses this effort.

Governments must keep conventional arms control near the top of their national and multilateral security agendas. NATO and other regional arrangements that offer the opportunity for sustained dialogue among the professional military establishments will help, and in the process promote important values of transparency, nonthreatening force structures and deployments, and civilian control of the military.

Cooperating for Peace

Around the globe, national military establishments in many—but not all—regions are shrinking and their role has come under profound reexamination as a result of the end of the Cold War and the sharp rise of economic globalization. With the end of the confrontation between East and West, military establishments in the former Warsaw Pact are being reconfigured and the forces of NATO and many Western nations are being reduced. The Commission believes that the general trend toward force reduction and realignment, the current absence of interstate war in the world, and the continuing development of international regimes form a foundation from which states can continue to reduce the conventional military threat that they pose to one another.

Security within States

Intrastate violence can result from active insurgencies, political terrorism, or organized crime. Four essential elements provide a framework for maintaining a just regime for internal stability:

- A corpus of laws that is legitimately derived and widely promulgated and understood

- A consistent, visible, fair, and active network of police authority to enforce the laws (especially important at the local level)

- An independent, equitable, and accessible grievance redress system, including above all an impartial judicial system

- A penal system that is fair and prudent in meting out punishment

These basic elements are vital yet hard to achieve, and they require constant attention through democratic processes.

Governments, international organizations, and private sector groups operating internationally have important roles to play in maintaining internal security. In general, outsiders can help by:

- Promoting norms and practices to govern interstate relations, to avoid and resolve disputes, and to encourage practices of good governance

- Reducing and eventually eliminating the many military threats and sources of insecurity between states, including those that contribute to instability within states

- Not exacerbating the interstate or intrastate disputes of others, either on purpose or inadvertently. The history of third-party intervention is replete with examples of interventions that were unwarranted, unwanted, or unhelpful.

Existing in a secure environment is only the beginning, of course. People may feel relatively free from fear of attack, but unless they also have the opportunity to maintain decent living standards, discontent and resentment can generate unrest.

Well-Being

Too many of the world's people still cannot take for granted food, water, shelter, and other necessities. The slippery slope of degradation—so vividly exemplified in Somalia in the early 1990s—leads to growing risks of civil war, terrorism, and humanitarian catastrophe.

Well-being entails access to basic necessities, including health services, education, and an opportunity to earn a livelihood. In the context of structural prevention, well-being implies more than just a state's capacity to provide essential needs. People are often able to tolerate economic deprivation and disparities in the short run because governments create conditions that allow them to improve their living standards and that lessen disparities between rich and poor.

The Commission believes that decent living standards are a universal human right. Development efforts to meet these standards are a prime responsibility of governments, and the international community has a responsibility to help through development assistance. Assistance programs are vital to many developing states, crucial to sustaining millions of people in crises, and necessary to help build otherwise unaffordable infrastructure. But long-term solutions must also be found through a state's own development policies, attentive to the particular needs of its society's economic and social sectors.

Helping from Within: Development Revisited

For a variety of reasons, many nations in the global South have been late in getting access to the remarkable opportunities now available for economic and social development. They are seeking ways to modernize in keeping with their own cultural traditions and distinctive settings.

The general well-being of a society will require government action to help ensure widespread economic opportunity. Whether and how to undertake such interventions in the economy is controversial and should be decided and implemented democratically by societies on their own behalf. The Commission emphasizes, however, that economic growth without widespread sharing in the benefits of that growth will not reduce prospects for violent conflict and could, in fact, be a contributing factor to exacerbating tensions. The resentment and unrest likely to be induced by drastically unbalanced or inequitable economic opportunity may outweigh whatever prosperity is generated by that opportunity.

Fundamentally, the distribution of economic benefits in a society is a political question resolved through decisions regarding the kind of economic organization a society will construct, including the nature and level of governmental engagement in private sector activity. Poverty is often a structural outgrowth of these decisions, and when poverty runs in parallel with ethnic or cultural divisions, it often creates a flash point. Peace is most commonly found where economic growth and opportunities to share in that growth are broadly distributed across the population.

There is great preventive value in initiatives that focus on children and women, not only because they are the main victims of conflict, but also because women in many vulnerable societies are an important source of community stability and vitality. For children, this emphasis entails a two-pronged approach that stresses, on the one hand, access to education and basic health services, and on the other, policies that prohibit the recruitment of child soldiers and the industrial exploitation of child labor. For women, this entails national programs that encourage education for girls, women-operated businesses, and other community-based economic activities. Moreover, in rebuilding violence-torn societies, women, usually the majority of the surviving population, must be involved in all decision making and implementation.

Making Development Sustainable

In at least three clear ways, natural resources lie at the heart of conflicts that hold the potential for mass violence through the deliberate manipulation of resource shortages for hostile purposes (for example, using food or water as a weapon); competing claims of sovereignty over resource endowments (such as rivers or oil and other fossil fuel deposits); and the exacerbating role played by environmental degradation and resource depletion in areas characterized by political instability, rapid population growth, chronic economic deprivation, and societal stress.

Global population and economic growth, along with high consumption in the North, have led to the depletion, destruction, and pollution of the natural environment. Nearly every region of the world has a major resource endowment that will require several states to cooperate to ensure that these resources are managed responsibly. Science and technology can contribute immensely to the reduction of environmental threats through low-pollution technologies. Greater effort is required to develop sustainable strategies for social and economic progress; in fact, sustainability is likely to become a key principle of development and a major incentive for global partnerships.

Helping from Outside: Development Assistance

Promoting good governance has become the keynote of development assistance in the 1990s, along with the building of fundamental skills for participation in the modern global economy. The new approach requires a state, at a minimum, to equip itself with a professional, accountable bureaucracy that is able to provide an enabling environment and handle macroeconomic management, sustained poverty reduction, education and training (including of women), and protection of the environment. The Commission believes that more strenuous and sustained development assistance can also reduce the risk of regional conflicts when it is used to tie border groups in one or more states to their shared interests in land and water development, environmental protection, and other mutual concerns.

The emphasis on good governance has also encouraged a more robust and responsible private sector development in many countries. There is rising economic activity in the private sector around the world.

Sustained growth requires investment in people, and programs must prevent deep, intergenerational poverty from becoming institutionalized. Development assistance can include transitional budgetary support, especially for maintenance and to buffer the human cost of conversion to market economies. Extensive technical assistance, specialized training, and broad economic education are all badly needed. So too is the building of indigenous institutions to sustain the vital knowledge and skills for development.

In sum, improving well-being requires a multifaceted approach. It means mobilizing and developing human capacities, broadening and diversifying the economic base, removing barriers to equal opportunity, and opening countries to participation in the global economy and the international community.

Justice

An understanding of and adherence to the rule of law is crucial to a healthy system of social organization, both nationally and internationally, and any effort to create and maintain such a system must itself rest on the rule of law. The rule of law is a goal in that it forms the basis for the just management of relations between and among people. It is also a means in that a sound legal regime helps ensure the protection of fundamental human rights, political access through participatory governance, social accommodation of diverse groups, and equitable economic opportunity.

Justice in the International Community

States' efforts in relation to justice should include ways to develop international law with particular emphasis on three main areas: human rights; humanitarian law, including the need to provide the legal underpinning for UN operations in the field; and nonviolent alternatives for dispute resolution, including more flexible intrastate mechanisms for mediation, arbitration, grievance recognition, and social reconciliation.

Justice within States

There is no more fundamental political right than the ability to have a say in how one is governed. Participation by the people in the choice and replacement of their government—democracy—assures all citizens the opportunity to better their circumstances while managing the inevitable clashes that arise. Democracy achieves this goal by accommodating competing interests through regularized, widely accessible, transparent processes at many levels of government. Sustainable democratic systems also need a functioning and fair judicial system, a military that is under civilian control, and police and civil services that are competent, honest, and accountable.

Effective participatory government based on the rule of law reduces the need for people to take matters into their own hands and to resolve their differences through violence. It is important that all groups within a society believe that they have real opportunities to influence the political process. The institutions and processes to ensure widespread political participation can vary widely.

Engineering transitions to participatory governance, or restoring legitimate governance following conditions of anarchy, may require temporary power sharing. Many forms of power sharing are possible, but all provide for widespread participation in the reconstruction effort, sufficient resources to ensure broad-based access to educational, economic, and political opportunities, and the constructive involvement of outsiders.

In the aftermath of authoritarian regimes or civil wars characterized by atrocities, the legitimacy of the reconciliation mechanisms is paramount. At least three ways exist to bring perpetrators to justice and help move societies forward: aggressive and visible use of the existing judicial system, establishment of a special commission for truth and reconciliation, or reliance on international tribunals.

International tribunals serve important accountability, reconciliation, and deterrence functions, inasmuch as they provide a credible forum to hear grievances and a legitimate process through which individuals, rather than an entire nationality, are held accountable for their transgressions. The International War Crimes Tribunal in The Hague, created in response to the conflicts in the former Yugoslavia and in Rwanda, reflects these aims. Notwithstanding a number of serious problems, the tribunals have set important precedents on several key legal issues. The Commission believes that the United Nations should move to establish an international criminal court, and it welcomes the secretary-general's proposal that an international conference be held in 1998 to finalize and adopt a treaty to establish such a court.

While the right to a say in how one is governed is a fundamental human right and the foundation of a political framework within which disputes among groups or their members can be brokered in nonviolent ways, merely giving people a say will not, of itself, ensure political accommodation. People must believe that their government will stay free of corruption, maintain law and order, provide for their basic needs, and safeguard their interests without compromising their core values.

Social Justice

While democratic political systems strive to treat people equitably, this does not mean that they treat all people the same. Just as efforts are made to accommodate the special needs of the very old, the very young, the poor, and the disabled, it is usually necessary to acknowledge explicitly the differences that may exist among various groups within a society and accommodate to the greatest extent possible their particular needs.

Among the most important needs are the freedom to preserve important cultural practices, including the opportunity for education in a minority language, and freedom of religion. One solution is to permit minorities to operate private educational institutions. Another is to mandate dual-language instruction. Simply put, vibrant, participatory systems require religious and cultural freedom.

THE RESPONSIBILITY OF STATES, LEADERS, AND CIVIL SOCIETY

Widespread deadly conflict threatens global stability by eroding the rules and norms of behavior that states have sought to establish. Rampant human rights abuses are often the prelude to violence. They reflect a breakdown in the rule of law, and if they are allowed to continue unchecked, the result will be weakened confidence in states' commitment to the protection of human rights, democratic governance, and international treaties. Moreover, the lack of a response—particularly by states that have an obvious capacity to act—will encourage a climate of lawlessness in which disaffected peoples or opposing factions will increasingly take matters into their own hands. In this regard, the Commission believes that, as a matter of fundamental principle, self-determination claims by national or ethnic communities or other groups should not be pursued by force. The international community should advance this principle and establish the presumption that recognition of a new state will be denied if accomplished by force. The effort to help avert deadly conflict is thus a matter not only of humanitarian obligation, but also of enlightened self-interest.

States and Their Leaders

Major preventive action remains the responsibility of states, and especially their leaders. States must decide whether they do nothing, act alone, act in cooperation with other governments, work through international organizations, or work with elements of the private sector. It should be an accepted principle that those with the greatest capacity to act have the greatest responsibility to do so.

The Commission is of the strong view that the leaders, governments, and people closest to potentially violent situations bear the primary responsibility for taking preventive action. They stand to lose most, of course, if their efforts do not succeed. The Commission believes that the best approach to prevention is one that emphasizes local solutions to local problems where possible, and new divisions of labor—involving governments and the private sector—based on comparative advantage and augmented as necessary by help from outside.

The array of those who have a useful preventive role to play extends beyond governments and intergovernmental organizations to include the private sector with its vast expertise and resources. The Commission urges the combining of governmental and nongovernmental efforts in a system of conflict prevention that takes into account the strengths, resources, and limitations of each component of the system.

It cannot be emphasized enough that governments bear the greatest responsibility to prevent deadly conflict. The following sections discuss the capacity for preventive action of the private and nongovernmental sectors and intergovernmental organizations. The Commission believes, however, that much of what these various agencies and organizations can do to help prevent deadly conflict will be aided or impeded by the actions of states.

Pivotal Institutions of Civil Society

Many elements of civil society can work to reduce hatred and violence and to encourage attitudes of concern, social responsibility, and mutual aid within and between groups. In difficult economic and political transitions, the organizations of civil society are of crucial importance in alleviating the dangers of mass violence. Many elements in the private sector around the world are dedicated to helping prevent deadly conflict and have declared a public commitment to the well-being of humanity in their various activities. They have raised considerable sums of money on the basis of this commitment, bringing them many opportunities but also great responsibilities.

Nongovernmental Organizations

Virtually every conflict in the world today has some form of international response and presence—whether humanitarian, diplomatic, or other—and much of that presence comes from the nongovernmental community. Performing a wide variety of humanitarian, medical, educational, and other relief and development functions, NGOs are deeply engaged in the world's conflicts and are now frequently significant participants in most efforts to manage and resolve deadly conflict.

As pillars of any thriving society, NGOs at their best provide a vast array of human services unmatched by either government or the market, and they are the self-designated advocates for action on virtually all matters of public concern. The rapid spread of information technology, market-driven economic interdependence, and easier and less expensive ways of communicating within and among states have allowed many NGOs—through their worldwide operations—to become key global transmission belts for ideas, financial resources, and technical assistance.

Three broad categories of NGOs offer especially important potential contributions to the prevention of deadly conflict: human rights and other advocacy groups, humanitarian and development organizations, and the small but growing number of Track Two groups that help open the way to more formal internal or international peace processes.

Human rights, Track Two, and grassroots development organizations all provide early warning of rising local tension and help open or protect the necessary political space between groups and the government that can allow local leaders to settle differences peacefully. Nongovernmental humanitarian agencies have great flexibility and access in responding to the needs of victims (especially the internally displaced) during complex emergencies. Development and prodemocracy groups have become vital to effecting peaceful transitions from authoritarian rule to more open societies and, in the event of a violent conflict, in helping to make peace processes irreversible during the difficult transitions to reconstruction and national reconciliation. The work of international NGOs and their connection to each other and to indigenous organizations throughout the world reinforce a sense of common interest and common purpose, and demonstrate the political will to support collective measures for preventive action.

Many NGOs have deep knowledge of regional and local issues, cultures, and relationships, and an ability to function in adverse circumstances even, or perhaps especially, where governments cannot. Moreover, nongovernmental relief organizations often have legitimacy and operational access that do not raise concerns about sovereignty, as government activities sometimes do.

Some NGOs have an explicit focus on conflict prevention and resolution. They may:

- Monitor conflicts and provide early warning and insight into a particular conflict

- Convene the adversarial parties (providing a neutral forum)

- Pave the way for mediation and undertake mediation

- Carry out education and training for conflict resolution, building an indigenous capacity for coping with ongoing conflicts

- Help to strengthen institutions for conflict resolution

- Foster development of the rule of law

- Help to establish a free press with responsible reporting on conflict

- Assist in planning and implementing elections

- Provide technical assistance on democratic arrangements that reduce the likelihood of violence in divided societies

Notwithstanding these valuable contributions, the Commission believes that NGOs must improve coordination with each other and with intergovernmental organizations and governments to reduce unnecessary redundancies among and within their own operations. Specifically, the leadership of the major global humanitarian NGOs should agree to meet regularly—at a minimum on an annual basis—to share information, and promote shared norms of engagement in crises. The Commission also recommends that the secretary-general of the UN follow through with his aim of strengthening NGO links to UN deliberation by establishing a means whereby NGOs and other agencies of civil society can bring relevant matters to the attention of appropriate organs of the United Nations.

Religious Leaders and Institutions

Five factors give religious leaders and institutions from the grass roots to the transnational level a comparative advantage for dealing with conflict situations. They have a

- Clear message that resonates with their followers

- Long-standing and pervasive presence on the ground

- Well-developed infrastructure that often includes a sophisticated communications network connecting local, national, and international offices

- Legitimacy for speaking out on crisis issues

- Traditional orientation to peace and goodwill

Because of these advantages, religious institutions have on occasion played a reconciling role by inhibiting violence, lessening tensions, and contributing decisively to the resolution of conflict.

Religious advocacy is particularly effective when it is broadly inclusive of many faiths. A number of dialogues between religions provide opportunities for important interfaith exchanges on key public policy issues. The Commission believes that religious leaders and institutions should be called upon to undertake a worldwide effort to foster respect for diversity and to promote ways to avoid violence. They should discuss as a priority matter during any interfaith and intrafaith gathering ways to play constructive and mutually supporting roles to help prevent the emergence of violence. They should also take more assertive measures to censure coreligionists who promote violence or give religious justification for violence. They can do so, in part, by promulgating norms for tolerance to guide their faithful.

The Scientific Community

The scientific community is the closest approximation we now have to a truly international community, sharing certain fundamental interests, values, standards, and a spirit of inquiry about the nature of matter, life, behavior, and the universe. This shared quest for understanding has overcome the distorting effects of national boundaries, inherent prejudices, imposed ethnocentrism, and barriers to the free exchange of information and ideas.

One of the great challenges for scientists and the wider scholarly community in the coming decades will be to undertake a much broader and deeper effort to understand the nature and sources of human conflict, and above all to develop effective ways of resolving conflicts before they turn violent.

Through their institutions and organizations, scientists can strengthen research in, for example, the biology and psychology of aggressive behavior, child development, intergroup relations, prejudice and ethnocentrism, the origins of wars and conditions under which wars end, weapons development and arms control, and innovative pedagogical approaches to mutual accommodation and conflict resolution. Other research priorities include exploring ways to use the Internet and other communications innovations to defuse tensions, demystify adversaries, and convey information to strengthen moderate elements. The scientific community should also establish links among all sides of a conflict to determine whether any aspects of a crisis are amenable to technical solutions and to reduce the risk that these issues could provide flash points for violence.

Educational Institutions

Education is a force for reducing intergroup conflict by enlarging our social identifications beyond parochial ones in light of common human characteristics and superordinate goals—highly valued aspirations that can be achieved only by intergroup cooperation. Pivotal educational institutions such as the family, schools, community-based organizations, and the media have the power to shape attitudes and skills toward decent human relations—or toward hatred and violence. These institutions can use the findings from research on intergroup relations and conflict resolution. The process of developing school curricula to introduce students to the values of diversity and to break down stereotypes should be accelerated.

The Media

Because many of today's wars occur in remote areas and have complicated histories, the international view of them has come to depend to a large extent on reporting by international journalists. A great challenge for the media is to report conflicts in ways that engender constructive public consideration of possibilities for avoiding violence. The media can stimulate new ideas and approaches to problems by involving independent experts in their presentations who can also help ensure factual, accurate reporting.

The media should develop standards of conduct in crisis coverage that include giving adequate attention to serious efforts under way to defuse and resolve conflicts, even as they give full international exposure to the violence itself. An international press council, consisting largely of highly respected professional journalists, could be helpful in this regard, especially in monitoring and enforcing acceptable professional practices. In addition, major networks should develop ways to expose publics to the circumstances and issues that could give rise to mass violence through regular public service programming that focuses on individual hot spots. Mass media reporting on the possibilities for conflict resolution, and on the willingness and capacity of the international community to help, could become a useful support for nonviolent problem solving.

Across the spectrum of activities, from worldwide broadcasts of violence and misery to the local hate radio that instigated killing in Rwanda and Bosnia, the media's interpretive representation of violent events has a wide and powerful impact. It is important to encourage the constructive use of the media to promote understanding and decent intergroup relations, even though these issues often do not come under the heading of "breaking news."

The Business Community

The business community is beginning to recognize its interests and responsibilities in helping to prevent the emergence of conditions that can lead to deadly conflict. Businesses should accelerate their work with local and national authorities in an effort to develop business practices that not only permit profitability but also contribute to community stability. This "risk reduction" approach to market development will help sensitize businesses to any potentially destabilizing violent social effects that new ventures may have, as well as reduce the premiums businesses may have to pay to insure their operations against loss in volatile areas.

The Commission believes that governments can make far greater use of business in conflict prevention. For example, governments might establish business advisory councils to draw more systematically on the knowledge of the business community and to receive advice on the use of sanctions and inducements. With their understanding of countries in which they produce or sell their products, businesses can recognize early warning signs of danger and work with governments to reduce the likelihood of violent conflict. However, business engagement cannot be expected to substitute for governmental action. The strength and influence of the business community give it the opportunity both to act independently and to put pressure on governments to seek an early resolution of emerging conflict.

The People

The people who may be the immediate victims of violence and the citizens of countries in a position to prevent violence have an important role to play as well. Mass movements, particularly nonviolent movements, have changed the course of history, most notably in India, where Mohandas Gandhi led his countrymen in nonviolent resistance to British rule. Hundreds of millions were moved by the example of a simple man in homespun who preached tolerance and respect for the least powerful of India's peoples and full political participation for all. In South Africa, the support of the black majority for international sanctions and the broadly nonviolent movement to end apartheid helped bring the white government to the realization

that the status quo could no longer be maintained. In the United States, the leadership of Martin Luther King, Jr., inspired both whites and blacks in a massive movement for civil rights. The power of the people in the form of mass mobilization in the streets was critical in achieving the democratic revolution in the Philippines in 1986 and in Thailand in 1992.

In 1997 the Nobel Peace Prize went to representatives of a grassroots movement to ban land mines. In 18 short months, this movement developed from a collection of diffuse efforts to a worldwide movement toward consensus among many of the world's governments—strong testimony to the power of an idea in the hands of the willing.

THE RESPONSIBILITY OF THE UNITED NATIONS AND REGIONAL ARRANGEMENTS

The United Nations

The UN can be an essential focal point for marshaling the resources of the international community to help prevent mass violence. No single government, however strong, and no nongovernmental organization can do all that needs doing—nor should they be expected to. One of the UN's greatest challenges is whether and how to adapt its mechanisms for managing interstate disputes to deal with intrastate violence. If it is to move in this direction, it must do so in a manner that commands the trust of member states and their voluntary cooperation.

Strengths of the UN

As the sole global collective security organization, the UN's key goals include the promotion of international peace and security, nonviolence except in self-defense, sustainable economic and social development, and fundamental human rights for all the world's citizens. Each of these goals is relevant to the prevention of deadly conflict. The global reach and intergovernmental character of the UN give it considerable influence when it can speak with one voice. The Security Council has emerged as a highly developed yet flexible mechanism to help member states cope with a remarkable variety of problems. The Office of the Secretary-General has considerable prestige, convening power, and the capacity to reach into problems early when they may be inaccessible to governments or private organizations. Many of the UN's functional agencies, such as the United Nations High Commissioner for Refugees (UNHCR), the United Nations Children's Fund (UNICEF), the United Nations Development Program (UNDP), the World Food Program (WFP), the World Health Organization (WHO) and, for that matter, the Bretton Woods financial institutions—the World Bank and the International Monetary Fund (IMF)—conduct effective programs of great complexity around the world. The UN system is vital to any effort to help prevent the emergence of mass violence. Its long-term programs to reduce the global disparity between rich and poor and to develop the capacity of weak governments to function more effectively are of fundamental importance to its role.

Its intergovernmental character gives the UN practical advantages for certain kinds of early preventive action—such as discreet, high-level diplomacy—that individual governments do not always have. Here, the Office of the Secretary-General has proven particularly valuable on a wide array of world problems in need of international attention. The secretary-general has brought to the attention of the

Security Council early evidence of threats to peace, genocide, large flows of refugees threatening to destabilize neighboring countries, evidence of systematic and widespread human rights violations, attempts at the forcible overthrow of governments, and potential or actual damage to the environment. The secretary-general has also helped forge consensus and secure early responses from the Security Council by deploying envoys or special representatives, assembling a group of member states to concentrate on a particular problem (so-called friends of the secretary-general), and speaking out on key issues such as weapons of mass destruction, environmental degradation, and the plight of the world's poor.

Limitations of the UN

The features that give the UN its potential often come at a price. Its global reach often demands some sacrifice of efficiency and focus, and the UN is, of course, fully dependent on its membership for political legitimacy, operating funds, and personnel to staff its operations and carry out its mandates. While member states seem in broad agreement that the UN should be concerned with a wide range of issues, there is far less agreement on what exactly the organization should do. Many countries, including some of the most powerful, use the UN as a fig leaf and a scapegoat to blur unwanted focus, to defuse political pressure, or to dilute or evade their own responsibilities. States—again, even the most powerful—often make commitments that they fail to honor.

Despite the lack of agreement on engagement in domestic conflicts by international organizations, the UN has been required to intervene in several. It shepherded the transition from war to peace in Cambodia, helped broker solutions to conflicts in new states such as the Former Yugoslav Republic of Macedonia and Georgia, marshaled an unprecedented humanitarian relief effort in Somalia, and dealt with refugees from the mass slaughter in Rwanda.

With the increasing number of conflicts within states, the international community must develop a new concept of the relationship between national sovereignty and international responsibility. The contradiction between respecting national sovereignty and the moral and ethical imperative to stop slaughter within states is real and difficult to resolve. The UN Charter gives the Security Council a good deal of latitude in making such decisions, but it also lays out a number of broad principles to guide the application of these decisions. The responsibility for determining where one principle or the other is to prevail resides with the Security Council and the member states on a case-by-case basis. It is precisely the sensitivity of such a responsibility that has led to the growing demand for reform of the Security Council in order to make it more representative of the membership and more legitimate in fulfilling its responsibilities.

Strengthening the UN for Prevention

The Commission believes that the UN can have a central, even indispensable, role to play in prevention by helping governments cope with incipient violence and organizing the help of others. Its legitimating function and ability to focus world attention on key problems, combined with the considerable operational capacity of many of its specialized agencies, make it an important asset in any prevention regime. Yet certain reforms are necessary to strengthen the UN for preventive purposes.

The Commission believes that the secretary-general should play a more prominent role in preventing deadly conflict through several steps:

- More frequent use of Article 99 of the UN Charter to bring potentially violent situations to the attention of the Security Council and, thereby, to the international community

- Greater use of good offices to help defuse developing crises

- More assertive use of the considerable convening power of the Office of the Secretary-General to assemble "friends" groups to help coordinate the international response

In addition, the Commission believes that:

- Member governments should be encouraged to make annual contributions to the Fund for Preventive Action established by the Norwegian government in 1996 for the use of the secretary-general. The secretary-general should use the fund to expand the pool of suitable candidates who serve as envoys and special representatives and to provide the resources necessary for training and support of their missions.

- The secretary-general should convene at least one meeting with the heads of the major regional organizations—as was done in August 1994—during each term of office. These meetings can be used to discuss, among other topics, potential violence in the regions, possible preventive strategies, and ways to coordinate regional and UN efforts.

- The secretary-general should establish a private sector advisory committee to draw more systematically on the expertise and insights of civil society for preventive action.

- The secretary-general should establish an advisory committee on science and technology, broadly composed of representatives from across the spectrum of the sciences, to offer advice and recommendations on a wide range of problems.

- The Security Council should call on the General Assembly to reconstitute the Collective Measures Committee to evaluate existing practices regarding the imposition and implementation of sanctions and to make recommendations regarding ways to improve their deterrent value. The Security Council should retain authority to decide when international norms have been violated and when and how the imposition of sanctions would be justified.

- UNICEF, UNDP, and UNHCR should integrate their new emphasis on prevention with a more activist UN High Commissioner for Human Rights to strengthen the UN's role in early warning, protection of human rights, and conflict prevention. The Office of the Secretary-General can play a key role in this integration.

Such measures, together with those offered by Secretary-General Kofi Annan and others in this report, would go a long way toward establishing a preventive orientation in the international community and laying the groundwork to develop standard practices that link UN actions with those of governments and NGOs.

Reform of the Security Council*

There is a compelling need to enlarge and modernize the Security Council to ensure that its membership reflects the world of today rather than 1945. One promising proposal is that put forward by Malaysian Permanent Representative, Tan Sri Razali Ismail, during his term as president of the General Assembly. In the Commission's view, the addition of new members should reflect not only the world's capacities but also the world's needs. The use of size, population, GDP, and level of international engagement (measured, for example, through such indices as participation in UN peacekeeping) might serve as criteria for permanent membership. The Commission would also propose to remove from the Charter the prohibition on election of any new nonpermanent members for successive terms, enabling other major powers with aspirations to continuous or recurring membership to negotiate their reelection on a continuous or rotating basis. The Commission believes that any new arrangement should be subject to automatic review after ten years.

The UN's Role in Long-Term Prevention

The long-term role of the UN in helping to prevent deadly conflict resides in its central purposes of promoting peace and security, fostering sustainable development, inspiring

---

* Commission member Sahabzada Yaqub-Khan dissents from the Commission's view on Security Council reform. In his opinion, the additional permanent members would multiply, not diminish, the anomalies inherent in the structure of the Security Council. While the concept of regional rotation for additional permanent seats offers prospects of a compromise, it would be essential to have agreed global and regional criteria for rotation. In the absence of an international consensus on expansion in the permanent category, the expansion should be confined to nonpermanent members only.

widespread respect for human rights, and developing the rule of international law. Three major documents combine to form a working program for the UN to fulfill these roles: *An Agenda for Peace*, published in 1992; *An Agenda for Development*, published in 1995; and *An Agenda for Democratization*, published in 1996. Each report focuses on major tasks essential to help reduce the global epidemic of violence, preserve global peace and stability, prevent the spread of weapons of mass destruction, promote sustainable economic and social development, champion human rights and fundamental freedoms, and alleviate massive human suffering. Each is an important statement of the broad objectives of peace, development, and democracy, as well as a valuable road map to achieving those objectives. In combination, they suggest how states might use the UN more effectively over the long term to reduce the incidence and intensity of global violence.

The International Financial Institutions

Although many people may have forgotten it, the international financial institutions (IFIs) are part of the UN system. Today, together with regional financial institutions, the World Bank and the IMF have a major interest and role to play in helping to prevent or cope with mass violence. Peace agreements need to be strengthened with economic development, and the Bank and the IMF have taken clear steps to focus on reconstruction to help prevent violence from reemerging.

The leverage of the IFIs could be used even more widely to provide incentives for cooperation in tense regions. Investment may act as a restraint on the causes of violence, and conditional assistance might be used to show

that loans and grants are available to those who cooperate with their neighbors.

The Commission believes that governments should encourage the World Bank and the IMF to establish better cooperation with the UN's political bodies so that economic inducements can play a more central role in early prevention and in postconflict reconstruction.

Regional Arrangements

The potential of regional mechanisms for conflict prevention deserves renewed attention in the next decade. These organizations vary in size, mandate, and effectiveness, but all represent ways in which states have tried to pool their strengths and share burdens.

Regional organizations have important limitations. They may not be strong enough on their own to counter the intentions or actions of a dominant state. Even if they are strong enough, regional organizations may not always be the most appropriate forums through which states should engage in or mediate an incipient conflict because of the competing goals of their member states or the suspicions of those in conflict. Nonetheless, if these organizations are inert or powerless in the face of imminent conflict, their function as regional forums for dialogue, confidence building, and economic coordination will also be eroded.

Regional efforts to promote cooperation, dialogue, and confidence building are, in many ways, still in the early stages. The histories of regional organizations are a process of adapting to regional and global exigencies. Today, the greatest of these exigencies is violent conflict within the borders of states. No region is unaffected by this phenomenon. If regional organizations are to be helpful in coping with these changing circumstances, member states must be prepared to commit the resources and demonstrate the political will to ensure that the regional efforts succeed.

The Commission believes that regional arrangements can be greatly strengthened for preventive purposes. They should establish means, linked to the UN, to monitor circumstances of incipient violence within the regions. They should develop a repertoire of diplomatic, political, and economic measures for regional use to help prevent dangerous circumstances from coalescing and exploding into violence. Such a repertoire would include ways to provide advance warning of conflict to organization members and to marshal the necessary logistics, command and control, and other functions that may be necessary to support more assertive efforts authorized by the UN.

TOWARD A CULTURE OF PREVENTION

This report emphasizes that any successful regime of conflict prevention must be multifaceted and designed for the long term.

Conflict, war, and needless human suffering are as old as human history. In our time, however, the advanced technology of destruction, the misuse of our new and fabulous capacity to communicate, and the pressure of rapid population growth have added monstrous and unacceptable dimensions to the old horrors of human conflict. We must make a quantum leap in our ability and determination to prevent the deadliest forms of conflict because they are likely to become much more dangerous in the next several decades. But the prevention of deadly conflict has a practical as well as a moral value; where peace and cooperation prevail, so do security and prosperity.

The inescapable fact is that the decision to use violence is made by leaders to incite susceptible groups. The Commission believes that leaders and groups can be influenced to avoid violence. Leaders can be persuaded or coerced to use peaceful measures of conflict resolution, and structural approaches can reduce the susceptibility of groups to arguments for violence.

Beyond persuasion and coercion, however, we must begin to create a culture of prevention. Taught in secular and religious schools, emphasized by the media, pursued vigorously by the UN and other international organizations, the prevention of deadly conflict must become a commonplace of daily life and part of a global cultural heritage passed down from generation to generation. Leaders must exemplify the culture of prevention. The vision, courage, and skills to prevent deadly conflict— and the ability to communicate the need for prevention—must be required qualifications for leaders in the twenty-first century.

There is a challenge to educate, a challenge to lead, and a challenge to communicate.

Current research is exploring practices within schools that can create a positive atmosphere of mutual respect and cooperative interactions among peers, as well as between students and teachers. The valuable potential of educational institutions for preventing deadly conflict is emphasized. Teaching children the values of cooperation and toleration of cultural differences helps to overcome prejudicial stereotypes that opportunistic leaders routinely use for their own destructive ends. Tapping education's potential for toleration is an important and long-term task. It is necessary not only to strengthen the relevant curricula in schools and universities, but also to use the educational potential of popular media, religious institutions, and the UN.

Although the prevention of deadly conflict requires many tools and strategies, bold leadership and an active constituency for prevention are essential for these tools and strategies to be effective. One of the central objectives of this Commission has been to help leaders to become better informed about the problems at hand and to suggest useful ways to respond. However, we recognize that raising leaders' awareness, although necessary, is not sufficient. We have also sought to offer practical measures by which leaders can be motivated, encouraged, and assisted to adopt a preventive orientation that is supported by the best knowledge and skills available.

Leaders must focus on generating a broad constituency for prevention. With a public that is aware of the value of prevention and informed of the availability of constructive alternatives, the political risks of sustaining preemptive engagement in the world are reduced. In practical terms, an enduring constituency for prevention could be fostered through measures that: identify latent popular inclinations toward prevention; reinforce these impulses with substantive explanations of rationales, approaches, and successful examples; make the message clearer by developing analogies from familiar contexts such as the home and community; and demonstrate the linkage between preventing deadly conflict and vital public interests. Such efforts are more likely to succeed if leaders can mobilize the media, the business community, and other influential and active groups in civil society.

Prevention entails action, action entails costs, and costs demand trade-offs. The costs of prevention, however, are minuscule when compared with the costs of deadly conflict and of the rebuilding and psychological healing in its aftermath. This report seeks to demonstrate the need for a new commitment—by governments, international organizations, opinion leaders, the private sector, and an informed public—to prevent deadly conflict and to marshal the considerable potential that already exists for doing so.

PREVENTING
DEADLY CONFLICT

Refugees from Rwanda stand in line for water.

CONFLICT PREVENTION IN THE TWENTY-FIRST CENTURY

Since the fall of the Berlin Wall, over four million people have been killed in violent conflicts. In January 1997, there were over 35 million refugees and internally displaced persons around the world.[1] The violence that generated this trauma has been in some cases chronic. In others, there have been tremendous spasms of destruction. For example, the 1990s have witnessed protracted violent confrontation in Bosnia and Chechnya and a massive genocide in Rwanda. The circumstances that led to the 1994 Rwandan genocide provide an extraordinary and tragic example of the failure of the world community to take effective preventive action in a deadly situation. With well over one-half million people killed in three months, this has been one of the most horrifying chapters in human history.[2]

Hopes for a better and saner world raised by the end of the Cold War have largely evaporated. Despite a massive and protracted effort toward global nuclear disarmament, no comprehensive approach to preventing a nuclear catastrophe has been articulated by governments, much less put in place. Although the nightmare of deliberate nuclear war has, for the time being, been dispelled, the risk of deliberate use of nuclear weapons by terrorists remains very much with us. Because of the degrading of stockpile controls, the danger of inadvertent use of nuclear weapons is now greater than it was during the Cold War.

Violent conflict continues at an alarming level, albeit now nearly exclusively within states. As a result, both policymakers and scholars have sought to go beyond the traditional ideas of containing and resolving conflict. While governments are understandably reluctant to become involved, either singly or collectively, in distant disputes that are both bloody and seemingly intractable, they recognize that they may nevertheless become embroiled in the widespread repercussions of these disputes. Therefore, a strong common interest has grown in recent years to find better ways to prevent violent conflict, with the immediate goal of identifying relatively modest measures which, if taken in time, could save thousands of lives.

Violent conflict can be traced to historical events, long-held grievances, economic hardship, attitudes of pride and honor, grand formulations of national interest, and related decisions by leaders or groups inclined to pursue their objectives by violence. Struggle, domination, and conflict have been recurrent features of human history, but mass violence with modern weapons does not, and thus should not, have to be a fact of life. Deadly conflict is not inevitable. The Carnegie Commission on Preventing Deadly Conflict does not believe in the unavoidable clash of civilizations or in an inevitably violent future. War or mass violence usually results from initial deliberate political calculations and decisions. This observation is perhaps the most significant lesson of the events in Rwanda in 1994.

THE LEGACY OF RWANDA

At this writing, the 1994 slaughter in Rwanda still reverberates in that country, in the region, and in capitals around the world. For the international community, the chief legacy of Rwanda is the knowledge that mass violence rarely happens without warning and that the absence of external constraints allows genocide to occur. Article II of the Convention on the Prevention and Punishment of Genocide (1948) defines genocide as

Many of the following acts committed with the intent to destroy, in whole or in part, a national, ethnical, racial or religious group, as such: (a) Killing members of the group; (b) Causing serious bodily or mental harm to members of the group; (c) Deliberately inflicting on the group conditions of life calculated to bring about its physical destruction in whole or in part; (d) Imposing measures intended to prevent births within the group; [and] (e) Forcibly transferring children of the group to another group.

The history of politically motivated animosity between Hutu and Tutsi in Rwanda dating back to colonial rule was widely known. A dramatically new situation was created when the Tutsi-led Rwandan Patriotic Front (RPF), supported by Uganda, invaded Rwanda in October 1990. The human rights group Africa Watch warned in 1993 that Hutu extremist leaders had compiled lists of individuals to be targeted for retribution—individuals who the next year were among the first victims.[3] The

Deadly conflict is not inevitable. War or mass violence usually results from deliberate political calculations.

implication of the RPF invasion and intensified warnings of a genocidal plot, received months before the plane crash that killed President Habyarimana of Rwanda and President Ntaryamira of Burundi, went unheeded by countries and international organizations in a position to thwart the plot. When the plane crash triggered the genocide, the reaction of the United Nations Security Council was to distance itself from the situation. The Security Council voted to withdraw all but 250 of the 2,500 troops of the United Nations Assistance Mission for Rwanda (UNAMIR), which had been authorized a year earlier by the Council to play a traditional peacekeeping role in support of the stillborn peace process. UNAMIR's mandate was so narrowly drawn and the force remaining in place so small that it could not intervene to halt the genocide.

It took four months for the UN to reverse itself and decide to send 5,000 peacekeeping troops to Rwanda with a mandate to protect civilians at risk and to provide security for humanitarian assistance. But member states took no concrete steps to act on their decision—no new UNAMIR troops were forthcoming—in part because troop-contributing countries had fresh memories of the bitter experience in Somalia. Meanwhile, perhaps 800,000 Rwandans had been slaughtered before an invading force of Tutsi-led exiles from neighboring Uganda routed the perpetrators of the genocide and sent two million Hutus fleeing into Zaire, Tanzania, and Burundi. Interspersed among the refugees were armed Hutu militia who had committed the genocide. They took control of the refugee camps, stole supplies intended for humanitarian relief, and embarked on an insurgency against the new government in Rwanda.[4] UN appeals for assistance to prevent further conflict went unheeded, and the violence spread and escalated, particularly in eastern Zaire. When Rwanda and other neighboring countries sent military forces into eastern Zaire, they set in motion an insurrection that eventually toppled the government of dictator Mobutu Sese Seko. We now know that while the world watched the dramatic march across Zaire of the Alliance of Democratic Forces for the Liberation of Congo-Zaire (ADFL), thousands of Hutu refugees were being systematically hunted down and slaughtered. These events only extended the cycle of deadly conflict within the region.[5]

Refugees facing an uncertain future in Zaire.

Since 1994, many knowledgeable people, including the commander of UNAMIR at the time, have maintained that even a small trained force, rapidly deployed at the outset, could have largely prevented the Rwandan genocide.[6] But neither such a force nor the will to deploy it existed at the time (see Box P.1). The Organization of African Unity (OAU) was incapable of such a preventive action, and no North Atlantic Treaty Organization (NATO) member was prepared to take such a step as part of a NATO intervention or on its own. When concerned governments finally turned to the United Nations and to the Security Council, there was neither a credible rapid reaction force ready to deploy nor the moral authority or will to assemble one quickly enough. The situation

was not helped by the fact that France and the United Kingdom were heavily involved militarily on the ground in the UN force in Bosnia; in the case of the United States, the political legacy of Somalia still seemed to haunt decision makers.

International relief and reconstruction efforts over the three years following the slaughter cost the international community more than $2 billion. Yet, according to one study, the estimated costs of a preventive intervention would have been one-third of this amount and would have very likely resulted in many thousands fewer casualties.[7]

The Rwandan tragedy is the kind of situation that is likely to recur when a great human disaster looms in a region of little strategic or economic concern to the major powers who currently constitute the crucial permanent membership of the Security Coun-

On April 6, 1994, President Habyarimana of Rwanda and President Ntaryamira of Burundi died when their plane was shot down while on approach to the Rwandan capital of Kigali. Within hours, sporadic violence broke out, and on April 7, the Rwandan prime minister was killed along with ten Belgian peacekeepers. Carnage quickly spread to the countryside, eventually claiming between 500,000 and 800,000 victims, mostly from the Tutsi minority but also members of the Hutu opposition. More killing was compressed into three months in Rwanda in 1994 than occurred in four years in Yugoslavia between 1991 and 1995.

In the midst of the slaughter, and with the UN force of 2,500 UN peacekeepers emasculated by the withdrawal of national contingents, the commander of the United Nations Assistance Mission for Rwanda (UNAMIR), Major General Romeo Dallaire of Canada, maintained that a capable force inserted within two weeks after the death of the presidents could have stopped much of the killing and removed the pretext for the continuation of the civil war. In his assessment, 5,000 troops operating under a peace enforcement mission (Chapter VII of the UN Charter) with air force, communications, and logistics support, could have: 1) prevented massive violence; 2) assisted in the return of refugees and displaced persons; 3) protected the flow of humanitarian aid; and 4) provided a secure environment to enable talks between Hutus and Tutsis to devise mechanisms to ease tensions between the ethnic groups. UN Secretary-General Boutros Boutros-Ghali also called for states to assemble and deploy such a force, but his calls fell on deaf ears.

With this history in mind, the Carnegie Commission on Preventing Deadly Conflict, the Institute for the Study of Diplomacy at Georgetown University, and the United States Army convened an international panel of senior military leaders to explore the Rwandan experience and assess the validity of General Dallaire's assertion. The panel generally agreed that early military intervention—within two weeks of the initial violence—by a force of 5,000 could have made a significant difference in the level of violence in Rwanda and that there was a window of opportunity for the employment of this force during April 7–21, 1994. The group acknowledged that such a force would have had to be properly trained, equipped, and supported, and possess a mandate from the Security Council to enable it to use "all means necessary" to protect vulnerable populations. In Rwanda in 1994, it is likely that 5,000 troops could have averted the slaughter of a half–million people.

Source: Scott R. Feil, *Preventing Genocide: How the Early Use of Force Might Have Succeeded in Rwanda* (Washington, DC: Carnegie Commission on Preventing Deadly Conflict, April 1998).

cil. To help prevent such mass violence, the Commission is convinced that reform of the Security Council to strengthen its legitimacy and efficacy in prevention is urgent. The Commission believes that Security Council membership needs to be expanded to reflect more accurately the distribution of power in the regions of the world of the twenty-first century (see pages 140–143). In the Commission's view, an expanded Security Council will be better able to finance and sustain measures necessary to prevent deadly conflict, including a Security Council rapid reaction capability.[8]

The Commission also believes that as part of that capability, a rapid reaction force is needed, the core of which should be contributed by sitting members of the Security Council.[9] The nucleus of such a force would be composed of a well-trained, cohesive infantry brigade with its own organic weapons, helicopters for in-country transportation, and compatible logistical and communication support. It would need the ability to react rapidly in potentially violent intrastate situations or in certain types of interstate crises but would not be a substitute for the normal range of UN peacekeeping operations. A more detailed discussion of this issue and recommendations that bear directly on the international community's ability to respond to circumstances of imminent mass violence can be found on pages 65–67.

IS PREVENTION POSSIBLE?

The Commission recognizes that its commitment to the possibilities and value of preventive action is not universally shared. Skeptics argue that preventing the outbreak of mass violence will often be difficult, costly, and hazardous—

perhaps even futile. Preventive measures must be applied in time in order to be effective, but no one can predict in advance the point at which a crisis will take an irreversible turn for the worse. On the receiving end, countries closest to the conflict may not want preventive assistance at a stage when it could be most effective. Countries involved in intrastate disputes often oppose the intervention of other states because they distrust their intentions or fear the consequences of intervention. Many countries resent intrusion into what are viewed as domestic affairs—maintaining law and order is still universally regarded as essentially a domestic problem. Countries often invoke the principle of national sovereignty as a barrier to early engagement, an issue this report takes up in greater detail in chapter 6.

For their part, the governments of states most capable of offering assistance—the wealthy industrialized countries—often perceive little or no national interest in engaging in some conflicts. There often may be no immediate imperative or strong interest for major states to act, aside from a strong humanitarian impulse. There is also a danger that frequent response can lead to "intervention fatigue."

The members of the Commission do not share the pessimism that underlies these views. While preventive efforts are certainly difficult, they are by no means impossible. They have been effective in a number of cases discussed throughout this report. Many preventive efforts are not well-known because they were undertaken quietly. As UN Secretary-General U Thant said of the preventive negotiations over the future of Bahrain in the late

> A rapid reaction force is needed, the core of which should be contributed by sitting members of the Security Council.

Mourners seek shelter during a sectarian attack at a funeral in Northern Ireland.

1960s, the perfect preventive operation "is one which is not heard of until it is successfully concluded, or even never heard of at all."[10] And indeed, intervention fatigue is itself an argument for more effective preventive action. Such action should be taken as early as practicable: the earlier the steps to avert a crisis, the lower the costs of engaging.

For every violent conflict under way today, there are many more disputes between deeply divided peoples and in deeply divided societies that have not escalated to warfare. This study is an attempt, in part, to understand why. In any event, the lack of an explicit, systematic, sustained focus on the prevention of deadly conflict means in practice that a preventive approach as recommended by the Commission has scarcely been tried.

TOWARD A NEW COMMITMENT TO PREVENTION

Preventive action to forestall violent conflict can be compared to the pursuit of public health. Thirty years ago, we did not know precisely how lung cancer or cardiovascular disease developed or how certain behavior, such as smoking or high-fat, high-cholesterol diets, increased the likelihood of contracting these diseases. With the advances in medicine and preventive health care over the past three decades, we have more accurate warning signs of serious illness, and we no longer wait for signs of such illness before taking preventive measures. So too in the effort to prevent deadly conflict, we do not yet completely understand the interrelationship of the various factors underlying mass violence. We know enough, however, about the factors involved to prescribe and take early action that could be effective in preventing many disputes from reaching the stage of deadly conflict.

This report points the way to a worldwide coordination of efforts toward this goal. This effort is, of course, only a beginning. By initiating discussions throughout the world and through a variety of publications, the Commission hopes to stimulate thinking and action on the prevention of deadly conflict. Our aim is to lift the task of prevention high on the world's agenda and to encourage the investment of both public and private resources in this vital endeavor. The Commission believes that all governments and peoples have a stake in helping to prevent deadly conflict, and that it is possible—indeed essential—to develop, in the light of experience, better and more effective approaches to this problem.

Conflict, war, and needless human suffering are as old as human history. In our time, however, the advanced technology of destruction, the misuse of our new and fabulous capacity to communicate, and the pressure of rapid population growth have added monstrous and unacceptable dimensions to the old horrors of human conflict. We must make a quantum leap in our ability and determination to prevent its deadliest forms because they are likely to become much more dangerous in the next several decades.

Preventing the world's deadly conflicts will be a highly complex undertaking requiring a concerted effort by a wide range of parties. Prevention will never be an easy, instinctive, or costfree cure for the global blight of mass vio-

lence. Preventing such violence requires early and concerted reaction to signs of trouble, and deliberate operational steps to stop the emergence and escalation of violence. Prevention will also require long-term policies that could reduce the likelihood of conflict by encouraging democratization, economic reform, and cross-cultural understanding. Prevention entails action, action entails costs, and costs demand trade-offs. The costs of prevention, however, are minuscule when compared with the costs of deadly conflict and the rebuilding and psychological healing in its aftermath. This report seeks to demonstrate the need for a new commitment—by governments, international organizations, opinion leaders, the private sector, and an informed public—to help prevent deadly conflict and to marshal the considerable potential that already exists for doing so.

The costs of prevention are minuscule when compared with the costs of deadly conflict.

Women and children make up the majority of the victims of conflict.

CHAPTER 1

AGAINST COMPLACENCY

FROM COLD WAR TO DEADLY PEACE

One hundred years ago, as the nineteenth century drew to a close, the mood was one of remarkably unrestrained optimism about the future. Decades of peace between the major global powers and unprecedented economic advances led many to believe that problems could be solved without resorting to deadly conflict. But the twentieth century proved to be the most violent and destructive in all human history, with armed conflict taking the lives of over 100 million people and political violence responsible for 170 million more deaths.[1]

A similar mood of optimism was evident as the Cold War ended. Perhaps with the shadow of nuclear holocaust lifted and a new spirit of superpower cooperation in the UN Security Council and elsewhere, we could look confidently forward to a new era of peaceful dispute resolution. Perhaps a commitment to trading with each other in an open-bordered, globalized economy would weaken the temptation to seek economic advantage through military conquest. Perhaps we now communicate with each other so much better—through travel, the global media, and new communications technology—that we would be much more reluctant to fight each other. Perhaps there have been so many advances over recent decades in health, education, and democratization that some crucial underlying causes of conflict have been ameliorated.

These hopes already ring hollow. The world has a long way to go before we can consign large-scale deadly conflict to history. Within a few short months of the Cold War's end, old aggressive nationalistic habits reasserted themselves with Iraq's invasion of Kuwait. The war in the Gulf was soon followed by bloody conflict in the Balkans and the Horn of Africa, and outright genocide in Bosnia and Rwanda. At the time of this writing, there is conflict in over two dozen locations around the world in which, over the years, tens of thousands have been killed and millions of persons displaced (see Figure 1.1).[2]

For many governments and their publics, the mounting losses from war have ceased to shock, as the rhythm of daily existence has settled into a routine of attack and counterattack. Yet wars have become ever more brutal. In some wars today, 90 percent of those killed in conflict are noncombatants, compared with less than 15 percent when the century began.[3] In Rwanda alone, approximately 40 percent of the population has been killed or displaced since 1994.[4]

Economic development has been set back by decades in some countries. In Lebanon, for example, GDP in the early 1990s remained 50 percent lower than it was before fighting broke out in 1974.[5] In 1993, 29 countries experienced conflict-related food shortages.[6] Civil war is blamed for

Figure 1.1
MAJOR ARMED CONFLICTS OF THE 1990s

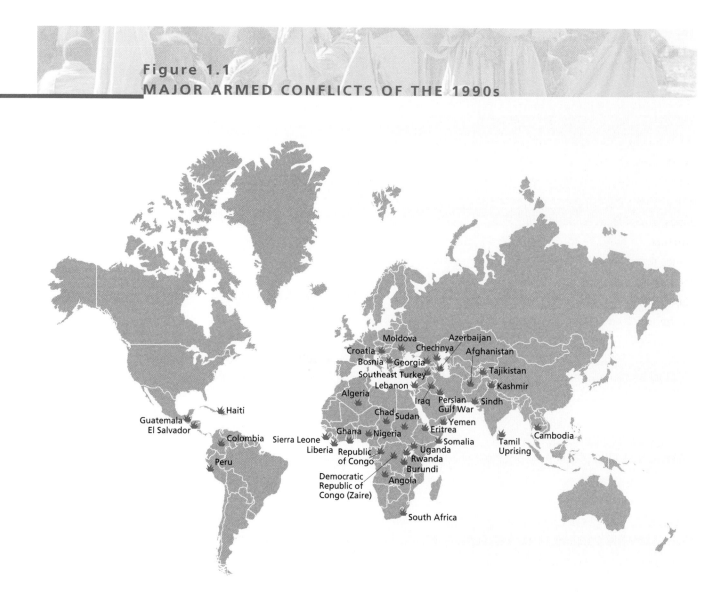

Note: Conflicts on this map had at least 1,000 deaths in any one year in the 1990s. There is no authoritative count of the dead in the recent campaign by Laurent Kabila in the Democratic Republic of Congo (Zaire). UN authorities suspect that more than 200,000 Rwandan refugees missing in Central Africa died in the campaign.

Sources: Stockholm International Peace Research Institute, *SIPRI Yearbook: Armaments, Disarmament and International Security,* 1991 to 1997 editions (New York: Oxford University Press: 1991-1997); Ruth Leger Sivard, *World Military and Social Expenditures 1996* (Washington, DC: World Priorities, 1996); "Were 200,000 Slaughtered?" *Foreign Report,* No. 2459, August 7, 1997; Amy Shiratori, "Ogata Urges Japan to Accept Refugees, Spare ODA Budget, " Asahi News Service, July 23, 1997.

the abandonment of an estimated 80 percent of Angola's agricultural land. In Burundi, already inadequate food production dropped 17 percent during recent periods of conflict.[7]

This chapter considers the world we face today and the phenomenon of violence that plagues so many countries. Two major factors—the steady growth of the world's population and the stunning advances of modern technology—are transforming the world. They are changing our lives at rates and with results—socially, politically, economically, and environmentally—difficult to predict, and both trends present formidable challenges to peacemakers. At the same time, modern weaponry has put enormous destructive power into the hands of the leaders and groups willing to use violence to achieve their goals. This chapter argues that while human development has managed great strides despite the many episodes of mass violence, we cannot be complacent about our future course.

A WORLD TRANSFORMING

Notwithstanding mass violence on a scale that dwarfs all previous centuries, those who survive in most countries now live longer, healthier lives in generally better circumstances than did their parents. Respect for human rights has become widely recognized as an important responsibility of governments and civil society. Concern for the condition of the planet has led to unprecedented international cooperation on many environmental issues.

While many elements of our changing world hold great promise for improvements in the human condition, the very process of rapid change inevitably creates new stresses, especially when accompanied by increased social and economic inequity. Over the past half-dozen years, nearly a quarter of the world's states have undergone political transformations. People and ideas have become more mobile within and between states. Immense wealth has been generated by new technology, but those left behind are increasingly conscious of their dimming prospects ever to share in this new wealth. Thus, many of the changes now under way could, if not managed properly, result in even greater risk of violent conflict.

ADVANCES IN HEALTH, EDUCATION, AND GOVERNANCE

In Health:

Between 1960 and 1994, life expectancy in developing countries increased by more than a third, from 46 to 62 years. In the same period, the infant mortality rate in developing countries fell by more than half, from 150 per thousand live births to 64. Between 1975 and 1995, maternal mortality rates fell by nearly one-half worldwide.

In Education:

Between 1970 and 1995, the literacy rate in developing countries rose from 43 percent to 70 percent. Between 1975 and 1995, females advanced twice as fast as males in both literacy and school enrollment in developing countries. Between 1960 and 1991, the net enrollment ratio in developing countries increased from 48 percent to 77 percent at the primary level.

In Governance:

Today, 117 countries, double the number in the 1970s, are either democracies or in the process of democratizing. In Latin America, 18 countries have made the transition from military to democratic governments since 1980, and since 1990, nearly 30 multiparty presidential elections have been held in Africa. The percentage of women in legislatures in 1995 was higher in developing than in developed countries, 12 percent compared with 9 percent.

Sources: United Nations Development Program, *Human Development Report 1997* (New York: Oxford University Press, 1997); Freedom House Survey Team, *Freedom in the World* (New York: Freedom House, 1996); Committee for the 1995 World Conference for Women, "Worldwide Facts and Statistics About the Status of Women" (New York: Committee for the 1995 World Conference for Women, 1995); United Nations Development Program, *Human Development Report 1996* (New York: Oxford University Press, 1996).

Figure 1.2
POPULATION PROJECTIONS

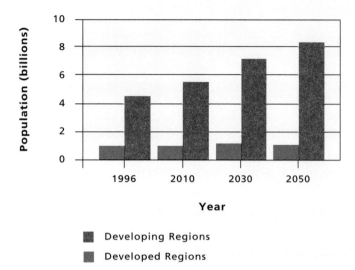

Source: United Nations Department for Economic and Social Information and Policy Analysis, *World Population Prospects: The 1996 Revision* (New York: United Nations Department for Economic and Social Information and Policy Analysis, Population Division, 1996), pp. 10, 12, 14. Figures are based on the "medium variant" population projection.

Rapid Population Growth

The UN projects that world population will increase by more than 50 percent before the year 2050. The population of the developed regions is projected to decrease, while populations in developing regions will increase by more than 80 percent (see Figure 1.2).[8]

In the coming decade, world economic output will also grow dramatically, but the benefits of this growth will be concentrated largely in already wealthy states and a handful of big emerging markets, thus adding to disparities between and within nations. The 50 poorest countries, home to one-fifth of the world's population, now account for less than two percent of global income, and their share continues to decrease.[9] Indeed, the poor in every country will experience the harshest effects and burdens of population increase. The income gap between wealthy and poor nations has doubled in the last 30 years and continues to grow.[10] And poverty seems to have a woman's face: of the 1.3 billion who live in poverty today, 70 percent are female.[11] With those having less becoming greater in number, the demands on governments will likely become even more difficult to manage and will create circumstances that could lead to increased conflict both within and between states.

Energy demands in the developing countries will more than double by 2010. According to some estimates, over the next decade annual energy infrastructure projects costing approximately $100 billion to $200 billion per year will be needed to support the economic growth of these countries.[12] The ability of these nations to feed their populations will also come under serious strain. The United Nations Food and Agriculture Organization (FAO) estimates that by 2010, developing countries will have to import more than 160 million metric tons of cereals, up from 90 million metric tons in the late 1980s.[13]

Most developing countries have also witnessed an abrupt rise in urbanization and a corresponding increase in unemployment as people move to the cities in search of work. Many find no jobs and more hardship in the cities, where urban infrastructure and services cannot support the swelling numbers. As urban centers become more crowded, housing conditions deteriorate, crime increases, and serious health problems emerge. In addition to these threats, women and children are particularly vulnerable to the dangers of sexual exploitation and are used as a cheap and plentiful (often coerced) source of labor.[14]

Beyond difficulties of urbanization and environmental stress brought on by competition for scarce resources, major problems of social adjustment, widespread resentment of the wealthy, and the deterioration of intergroup relations confront governments and leaders everywhere. Obviously, new strategies are needed to cope with these issues.

In sum, we face a world in the next century that will have nearly twice as many people consuming twice the resources but fed from considerably less arable land, with less water for irrigation and drinking available where people's needs are greatest. Some nations face the prospect of dependence on outside help for the subsistence of their people and therefore, perhaps, for the very existence of their states.[15] Pushed by growing populations, governments and markets will continue to seek ways to adapt. They are both aided and frustrated in these efforts by the explosive pace of technological advancement.

The Expansion of Technology

One of the most striking facts of our time is the rise of technology as a dominant influence in the lives of most people. Technology now presents unimaginable benefits, opportunities, and choices, but it also poses grave hazards.

Advances in information technology have decreased the cost of processing and transmitting data by factors of a thousand to a million, an efficiency gain unmatched in history.[16] The number of people around the world with access to the Internet is growing at a rate of ten percent per month.[17]

Countries in which more than half the population did not have access to safe drinking water (1990–1996)

Ethiopia	75%
Zambia	73%
Haiti	72%
Papua New Guinea	72%
Angola	68%
Sierra Leone	66%
Malawi	63%
Uganda	62%
Tanzania	62%
Democratic Republic of Congo	58%

Source: United Nations Development Program, *Human Development Report 1997* (New York: Oxford University Press, 1997), pp. 166–167.

Technical advances have also spurred the growth and integration of a global economy. By the mid-1990s over $1 trillion changed hands each day, a fact that takes on greater significance when one considers that "a new global work force has developed that works in cyberspace and that, like much of the world's financial markets, operates beyond the reach of governments."[18] These advances in certain ways limit the ability of governments and financial institutions to regulate financial flows and global markets, which makes them increasingly vulnerable to rogue trading and other illegal behavior.

The benefits of technology do not fall equally among or

The 50 poorest countries, home to one-fifth of the world's population, now account for less than two percent of global income, and their share continues to decrease.

within nations. The ability to exploit technological innovation favors those who already operate in technologically sophisticated ways.

For those less fortunate, global competition for market shares and capital flows has made it more difficult for governments to protect the jobs, wages, and working conditions of their citizens.[19] For example, new chemically and biologically engineered food and other products aimed at satisfying consumer preferences in rich countries can cause sudden drops in the export earnings of poor countries, creating a dramatic economic downturn that can fuel social and political upheaval. Advances in technology in one area of the world can thus unintentionally contribute to the emergence of violent conflict elsewhere.

An AK-47 costs as little as $6; ammunition is plentiful and cheap.

The world of the next century will be markedly more crowded, interdependent economically, closely linked technologically, increasingly vulnerable ecologically, and progressively more interconnected culturally.[20] Trends in this direction have long been apparent, but what has only recently come into sharper focus is the importance of managing the pace of change and its widespread repercussions. Contributing to this focus is the highly destructive power and universal availability of modern weaponry.

MODERN WEAPONRY: Lethal and Available

Far too many weapons—conventional and unconventional—can today fall easily into dangerous hands. The worldwide accessibility of vast numbers of lethal conventional weapons and ammunition makes it possible for quite small groups to marshal formidable fire power. One person armed with an M-16 or AK-47 can kill dozens. A militant with one shoulder-fired ground-to-air missile can bring down a commercial aircraft carrying over 400 people. Civil society is extremely vulnerable to such threats. A few well-armed individuals can seriously disrupt public order. The threat of terrorists has had a profound effect on daily life and government policies throughout the world. In short, the power of modern weaponry—conventional, chemical, biological, and nuclear—is unprece-

EMERGING MARKETS

World GDP increased over 100 percent between 1970 and 1995. Emerging markets contributed substantially to this increase, especially China, South Africa, India, and Mexico. Formerly considered minor economic players, they have demonstrated their capacity for sustained economic growth and development, becoming significant forces in the international economy. In fact, in 1995, the top ten emerging markets accounted for 10.2 percent of world economic output. This share is expected to increase in the future.

Source: International Monetary Fund, *International Financial Statistics Yearbook* (Washington, DC: International Monetary Fund, 1997), pp. 146-147. See also Jeffrey E. Garten, *The Big Ten: The Big Emerging Markets and How They Will Change Our Lives* (New York: Basic Books, 1997), p. 27.

dented in human experience, and the ability to produce and sell this weaponry is still largely uncontrolled.

Conventional Weapons

Conventional weapons are cheap and in ample supply. In many countries, guns are more readily available than basic food or medicine. An AK-47 costs as little as $6; ammunition is plentiful and cheap.[21] A land mine costs as little as $3, and those already deployed probably number over 100 million worldwide.[22] Nearly all of the large, wealthy, established states and many emerging states sell arms, and their aggressive marketing and easy financing have generated huge inventories and a steady global arms flow (see Table 1.1).

Countries of the developing world, where most of today's conflicts are being fought, spent over $150 billion in 1995 on defense.[23] Even as governments in many of these states have lost the ability to provide basic services for their populations, they still find ample resources to buy arms (see Table 1.2). Even as donor states offer funds and other assistance to help ease the ravages of war, many of these same countries, attracted to the lucrative arms trade, continue to sell the weapons and ammunition that fuel the ongoing violence.

Chemical and Biological Weapons

Chemical and biological weapons pose new dangers to poor and rich countries alike. The Iraqi government, for example, used deadly gas against its Kurdish population in 1988, and in 1995 the Japanese sect Aum Shinrikyo used sarin gas in a Tokyo subway, resulting in ten killed and over 5,000 injured—some perma-

LAND MINES

- Over 100 million land mines are deployed in more than 64 countries, with an estimated clearance cost of $33 billion.
- Some estimates suggest that every two minutes someone around the world is killed or maimed by a land mine.
- Antipersonnel land mines claim more than 25,000 casualties each year.
- Most victims of land mines are civilian women and children.
- In Afghanistan, Angola, and Cambodia, there are an estimated 28 million mines and over 22,000 casualties annually.
- Land mines strewn throughout half of Africa's countries kill over 12,000 people annually.
- A mine costs as little as $3 to make and up to $1,000 to clear.
- For every mine cleared by the international community, 20 new mines are deployed.

Sources: Fact Sheet: Banning Anti-Personnel Landmines, White House Office of the Press Secretary, May 16, 1997; United Nations Children's Fund, *State of the World's Children 1996* (New York: Oxford University Press, 1996); Isebill V. Gruhn, "Banning Land Mines," in *IGCC Policy Brief*, Institute on Global Conflict and Cooperation, March, 1996; Lloyd Axworthy, "The Ottawa Process: Towards a Global Ban on Anti-Personnel Mines," (Washington, DC: The Embassy of Canada, May 1997); United Nations, *Assistance in Mine Clearance: Report of the Secretary-General*, Document A/49/357, United Nations, September 6, 1994; United States Department of State, Bureau of Political-Military Affairs, *Hidden Killers: The Global Landmine Crisis*, Office of International Security and Peacekeeping Operations, 1994.

nently.[24] Governments and disaffected groups still seek these inexpensive weapons of mass destruction, some of which can be produced from ingredients normally sold for commercial purposes.

Table 1.1
THE TEN LEADING SUPPLIERS OF MAJOR CONVENTIONAL WEAPONS, 1992-1996 (Indexed value of exports in millions of US$)

	1992	1993	1994	1995	1996	1992–1996
U.S.	14,187	14,270	12,029	10,972	10,228	61,686
Russia	2,918	3,773	763	3,505	4,512	15,471
Germany	1,527	1,727	2,448	1,549	1,464	8,715
UK	1,315	1,300	1,346	1,568	1,773	7,302
France	1,302	1,308	971	785	2,101	6,467
China	883	1,234	718	949	573	4,357
Netherlands	333	395	581	430	450	2,189
Italy	434	447	330	377	158	1,746
Czech Republic[a]	214	267	371	195	152	1,199
Israel	192	271	207	352	168	1,190
Total	23,305	24,992	19,764	20,682	21,579	110,322

Note: The countries are ranked according to 1992-1996 aggregate exports. Figures are "trend-indicator" values at constant 1990 prices. See *SIPRI Yearbook 1997* for details of methodology.

[a] For 1992, the data refer to the former Czechoslovakia; for 1993-1996, the data refer to the Czech Republic.

Sources: Stockholm International Peace Research Institute, *SIPRI Yearbook 1997: Armaments, Disarmament and International Security* (New York: Oxford University Press, 1997), p. 268. See also, Richard F. Grimmett, "Conventional Arms Transfers to Developing Nations, 1989-1996," Congressional Research Service, The Library of Congress, Washington, DC, August 17, 1997.

The potency of these weapons is frightening. According to one analysis, "an ounce of type-A botulinal toxin, properly dispersed, could kill every man, woman, and child in North America. . . just eight ounces of the substance could kill every living creature on the planet."[25] Many lethal gasses are colorless and odorless and can lead to immediate or slow, agonizing death for thousands. These weapons can be delivered in missiles or dropped from planes, exploded in ground ordnance, set in time-delay devices, released via remote control, or put in water supplies. Large concentrations of unsuspecting civilians, especially in urban settings, are vulnerable, as the Aum Shinrikyo episode demonstrated.

To be sure, the 1972 Biological Weapons Convention prohibits the development, production, stockpiling, acquisition, retention, and transfer of biological agents for offensive purposes. Nevertheless, there are difficult problems of distinguishing hostile and peaceful purposes. There are currently no standards to resolve these problems, nor is there a suitable process in place for making progress.

Unlike standard weapons, many biological agents are produced naturally; their existence does not depend on a design bureau or a manufacturing organization. Moreover, although the development of biological weapons must overcome technical problems and uncertainties, much relevant information about biological agents is generated by medical science and is easily available throughout the world. So are the pathogens themselves. As a result, development and production experiments could be undertaken in virtually any country in small-scale operations that would be difficult to locate. These characteristics preclude reliance on a system of control similar to those developed, for example, for fissionable materials or for major items of military hardware.

The Continuing Nuclear Threat

A pervasive sense that progress has been made in reducing the dangers posed by superpower arsenals belies the menace posed by nuclear proliferation. Weapons stockpiles, loose or nonexistent controls, and the lucrative market in trafficking nuclear materials and know-how create a substantial potential for two kinds of nuclear threats: deliberate use and inadvertent use.

It is not difficult to imagine at least three plausible circumstances in which nuclear weapons might be used deliberately: in the context of a dispute between states in which at least one has nuclear capabilities, by so-called "outlaw" states who perceive themselves unacceptably threatened, or by a terrorist group. Chapter 4 discusses ways to prevent these circumstances from materializing.

While the potential for such deliberate use of nuclear weapons may seem obvious, far less apparent, although no less dangerous, is the significant potential that also exists for an inadvertent nuclear detonation. Such an outcome could result if the nuclear-capable states—particularly the United States and Russia—do not take steps to strengthen and broaden the process by which they manage and reduce their existing nuclear capability. Specifically, Russia's nuclear arsenal cannot be safely sustained at current levels or deployments—two factors that are strongly influenced by the

posture of the United States. The safe management and redeployment of Russian weapons is essential to avoid the prospect that instability in the former Soviet Union could trigger an inadvertent nuclear interaction. This report will discuss how improved early warnings, accountability, and physical security regimes can help prevent inadvertent nuclear use.

THE COST OF DEADLY CONFLICT

Against the backdrop of population growth, technological change, and the availability of destructive weaponry, the potential for violent conflict looms large. What are the consequences of such conflict? What are the long-term effects of los-

Table 1.2
THE WORLD'S SPENDING PRIORITIES (1996 US$)

Military Expenditures per Soldier

World	31,480
Developed	123,544
Developing	9,094

Education Expenditures per Student

World	899
Developed	7,675
Developing	143

Health Expenditures per Capita

World	231
Developed	1,376
Developing	22

Source: Ruth Leger Sivard, *World Military and Social Expenditures 1996* (Washington, DC: World Priorities, 1996), pp. 44-49.

> **Russia's nuclear arsenal cannot be safely sustained at current levels or deployments—two factors that are strongly influenced by the posture of the United States.**

During Mozambique's 16-year civil war:

- 490,000 children died from war-related causes.

- 200,000 children were orphaned or abandoned by adults.

- At least 10,000 children served as soldiers during the conflict.

- Over 40 percent of schools were destroyed or forced to close.

- Over 40 percent of health centers were destroyed.

- Economic losses totaled $15 billion, equal to four times the country's 1988 GDP.

- Industries were so damaged that postwar production equaled only 20 to 40 percent of prewar capacity.

Sources: United Nations Children's Fund, *State of the World's Children 1996* (New York: Oxford University Press, 1996); Michael Cranna, ed., *The True Cost of Conflict* (New York: The New Press, 1994); United States Mission to the United Nations, *Global Humanitarian Emergencies, 1996* (New York: United States Mission to the United Nations, 1996).

ing doctors, lawyers, teachers, or other professionals and the destruction of schools and factories? How long does it take to rebuild? Who pays? What opportunities are lost forever? How does one begin to calculate what it means to a country to lose a generation of its children to war?

While it is difficult to measure the overall effects of a lost generation in countries ravaged by protracted civil war, the social effects of war can be felt in such ways as major changes in the size and composition of the labor force, in economic production, and in community stability.[26] In modern wars nations lose their most precious resource—their people—and the capacity to rehabilitate those that survive. In Cambodia, for example, thousands

of people have lost limbs to land mines, with the effects on women and children particularly devastating.[27] Those who survive often harbor bitterness that fuels future violence.

Postwar rebuilding is an extremely slow, costly, and uncertain process (see Table 1.3). The cost of reconstruction in Kuwait after the six months of Iraqi occupation that ended with Operation Desert Storm was estimated at $50 billion to $100 billion, the equivalent of up to four times Kuwait's preconflict annual GDP.[28] Iraq, under a sanctions regime imposed in April 1991, showed that by summer 1997 there was little prospect for a quick return to normal living. Efforts to restore adequate shelter, water, and power to the innumerable ruined cities and towns of Afghanistan, Bosnia, Cambodia, Chechnya, Somalia, and Sudan will take years. Renewed violence, growing crime, and corrupt government are ever-present dangers, and where capable government is absent, the threat of widespread violence is often present.

In addition to the price paid by those actually in violent conflict, many peoples and countries well beyond the boundaries of the fighting face consequences and bear significant costs as well. Other states, international organizations, and nongovernmental organizations (NGOs) become involved in efforts to manage or resolve conflict and deal with the enormous human suffering, and the demand for help has only increased (see Figures 1.3 and 1.4).

The United Nations High Commissioner for Refugees (UNHCR) has seen its expenditures increase along with the growing millions of refugees and displaced persons, from under $600 million in 1990 to an estimated $1.4 billion in 1996.[29] The members of the Organization for Economic Cooperation and Development (OECD) collectively contribute up to $10 billion annually in emergency

Table 1.3
WORLD BANK LOANS AND ASSISTANCE FOR RECONSTRUCTION AND REDEVELOPMENT
(Jan. 1993 – Sept. 1997)

Croatia	$265 million
Cambodia	$237 million
Angola	$197 million
Lebanon	$175 million
Bosnia	$150 million
Rwanda	$120 million
Eritrea	$25 million

Sources: World Bank, *World Bank Annual Report, 1996* (Washington, DC: World Bank, 1996); Country Overviews for Bosnia, Cambodia, Croatia, and Lebanon, http://www.worldbank.org; and conversations with World Bank economists for Angola, Cambodia, Eritrea, and Rwanda.

humanitarian assistance. They spend nearly $59 billion on overseas development assistance, much of this to help countries ravaged by war.[30] Additionally, the International Committee of the Red Cross (ICRC), which assists all victims during and after international conflict and internal strife, had a budget in 1996 of nearly $540 million.[31]

The major global humanitarian NGOs have thousands of people operating around the world in countries beset by war. CARE International, for example, had operations in 24 countries in 1995 that were in conflict; Médecins Sans Frontières had more than 2,500 people in the field in 1995.[32] Religious, relief, and development organizations alone operated programs that cost more than $800 million in 1995.[33] In short, once war has broken out, the costs of the violence soar.

A HISTORIC OPPORTUNITY: Toward Prevention

The end of the Cold War was a turning point in history that brought a largely peaceful end to the rivalry between the nuclear powers, which could have destroyed human society. Current agreement between these powers on many issues has improved prospects for a more unified international response to crises. This ability to agree, combined with a growing (although still inadequate) consensus about the importance of human rights and democratic

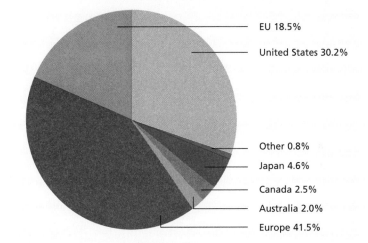

Figure 1.3
HUMANITARIAN ASSISTANCE FOR COMPLEX EMERGENCIES, 1996

EU 18.5%
United States 30.2%
Other 0.8%
Japan 4.6%
Canada 2.5%
Australia 2.0%
Europe 41.5%

Note: The term "complex emergencies" does not encompass natural disasters. Total for the European Union does not include aid accorded by member states (amounting to approximately US$922 million) independent of their EU allotment. Total for Europe includes aid accorded by European states not members of the EU and by member states independent of their EU allotment.

Source: United Nations Department of Humanitarian Affairs, "Total Humanitarian Assistance in 1996 (Global) as of 1 January 1997," *Donor Humanitarian Assistance Database,* located at http://www.reliefweb.int

Figure 1.4
WHO BEARS THE BURDEN OF
REFUGEES AND ASYLUM
SEEKERS?

Share of Refugee and Asylum-Seeking Populations by Country of Asylum, 1996

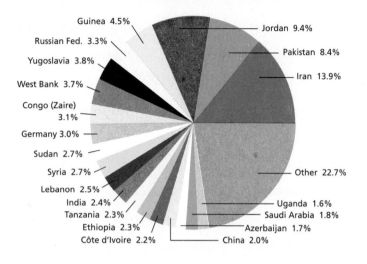

Guinea 4.5%
Russian Fed. 3.3%
Yugoslavia 3.8%
West Bank 3.7%
Congo (Zaire) 3.1%
Germany 3.0%
Sudan 2.7%
Syria 2.7%
Lebanon 2.5%
India 2.4%
Tanzania 2.3%
Ethiopia 2.3%
Côte d'Ivoire 2.2%
China 2.0%
Azerbaijan 1.7%
Saudi Arabia 1.8%
Uganda 1.6%
Other 22.7%
Jordan 9.4%
Pakistan 8.4%
Iran 13.9%

Source: U.S. Committee for Refugees, *World Refugee Survey 1997* (Washington, DC: Immigration and Refugees Services of America, 1997), pp. 4-5.

governance, provides the opportunity for a new international effort to curb violent conflict. This opportunity must be seized by responsible leaders worldwide through economic, political, and social policies designed to develop an awareness of the value of prevention, a grasp of what preventive strategies work best under various conditions, and a cooperative orientation to draw on all of the available resources—government and nongovernment alike. Such cooperation is essential if we are to solve the global problems of violence, environmental degradation, public health, and poverty.

While many dangers cloud our future and prompt this warning against complacency, it is reasonable to approach the coming decades with qualified hope. Economic and social changes on the horizon could lead to greater understanding among cultures and raise the living standards of most of the world's population in an equitable way.

To make this hope a reality, all of the relevant players in the international community must put far more effort into preventive strategies. National leaders, global and regional organizations, and the key institutions of civil society—nongovernmental organizations, educational and scientific institutions, religious institutions, the media, and the business community—all have crucial roles to play. The task that the Carnegie Commission on Preventing Deadly Conflict has set itself in this report is to identify those roles and suggest how they might best be carried out.

Two women pause among the ruins of Grozny, Chechnya.

CHAPTER 2

WHEN PREVENTION FAILS

How and Why Deadly Conflict Occurs

UNDERSTANDING VIOLENT CONFLICT

In the post–Cold War era, most violent conflict can be characterized as internal wars fought with conventional weapons, with far greater casualties among civilians than soldiers. None is spontaneous: someone is leading the groups that are willing to fight. This harsh reality may help us understand a simple truth: war remains primarily an instrument of politics in the hands of willful leaders.

Yet in many parts of the world, diverse peoples coexist in peace. Cultural distinctions, religious differences, or ethnic diversity may sharpen disagreements, but these factors do not alone determine why these differences become violent. Serbs, Croats, and Bosnians coexisted in relative calm since World War II, and in some respects even for centuries, before the violence erupted in the former Yugoslavia in 1991. Chechens had declared independence from Russia three years before the shelling of Grozny began in 1994.

While disputes between groups are common, the escalation of these disputes into lethal violence cannot be explained merely by reference to sectarian, ethnic, or cultural background. Indeed, in the Commission's view, mass violence is never "inevitable." Warfare does not simply or naturally emerge out of contentious human interaction. Violent conflict is not simply a tragic flaw in the cultural inheritance and history of certain groups.

Violent conflict results from choice—the choice of leaders and people—and is facilitated through the institutions that bind them. To say that violent clashes will inevitably occur and can only be managed, a view implicit in much of the contemporary literature on mediation and conflict resolution, will not do.[1] The factors that lead to the choice to pursue violence are numerous and complex, and this chapter seeks to illuminate how they emerge. What are the political, economic, and social circumstances that lie behind decisions for violent action? Why do leaders and groups choose deadly conflict? Can anything be done to make them choose differently?

Many of the factors that can lead to violent conflict—between and within states—are in fact sufficiently well understood to be useful in prevention. The causes of war in general and specifically of war in the pre–Cold War period have been well studied. What do these studies suggest about the causes of conflict?

In the post–Cold War era, most violent conflict can be characterized as internal wars fought with conventional weapons, with far greater casualties among civilians than soldiers.

Conflict between States

Violent conflict has often resulted from the traditional preoccupation of states to defend, maintain, or extend interests and power.[2] A number of dangerous situations today can be understood in these terms. The newly independent states of the former Soviet Union harbor thinly veiled concerns that Russia's active interest in disputes that lie beyond its present borders may lead to intervention. In the Middle East, much of the maneuvering among the various governments reflects calculated efforts to maximize power and minimize vulnerability. In East and Southeast Asia, some states are wary of their territorial disputes with a resurgent China, fearing that they could become unmanageable. In South Asia, the long festering dispute over Jammu and Kashmir has bedeviled relations between India and Pakistan, impairing the economic and social development of almost one-fifth of humanity. Greece and Turkey have come dangerously close to war several times over the past decades, and border disputes between Ecuador and Peru and Nigeria and Cameroon have led to repeated though relatively minor violence.

Yet, remarkably, no significant interstate wars rage in 1997. Since the end of the Cold War, most states have managed—often with help from outside—to stay back from the brink.

The fact that there are fewer instances of interstate war in the post–Cold War period is remarkable in view of the number and size of states around the world in the throes of profound political, social, and economic transition, especially where large groups of one country's population have close cultural and ethnic ties with another country. In many cases the transition process is painful and protracted and has created a volatile political climate, sometimes because of the absence of established political institutions that have the confidence of the public and the flexibility to absorb the shock of radical changes. Many economies are in disarray, and social cohesion is severely strained.

The absence of major interstate conflict is all the more remarkable given the existence of the many familiar motives that have fueled interstate conflict in the past. Disputes over territory and boundaries, profitable natural resources such as oil or necessities such as water, kindred populations across borders, and the complicating factor of national honor, still chafe relations between neighbors. Yet states now appear to work hard to prevent these continual sources of friction from turning violent. Moreover, as the Cold War recedes, war between or among the most powerful countries appears, for the time being at least, to be unlikely. However, and ironically, as interstate wars wane, violent intrastate conflict has exploded.

Conflict within States

The internal conflicts of the post–Cold War period have involved both states in transition (about a dozen) and established states, many with long histories of internal discord (some 25 in all).

A significant source of conflict is to be found in the competition to fill power vacuums, especially during times of transition within states and often as a result of the end of the Cold War and the collapse of the Soviet Union.[3] During the Cold War, many regimes

Remarkably, no significant interstate wars rage in 1997.

Africa

Nigeria	Cameroon

Asia

Armenia	Azerbaijan
China	Vietnam
India	Pakistan
North Korea	South Korea

Europe

Bosnia	Serbia
Croatia	Serbia
Greece	Turkey

Middle East

Iran	Iraq
Israel	Syria

South America

Ecuador	Peru

around the world maintained power through repressive measures made possible by substantial help from major powers on opposite sides of the East–West divide. Powerful states helped maintain these repressive regimes, in part to ensure that the other side in the Cold War did not gain control, and in part to avoid the risk that local conflicts might escalate into a direct confrontation between the superpowers. In Angola, Central America, and the Horn of Africa, for example, the superpowers in effect fought by proxy through local factions. The end of the Cold War eliminated this practice. Unable to maintain a hold on power without

massive help from outside, many regimes have found themselves challenged by internal groups, and those challenges have often led to violence.

Since the fall of the Berlin Wall, more than 50 states have undergone political transformation.[4] Such states may be prone to violence because of the inherent dangers that exist where habits of democratic governance have not yet fully taken hold and where deeply contentious issues of minority status and entitlement remain unsolved.[5] Political alienation can be extremely destructive in such cases.

Other explanations for conflict can be derived from economic factors, such as resource depletion, rising unemployment, or failed fiscal and monetary policies, particularly when discriminatory economic systems create economic disparities along cultural, ethnic, or religious lines.[6] The efforts of some countries to modernize—to become competitive in the global economic system and to meet the needs of growing populations—are often accompanied by cultural clashes started by people wanting to maintain traditional ways of life. Few doubt that economic conditions contribute to the emergence of mass violence, although experts disagree about exactly how the stresses of economic transformation contribute to violent outbreaks.

Outsiders may exacerbate internal conflicts. Neighbors often become involved because of fear of spillover effects (e.g., outflow of refugees or soldiers regrouping), pressure from domestic constituencies, perceived economic interests, or threats to their citizens abroad. Insurgents sometimes are able to entice

War remains primarily an instrument of politics in the hands of willful leaders.

A wounded child in a Médecins Sans Frontières hospital in Burundi.

foreign intervention by appeals to religious and ethnic solidarity, or by using local resources to pay for foreign mercenaries. Intervention can range from supplying weapons and support to direct participation with organized military forces. Turkey has accused Syria of providing financial support and a safe haven for Kurdistan Workers' Party (PKK) terrorists. Russia is thought by some surrounding countries to have a hand in violence around its periphery.[7] Croatia allowed Iranian arms to go through to the Bosnian government forces—apparently with at least tacit U.S. support—despite the UN arms embargo. Indeed, outside actors play a catalytic role in internal conflict, even if they stand by and do nothing.

At the moment there is no specific international legal provision against internal violence (apart from the Genocide Convention and more general prohibitions contained in international human rights instruments), nor is there any widely accepted principle that it should be prohibited. Yet, the Commission believes that, as a matter of fundamental principle, self-determination claims by national or ethnic communities or other groups should not be pursued by force.

In other contexts we do recognize that situations can arise where groups within states may, as a last resort, take violent action to resist massive and systematic oppression, in the event that all other efforts, including resort to international human rights machinery, have failed. This is violence in defense of human security—as was the case, for example, in South Africa. This case also illustrates an actively helpful role for the international community in diminishing oppression and paving the way toward nonviolent resolution of underlying problems. The international community should advance this fundamental principle and establish the presumption that recognition of a new state will be denied if accomplished by force.

In summary, the Commission's strong view is that the words "ethnic," "religious," "tribal," or "factional"—important as they may be in intergroup conflict—do not, in most cases, adequately explain why people use massive violence to achieve their goals. These descriptions do not, of themselves, reveal why people would kill each other over their differences. To label a conflict simply as an ethnic war can lead to misguided policy choices by fostering a wrong impression that ethnic, cultural, or religious differences inevitably result in violent conflict and that differences therefore must be suppressed. Time and again in this century, attempts at suppression have too often led to bloodshed, and in case after case, the accommodation of diversity within appropriate constitutional forms has helped prevent bloodshed.

In the Commission's view, mass violence almost invariably results from the deliberately violent response of determined leaders and their groups to a wide range of social, economic, and political conditions that provide the environment for violent conflict, but usually do not independently spawn violence. The interplay of these predisposing conditions and violence-prone leadership offers opportunities for prevention.

LEADERS AND GROUPS

Within diverse political, economic, and social environments, many factors heighten the likelihood of violence—political and economic legacies of colonialism or of the Cold War, problematic regional relationships, religious or ethnic differences sustained by systematic cultural discrimination, political or economic repression, illegitimate government institutions, or corrupt or collapsed regimes. Rapid population growth or drastic economic changes generate extreme social and economic frictions, and a shortage of vital resources can also exacerbate feelings of deprivation, alienation, hatred, or fear. Other factors can worsen the situation, including sudden changes of regime, disturbances in neighboring areas, and, as discussed, the ready availability of weapons and ammunition.[8] A dramatic event, such as the plane crash that killed the presidents of Rwanda and Burundi and precipitated the 1994 genocide in Rwanda, can trigger or be used as the pretext for an outbreak of violence. Demagogues and criminal elements can easily exploit such conditions. Indeed, it may be possible to predict violent conflict from some of these factors. For example, the UN High Commissioner for Refugees (UNHCR) foresees a high risk for refugee disasters when minority populations are present in economically depressed areas that border kin states.[9]

Time and again in this century, suppression of ethnic, cultural, or religious differences has led to bloodshed.

The political interaction between societies and their leaders helps to explain why, under some circumstances, violence breaks out between groups—both within and across state boundaries—and why with other groups in very similar circumstances it does not. Mass violence results when leaders see it as the only way to achieve their political objectives, and they are able to mobilize groups to carry out their strategy. Without determined leaders, groups may riot but they do not start systematic, sustained campaigns of violence to achieve their goals; and without mobilized groups, leaders are unable to organize a fight.

This is not to say that deliberate choices by leaders are the only cause of violence. Miscalculation and unforeseen events also contribute to the outbreak of violent conflict. Nonetheless, the state of mind of leaders is almost always an important factor. Their judgments are usually strongly influenced by two calculations: whether they think that violence will achieve their aims, and whether they think they must use violence to survive. A central question concerns how leaders' interests in pursuing certain objectives—for example, group emancipation, regime change, or self-aggrandizement—develop into pursuing violence to achieve those objectives.

Obviously, not all leaders who turn to violence are evil. Leaders and their followers, seeing their goals to be in direct conflict with those of their opponents, may discern no effective alternatives to violence and believe they can win.[10] And where there are no mediating structures of governance or help from outside that both sides trust, advocates of violence will usually prevail. Sometimes external factors, such as the threat of outside intervention or the effects of the fighting on bordering areas or states, may influence a leader's decisions regarding whether or when to initiate violence. Certainly, domestic circumstances and relationships with followers, as well as with rival leaders, help to explain why violence is chosen, especially when alternative methods of settling a dispute exist. In many cases, particularly in a crisis, leaders may maintain only a tenuous authority and therefore respond to the group demands for action.

These demands and, more broadly, a group's susceptibility to violence, typically develop from a combination of factors. Such factors include conflicting claims and objectives, hatred or fear of others, the conviction that there is no alternative to violence, a sense that the group could prevail in a military contest, and an assessment that fighting will provide better prospects for the future.[11] Yet even when such factors exist, and despite the dire predictions of observers who believe warfare is inevitable, violence does not always arise. Why?

AVOIDING THE WORST CASE

To understand how violence can be avoided even in the context of grave, profound conflict, it is useful to look at transitions where mass violence could have been expected to break out, but did not. The transitions of South Africa and the Soviet Union offer two prominent examples.[12] The striking transformation of these countries in relative peace points out the importance of three factors that might help forestall mass violence: *leadership, social cohesion* (magnified in a robust civil society that offers a vibrant atmosphere for citizen interaction, or in accepted patterns of civil behavior able to absorb the shocks of rapid

Leadership and reconciliation: President Nelson Mandela with Betsie Verwoerd, widow of Hendrik Verwoerd, the South African prime minister who ruthlessly enforced apartheid, March 1996.

change), and concerted *international engagement*. Later sections of this report will examine these factors in greater detail.

South Africa

South Africa's transition began toward the end of the 1980s and the latter days of P.W. Botha's presidency—a regime marked by some of the most severe repression of the apartheid era.[13] As Communism entered its final phase in Europe and political transformation of the countries of the Warsaw Pact began, the South African government began a secret dialogue with representatives of the African National Congress (ANC). Even among members of the inner circle of the ruling National Party (NP), few realized that a dialogue had begun between Botha himself and Nelson Mandela.

Mandela met with Botha in the summer of 1989, shortly before the latter's resignation. The dialogue continued with Botha's successor, F.W. de Klerk, and on February 2, 1990, de Klerk announced that Mandela would be released from jail after 27 years. He also lifted the ban on the ANC and other opposition parties.[14] This unexpected move marked the beginning of formal negotiations to move South Africa away from apartheid and toward democracy.

The negotiating process was painstaking, beset with obstacles, and accompanied by periodic outbreaks of political violence. Each stalemate was met by public threats to break off the talks. At crucial moments, help provided by the UN and certain private sector agencies was able to assist in restoring the negotiating process.[15] In November 1993, an interim constitution was adopted, and in 1994, the first open elections in South African history were held. Local elections and the adoption and ratification of a final constitution in 1996 consolidated the new democracy.

Leadership, civil society, and international engagement account for much of the success—that is, the relative peace—of the transition. Indeed, enlightened leadership on both sides may prove to be the most important factor. For his part, de Klerk did not have full support within his own party. Significant segments of the Afrikaner and English-speaking populations were (and indeed remain) opposed to the process of accommodation with black South Africans. Some elements of the black population contemplated intensifying the armed struggle to defeat fully the old regime. Yet under the extraordinary leadership of Mandela and others, they did not. Mandela's willingness to forgive his captors for his 27-year imprisonment established a tone of national reconciliation.

Moreover, within the black community, an active civil society—trade unions, women's groups, professional organizations, human rights groups, and community-based education programs—provided an opportunity for the development of black leadership, strong social structures, and alternative means of political participation. Many people active in these groups would later assume leadership roles in the ANC-led government. The respect that these leaders gained through years of community activism has helped carry South Africa through its transition.

Finally, black and white South Africans alike acknowledge and credit the importance of concerted international action in pushing the country toward change and in helping that change come about. The controversial economic sanctions imposed by the international community against South Africa in 1979, though incapable of bringing about immediate change, had a cumulative impact on the South African economy and on its leaders. By the end of the 1980s, particularly as financial sanctions impeding the flow of capital to South Africa took greater effect, it was increasingly obvious that sufficient economic growth was impossible without reintegration into the world economy. With the collapse of the Soviet Union and subsequent marginalization of South Africa's position as a self-styled regional bulwark against Communism, it also became evident that reintegration into the global economy would take place only after the integration of South Africa's own society. International sanctions became an important bargaining chip in the negotiation process—a chip the ANC would not finally trade in until late in 1993 when Mandela called for the lifting of all sanctions.

The striking transformation of South Africa and the Soviet Union in relative peace points out the importance of three factors that might help forestall mass violence: leadership, social cohesion, and concerted international engagement.

President Gorbachev leaves the May Day parade on Red Square, Moscow, May 1, 1989.

While the international community attempted to weaken the apartheid state, it also worked to build the economic, political, and social resources of the black community. Governments and private organizations contributed millions of dollars to the development of a civil society whose leaders and organizations have contributed so much to the success of South Africa's transition.

Finally, symbolic gestures reinforced the international community's commitment to the creation of a democratic South Africa and encouraged South Africa's leaders to stay on the peaceful path to change. The award of the 1993 Nobel Peace Prize to de Klerk and Mandela, for instance, did more than just recognize the remarkable progress that had been made. In focusing the attention of the international community on South Africa, it strengthened the two leaders in their efforts to conclude final power-sharing agreements.[16]

The Soviet Union

Although there were clear signs of decay within the Soviet Union by the early 1980s, few would have predicted that within a decade, Eastern Europe would be free and the Soviet Union itself would dissolve into 15 separate states in a largely nonviolent process. An examination of this historic and relatively peaceful transition reveals that, here too, leadership, social cohesion, and international engagement all played significant roles.

From the time Mikhail Gorbachev embarked on a course of reform in 1985, to the crisis of the attempted coup in August 1991

President Clinton brings together Prime Minister Yitzhak Rabin and Chairman Yasir Arafat at the Israel-PLO Peace Treaty signing ceremony, September 13, 1993.

and beyond, leadership from the Kremlin and the capitals of the newly independent states was essential to the process of peaceful transition.[17] Gorbachev recognized that the economy and society of the Soviet Union, weakened by the decades-long emphasis on military competition with the West and the nature of the totalitarian system, were unsustainable. He set the forces of change in motion and soon learned that he could not control those forces. Widely criticized for his efforts in the years since he left office, Gorbachev nevertheless manifested a strong commitment to effecting a peaceful change and to bringing into practice the values of democracy. His commitment to nonviolence

set the tone for the peaceful dissolution of the Soviet Union and the Warsaw Pact. Faced with the prospect of propping up faltering East European Communist regimes by force, Gorbachev broke ranks with his predecessors and elected not to send in troops to preserve the old order.

Gorbachev's turn away from the habit of automatic crackdown may also have influenced events in the remarkably bloodless reversal of the attempted coup of 1991. Although Gorbachev became unpopular in Russia for presiding over the collapse of the Soviet economy and political system, there was no widespread popular support for a return to the old ways. The coup leaders underestimated the power of the unleashed forces of political liberalization. The resounding cry of opposition to the illegal seizure of power from supporters of democratic reform led by Boris Yeltsin—one of Gorbachev's most bitter political rivals—was instrumental in consolidating popular resistance to a return to government-by-force.

Other internal factors in the Soviet Union contributed to the peaceful outcome of these dramatic events. While the institutions and habits of civil society had been repressed during 70 years of totalitarian rule, the seeds of civil society found fertile ground among the highly literate population and the highly developed (although state-dominated) social institutions of the Soviet Union. Labor unions took on a new life and emerging grassroots political and religious organizations became increasingly active and helped provide a measure of organizational stability in the last days of the Soviet Union. As did the newly free press; the independent radio broadcasts from Yeltsin's stronghold at the Russian White House during the coup gave ordinary citizens a different version of events from those that they received from the official television station.

The international community played a vital role in helping to moderate the Soviet transition. Its broad support gave Gorbachev room to maneuver with respect to the hard-line elements in the Kremlin who might otherwise have been moved to respond more forcefully to hold the country together. An enabling international environment made it possible for reformers inside to argue that Russian security was not being threatened by the unfolding events, leaving little room for extremist voices to gain popular support during the height of political upheaval.[18]

These cases illustrate an important point about international engagement. It may be clear in certain cases to those closest to a conflict that international engagement can help avoid mass violence. It is not always clear, however, what outsiders should do or how they can be persuaded to act wisely and in a timely manner.

WHAT CAN BE DONE? WHAT ARE THE TASKS? WHAT WORKS?

Just as in the practice of good medicine, preventing the outbreak, spread, and recurrence of the disease of deadly conflict requires timely interventions with the right mix of political, economic, military, and social instruments. Subsequent chapters of the report will seek to spell out how all these instruments might work.

Violent conflict can usually be foreseen.

The circumstances that give rise to violent conflict can usually be foreseen. Early indicators include widespread human rights abuses, increasingly brutal political oppression, inflammatory use of the media, the accumulation of arms, and sometimes, a rash of organized killings. Such developments, especially when combined with chronic deprivation and increasing scarcity of basic necessities, can create an extremely volatile situation. Successful prevention of mass violence will therefore depend on retarding and reversing the development of such circumstances.

When efforts to forestall conflict do not succeed, it is essential at least to prevent the conflict from spreading. Such efforts include political and diplomatic measures to

Removal of nuclear weapons from Ukraine.

A further important element in this equation, particularly in the context of avoiding conflict between states, is the development of effective international regimes for arms control and disarmament, for rule making and dispute resolution, and for dialogue and cooperation more generally. All of these can be important in preventing disagreements or disputes from escalating into armed conflict.

The preventive needs identified above involve avoiding the outbreak, escalation, or recurrence of mass violence. It is difficult in practice, however, to develop effective policies merely of avoidance. It may therefore be more useful to think of prevention not simply as the avoidance of undesirable outcomes but also as the creation of preferred circumstances. This approach was one of the basic strategies of the Marshall Plan and other economic and political initiatives in Europe after World War II: to build capable and self-reliant partners within Europe, to strengthen relations between Europe and North America, and to reduce tensions between former adversaries and integrate them into

help manage and resolve the conflict as well as humanitarian operations to relieve victims' suffering. When a cessation of hostilities is achieved, the task of securing peace despite distrust and hatred usually proves to be long, frustrating, and expensive, but it is essential in order to break the cycle of violence.

a more cohesive political and economic community. A similar effort was undertaken with respect to Japan. The countries devastated by war needed to become flourishing societies for their own future peace and benefit, and in so doing, they would become more able to withstand the pressures of totalitarianism, both internally and externally.

PREVENTING DEADLY CONFLICT

To move policies of prevention toward greater pragmatic effect, therefore, the broad objectives identified above might be stated more fully as:

- Promote effective international regimes—for arms control and disarmament, for economic cooperation, for rule making and dispute resolution, and for dialogue and cooperative problem solving.

- Promote stable and viable countries—thriving states with political systems characterized by representative government, the rule of law, open economies with social safety nets, and robust civil societies.

- Create barriers to the spread of conflict within and between societies—by means such as the suffocation of violence through various forms of sanctions (including the denial of weaponry and ammunition, or restricting access to the hard currency resources necessary to fund continued fighting), the preventive deployment of military resources when necessary, and the provision of humanitarian assistance to innocent victims.

- Create a safe and secure environment in the aftermath of conflict by providing the necessary security for government to function, establishing mechanisms for reconciliation, enabling essential economic, social, and humanitarian needs to be met, establishing an effective and legitimate political and judicial system, and regenerating economic activity.

Strategies for prevention fall into two broad categories: operational prevention (measures applicable in the face of immediate crisis) and structural prevention (measures to ensure that crises do not arise in the first place or, if they do, that they do not recur). The following chapters develop these strategies and offer a view as to how governments, international organizations, and the various institutions of civil society might best help implement them.

It may be more useful to think of prevention not simply as the avoidance of undesirable outcomes, but also as the creation of preferred circumstances.

A UN soldier on the border of Serbia.

CHAPTER 3

OPERATIONAL PREVENTION

Strategies in the Face of Crisis

LOOKING AT THE WHOLE PROBLEM

Realistic prospects often exist to prevent or curtail violence. In Rwanda, for example, there were at least two opportunities for the international community to exert influence to prevent the disaster. The first came during the months preceding the genocide. As the Arusha Accords were being negotiated, decision makers in the major capitals were warned repeatedly in public and private forums that the Hutu extremists were preparing to unleash a campaign of massive violence against the Tutsi minority. But countries in the region and the wider international community took no action to forestall such preparations. The second opportunity came when the violence began to flare in Kigali. Yet again, the international community failed to respond to calls from the UN secretary-general for the deployment of a military force to stop the bloodshed.[1]

In contrast, violence has been averted in several countries because opportunities were seized by the international community. The UN Security Council took the remarkable step in 1992 of deploying the first-ever *preventive* peacekeeping force in Macedonia to stem spreading violence in the Balkans.[2] In Guatemala in 1993, the Organization of American States (OAS) quickly supported institutions of civil society to resist successfully the disruption of constitutional government by President Jorge Serrano.[3] The same year, the OAU intervened to protect a fragile democratic process in the Republic of Congo.[4] Regrettably, by 1997 the round of violence that began with the Rwandan genocide had spread across central Africa, and a resurgent local conflict in Congo overwhelmed the diplomatic efforts of the OAU and the UN. The fighting in Congo illustrates the recurring nature of the prevention challenge, especially in a region where bullets can still trump ballots and overthrow a fragile democracy.

This chapter discusses operational prevention, that is, strategies and tactics undertaken when violence appears imminent. The responsibility for taking these measures falls both to those closest to an unfolding crisis and also to those more removed. Since the parties in a crisis often cannot find nonviolent solutions on their own, the help of outsiders is, in many instances, necessary. It is of vital importance, however, that the economic, military, or diplomatic action and policies of outsiders avoid exacerbating dangerous situations. Even well-intentioned efforts, if not carefully planned, can have adverse effects.

This chapter lays out a framework for such involvement and discusses the various measures that can be used to avoid imminent violence:

- Early warning and response
- Preventive diplomacy
- Economic measures, such as sanctions and incentives
- The use of force

Although this chapter is primarily focused on and will draw on many examples from intrastate disputes, all these measures can be used whether a crisis occurs within a state or between states. In both cases, successful operational prevention involves shared efforts, with the actions and responsibilities of national leaders linked to help as and where needed from other governments, international organizations, and the national and international nongovernmental sector.

A FRAMEWORK FOR ENGAGEMENT

Operational prevention relies on early engagement deliberately designed to help create conditions in which responsible leaders can resolve the problems giving rise to a crisis. It involves four key elements that, while not a guarantee of success, certainly increase its prospects: 1) a lead player—an international organization, country, or even prominent individual around which or whom preventive efforts can mobilize; 2) a coherent political-military approach to the engagement designed to arrest the violence, address the humanitarian needs of the situation, and integrate all political and military aspects of the problem; 3) adequate resources to support the preventive engagement; and, particularly applicable to intrastate conflict, 4) a plan for the restoration of host country authority.[5]

These elements provide a framework for applying various preventive political, economic, social, and military measures. These steps may not be sufficient, in themselves, to head off violence indefinitely, but they can help open up the political space and time necessary to pursue other means to resolve the dispute.[6] The following discussion explores this framework and many of the measures the Commission believes can be used to prevent the emergence of mass violence.

The Need for Leadership

Governments, international organizations, and even nongovernmental agencies or prominent individuals can provide the necessary leadership around which preventive efforts can mobilize. Effective leadership derives from a special relationship or capacity that makes an organization, a government, or an agency the logical focal point for rallying the help of the international community. To cite but two examples, U.S. leadership in the Gulf War, supported strongly by UN Security Council resolutions, was critical in maintaining unity within a diverse coalition of nations,[7] and in the early 1990s, the UN led an ambitious international peace initiative in Cambodia.[8] In most cases, the active support of the members of the UN Security Council—especially the permanent members—is important to success.

For a number of crisis responses, the absence of international leadership has given

Operational prevention relies on early engagement to help create conditions in which responsible leaders can resolve the problems giving rise to a crisis.

them a random quality that inevitably reduces their individual and collective effectiveness. A major evaluation of emergency assistance to Rwanda, for example, concluded that "the Rwanda crisis has been characterized by the lack of a coordinated political strategy within the international community for 'managing' the crisis."[9] Thus, even when much is done to attend to the short-term humanitarian needs generated by conflict, frequently a good deal of "wheel-spinning" occurs; little headway is made in reducing basic tensions or containing the spread of violence. With a leader to help shape a constructive effort and maintain political support, these problems can be avoided.

A Comprehensive Political–Military Response

Preventive responses must seek not only to reduce the potential for violence, but also to create the basic conditions to encourage moderation and make responsible political control possible. In the acute phase of a crisis, assertive efforts may be necessary to deny belligerents weapons and ammunition, and these military steps may very well need to be complemented by economic steps to deny access to the hard currency necessary to procure weapons and pay combatants (steps that themselves demand that outsiders refrain from providing weapons, funds, and other resources to factions in conflict). In addition, humanitarian assistance will usually be needed to help noncombatant victims of the crisis, and such assistance must be carried on in close coordination with the other political, military, and economic programs under way. This is easier said than done, however, as belligerents now frequently try to deny the provision of food and other humanitarian assistance to gain an advantage in the conflict.[10]

An integrated response should bring together the efforts of governments, international organizations, NGOs, and private relief agencies. It should also coordinate the efforts of outside parties with those of the responsible leadership on the ground.

Well before civil strife or other sources of crisis yield high levels of violence, they will generate refugees and displaced persons who need emergency humanitarian assistance. A number of states, international agencies, and private sector groups routinely provide for these needs. A serious question surrounds how to provide that assistance in ways that do not exacerbate or prolong the crisis or lead to permanent displacement of large numbers of people. To meet this challenge, humanitarian assistance groups, often led by the UN High Commissioner for Refugees (UNHCR), have begun to expand the boundaries of their operations, both in time and in scope.[11]

UNHCR and other relief agencies have become more vocal and active in identifying and addressing dangerous circumstances *before* they generate large numbers of refugees and displaced persons.[12] In May 1996, for example, in an effort to reduce the potential for massive population movements, UNHCR cosponsored a conference with the Organization for Security and Cooperation in Europe (OSCE) and the International Organization for Migration (IOM) to address the problem of refugees, displaced persons, other forms of involuntary displacement, and returnees in the Commonwealth of Independent States (CIS). The conference sought to devise an integrated strategy

An integrated response should bring together the efforts of governments, international organizations, NGOs, and private relief agencies.

that would enable the countries of the CIS to prevent further population displacement, and a major conclusion of this gathering was that the effects of massive population migration reverberate well beyond the locales where the crises occur. Entire regions are affected, and often the entire international community is called upon to help deal with these situations.[13]

In part because of the changing nature of post–Cold War crises, UNHCR has broadened its approach to relief, moving well beyond its traditional mandate to provide essential food, medicines, shelter, and refugee protection. It now also emphasizes the importance of rebuilding and strengthening a sense of community through strategies that give priority to more permanent shelter, education, and women's initiatives.[14] Similarly, CARE USA has launched new programs on girls' education, family planning, and microenterprise.[15] Measures such as these can be valuable complements to governmental efforts to find a political solution to a crisis, but they cannot substitute for such efforts.

Resources

As a crisis escalates, and even as efforts begin to help defuse its effects, political rhetoric to mobilize preventive efforts often outpaces the flow of resources, which consists of cash and contributions "in kind" by governments, the International Committee of the Red Cross, and global NGOs such as CARE and Oxfam.[16] Sig-

nificant resources also come from many smaller humanitarian organizations such as Médecins Sans Frontières, and other private sector agencies. While these nongovernmental and private sector organizations may not play leading roles in either mobilizing the overall international response to a crisis or in developing the overall plan of engagement, their services and resources are vital to the larger effort and should be systematically integrated into the overall approach. This report takes up the role of these important actors in chapter 5.

Transition to Host Nation Control

The international response to a potentially explosive intrastate situation must, *from its outset,* plan for the full restoration of authority and responsibility to the leaders of the country in crisis. The participation of community and national leaders in all aspects of the international response helps allay fears regarding the motives of outside parties, and a plan to restore local authority also reassures outsiders that their job will come to an end. While many governments may be willing to help in a crisis, few if any are willing to stay indefinitely. Competing domestic demands and other international concerns drastically restrict even a willing government's ability to engage in a costly international effort over the long term. In fact, it is becoming clear that many of the permanent members on the UN Security Council are simply reluctant to become involved at all in situations that appear intractable and by any measure costly.[17] Even traditionally active countries have limits. Canada's decision in 1993 to withdraw from UNFICYP—the UN peacekeeping mission in Cyprus—ended its commitment of nearly 30 years.

The Commission believes that the primary responsibility to avoid the reemergence of violence once peace has been achieved belongs to the people and their legitimate leaders; they must resume complete responsibility for their own affairs at the earliest opportunity. In rebuilding violence-torn societies, women, usually the majority of the surviving population, must be involved in all decision making and implementation.

These elements form a framework for operational prevention, and within this framework a number of specific measures can be applied. The first critical task in prevention is to determine where and when the most disastrous conflicts and confrontations are likely to occur. The capacity to anticipate and analyze possible conflicts is a prerequisite both for any prudent decision to act and for effective action itself.

EARLY WARNING AND EARLY RESPONSE

To repeat, the circumstances that give rise to violent conflict can usually be foreseen.[18] This was certainly true of violence in Bosnia in 1992 and in Rwanda in 1994. Ample warning of the deteriorating circumstances was available in both cases—in the open media and through government intelligence information channels. It is not plausible for governments to claim that there was a lack of timely warning of crises on such a

The United Nations airlifts wounded civilians from Gorazde to Sarajevo.

scale as these. This argument is simply unconvincing in an age when major governments operate extensive, sophisticated early warning and intelligence networks worldwide. These governments, as well as the major regional players, often *do* know about incipient catastro-

Box 3.1

INDICATORS OF STATES AT RISK

The following indicators have been cited as particularly relevant to the identification of states that may be in danger of collapse:

- Demographic pressures: high infant mortality, rapid changes in population, including massive refugee movements, high population density, youth bulge, insufficient food or access to safe water, ethnic groups sharing land, territory (i.e., groups' attachment to land), environment (i.e., the relationship between ethnic groups and their physical settings)
- A lack of democratic practices: criminalization or delegitimization of the state, or human rights violations
- Regimes of short duration
- Ethnic composition of the ruling elite differing from the population at large
- Deterioration or elimination of public services
- Sharp and severe economic distress: uneven economic development along ethnic lines and a lack of trade openness
- A legacy of vengeance-seeking group grievance
- Massive, chronic, or sustained human flight

The Commission recognizes that such lists do present problems—nearly every country might have at least one of the above characteristics. Yet a critical mass of these symptoms could very well serve as a credible warning signal of developing problems.

Sources: Daniel C. Esty, Jack A. Goldstone, Ted Robert Gurr, Pamela T. Surko, and Alan N. Unger, *Working Papers: State Failure Task Force Report*, November 30, 1995; Pauline H. Baker and John A. Ausink, "State Collapse and Ethnic Violence: Toward a Predictive Model," *Parameters* 26, No. 1 (Spring 1996), pp. 19-36.

phes, and in most cases they have a sense of what should, and could, be done to reduce the chance of catastrophe.

What Kind of Warning Is Most Useful?

Because dangerous circumstances rarely degenerate without warning into violence, what is needed is not simply more information, but rather the right kind of information and a reliable interpretation of its meaning. Every major government maintains an active watch over the world's "hotspots," and many have developed capabilities to track and predict developing trends (see Box 3.1).

Yet even practical early warning will not ensure successful *preventive* action unless there is a fundamental change of attitude by governments and international organizations. A systematic and practical early warning system should be combined with consistently updated contingency plans for preventive action. This would be a radical advance on the present system where, when a trigger event sets off an explosion of violence, it is usually too difficult, too costly, and too late for a rapid and effective response.

Thus, in addition to the relatively easy identification of major hotspots and checklists of problem conditions, policymakers also need *specific* knowledge of the major elements of destabilization and the way in which they are likely to coalesce to precipitate an outbreak of violence. For effective preventive action, however, an additional step is necessary. Policymakers need to identify the issues, factors, and conditions that will encourage and sustain *local* solutions, an effort that may very well involve providing support for "responsible" or "moderate" leaders. But two cautions are in order. First, if outsiders back these moderate leaders with too heavy a hand, the solutions arrived at will be seen as illegitimate and not sufficiently "local." Second, "moderate" in these circumstances is often relative and ephemeral. Today's moderate leader could prove to be increasingly extreme as time passes and circumstances change.

Two conclusions can be drawn from these observations. First, during the early stages of a crisis, policymakers should not only be attentive to how circumstances could worsen, but also be alert for opportunities to make constructive use of local issues and processes that could help avoid violence. Second, they should exercise great care as to whom they support and how that support is offered.

Big events are often triggered by small incidents, but seldom by small causes. By 1994 it was well known that Rwanda was one of the poorest countries in Africa and that its economy was heavily dependent on coffee. When the International Coffee Agreement collapsed in 1987 and the price of coffee fell to half its 1980 value, knowledgeable people knew that it would have a particularly damaging effect on what was an already ethnically charged situation. This situation was dramatically polarized by the October 1990 RPF invasion. By the same token, while it was not possible to predict precisely that a plane crash involving the death of the presidents of Rwanda and Burundi would precipitate the slaughter of nearly one million people, there were many earlier indications of the likelihood of genocide in Rwanda. Yet in 1994, no effective plan for preventive action was in place for decisive Security Council action.

Many policymakers point to the impossibility of reliably predicting the "trigger" as an important reason for the failure to act. Yet the claim to need advance knowledge of precise "triggers" is undermined by actions that states sometimes take without a trigger. In 1992, the Bush administration mounted a much needed humanitarian operation in Somalia, not in response to any particular event on the ground, but rather in response to an awareness that 1,000 people per day were dying and the increasing public sense within the United States that something needed to be done to deal with the growing number of crises around the world.[19]

For effective preventive action, policymakers need to identify the issues, factors, and conditions that will encourage and sustain *local* solutions.

Who Can Best Provide Useful Early Warning?

Governments, international organizations, NGOs, business enterprises, religious leaders, scientific groups, the media, and even the public at large all have, in their different ways, a capacity for early warning. Governments, of course, have already developed procedures and

A Unified Task Force (UNITAF) soldier guards workers unloading food at a Mogadishu warehouse.

systems to keep themselves abreast of the essential information necessary to operate in dangerous circumstances. But many of these other groups and agencies also have a capacity to warn.

NGOs, for example, are often the first to be aware of and to act in crisis areas, and they have a wealth of information regarding the conditions and grievances that give rise to violence. (Indeed, the disruption of normal NGO operations is itself an early warning signal that conditions are deteriorating dangerously, a signal that governments often miss.) In Cambodia, for instance, while outside links with leaders were largely nonexistent throughout the 1980s, NGOs maintained a presence in much of the country and provided a rich source of information from which the international community was able to draw.

There are, of course, problems involved when humanitarian and other nongovernmental and private sector groups take on an increased information and early warning role. The information these groups provide is not always accurate or balanced. Many conflicts today occur in relatively remote regions where accurate information about the competing sides and their partisans is hard to come by, which makes it difficult to form a valid picture of the overall situation. Moreover, humanitarian groups, business enterprises, and religious institutions that operate regularly within or near crisis areas develop their own agendas that often do not conform to those of governments, the parties to the dispute, or outsiders. Thus, what might appear to one group as an unambiguous opportunity for action may be seen as the opposite by another. In addition, humanitarian and other groups are understandably reluctant to provide information that can be used to undermine one or another of the parties and generate allegations of spying and heightened dangers for their field staff.[20] Episodes of kidnapped or murdered aid workers send a chilling message that they are no longer immune from the very violence they seek to end.

Governments and international organizations are ultimately best suited to alert the broader international community to a coming crisis and to assess the validity of the information available from other sources. But they seldom do so; there are no mechanisms in place for governments or the decision-making bodies of the major regional organizations to acquire systematically the information that international and national NGOs, religious leaders and institutions, the business community, or other elements of civil society have accumulated from years of involvement. Moreover, few habits and practices have been developed to encourage such an exchange. There are signs that this may be changing, however. In a major report on UN reform issued in July 1997, UN Secretary-General Kofi Annan recognized the importance of NGOs and other elements of civil society and acknowledged the essential contribution they make to UN operations.[21]

Who Should Be Warned?

While the answer to this question may seem obvious, it poses a legitimate challenge to proponents of early preventive action. Logically, early warning should be given first to those who can take constructive action. This generally means governments and groups likely to be immediately involved in the crisis, governments and leaders nearest to the scene of conflict, the United Nations (particularly the UN Security Council), and regional organizations. Religious organizations may also be warned, particularly of situations in which local religious leaders and institutions could play positive roles or in which they are playing a particularly unhelpful role of exacerbating tensions.

In addition, those who can induce governments, organizations, and agencies to act (e.g., media organizations, business communities, NGOs, concerned publics) should be kept informed. The role of an informed public may be especially important because public expectations can be a significant factor in motivating governments to act. Attentive, expert, and activist communities in many countries often know about problems before they become desperate and can encourage governments to take positive and timely action.

Before even a rudimentary strategy for preventive action can be developed, however, the weak links in the warning-response chain must be strengthened. Four problems in particular are noteworthy. First, the difficulty is not in identifying potential trouble spots, but rather in understanding situations well enough to map

> NGOs are often the first to be aware of and to act in crisis areas, and they have a wealth of information regarding the conditions and grievances that give rise to violence.

their trends and forecast which ones are likely to explode and when. Second is the related problem of unjustified or premature warning which gives rise to a "cry wolf" reaction among policymakers. The fear that actions taken may prove to have been premature or unnecessary may, in many instances, be stronger than the fear that inaction may allow a crisis situation to explode. Third, those in a position to take early action often find themselves overwhelmed by other pressures and crises. Attention to what are considered relatively distant, merely potential problems is considered a luxury they cannot afford. Finally, while decision makers may take a crisis very seriously, a reluctance to act in the face of warning may arise because they are deterred by the prospects of a slippery slope of increasing involvement in the crisis. These problems make the task of formulating a response to a crisis difficult. But they do not relieve governments of the need to respond to the increasing expectations their citizens have that something will be done to deal with the unfolding events.

In sum, it is difficult for major governments to claim that they did not know that violence on the scale of a Rwanda or Bosnia could happen. Similarly, it is implausible for such governments, especially in the larger, more powerful and wealthy states, to claim that nothing could be done to avert such crises. Increasingly, they are being held accountable not only for "What did they know and when did they know it?" but also for "What could they have done and when should they have done it?" To prevent deadly conflict, the problem is less one of early warning than of early action. As a first step, diplomatic engagement can help overcome this problem.

PREVENTIVE DIPLOMACY

Simply knowing about a developing crisis is not enough. As a minimum step to arrest potential violence and to address humanitarian needs—but without precipitating unwanted and indefinite involvements in remote crises—governments should explore the possibilities of expanded frontline preventive diplomacy by using ambassadors, senior foreign office officials, and personal envoys of the UN secretary-general.[22] When crisis threatens, traditional diplomacy continues, but more urgent efforts are also made—through bilateral, multilateral, and unofficial channels—to pressure, cajole, arbitrate, mediate, or lend "good offices" to encourage dialogue and facilitate a nonviolent resolution of the crisis.

Of special importance is the need to strengthen the secretary-general's capacity for preventive diplomacy. It was with this in mind that Norway in 1996 initiated a Fund for Preventive Action to increase the capacity of the secretary-general to act quickly and effectively when early action is required.[23] This report makes a number of recommendations regarding ways to strengthen the Office of the Secretary-General in chapter 6.

Preventive diplomacy must overcome several obstacles. One of the greatest challenges is suspicion of the motives of those who would practice it. Another is the charge that much of

It is difficult for major governments to claim that they did not know that violence on the scale of a Rwanda or Bosnia could happen. Similarly, it is implausible for such governments, especially of the larger, more powerful, and wealthy states, to claim that nothing could be done to avert such crises.

this is really little more than traditional diplomacy—statecraft and foreign policy that have long been composed largely of diplomatic and political efforts to forestall undesirable events. A key difference today, however, is that diplomats and politicians need to find ways to cope with crises anywhere in the world and within states as well as between them, not only because these crises are tragic in themselves, but also because they are increasingly costly for neighboring countries and many countries beyond.

Therefore, diplomacy today is tied, perhaps as never before, to a complex web of economic and social relationships that span the globe. The diplomat's job is at once easier and harder. It is easier because states and peoples relate to each other in multiple dimensions at all levels of society, and the welter of contacts may enhance mutual understanding and help establish wider bases for cooperation. The job is harder, in part, because nonstate actors are increasingly important in international relations and often operate beyond diplomats' reach. One result is that it is now effectively impossible to isolate a state from the international system, and this fact makes it easier for targeted states to deflect pressure. Nevertheless, in deteriorating circumstances, a number of diplomatic steps may help manage the crisis successfully and prevent the emergence of violence.

First, states should resist the traditional urge to suspend diplomatic relations as a substitute for action and instead maintain open, high-fidelity lines of communication with leaders and groups in crisis. It may be counterproductive to deny governments an important means of managing a problem precisely at a time when reliable firsthand information is essential.

Second, governments and international organizations must express in a clear and compelling way the interests in jeopardy. This step is essential to help mobilize support for preventive action, and it is especially important should it prove necessary later—as is often the case—to use more assertive measures to draw clear lines against unacceptable behavior.

Decision makers often run into domestic difficulties when they contemplate more assertive measures to deal with a crisis, in large measure because they have not laid the groundwork at home to prepare their parliaments or legislatures and publics for such steps. It is essential to articulate clearly, early, and repeatedly the national interests involved in engaging constructively to prevent a worsening of the crisis. This preparation can include providing information about the developing crisis; offering regular explanations of how national interests are served through preventive engagement; initiating and supporting public dialogue on the broad options available for dealing with the crisis; and developing a decisive strategy to manage the situation.

Third, the crisis should be put on the agenda of the UN Security Council or of the relevant international organization, or both, early enough to permit preventive action. At the same time, a means should be established to track developments in the crisis to provide regular updates. In addition, as mentioned earlier, a mechanism should be established to incorporate information from NGOs and other nongovernmental actors to augment Security Council deliberations on unfolding events.[24] Exposing brewing crises in these ways helps to illustrate the broader context—and perhaps higher stakes—of the crises. It also demonstrates to concerned publics that serious efforts are under way to resolve the problems.[25]

Fourth, whatever the case for broadening the multilateral context of an unfolding crisis, governments should be attentive to opportunities to support quiet diplomacy and dialogue with and between moderate leaders in the crisis. Special envoys and representatives of key states or regional organizations, or on behalf of the UN, have time and again demonstrated their value, particularly in the early stages of a crisis. In reviewing the role of "quiet diplomacy" by mediators, one scholar identified the following elements of successful negotiation: 1) sensing when conflicting parties are open to outside engagement; 2) maintaining the confidentiality of negotiations; 3) judiciously using incentives to carry negotiations through stalemates; 4) creating a deadline for agreements; 5) tackling easier issues first—with the momentum created by early agreements easing more difficult negotiations; 6) understanding the honor and symbolism that parties may ascribe to certain issues; and 7) maintaining the trust of all parties through open, honest dialogue.[26]

In the fluid circumstances of the post–Cold War era, diplomatic and political strategies to avert a looming crisis demand creative ways of defusing tensions and facilitating mutual accommodation among potential belligerents. These strategies can include a serious discussion of peaceful border adjustments or revisions, new constitutional arrangements, forms of regional or cultural autonomy, or even, in unusual circumstances, partition. Potential solutions may lie in various forms of power sharing—discussed further in the next chapter—to help assure groups that their interests are not at the mercy of a simple majority, however assembled.[27]

In Europe, the OSCE has developed "missions of long duration" that have been deployed to some 12 countries. The details of the mandates vary, but these missions emphasize the protection of fundamental human rights through international presence, first-hand information gathering, situation monitoring, and technical advice and assistance to host countries. These missions are usually made up of civilian and military members and have a minimum mandate of six months, although most have lasted much longer. Missions of long duration provide a virtual permanent presence on the ground and as a result are able to provide the Permanent Council, the Chairman-in-Office, the High Commissioner on National Minorities, and other OSCE bodies with first-hand accounts of unfolding events. They are frequently led by senior diplomats with extensive regional expertise and practical experience in intercultural communication, negotiation, mediation, and confidence-building measures.[28]

Official diplomacy can be greatly strengthened by private sector activity. So-called Track Two diplomacy, long an informal staple in international negotiations and used by leaders who wanted to take informal soundings of adversaries' intentions, is increasingly the diplomacy of choice for problems beyond the reach of official efforts.

Indeed, some governments have found NGOs very useful in brokering political agreements and supplementing governmental roles. In the Middle East peace process, for example, a Norwegian research institute with its roots in the trade union movement was critical in breaking the ice and laying the groundwork for the

States should resist the traditional urge to suspend diplomatic relations as a substitute for action, and instead maintain open, high-fidelity lines of communication with leaders and groups in crisis.

UN peacekeepers on patrol in Bosnia.

Oslo Agreements in 1993. In Guatemala, Norwegian church organizations were instrumental in facilitating the dialogue between the parties to the conflict. In Tajikistan, a joint U.S.-Russian task force of private citizens with deep experience in conflict mediation and resolution, sponsored by the Kettering Foundation of Dayton, Ohio, had by mid-1997 brought the Tajik factions together nearly 20 times to establish a foundation for formal negotiations. Other groups in the United States and Europe that are engaged in unofficial preventive diplomacy include The Carter Center's International Negotiation Network, the Conflict Management Group, the Institute for Multi-Track Diplomacy, International Alert, the International Crisis Group, the Project on Ethnic Relations (see Box 3.2), and Search for Common Ground. These organizations have played active roles in building relationships between conflicting parties and with interested governments, training in diplomacy and conflict resolution, and providing good offices to parties that are committed to the peaceful resolution of conflict.[29]

Those well-practiced in the art of nongovernmental diplomacy (including Track Two, multitrack, and citizen diplomacy) uniformly point up the value of building trust through long-term commitments to dialogue and intergroup relations and active training programs that make aggressive use of facilitated dialogues, high technology access to ideas and people via the Internet, and cross-cultural or intergroup exchanges. In addition to the substantive progress that these efforts make in bridging the differences that often divide hostile neighbors, they generate impressive lists of "alumni" who carry their experiences back to their communities and influence them in later years when many of them assume positions of leadership.[30]

In sum, a wide array of political and diplomatic steps are possible, early, to help defuse an unfolding crisis. Sometimes, however, stronger measures are called for to send a sharper message to leaders that the path they have chosen to pursue their aims is an unacceptable one.

ECONOMIC MEASURES

In circumstances of incipient conflict, a number of economic measures are at the disposal of states and international organizations. Beyond sanctions, other tools such as inducements, conditionality, and the dispute resolution mechanisms of international trade organizations may help influence potential belligerents to avoid a violent course.

Sanctions

Sanctions can play an important role in support of preventive diplomacy, notwithstanding the fact that practical questions remain about governments' abilities to use them effectively. Governments use sanctions to serve three broad policy functions: to signal international concern to the offending state (and, by example, to others), to punish a state's behavior, and to serve as an important precursor to stronger actions, including, if necessary, the use of force. Sanctions are often used as a first step and as a means to signal the targeted state that more drastic action could be forthcoming if corrective steps are not taken.

In fact, sanctions regimes have been in virtually constant use in recent years, suggesting that governments view this measure as an effective means of influence. The fact that many states seem to place great store by them sharply contrasts with the general view that sanctions are cumbersome, costly, slow to produce results, a cynical gesture (to deflect pressure for stronger measures), or completely ineffective, and that sanctions also tend to penalize innocents as much as or more than culpable leaders. These difficulties are real. If sanctions are to prove more useful in preventing mass violence, their deterrent value must be strengthened.[31]

States can improve their ability to use sanctions by developing national infrastructure and procedures to ensure that sanctions take effect quickly and by facilitating improved international coordination. Few countries have the necessary laws and administrative arrangements in place to impose sanctions in a timely and effective manner. Many valuable lessons in

Sanctions serve three broad policy functions: to signal international concern to the offending state, to punish a state's behavior, and to serve as an important precursor to stronger actions, including, if necessary, the use of force.

Box 3.2
THE PROJECT ON ETHNIC RELATIONS

The Project on Ethnic Relations (PER), founded in 1991, works to encourage the peaceful resolution of ethnic conflicts in the new democracies of Central and Eastern Europe and the Russian Federation. It provides the opportunity for dialogue among government officials and ethnic leaders in emerging democracies, while increasing the visibility of individuals and institutions of moderate views through international recognition, validation, and support. PER assists in the development of national and local institutions for dealing with ethnic conflicts and trains a new generation of specialists to carry out practical and analytical work in the management of international conflicts. With the help of PER, national groups from different countries organize regionally and gain access to information and assistance from other nations. PER also consults with international and European intergovernmental organizations on strategies for dealing with ethnic tensions.

PER is involved in brokering ethnic disputes in Bulgaria, Hungary, Romania, Slovakia, the former Yugoslavia, and other countries. An example is its contribution to reducing the high potential for interethnic conflict in Romania and Slovakia. PER played a key role in bringing the Hungarian minorities in both countries and Romanians and Slovaks to the conference table. Moderates on both sides were able to develop partnerships, begin to devise peaceful solutions and compromises, and create an atmosphere of mutual respect. While the issues are not yet fully resolved, conditions now exist for a genuine reconciliation. In Romania, the ethnic Hungarian party became a coalition partner in a new Romanian government in 1997 and relations have improved between Hungary and Romania. In Slovakia, PER brought the ruling coalition, the opposition parties, and the ethnic Hungarian leadership to the table and helped negotiate a first-time agreement to work on their differences. While the situation is still at an early stage and operating in difficult circumstances, PER has helped the key actors to continue to communicate.

There is nothing inevitable about interethnic conflict, according to PER, but the potential for conflict exists anywhere that ethnic groups interact, especially if leaders mobilize that potential. PER has found a number of methods to reduce those chances: 1) create credible, neutral forums for dialogue early and maintain momentum; 2) work within political realities; 3) redefine the self-interests of parties; 4) act with the backing of powerful nations; 5) work regionally and avoid concentrating on one country or minority issue; 6) maintain communication with opinion leaders such as the mass media; 7) avoid the role of the minority rights advocate; and 8) encourage authentic, indigenous solutions from within existing political processes.

Source: Allen H. Kassof, remarks to Carnegie Corporation of New York Board of Trustees, January 9, 1997.

this regard were learned during the establishment of the elaborate network of sanctions assistance monitoring teams (SAMs) surrounding the Federal Republic of Yugoslavia beginning in 1993. These procedures should be standardized and made available to other states, with small amounts of UN technical assistance, so that sanctions regimes can be rapidly deployed as part of a broader strategy to help prevent and resolve future conflicts.[32]

The application of economic sanctions requires detailed planning, implementation, monitoring, and enforcement. As sanctions regimes become increasingly complex technically, juridically, and administratively, few governments have developed corresponding legal and administrative infrastructures to guarantee the effectiveness of the process by which sanctions are imposed and monitored. Sanctions regimes require the involvement of agencies throughout government—including those responsible for foreign affairs, economic policies, legal issues, and military strategy.

A step toward building national capacities for sanctions would be to survey national structures and develop a database of operating practices and procedures. Various models of national sanctions legislation and structures could be identified, so that when a new regime is mandated by the Security Council, it can be implemented quickly. Standard guidelines for creating and maintaining national monitoring and enforcement measures might also be devised. As with the case of SAMs in the former Yugoslavia, the UN and concerned governments have demonstrated that they can cooperate to develop the necessary local infrastructure to implement effective sanctions.[33]

Sanctions should be part of a broader influence strategy that puts maximum political and economic pressure as precisely as possible on the offending parties—preferably regimes or specific leaders, rather than whole populations. Sanctions regimes, if they are focused on commodities exclusively, must be swiftly and comprehensively imposed to be most effective. Graduated, piecemeal approaches are unlikely to work.[34] Sanctions regimes should be supported, where necessary, with the forceful measures suitable to ensure compliance and demonstrate resolve. Diplomatic and other political communications should be clear on the behavior necessary for sanctions to be lifted and, where possible, accompanied by an incentive package to comply. Public information outlets at home and abroad should convey these same messages.

Such a comprehensive view of sanctions means identifying in each case the measures and approaches most likely to affect the leaders and decision makers who are being targeted. Greater international cooperation will be required to achieve these aims and minimize loopholes. Sustained and skillful efforts are needed to produce the diplomatic consensus required to ensure both the legitimacy and effectiveness of sanctions.

Sanctions are sometimes imposed for lack of better alternatives and without much expectation of effectiveness. Indeed, sanctions often seem to exact a price from the target state—usually at the expense of the most vulnerable sectors of the population—without effecting a change in the target government's behavior. The Commission believes that sanctions would be more effective if outside governments communicated more explicitly to the target state's leaders the future consequences of their actions. To do this, detailed knowledge of a potential target state and its economy is necessary.

International corporations often have an extremely good understanding of what eco-

Sanctions should be part of a broader influence strategy that puts maximum political and economic pressure as precisely as possible on the offending parties.

nomic levers can influence governments. As foreign direct investment and international trade have expanded in recent years, the international business community has become increasingly knowledgeable about the conditions that could lead to international pressure to use sanctions, the likely impact of sanctions, and ways to make them more effective.[35] Unfortunately, consultation between policymakers and international business leaders has been limited. While, in part, this can be attributed to a divergence of interests over the use of economic sanctions, much of it can also be ascribed to weak channels of communication. Recent steps to improve cooperation include discussion of a possible UN international business advisory group on sanctions and several private sector initiatives aimed at minimizing economic disruption caused by sanctions.[36]

States that impose sanctions should also take steps in accordance with Article 50 of the UN Charter to reduce unwanted or undesirable effects and minimize the privation and suffering of innocent civilians and the economic losses often suffered by neighboring countries.[37] One way, as noted above, is to impose commodities sanctions regimes swiftly and comprehensively in order to achieve maximum effect and thereby help reduce the time such regimes must be in place.

The UN is indispensable to mandating and implementing sanctions, but the Commission also recognizes the potential preventive value of informal measures undertaken by neighboring states or other regional arrangements. Such informal moves can often be implemented quickly, sending a clear signal that unacceptable behavior has generated this response.

But even sharper measures are possible. "Targeted" sanctions offer a way to focus the penalty more directly on those most responsible for the crisis. Such "targeted" sanctions include freezing leaders' personal assets, or denying them access to hard currency. In this regard, financial information can be shared among cooperating nations to identify and restrict the cash flows of leaders who threaten to use violence. While these leaders may still be able to hide assets, they would have great difficulty using them without being detected. Restricting their access to hard currency can limit their ability to keep arms and ammunition flowing and can also jeopardize their hold on power.[38]

The Commission recognizes that targeted sanctions are extremely intrusive and set a stark precedent for dealing with ruthless behavior. Such sanctions therefore must be subjected to strict scrutiny and fully vetted by international deliberative bodies to establish a legal justification and basis for their imposition before they are used.

Although the Commission sees much promise in the use of economic sanctions as a tool for preventing violence, it recognizes that sanctions mandated by the UN since 1990 have lasted longer, and been less effective and more costly than their proponents had originally hoped. Obviously, much needs to be done to improve them. To begin, sanctions must be considered in the context of a broader influence strategy. Such a strategy would take account of the target state's vulnerabilities and the role of neighboring states and regional arrangements.

Targeted sanctions, i.e., freezing leaders' personal assets or denying them access to hard currency, offer a way to focus the penalty more directly on those most responsible for the crisis.

Mozambican/Norwegian demining team working to clear land.

Inducements

Although there has been much research on the use of economic sanctions in international relations, there has been far less work on the role of political or economic inducements—the use of "carrots" instead of or in addition to "sticks"—to influence other leaders and states.[39] Yet in practice, inducements are very often an integral part of diplomacy. They could have greater preventive potential if they were better understood.[40]

Essentially, the inducement process involves the granting of a political or economic benefit in exchange for a specified policy adjustment. Inducement policies strive to make cooperation and conciliation more appealing than aggression and hostility. Examples of inducements include: favorable trade terms, tariff reductions, direct purchases, subsidies for exports or imports, economic and military aid, favorable taxation, granting access to advanced technology, military cooperation, and the many benefits that accrue to members in good standing in international organizations. Often policymakers juggle a variety of political, military, and economic elements as part of an overall package of inducements.

It would require developing a legal justification and a framework for imposing sanctions and monitoring their implementation. It would also require specifying the steps by the target state that would avoid sanctions or cause them to be lifted.

A study sponsored by the Commission concludes that inducements are most effective when used early and that they are especially influential when used against the backdrop of sanctions—where benefits of cooperation can be weighed against stark punishments for pursuing a course of violent action.[41] The proportion of these positive and negative approaches to be applied in a particular situation depends on the nature of the problem and the objectives being served. While inducement strategies are preferable for laying a groundwork for peace and cooperation and preventing the initial outbreak of violence, coercive measures may be more appropriate and effective when unacceptable behavior is clearly indicated. Here too, however, careful consideration of the political and economic needs of the target state can assist the international community in devising a balance between positive and negative approaches (see Box 3.3).

While inducements are not appropriate in every setting and may be considered appeasement if employed in the face of overt military aggression, they can have significant advantages over punitive approaches. Conciliatory gestures frequently lead to cooperative responses, while threats often initiate spirals of hostility and defiance.[42] If such lessons are applied to preventive action and new ways are created to use inducements judiciously, chances can be improved that a violent outbreak might be averted.

Conditionality

One particularly potent inducement for effective preventive action may be "conditionality," or the forging of links between responsible, nonviolent behavior and the promise of greater reward through growing integration into the community of market democracies. Increasingly, through bilateral programs and through pressure on the international financial institutions, states are attaching good governance conditions to the development assistance provided to emerging economies. In several countries, for example, Malawi and Kenya, bilateral and international financial aid was suspended for a time in an effort to promote democratization.[43] Associating assistance with responsible governance in this way may give the international community a powerful source of leverage with those who persistently use violent means to pursue their aims, provided that such policies are applied with consistency in similar situations.

States that attach conditions to their aid are not themselves above scrutiny, however. The potential leverage of conditionality is diminished when donor states demand higher standards of behavior than they themselves are prepared to observe. No longer can established, wealthy states simply dictate behavior to the less powerful. Consistent standards must be devised that apply to all states equitably. Perhaps nowhere is this kind of reciprocal accountability in greater evidence than on questions related to the proliferation of nuclear weapons and their eventual elimination. So-called threshold states are unwilling to sign up to rules and regimes for managing the problem of nuclear proliferation until they are satisfied that future arrangements will apply with equal force and effect to the existing nuclear states.

Economic Dispute Resolution Mechanisms

Every major international trade organization has mechanisms to help broker disputes that may arise among members, and members commit themselves to pursue their grievances through these organizational processes and to

Inducements are most effective when used early and against the backdrop of sanctions.

Box 3.3
NORTH KOREA
The Role of Inducements

The North Korean capability for nuclear weapons construction was first confirmed by U.S. intelligence sources in 1988. Uneasy about the construction of two nuclear facilities and a plutonium reprocessing capability, the Bush administration made efforts to secure North Korean cooperation on the issue of nonproliferation.

North Korea was a signatory of the Non-Proliferation Treaty (NPT) as well as treaties such as the Agreement on Reconciliation, Nonaggression, Exchanges, and Cooperation (1991)—also known as the Basic Agreement—and the Joint Declaration on the Denuclearization of the Korean Peninsula (1991). Yet the 1992 discovery of North Korean "cheating" by the International Atomic Energy Agency (IAEA) led to a breakdown in relations and North Korea's March 1993 announcement of plans to withdraw from the NPT.

Despite initial difficulties, bilateral discussions between the United States and North Korea postponed North Korean withdrawal from the NPT and eventually led to the Geneva Agreed Framework of 1994. According to the framework, North Korea agreed to freeze its nuclear program, rejoin the ranks of the NPT nations, and dismantle specified reactors. In exchange, the United States was to organize an international consortium that offered North Korea two light-water reactors and an annual supply of oil.

The framework was achieved with the combined use of inducements and sanctions. The U.S. and North Korea met in high-level talks, a move that was seen to legitimize the North Korean government as a party in the negotiations. In exchange for North Korean cooperation, the U.S. offered to limit its military training operations with South Korea, provide negative security assurances, lift trade restrictions, and provide proliferation-resistant light-water reactor technology and other energy sources. An IAEA cutoff of economic assistance (eventually imposed on June 10, 1993), a U.S. drive for UN-sponsored sanctions, continued isolation of the North Korean economy through trade restrictions, and the unspoken threat of potential military action were held out as "sticks" to punish North Korean resistance or reluctance.

While many in the international community had doubts about the willingness of North Korea to abide by the agreement, implementation of the framework has generally proceeded smoothly. Argument continues in nuclear circles as to whether the framework gives too much to North Korea while not demanding enough in return. Yet a blend of promised benefits and threatened sanctions successfully halted North Korean attempts to build a nuclear weapons program and eased tensions on the Korean peninsula.

Source: Scott Snyder, "North Korea's Nuclear Program: The Role of Incentives in Preventing Deadly Conflict," in *The Price of Peace: Incentives and International Conflict Prevention*, ed. David Cortright (Lanham, MD: Rowman & Littlefield, 1997).

be bound by their findings. The dispute resolution mechanism of the World Trade Organization (WTO) is typical: following the identification of a grievance, a panel of experts may be assembled to rule on the merits. If found in violation, an offending party is required to bring its policies or practices into compliance within a reasonable period of time or face a damage judgment. If corrective action is not taken, the aggrieved party may retaliate by raising duties. Decisions may be appealed, and uncorrected behavior can lead to more serious measures, such as sanctions or expulsion from the organization.[44]

Other organizations, arrangements, and agreements, such as the European Union (EU), the North American Free Trade Agreement (NAFTA), the Mercado Común del Sur (MERCOSUR), and the Bank for International Settlements, all have dispute resolution mechanisms that may be activated to reduce points of friction among members. Because these mechanisms are designed to work between governments, however, they are less suitable for brokering internal economic disputes, and governments do not appear uniformly eager to invite outside engagement on such matters. Nevertheless, some similar mechanisms may be adaptable for use by governments in their internal affairs, and they remain in any case important tools to help manage disputes between states. Given the great significance of economic issues in an increasingly interdependent world, the lessons learned from these mechanisms for nonviolent dispute resolution deserve closer attention (see Box 3.4).

Notwithstanding the utility of the foregoing diplomatic and economic measures to help prevent the outbreak of mass violence,

some circumstances may demand more assertive steps to limit the possibility for violence.

FORCEFUL MEASURES

Basic Principles

The threat or use of forceful measures might seem at odds with the Commission's focus on prevention of deadly conflict. But situations will arise where diplomatic responses, even when supplemented by strong economic measures, are insufficient to prevent the outbreak or recurrence of major violence. The question is when, where, and how should individual nations and global and regional organizations be willing to apply forceful measures to curb incipient violence and prevent potentially much larger destruction of life and property. The Commission believes that there are three broad principles that should govern any such decision.

First, any threat or use of force must be governed by universally accepted principles, as the UN Charter requires. Decisions to use force must not be arbitrary or operate as the coercive and selectively used weapon of the strong against the weak.

Chapter VII of the UN Charter enables the Security Council to authorize any measures, including armed force—by individual states or organized groups of states—which it deems necessary to "maintain or restore international peace and security." The classic use of this peace enforcement process is in response to cross-border aggression, as in the case of the Iraqi invasion of Kuwait. With the post–Cold War shift in preoccupation from international

Associating assistance with responsible governance may give the international community a powerful source of leverage.

Box 3.4
CONFLICTS AT SEA

There is a rich history of international regimes created to manage conflicts at sea. The importance of sea lanes and waterways and the international nature of the world's oceans have made maritime law one of the oldest forms of international law. Two types of potential maritime conflicts are disputes over: 1) stationary assets that give access to resources or control the flow of resources; and 2) migratory maritime resources such as fish.

Examples of the former group include the Spratly Islands and the Strait of Hormuz. The Spratlys sit astride key South China Sea shipping lanes and oil and mineral reserves. Brunei, China, Malaysia, the Philippines, and Vietnam each claim all or part of the archipelago. The bulk of oil from the Persian Gulf is carried by tankers that pass through the Strait of Hormuz. Japan receives two-thirds of its imported oil from the Gulf and Asia and Latin America each receive three-quarters of their imported oil from that region. At its narrowest the strait is only 20 $^{3}/_{4}$ nautical miles wide. Geology and claims to coastal waters extending to 12 nautical miles squeeze international shipping lanes.

Examples of the latter type of conflict include disputes over migratory fish stocks. NATO members Canada and Spain have had an ongoing confrontation over fishing rights since May 1994, when Canada placed a fishing ban on waters off its east coast in addition to its exclusive territorial waters that extend for 200 miles. The conflict flared up with the March 1995 machine-gunning and seizure of a Spanish vessel illegally fishing in Canada's North Atlantic waters. The dispute between the United States and Canada over salmon has erupted periodically and has prompted clashes such as the April-May 1997 Canadian seizure of U.S. fishing boats and the blockade of a passenger ferry sailing between Alaska and Washington state by Canadian fishermen.

continued on page 61

conflicts to those within state boundaries, there has been a greater willingness to apply the concept of "threat to international security" more liberally, and to see a number of internal conflicts as having this character.

Some have gone further, arguing that the UN's basic responsibility is to protect *human* security when it has been imperiled on a vast scale, and that this—together with the obligation of member states through the UN Charter and other instruments to protect basic human rights—may be a sufficient foundation in certain cases for forceful measures.[45] While it cannot be said that this approach has had much overt acceptance, it has been an important tacit rationale for enforcement operations in support of humanitarian objectives (as in Somalia in 1993), and it has given some encouragement to those inclined to take a broad view of what constitutes an "international" security problem.

Chapter VI of the Charter, relating to the settlement of disputes by negotiation, mediation, "or other peaceful means," has been the banner under which a number of military and police deployments have in fact occurred in the past. These deployments have been more for the now-traditional peacekeeping functions of monitoring, supervising, and verifying cease-fires and related agreements (as, for example, in Cyprus since 1964) than for applying force

National governments have developed sophisticated maritime dispute resolution mechanisms. The United Nations Convention on the Law of the Sea entered into force on November 16, 1994, and established the global regime covering the seas; 177 countries are party to the agreement. The International Tribunal for the Law of the Sea is the convention's main body for the peaceful resolution of disputes. Four interstate disputes await settlement under the United Nations Convention: Cameroon/Nigeria, Guinea-Bissau/Senegal, Qatar/Bahrain, and Yemen/Eritrea. In each of these cases, states disagree over the location of a border or sovereignty over offshore islands. The UN has also created mechanisms for controlling disputes over mobile resources. The United Nations Agreement for the Implementation of the Provisions of the United Nations Convention on the Law of the Sea of December 10, 1982, relating to the Conservation and Management of Straddling Fish Stocks and Highly Migratory Fish Stocks was open for signature from December 4, 1995, to December 4, 1996. The agreement will enter into force 30 days after the deposit of the thirtieth ratification.

Sources: British Petroleum 1992 figures cited in Keith McLachlan, "Hydrocarbons and Iranian Policies toward the Gulf States: Confrontation and co-operation in island and continental shelf affairs," in *Territorial Foundations of the Gulf States*, ed. Richard Schofield (London: UCL Press, 1994), pp. 223-236; R.K. Ramazani, *International Straits of the World: The Persian Gulf and the Strait of Hormuz* (Alphen aan den Rijn, Netherlands: Sijthoff and Noordhoff, 1979), p. 2; Mark Hume, "U.S. Advantage in Salmon Wars," *The Montreal Gazette*, May 29, 1997, p. A15; United Nations Division for Ocean Affairs and the Law of the Sea, *Oceans and Law of the Sea*, http://www.un.org/Depts/los/; United Nations Conference on Straddling Fish Stocks and Highly Migratory Fish Stocks, "Agreement for the Implementation of the Provisions of the United Nations Convention on the Law of the Sea of 10 December 1982 Relating to the Conservation and Management of Straddling Fish Stocks and Highly Migratory Fish Stocks," September 8, 1995, A/CONF.164/37 (1995); Nick Cumming-Bruce, "Malaysia Buys into Military Build-Up," *The Guardian* (London), October 23, 1996, p. 14; Vipal Monga, "Daley Expresses Doubts on a Quick Resolution of Pacific Salmon Dispute," *Journal of Commerce*, August 7, 1997, p. 3A.

to prevent additional outbreaks of violence. It has always been accepted that a mission mandated under Chapter VI could apply force in self-defense, perhaps now extended to include "in defense of the mission," but that is as far as the authority reaches.

There is a conceptual "gray zone" between Chapters VI and VII of the UN Charter in which the UN has increasingly found itself operating—the so-called "Chapter VI and a half" situation, in which the Security Council has been unwilling to give a full Chapter VII enforcement mandate (or to make available the resources to enable it to be carried out effectively), but at the same time has given military and police peacekeeping personnel tasks that require threats of force or, in extreme situations, the use of force.

Multidimensional UN peacekeeping operations—that involve not only monitoring and supervising, but also active support of humanitarian objectives and maintenance of law and order—are not new (having begun in the Congo in the early 1960s), but they have become more common since the end of the Cold War. The record of such ambiguously mandated operations has been mixed: successful enough in Cambodia and Mozambique (mainly because the enforcement role was not fully tested), but unable to prevent massacres from 1994 to 1997 in Rwanda and Zaire, as well as in 1995 in Srebrenica, Bosnia.

The message from all this is clear enough. If the UN contemplates missions in situations where the threat or use of force may be required to avert major violence, it must determine from the outset its source of authority in the Charter, specifically mandate the mission accordingly, and provide the resources needed to do the job effectively. It cannot be left for later discussion or to the commander in the field to decide whether there is some acceptable principle, in international law and practice, on which to rely when applying force: that responsibility has to be borne by the Security Council.

Second, the threat or use of force should not be regarded only as a last resort in desperate circumstances. Governments must be attentive to opportunities when demonstrations of resolve can establish clear limits to unacceptable behavior. Familiar examples of such uses of force include the deployment of military forces to areas of potential conflict and the mobilization of forces to heightened states of readiness.[46]

Many thoughtful observers view the use of force only as a last resort. They believe that using forceful measures where necessary to back up diplomatic and economic steps comes dangerously close to starting down the slippery slope of entanglement, or that such steps amount to unacceptable intervention. But the Commission believes that there are acceptable ways to take firm measures early enough to prevent or limit violent conflict. To be sure, taking such steps as deploying warships or conducting fly-overs in a show of force requires a careful consideration of next steps if the measures do not have the intended effect. While this is also true of other means of influence, it is an especially important factor to consider when contemplating threats or use of force.

Therefore, the use of such measures must be carefully integrated with other policy instruments, calibrated to the interests engaged, and supported by consistent political and diplomatic signals to underscore the seriousness of purpose. The aim is to use threats or actual use of force judiciously to set clear and convincing limits on unacceptable behavior.

Third, states—particularly the major powers—must accept that the threat or use of force, if it does become necessary, must be part of an integrated, ideally multilateral strategy, and used in conjunction with political and economic instruments.[47] The use of force must also be guided by prudence and responsibility. One way to achieve these aims is to institutionalize the emerging view that when employing force for preventive purposes, states should only do so with a UN Security Council resolution specifying a clear mandate that details the arrangements under which force will be used and the institutions that will be involved in the action. Consultation with other multilateral institutions or regional organizations is essential to establish the legitimacy of such a force. The effectiveness of the deployed force will depend, in part, on the perception of its legitimacy and integrity in discharging its mandate—a perception that itself will require greater confidence in the organization and, in particular, the representativeness of the Security Council (which is in much need of reform—an issue taken up in greater detail in chapter 6).

The Commission does not mean to suggest that there are no circumstances under which the unilateral use of force might be contemplated. Indeed, the Charter authorizes unilateral force in certain circumstances. For the kinds of preventive action contemplated here, however, a multilateral response should be the norm, as envisaged in the UN Charter, and a norm that should apply to large as well as small states.

There are three distinct kinds of operations where the use of force and forces—that is, military or police personnel—may have an important role in preventing the outbreak or recurrence of violent conflict: postconflict peacekeeping, preventive deployments, and "fire brigade" deployments. Only the third of these involves personnel on the ground having the mandate or capacity to apply forceful measures (other than in self-defense)—but the credibility of all three as preventive strategies depends on the perception that if peace breaks down, forceful measures to restore it may well be forthcoming.

Peacekeeping and Maintaining Civil Order

In the aftermath of cease-fires and more substantial peace settlements, traditional lightly armed peacekeeping missions can help monitor and restrain tense situations. The UN has deployed many missions of this type, including its very first peacekeeping operation, the United Nations Truce Supervision Organization set up in Palestine in 1948, and troops deployed under UN auspices in Cyprus in 1963. Their primary role has been to monitor, supervise, and verify cease-fires and settlement terms.

Though mentioned nowhere in the UN Charter, peacekeeping missions have become an integral aspect of the organization's effort to maintain peace and security. These operations have been most effective when deployed in very specific circumstances where the parties to a conflict are separated along clearly demarcated boundaries and when they agree to a cease-fire

and the presence of the outside forces. These missions serve several purposes, including to signal the interest and engagement of the international community, to observe and monitor relations between antagonistic parties, and to act as a deterrent against renewed fighting.

More recent UN peacekeeping operations have been multifunctional in character, with tasks extending beyond basic monitoring and supervision to involvement in maintaining law and order, infrastructure rebuilding, and assisting to reestablish effective governance. Examples of successful "expanded" peacekeeping missions include those deployed in Namibia and Cambodia. In Namibia the United Nations Transition Assistance Group (UNTAG), in addition to its core peacekeeping mission, negotiated the repeal of discriminatory laws, the granting of amnesty for exiles, and the release of prisoners and detainees, in addition to registering voters for elections and supervising those elections. Likewise, the United Nations Transitional Authority in Cambodia (UNTAC) administered elections, a landmine clearing program, and the rehabilitation of the civil administration.[48]

Experience in a number of UN missions—Bosnia, Cambodia, Haiti, Rwanda, Somalia, Western Sahara, and elsewhere—reflects the particular need to plan carefully and execute responsibly law-and-order operations to establish and maintain legitimate civil control. An international policing force can

When employing force for preventive purposes, states should only do so with a UN Security Council resolution specifying a clear mandate that details the arrangements under which force will be used.

Box 3.5
PREVENTIVE DEPLOYMENT: A First

In December 1992, the Former Yugoslav Republic of Macedonia became the site of the first—and to date, only—preventive deployment of United Nations peacekeeping units. Newly independent, Macedonia was susceptible to conflict due to hostile neighboring states, including Greece and Serbia, ethnic tensions between Macedonians and Albanians and other minorities, and upheaval in nearby Kosovo. Subsequent economic difficulties due to a Greek embargo and UN sanctions on Serbia enhanced the potential for conflict.

Following the request of David Owen and Cyrus Vance, the European Union and UN mediators for the former Yugoslavia, and in response to the initial request of Macedonian president Kiro Gligorov, the UN Security Council authorized the formation of the UN Preventive Deployment Force (UNPREDEP), originally as part of the UN Protection Force (UNPROFOR). Shortly after the passage of Security Council Resolution 795, the first UN personnel were deployed in Macedonia. The first contingent was made up of Canadian troops, who arrived in early January 1993. They were replaced in February by a Nordic battalion composed of soldiers from Denmark, Finland, Norway, and Sweden. The United States sent additional troops in 1993 for a total UNPREDEP military contingent of 1,050. UN military observers (UNMOs) and UN civilian police (UNCIVPOL), almost 50 in all, were drawn from various countries, as were additional civilian affairs personnel and administrative staff.

UNPREDEP functions mainly as an early warning system deployed along Macedonia's borders with Albania and the Federal Republic of Yugoslavia (Serbia and Montenegro). Military responsibilities consist of monitoring and reporting developments that could undermine the region's stability and threaten peace. Troops patrol border crossings, customs stations, and villages and are stationed at operation posts along the border. They are not authorized to engage in combat but serve a deterrent function. The civilian component of the operation tracks political, economic, and social conditions within the country. UN civilian police monitor the work of local police forces in maintaining order and protecting human rights. Civil affairs officers have advised government officials, monitored presidential and parliamentary elections, performed fact-finding missions, helped defuse tensions among parties, and aided with the targeting of humanitarian assistance.

While tensions in the region remain high and deployment is still necessary, the Macedonian experience provides important lessons for preventive peacekeeping operations. Factors that contributed to the success of the mission include the timing of the implementation, the relatively low intensity of tensions along the line of deployment, a clear objective and mandate, considerable interest of the international community, cooperation with regional and nongovernmental organizations, and the strong support of the Macedonian government, most opposition political parties, and leaders of indigenous ethnic communities.

Source: Alice Ackermann and Antonio Pala, "From Peacekeeping to Preventive Deployment: A Study of the United Nations in the Former Yugoslav Republic of Macedonia," *European Security* 5, No. 1 (Spring 1996), pp. 83-97.

monitor situations of potential unrest, provide security for humanitarian operations, establish a presence through patrols and precincts to help keep tensions in check, retrain or replace problematic elements within the host country's own police force, and restrain gang or other organized criminal activities until local authorities can resume complete control.[49] Strengthening local policing capacities through international, regional, or ad hoc arrangements may reduce the necessity for military interventions. Technological innovations that permit law enforcement and military forces to use less-than-lethal means for keeping order may increase the effectiveness of their operations.[50]

Policing cannot by itself ensure civil control. Good police practices are not a substitute for political systems providing alternative outlets for grievances. Success depends on the degree to which policing practices are supported (and regulated) by legitimate governmental, judicial, and penal systems underwritten by the rule of law.

"Thin Blue Line" Preventive Deployments

Until recently, peacekeeping operations—both traditional and expanded—were only used in the aftermath of conflict to help reconcile the parties and to prevent the recurrence of fighting. A new concept has now emerged with the deployment in late 1992 of a small force of troops and civilian monitors to the Former Yugoslav Republic of Macedonia with the objective, so far successful, of preventing the spread of hostilities from other areas of the former Yugoslavia (see Box 3.5). The essence of the strategy is a preventive military rather than diplomatic response involving the positioning of troops and related personnel on one or both sides of a border between parties in dispute to prevent escalation into armed conflict. While this is only a "thin blue line" of forces, as with classic peacekeeping, the deterrent lies in the fact that the Security Council has expressed its interest in the situation, all the relevant parties are under close international scrutiny, and there is at least an implication of willingness to take action if there is any resort to violence.[51] The success to date of the deployment in Macedonia may suggest that this measure could prove a particularly effective preventive device. One potential disadvantage, as the experience in Cyprus illustrates, is that sometimes the international community must be prepared to stay for an extended, perhaps even indefinite, period of time.

The record of international crises points out the need in certain cases to respond rapidly and with force...

"Fire Brigade" Deployments

Much debate has swirled around the idea of establishing a rapid reaction capability within the UN or through other regional arrangements to give the international community a means to respond quickly to an emerging crisis. Many political difficulties attach to such a capability, however, and governments have in large measure proved unwilling to take the steps necessary to establish such a force.[52]

As discussed in the prologue to this report, the Commission supports the establishment of a rapid reaction force, the core of which would be made up of 5,000 to 10,000 troops from members of the Security

...The operational integrity of such a force requires that it not be assembled in pieces or in haste.

Council. The force would also need a robust planning staff, a standing operational headquarters, training facilities, and compatible equipment.

The Commission offers two arguments for such a capability: first, the record of international crises points out the need in certain cases to respond rapidly and with force; and second, the operational integrity of such a force requires that it not be assembled in pieces or in haste. A standing force may well be a necessity for effective prevention.

Currently, the UN Security Council is ill-equipped to implement quick decisions to establish a military presence on the ground in a crisis. The political machinery and the logistical and financial structure necessary to make things happen within days does not exist. Transportation, communications, and supply functions are contracted out through a competitive, laborious, and time-consuming system. Crisis military staffing is ad hoc and drawn from standing organizations within the UN. While the UN has a military staff of about 145 officers, it is neither permitted to field a force without Security Council authorization, nor is it capable of doing so.

This lack of capacity creates genuine operational hazards. Because of the uncertainties in war and other conflict situations, military commanders desire as much clarity as possible in defining their operations. This clarity includes confirming the legitimacy of the chain of command and mobilizing adequate resources and troop strength to carry out the mission. In complex international operations, the military mission can easily be jeopardized by unclear mandates or a confused chain of command. Obviously, all uncertainty cannot be eliminated, but considerable improvements can certainly be achieved in multinational operations. The chain of command must be clear, unified, and legitimate. The existence of a standing rapid reaction capability would help ensure that these requirements are fulfilled.

In an enlarged Security Council, member states should be prepared to accept as the price of being on the Council the obligation to contribute to the deployment of a well-trained and well-equipped rapid reaction force for short-term missions. Of course, smaller countries would not be expected to make the same contribution as larger countries, and any country on the Security Council would be able to choose, for national reasons, not to deploy their forces in any particular mission. Countries not on the Security Council who wish to contribute to the rapid reaction force would be welcome to do so. The interest shown in the concept of such a force by Canada, Denmark, Norway, the Netherlands, and other countries is a sign that the political will exists.

It seems clear that because of its unparalleled capabilities in certain areas, the United States should be called upon to bear a large, perhaps primary, responsibility for the logistical, communications, and intelligence support, including heavy lift aircraft able to fly the force within days anywhere in the world for

Security Council members should be prepared to accept as the price of being on the Council the obligation to contribute to the deployment of a well-trained and well-equipped rapid reaction force for short-term missions.

UN missions. This would mean that the United States would not always be expected to contribute ground troops, although at times that too may be necessary.

The Security Council should immediately establish a working group to develop the operational requirements for such a capability and make recommendations for Council decision regarding the guidelines for raising and funding such a force. The force would be under the authority of the Security Council and its deployment subject to a veto by any of the permanent members.[53]

In the end, of course, the use of such a capability may mean that other efforts to forestall violence have not been effective. The foregoing discussion has illuminated measures that can help defuse a crisis that has reached an acute phase. But the question remains: What can be done to prevent crises from getting to that point to begin with? In other words, what conditions inhibit the rise of violence and how can these conditions be established and maintained? We take up these questions in our discussion of structural prevention in chapter 4.

Voters in Greater Johannesburg wait to cast ballots
in the historic 1994 all-race election.

CHAPTER 4

STRUCTURAL PREVENTION

Strategies to Address the Root Causes of Deadly Conflict

Structural prevention—or peace building—comprises strategies to address the root causes of deadly conflict, so as to ensure that crises do not arise in the first place, or that, if they do, they do not recur. Those strategies include putting in place international legal systems, dispute resolution mechanisms, and cooperative arrangements; meeting people's basic economic, social, cultural, and humanitarian needs; and rebuilding societies that have been shattered by war or other major crises.

It will be seen that peace-building strategies are of two broad types: the development, by governments acting cooperatively, of international regimes to manage the interactions of states, and the development by individual states (with the help of outsiders as necessary) of mechanisms to ensure bedrock security, well-being, and justice for their citizens. Too often in the past, these activities have been given less attention than they deserve, partly because their conflict prevention significance has been less than fully appreciated.

This chapter discusses both the international and national dimensions of structural prevention. It argues that, while there are no vaccines to immunize societies against violence, a number of measures promote conditions that can inhibit its outbreak. By and large, these measures must be generated and sustained in the first instance within states, through a vibrant social contract between societies and their governments. This positive interaction allows citizens to thrive in a stable environment based on equity and justice in their political and economic lives, and it is characteristic of successful states. The central argument of this chapter is that such states are less likely to succumb to widespread internal violence and less likely, as well, to fight other states.

There are many international laws, norms, agreements, and arrangements—bilateral, regional, and global in scope—designed to minimize threats to security directly.[1] Numerous arms control treaties exist, as do legal regimes like the Convention on the Law of the Sea, and dispute resolution mechanisms like the International Court of Justice and that in the World Trade Organization. These various regimes help reduce security risks by codifying the broad rules by which states can live harmoniously together and by putting in place processes by which they can resolve disputes peacefully as they arise. They also provide institutional frameworks through which states can engage in dialogue and cooperate more generally on matters affecting their national interests. As noted earlier, in 1997 no open hostilities existed between states; the peace that prevails is in part due to the effectiveness of these regimes.[2]

This report argues that whatever model of self-governance societies ultimately choose, and whatever path they follow to that end, they must meet the three core needs of security, well-being, and justice and thereby give people a stake in nonviolent efforts to improve their lives. Meeting these needs not only enables people to live better lives, it also reduces the potential for deadly conflict.

SECURITY

People cannot thrive in an environment where they believe their survival to be in jeopardy. Indeed, many violent conflicts have been waged by people trying to establish and maintain their own security.

There are three main sources of insecurity today: the threat posed by nuclear and other weapons of mass destruction; the possibility of conventional confrontation between militaries; and internal violence, such as terrorism, organized crime, insurgency, and repressive regimes.

Nuclear Weapons

As Presidents Ronald Reagan and Mikhail Gorbachev made clear, any use of nuclear weapons would be catastrophic. Moreover, the proposition that nuclear weapons can be retained in perpetuity and never be used—accidentally or by design—defies credibility. As already pointed out with respect to nuclear proliferation, the retention of nuclear weapons by any state stimulates other states

and nonstate actors to acquire them. Given these facts, the only durably safe course is to work toward elimination of weapons within a reasonable time frame, and for this good purpose to be achieved, stringent conditions have to be set to make this feasible with security for all. These conditions must include rigorous safeguards against any nuclear weapons falling into the hands of dictatorial and fanatical leaders. Steps that should be taken promptly in this direction include developing credible mechanisms and practices: 1) to account for nuclear weapons and materials; 2) to monitor their whereabouts and operational condition; and 3) to ensure the safe management and reduction of nuclear arsenals.

As the Canberra Commission on the Elimination of Nuclear Weapons pointed out in 1996, "The opportunity now exists, perhaps without precedent or recurrence, to make a new and clear choice to enable the world to conduct its affairs without nuclear weapons" (see Box 4.1).[3] The work of the Canberra Commission represents a major step forward and deserves serious consideration by governments working to reduce the nuclear threat.

The Committee on International Security and Arms Control of the U.S. National Academy of Sciences has called for extensive improvements in the protection of nuclear weapons and fissile materials. It underscored the call for aggressive efforts to promote transparency—that is, open practices—with respect to the production, storage, and dismantling of nuclear warheads, and for efforts to ban nuclear weapons completely from specific regions and environments. In addition, the committee placed a premium on developing diplomatic strategies to clarify and to allay the legitimate security concerns of undeclared nuclear states

Box 4.1
THE CANBERRA COMMISSION ON
THE ELIMINATION OF NUCLEAR WEAPONS

The Canberra Commission advocates that the five nuclear weapons states commit themselves to the elimination of nuclear weapons within a reasonable time frame. To date, the states' existing collective and unilateral commitments in this direction have neither led to sufficient concrete steps nor been free of ambiguity with respect to the goal of elimination. Such a commitment, made at high political levels, would change instantly the underlying nuclear weapons paradigm, the thrust of defense planning, and the timing—or indeed the necessity—for modernization and testing programs.

The seriousness of this commitment could be confirmed, the physical safety of the world improved, and the process of elimination significantly advanced if the following immediate steps were taken by nuclear weapons states:

- Taking all nuclear forces off alert
- Removing warheads from delivery vehicles
- Ending deployment of nonstrategic nuclear weapons
- Initiating negotiation to further reduce U.S. and Russian nuclear arsenals
- Agreeing to reciprocal no-first-use undertakings and to nonuse in relation to nonnuclear weapons states

The Canberra Commission proposes that these immediate steps by nuclear weapons states should be supported by all states through:

- Comprehensive disclosure of fissile material stocks
- Universal adherence to the Comprehensive Test Ban Treaty (CTBT)
- Negotiation of a fissile materials cut-off convention

The Canberra Commission also maps the series of steps necessary to prevent horizontal proliferation, to develop effective verification arrangements for a nonnuclear world, and to lay the foundations for the final achievement of a "zero nuclear weapons" world.

Source: Canberra Commission on the Elimination of Nuclear Weapons, *Report of the Canberra Commission on the Elimination of Nuclear Weapons* (Canberra Commission on the Elimination of Nuclear Weapons, August 1996). The members of the Canberra Commission, established by the Australian government in 1995 to propose practical steps toward a nuclear free world, were Celso Amorim, Lee Butler, Richard Butler (Convenor), Michael Carver, Jacques-Yves Cousteau, Jayantha Dhanapala, Rolf Ekeus, Nabil Elaraby, Ryukichi Imai, Ronald McCoy, Robert McNamara, Robert O'Neill, Qian Jiadong, Michel Rocard, Joseph Rotblat, Roald Sagdeev, and Maj Britt Theorin.

in order to freeze, reduce, and eventually eliminate undeclared programs (see Box 4.2).[4]

The Commission takes note of these calls, especially at this time when real progress in arms control has all but come to a complete halt, a development that raises deeply troubling issues regarding the possibility of an inadvertent nuclear attack during a crisis. As chapter 1 observed, while the threat of deliberate use of nuclear weapons by one of the major nuclear states has greatly diminished, the threat of

Box 4.2
REDUCING THE THREAT OF WEAPONS
OF MASS DESTRUCTION

The disintegration of the Soviet Union in 1991 left an estimated 30,000 nuclear weapons, 2,500 nuclear delivery systems, and 40,000 metric tons of chemical weapons scattered throughout Russia, Belarus, Kazakstan, and Ukraine. In addition, Russia possessed at least 40,000 metric tons of chemical weapons and a robust biological weapons capability. The potential for political, social, and economic unrest in the former Soviet Union (FSU) raised concern that these weapons of mass destruction, materials, and expertise might fall into the wrong hands.

To combat this threat the U.S. Congress in 1991 passed the Soviet Nuclear Threat Reduction Act (commonly known as the Nunn-Lugar program, after the bill's chief sponsors). Since this time, the Nunn-Lugar program has authorized $1.5 billion for the Cooperative Threat Reduction Program (CTR) administered by the U.S. Department of Defense. CTR provides funding and assistance to FSU states for the dismantlement and destruction of weapons of mass destruction; transportation, storage, and safeguarding of weapons; strengthening the security of fissile materials; and enhancement of safeguards against proliferation.

While CTR has not been involved in the actual dismantlement of nuclear warheads in Russia, it has directly supported the dismantling of silos, submarines, missiles, and bombers. Rather than stipulate a specific level of weapons reductions, the Nunn-Lugar program supports Russia's efforts to comply with the Strategic Arms Reduction Treaty (START). To date, the United States has provided support for the following:

- Removal of over 1,200 strategic warheads from deployed systems
- Elimination of 230 submarine-launched ballistic missiles (SLBMs)
- Elimination of 445 intercontinental ballistic missile (ICBM) silos
- Elimination of approximately 35 strategic bombers
- Elimination of 1,500 missiles

The Nunn-Lugar program was instrumental in the decision of Belarus, Kazakstan, and Ukraine to return all nuclear warheads to Russia and become nonnuclear states.

Sources: Arms Control and Disarmament Agency, "U.S. Nunn-Lugar Safety, Security, Dismantlement Program," Arms Control and Disarmament Agency Fact Sheet, May 20, 1996; Craig Cerniello, "U.S. Security Assistance to the Former Soviet Union," *Arms Control Today* (September 1996), pp. 25-26; Dunbar Lockwood, "The Nunn-Lugar Program: No Time to Pull the Plug," *Arms Control Today* (June 1995), pp. 8-13; William J. Perry, *Report of the Secretary of Defense to the President and the Congress* (Washington, DC: U.S. Government Printing Office: 1996), pp. 63-70; U.S. Department of Defense, *Cooperative Threat Reduction* (Washington, DC, April 1995); U.S. Government Accounting Office, *Weapons of Mass Destruction, Status of the Cooperative Threat Reduction Program*, Report to Congressional Requestors (September 1996).

inadvertent use has actually risen—largely due to the serious gaps that exist in control of the Russian nuclear arsenal and associated weapons-grade materials. But Russia cannot reasonably be expected to reduce the number of its warheads as long as the United States maintains its current levels. Major reductions would be beneficial for both countries and for their worldwide influence in reducing the nuclear danger.

An equitable outcome with respect to the ultimate force levels of these two nuclear powers, therefore, must be a priority. Unless it is, the arms reduction process on which the continuing viability of the Non-Proliferation Treaty (NPT) depends will remain in jeopardy.

Perhaps of greater urgency, the current operational conditions of much of the Russian inventory cannot be safely sustained. Starkly put, Moscow simply has little capacity to maintain 1,000 warheads, much less the several thousands now permitted under existing START I and START II agreements. This situation must be addressed.

Since nuclear arms are the deadliest of weapons, they create an especially critical problem of prevention. The Commission believes that preventive efforts against violence with conventional or other weapons of mass destruction would be strongly reinforced if fuller efforts were made to control the nuclear danger.

The world would be a safer place, and the risks of deadly conflict would be reduced, if nuclear weapons were not actively deployed. Much of the deterrent effect of these weapons can be sustained without having active forces poised for massive attack at every moment. The countries that maintain these active forces are the ones most threatened by the active forces of other countries, but the entire world is exposed to the consequences of an operational accident or an inadvertent attack. As long as any active deployments are maintained, moreover, the incentive and opportunity for proliferation will remain. The dramatic transformation required to remove all nuclear weapons from active deployment is feasible in technical terms, but substantial changes in political attitudes and managerial practices would be necessary as well. The Commission endorses the ultimate objective of elimination long embodied in the Non-Proliferation Treaty and recently elaborated in the reports by the Canberra Commission and the National Academy of Sciences. Precisely because of the importance of that objective, we wish to emphasize the conditions that would have to be achieved to make elimination a responsible and realistic aspiration.

In a comprehensive framework to achieve that objective, the foremost requirement would be an international accounting system that tracks the exact number of fabricated weapons and the exact amounts of the fissionable materials that provide their explosive power. This accounting is now done individually by the five countries that maintain acknowledged nuclear weapons deployments and presumably by the three countries that are generally believed to have unacknowledged weapons inventories or capability. These countries do not provide enough details to each other or the international community as a whole to the extent that would be required to

The world would be a safer place, and the risks of deadly conflict would be reduced, if nuclear weapons were not actively deployed.

determine how many nuclear weapons and how much fissionable material actually exists, where it is, and what the arrangements for its physical security are. Unless these basic features are known and monitored with reasonable confidence by an agreed mechanism, it will not be possible to reach agreement on removing nuclear weapons from active deployment.

For technical as well as political reasons, it will inevitably require a considerable amount of time to develop an accounting system that could support a general agreement to eliminate active nuclear weapons deployments. The requisite accuracy is not likely to be achieved until such a system has been in operation over a substantial period of time. The Commission strongly recommends that efforts be initiated immediately to create such a system as a priority for the prevention of deadly conflict.

Concurrently, governments should eliminate the practice of alert procedures (e.g., relying on continuously available weapons) and set an immediate goal to remove all weapons from active deployment—that is, to dismantle them to the point that to use them would require reconstruction. In addition, the major nuclear states should reverse their commitment to massive targeting and establish a presumption of limited use. Finally, as this process proceeds, multilateral arrangements will need to be made to ensure stability and the maintenance of peace and security in a world without nuclear weapons.[5]

Regional Contingencies

Managing the volatile relationship between the United States and the Soviet Union during the Cold War rested on high-quality deterrence and avoiding the conditions that could lead to a massive accident. It was important that the two superpowers were not immediate neighbors in any meaningful sense and—with the important exception of the Cuban Missile Crisis in 1962—never posed any direct threat to each other. The geographic distance between Washington and Moscow was an important component of the deterrent relationship. It helped account for the fact that circumstances never arose to produce the simultaneous mobilization of forces against each other that could have led to a nuclear attack.

In several regions of the world today, however, volatile circumstances involve neighbors, one or more of which may possess nuclear weapons. These circumstances give added impetus to developing improved methods of accounting and safeguarding nuclear weapons and materials. The aim must be to remove the specter of nuclear weapons far to the background of any conventional confrontation. For this to happen, the nuclear states must demonstrate that they take seriously Article VI of the NPT (which calls for signatories to make good faith progress toward complete disarmament under strict and effective international control). Movement along the lines discussed above can help send that message throughout the world.

Biological and Chemical Weapons

Although there have been numerous protocols, conventions, and agreements on the control and elimination of biological and chemical weapons, progress has been slowed by a lack of binding treaties with provisions for implementation, inspection, and enforcement.[6] The 1972 Biological Weapons Convention, for instance, includes no verification measures, and the 1993 Chemical Weapons Convention has yet to be ratified by a number of the major producers, including Russia.

As chapter 1 argued, it is impossible to control completely or deny access to materials and information regarding biological weapons. But it may be possible to gain greater control through mechanisms to monitor the possession and the construction of facilities for the most dangerous pathogens. A registry could be established in which governments and other users would register strains under their control and detail the purposes of experimentation. Registrants would be required to publish the results of their experiments. This registry would seek to reinforce the practice of systematic transparency and create a legal and professional expectation that those working with these strains would be under an obligation to reveal themselves. In addition, the professional community of researchers and scientists must engage in expanded and extensive collaboration in this field and establish close connection to the public health community. Here too, the United States and Russia should set an example for others.

The Commission believes that governments should seek a more effective categorical prohibition against the development and use of chemical weapons. The international community needs systematic monitoring of chemical compounds and the size of stockpiles to ensure transparency and to guard against misuse.[7]

If progress on these fronts is to be made, complex disagreements within both the international community and individual states must be addressed. Notwithstanding its shortcomings, the experience gained on the nuclear front has created important expectations of transparency, accountability, and reciprocity, and may help improve the control of biological and chemical weapons (see Box 4.3).[8]

Conventional Weapons

As noted in earlier chapters, violent conflict today is fought with conventional weapons. The Commission recognizes that all states have the right to maintain adequate defense structures for their security and that achieving global agreement on the control of weapons will be difficult. Nevertheless, progress should be possible to control the flow of arms around the world. The global arms trade in advanced weapons is dominated by the five permanent members of the UN Security Council and Germany. Jointly, they account for 80–90 percent of such activity.[9] The Middle East remains the largest regional market for weapons, with Saudi Arabia the largest single purchaser. East Asia, with even wealthier states modernizing their defense forces, is also a huge weapons market. To date, few efforts to control the flows of conventional weapons have been undertaken (see Box 4.4).

The trade in small arms and ammunition—which account for the majority of deaths in today's conflicts—remains largely unregulated, a condition that is also exploited by private arms dealers and transnational criminal elements, including narcotics cartels.[10] The first step toward regulation has been documenting arms transfers, notably the UN Register of Conventional Arms and the Wassenaar Arrangement.

Governments should seek a more effective categorical prohibition against the development and use of chemical weapons.

Box 4.3
DECREASING THE THREAT OF BIOLOGICAL
AND CHEMICAL WEAPONS

The Chemical and Biological Arms Control Institute has identified several measures to decrease the threat of these weapons of mass destruction:

- Better coordination of policy tools, for example, intelligence, export controls, diplomacy, and military force. The international community must formulate a coherent strategy to control chemical and biological weapons, appreciating technological constraints and promoting adequate response capabilities.
- More efforts to understand the terrorist threat by studying groups that might try to acquire weapons
- Isolation of rogue states that do not sign the Chemical Weapons Convention (CWC) or the Biological Weapons Convention (BWC) to convince them that the international community will prevent them from obtaining chemical and biological weapons, or deny them any benefits from the use of such weapons
- Resolution of differences between developed and developing countries over the sharing of technology and export controls, as they relate to the control of chemical and biological weapons

Chemical and biological weapons pose different problems from nuclear arms, and controlling them demands different measures. For chemical weapons:

- Effective implementation of the CWC is a high priority. After an initial grace period, compliance must be rigorously verified to ensure the credibility of the CWC. Success of the CWC will help other arms control efforts.
- All countries must sign the CWC. Russia, in particular, may need help with financial problems posed by the convention.
- Defense against chemical weapons must be strengthened because they probably will not be eliminated in the next ten years. Timely and accurate detection and identification, protective equipment, medical research, and training should be improved.

For biological weapons:

- The BWC protocol negotiations must be completed. This will require a realistic formulation of a declaration/inspection process that may not allow the same access provided by the CWC because of the differences in the science involved and the way the treaties are written, but which can, nevertheless, bolster confidence in compliance.
- The concerns of the United States and the United Kingdom over Russian compliance with the BWC must be alleviated.
- Policymakers must be better informed about biological weapons. Such an education process should include additional research, outreach, and training.

Source: Michael L. Moodie, "Chemical and Biological Weapons: The Unfinished Agenda," Chemical and Biological Arms Control Institute, May 27, 1997.

The UN Register of Conventional Arms, established in 1991, provides for the voluntary disclosure of national arms transfers of major conventional weapons systems. Although a valuable source of information on arms transfers, the register's effectiveness suffers as a result of shortcomings, most notably the failure of many countries to submit information on transfers: some states failed to respond after the first two years, while others filed "nil returns," indicating no such arms exchanged.[11] In short, the quality and quantity of information in the register is not adequate to provide true transparency for conventional armaments.

The Wassenaar Arrangement for Export Controls for Conventional Arms and Dual-Use Goods and Technologies was created in 1995 as a follow-on to the NATO-based Coordinating Committee on Multilateral Export Controls (COCOM). Named after the suburb of The Hague where the agreement was signed, the arrangement includes 33 participating countries and seeks to avoid destabilizing transfers of weapons and sensitive technologies through the coordination of national export control policies. To date, it has focused nearly exclusively on major weapons systems and not on small arms, but one option under discussion is to restrict all conventional arms transfers into certain areas at risk for renewed violent conflict or under UN sanctions.

Again, the results have been less than promising. The group concluded its December 1996 plenary session without reaching its goal of enhancing new export control guidelines. However, participation in the exchange of conventional arms and dual-use technology transfer information between members has greatly improved since the first exchange in September

The UN Register of Conventional Arms was created as a means to ensure transparency in armaments with the goals of serving as a confidence-building mechanism and promoting stability and restraint among member states. Under the register, states submit data relating to arms levels, transfers, imports, and exports. States are also encouraged to submit information relating to their arms import and export policies as well as legislation and administrative procedures. The categories of weapons included in the register are limited to battle tanks, armored combat vehicles, artillery systems, combat aircraft, attack helicopters, warships, and missiles and missile launchers.

Source: United Nations, "General and Complete Disarmament, Part L: Transparency in Armaments," A/RES/46/36L, December 6, 1991, in *General Assembly Official Records: 46th Session, Supplement No. 49* (A/46/49), pp. 73-76.

1996.[12] Nevertheless, without ongoing consultations or veto powers for its members, it is unclear whether the Wassenaar Arrangement can effectively serve as a forum for resolving disputes over transfers of conventional weapons and dual-use technology (see Box 4.5).

The Conventional Armed Forces in Europe Treaty (CFE) is the only international agreement to impose limits on conventional arms. In force in 1992, the CFE limits five types of conventional weapons: tanks, armored combat vehicles, artillery, attack helicopters, and combat aircraft. A side agreement known as CFE-1A places limits on manpower in Europe. The treaty provides for a multilayered verification system consisting of on-site inspections and national and multinational technical means. More than 50,000 pieces of military equipment have been destroyed or converted to other uses under the treaty. The states party to the treaty engaged in CFE Treaty

Box 4.4
INTERNATIONAL CODE OF CONDUCT
ON ARMS TRANSFERS

In an effort to restrict the global transfer of arms, particularly to authoritarian regimes, Oscar Arias Sánchez, Nobel Peace laureate and former president of Costa Rica, invited fellow peace laureates to develop an "International Code of Conduct on Arms Transfers." Under the International Code of Conduct, unveiled in May 1997, to be eligible for arms transfers, a government would be obligated to meet a number of internationally recognized standards: being chosen in free and fair elections; protecting citizens' human rights; permitting the expression of political views; having civilian control over its armed forces and transparency in military spending; and not being engaged in civil war, international conflict, or sponsoring international terrorism. In addition, all nations would be required to participate in the United Nations Register of Conventional Arms and to respect international arms embargoes and military sanctions. The code covers all arms transfers, including conventional weapons, munitions, subcomponents and delivery systems; military and security training; and sensitive military and dual-use technologies.

To date, the International Code of Conduct has been endorsed by more than a dozen Nobel Prize laureates. Similar codes of conduct on arms transfers have also been proposed in the United Nations, the Organization for Security and Cooperation in Europe, the European Union, the United States, and South Africa. Proponents of the initiative believe that strict adherence to the International Code of Conduct will reduce levels of conflict while promoting democracy and human rights.

Sources: Oscar Arias Sánchez, the Dalai Lama, Donald Gann, Gururaj Mutalik, Jose Ramos Horta, Susan Waltz, Elie Wiesel, and Betty Williams, "The Commission of Nobel Peace Laureates' International Code of Conduct on Arms Transfers: A Joint Statement for Peace and Human Rights," New York, May 29, 1997; speech by Oscar Arias Sánchez at the public presentation of the Commission of Nobel Peace Laureates' "International Code of Conduct on Arms Transfers," New York, May 29, 1997; Oscar Arias Sánchez, "A Precondition for Peace and Prosperity in the 21st Century: A Code of Conduct on Arms Transfers," speech to the State of the World Plenary Session, San Francisco, October 3, 1996; British American Security Information Council (BASIC) and Arias Foundation for Peace and Human Progress, "The International Code of Conduct on Arms Transfers: Fact Sheet," May 1997.

Review Conferences to adapt the treaty to the changing security situation of Europe.[13]

Within countries, some efforts to rein in small arms through exchange or buy-back programs have met with a measure of success. Nations such as El Salvador, inundated with weapons acquired during civil war, have initiated gun buy-back programs.[14] In Mozambique, a small church-based buy-back program provides farms tools, sewing machines, and other essential household items in return for guns and armaments.[15] These models may be adaptable to other regions by governments committed to controlling conventional weapons.

As previously mentioned, the momentum behind steps to reduce and restructure conventional military establishments will likely continue for many states. Governments must keep conventional arms control near the top of their national and multilateral security agendas to preserve the gains that have been made. NATO and other regional arrangements that offer the opportunity for sustained dialogue among the professional military establishments will help, and in the process promote important values of transparency, nonthreatening force structures and deployments, and civilian control of the military.

Box 4.5
PROPOSAL FOR CONTROLLING LIGHT
WEAPONS PROLIFERATION

Many groups have proposed regimes to control light weapons. One such group, Saferworld, a London-based nongovernmental organization, has proposed an initiative for the European Union (EU) to help constrain the proliferation of light weapons. They propose a presumption of denial of weapons transfers to areas in conflict or tension or with serious human rights abuses, and to any destinations posing a significant risk that weapons will be diverted. Saferworld's recommendations for action by EU states include: establishing systems for registering and tagging all weapons and ammunition; making arms exports conditional on the supplier state having the right to check information on end-use after delivery and to be consulted if the recipient is considering re-export or change of use; introducing a compulsory registration system for arms traders; and reviewing member states' regulations to ensure their right to impose and revise arms embargoes.

In addition, the proposal asserts that the EU and its member states should endorse and, where appropriate, adopt the 'Security First' approach to providing assistance to conflict-prone countries or regions, whereby assistance to promote security, demobilization, and disarmament is integrated from the beginning with economic and social development programs. In exchange for such assistance, the EU could reasonably expect its recipient country partners to commit themselves to some agreed measures, such as participating in regional transparency or confidence-building measures or implementing controls on arms flows to the best of their ability.

While Saferworld focused recommendations on the EU, the proposal advocates that the policies be implemented by all arms exporters. Moreover, Saferworld also argued that the UN Register of Conventional Arms could usefully be extended to cover some of the 'heavier' light weapons, such as light mortars or machine guns. Beyond this, the proposal argues that new transparency arrangements should be developed at either a global or regional level, including information exchanges on relevant national legislation and regulations.

Sources: Owen Greene, *Tackling Light Weapons Proliferation: Issues and Priorities for the EU* (London: Saferworld, 1997). Natalie J. Goldring, "Bridging the Gap: Light and Major Conventional Weapons in Recent Conflicts," British American Security Information Council (BASIC), Washington, DC, 1997; paper prepared for the annual meeting of the International Studies Association, Toronto, Ontario, March 1997.

Cooperating for Peace

Around the globe, national military establishments in many—but not all—regions are shrinking and their role has come under profound reexamination as a result of the end of the Cold War and the sharp rise of economic globalization. With the end of the confrontation between East and West, military establishments in the former Warsaw Pact are being reconfigured and the forces of NATO and many Western nations are being reduced. Moreover, rapid and widespread global economic competition has put pressure on governments to redirect resources away from military expenditures toward social programs and other initiatives to accelerate economic growth, and this appears to be the likely course for many states for the foreseeable future.

The Commission recognizes, of course, that this phenomenon is not universal. A noteworthy exception to this trend is East

Asia, where many nations have increased their military expenditures.[16] Some states continue to support disproportionately large military establishments at huge cost. In North Korea and the former Yugoslavia (Serbia and Montenegro), for example, military spending accounts for more than 20 percent of the gross domestic product.[17] The Commission believes, however, that the general trend toward force reduction and realignment, the current absence of interstate war in the world, and the continuing development of international regimes form a foundation from which states can continue to reduce the conventional military threat that they pose to one another.

One important regional initiative to help improve the security climate is NATO's Partnership for Peace (PFP). This program, formalized by the North Atlantic Council in January 1994, allows non-NATO states, particularly

An Afghan gardener pots plastic flowers in the shells of Soviet bombs.

the former Communist nations of Eastern Europe, to enter into bilateral agreements with the North Atlantic Alliance, provided that they agree to the principles of the North Atlantic Treaty. PFP invited these states to participate in political and military bodies of NATO to widen and deepen European security and cooperation. Twenty-seven states participated in PFP in 1997. This ambitious program has helped underscore the importance and viability of three essential factors to reduce conventional military threats: transparency—that is, mutual awareness of defense expenditures and force composition—nonoffensive force structures and deployments, and civilian control of the military as an essential feature of democratic governance. The goals of the Partnership for Peace are also reinforced through bilateral programs of major NATO members.[18]

Beyond NATO, other regional organizations have an active agenda to reduce threats and build confidence. In Asia, the ASEAN Regional Forum was created for just such a purpose and now brings together some 20 nations for regular consultations.[19] The Organization for Security and Cooperation in Europe (OSCE) has in the past two decades proved to be a valuable forum for confidence building in Europe.

Finally, many states pursue a number of specialized military-to-military initiatives, tailored to their specific circumstances, to help reduce external threats. The South African government, for example, has undertaken military cooperation programs with other nations of the Southern African Development Community, many of whom were involved in military confrontations with South Africa during the apartheid era. Israel and Egypt have maintained a peaceful border (albeit with significant outside help) for over 20 years. Brazil and Argentina have created the Argentinean-Brazilian Agency for Accounting and Control of Nuclear Materials (ABACC) and established a Common System of Accounting and Control of Nuclear Materials (SCCC). These steps have proven an invaluable means of developing trust and cooperation between Brazil and Argentina and have spawned a number of agreements, safeguards, protocols, and subsidiary organizations.[20]

But while the general international environment is moving to greater stability between states—indeed many countries exist today in regions or subregions with absolutely no fear of outside military exploitation—in many countries a major risk still arises from internal threats.

Security within States

Intrastate violence can result from active insurgencies, political terrorism, or organized crime. Four essential elements provide a framework for maintaining a just regime for internal stability: a corpus of laws that is legitimately derived and widely promulgated and understood; a consistent, visible, fair, and active network of police authority to enforce the laws (especially important at the local level); an independent, equitable, and accessible grievance redress system, including above all an impartial judicial system; and a penal system that is fair and prudent in meting out punishment.[21] These basic elements are vitally significant yet hard to achieve, and they require constant attention through democratic processes.

Of course, not all states are democratic; some are centralized and repressive while others have weak or corrupt central governments. In such cases, this framework will not be used until major reform is undertaken. It is often the case that precisely because chances for such reforms are so remote that internal violence erupts and can last for years. Later in this chapter we discuss transitions from authoritarian to democratic government.

Important factors contributing to internal security can be derived from peace agreements that ended civil wars in Guatemala, El Salvador, Lebanon, Mozambique, and Nicaragua. These agreements have several common elements: a focus on devising and implementing long-term change; the promotion and establishment of mechanisms for national consensus building (e.g., constituent assemblies); provisions for the maintenance of a close and ongoing relationship between the former warring parties, including the establishment and maintenance of acceptable power-sharing arrangements; and an emphasis on cooperating on long-term arrangements for economic opportunity and justice.[22]

Other governments, international organizations, and private agencies operating internationally have important roles to play in maintaining internal security. The UN contributed greatly to building peace in several of the countries mentioned above. In general, outsiders can help by

- Promoting norms and practices to govern interstate relations, to avoid and resolve disputes, and to encourage practices of good governance

- Reducing and eventually eliminating the many military threats and sources of insecurity between states, including those that contribute to instability within states

- Not exacerbating the interstate or intrastate disputes of others, either on purpose or inadvertently. The history of third-party intervention is replete with examples of interventions that were unwarranted, unwanted, or unhelpful.

Existing in a secure environment is only the beginning, of course. People may feel relatively free from fear of attack, but unless they also believe themselves able to maintain a healthy existence and have genuine opportunities to pursue a livelihood, discontent and resentment can generate unrest.

WELL-BEING

What is the relationship between economic well-being and peace? If the relationship is clearly positive, what strategies to promote economic prosperity work best under what conditions? We have learned important lessons from successes and failures in Africa, Asia, and Latin America during the past half-century.

Too many of the world's people still cannot take for granted food, water, shelter, and other necessities. Why are there still widely prevalent threats to survival when modern science and technology have made such powerful contributions to human well-being? What can we do to diminish the kind of vulnerability that leads to desperation? The slippery slope of degradation—so vividly exemplified in Somalia in the early 1990s—leads to growing risks of civil war, terrorism, and humanitarian catastrophe.

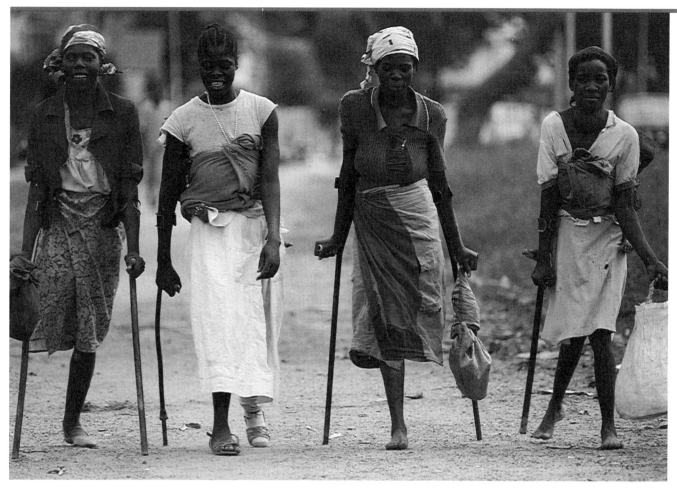

Angolan women maimed by land mines.

Basic well-being entails access to adequate shelter, food, health services, education, and an opportunity to earn a livelihood. In the context of structural prevention, well-being implies more than just a state's capacity to provide essential needs. People are often able to tolerate economic deprivation and disparities in the short run because governments create conditions that allow people to improve their living standards and that lessen disparities between rich and poor. To this extent, well-being overlaps with political and social justice, discussed below.

The Commission believes that decent living standards are a universal human right. Development efforts to meet these standards are a prime responsibility of governments, and the international community has a responsibility to help governments through development assistance. Assistance programs are vital to many developing states, crucial to sustaining millions of people in crises, and necessary to help build otherwise unaffordable infrastructure. But long-term solutions must also be found through states' own developmental policies, attentive to the particular needs of a society's economic and social sectors. In addition, the careful management of existing natural resources is becoming increasingly vital to the welfare of all societies.

Helping from Within: Development Revisited

For a variety of reasons, many nations in the global South have been late in getting access to the remarkable opportunities now available for economic and social development. They are seeking ways to modernize in keeping with their own cultural traditions and distinctive settings. How can they adapt useful tools from the world's experience for their own development?

The general well-being of a society will require government action to help ensure widespread economic opportunity. Whether and how to undertake such strategies is controversial and should be decided and implemented democratically by societies on their own behalf. The Commission emphasizes, however, that economic growth, by itself, will not reduce prospects for violent conflict and could, in fact, be a contributing factor to internal conflicts. The resentment and unrest likely to be induced by drastically unbalanced or inequitable growth may outweigh whatever prosperity that growth generates. In contrast, equitable access to economic growth and, importantly, economic opportunity inhibits deadly conflict.[23]

Unfortunately, the current international economic environment is not particularly sympathetic to this view, emphasizing instead short-term bottom-line performance as a measure of economic competitiveness and vitality. Clearly, in many states economic growth must sharply increase to meet the needs of burgeoning populations. But if this complex equation is to be managed with as little potential for deadly violence as possible, governments must reorient their thinking away from an overemphasis on short-term performance. Otherwise, there will be an avoidable excess of human suffering—with associated resentment and hence the seedbed for hatred and violence, even terrorist movements.

Fundamentally, the distribution of economic benefits in a society is a function of political decisions regarding the kind of economic system a society will construct, including the nature and level of governmental engagement in private sector activity. Poverty is often a structural outgrowth of these decisions, and when poverty runs in parallel with ethnic or cultural lines, it often creates a flashpoint. Peace is most commonly found where economic growth and opportunities to share in that growth are broadly distributed across the population.

There is great preventive value in initiatives that focus on children and women, not only because they are the main victims of conflict, but also because women in many vulnerable societies are an important source of community stability and vitality. For children, this emphasis entails a two-pronged approach that stresses, on the one hand, broad opportunities for education and basic health services, and on the other, policies that prohibit the recruitment of child soldiers and the industrial exploitation of child labor. For women, this entails national programs that encourage education for girls, women-operated businesses, and other community-based activities.

> There is great preventive value in initiatives that focus on children and women, not only because they are the main victims of conflict, but also because women in many vulnerable societies are an important source of community stability and vitality.

A growing body of evidence shows that the education of women and girls is a remarkably promising route for developing countries. The need to improve the educational attainment and status of women is an objective of intrinsic value, but it has the added practical value of far-reaching significance in widening women's skills and choices as well as in improving their health and nutrition. It is an investment in future economic growth and well-being even when women do not participate in wage employment. Most girls in developing countries become mothers, and their influence on their children is crucial. Health studies show that the more educated the mothers, the less likely that their children will die, regardless of differences in family income. Education helps delay marriage for women, partly by increasing their chances for employment, and educated women are more likely to know about and use contraceptives.[24]

Almost all countries committed themselves to the goal of eradicating severe poverty at the World Summit for Social Development in 1995.[25] Daunting though this aim is, the opportunities of the global economy and the lessons learned in development make this a reasonable goal in the next few decades. The UN Development Program's *Human Development Report 1997* formulates six priorities for action:

- Everywhere the starting point is to empower women and men—and to ensure their participation in decisions that affect their lives and enable them to build their strengths and assets.

- Gender equality is essential for empowering women—and for eradicating poverty.

- Sustained poverty reduction requires "pro-poor" growth in all countries—and faster growth in the 100 or so developing and transition countries where growth has been failing.

Women attend a literacy class in Bangladesh.

- Globalization offers great opportunities—but only if it is managed more carefully with more concern for global equity.

- In all these areas, the state must provide an enabling environment for broad-based political support and alliances for "pro-poor" policies and markets.

- Special international support is needed for special situations—to reduce the poorest countries' debt faster, to increase their share of aid, and to open agricultural markets for their exports.[26]

A complementary approach to economic development is made in the World Bank's *World Development Report 1996*. It derives lessons of experience from economies in transition from central planning to market-based operation—as they build essential institutions to support efficient markets with adequate social safety nets.

Decent living standards are a universal human right.

What can these countries learn from each other? What does the experience of transition to date suggest for the many other countries grappling with similar issues of economic reform? What are the implications for external assistance—and for the reform priorities in the countries themselves? The World Bank's report observes:

- Consistent policies, combining liberalization of markets, trade and new business entry with reasonable price stability, can achieve a great deal—even in countries lacking clear property rights and strong market institutions.

- Differences between countries are very important, both in setting the feasible range of policy choices and in determining the response to reforms.

- An efficient response to market processes requires clearly defined property rights—and this will eventually require widespread private ownership.

- Major changes in social policies must complement the move to the market—to focus on relieving poverty, to cope with increased mobility, and to counter the adverse intergenerational effects of reform.

- Institutions that support markets arise both by design and from demand.

- Sustaining the human capital base for economic growth requires considerable reengineering of education and health delivery systems. International integration can help lock in successful reforms.

These judgments reinforce the Commission's belief that diligent programs that help cultivate the human resources of a country, in ways that ensure widespread access to economic opportunity, will help create conditions that inhibit widespread violence.

Making Development Sustainable

Global population and economic growth, along with high consumption in the North, have led to the depletion, destruction, and pollution of the natural environment. Science and technology can contribute immensely to the reduction of environmental threats through low-pollution technologies. Greater effort is required to develop sustainable strategies for social and economic progress; in fact, sustainability is likely to become a key principle of development and a major incentive for global partnerships.

In at least three clear ways, the use and misuse of natural resources lie at the heart of conflicts that hold the potential for mass violence: 1) the deliberate manipulation of resource shortages for hostile purposes (for example, using food or water as a weapon); 2) competing claims of sovereignty over resource endowments (such as rivers or oil and other fossil fuel deposits); and 3) the exacerbating role played by environmental degradation and resource depletion in areas characterized by political instability, rapid population growth, chronic economic deprivation, and societal stress.

Serious issues of international equity will be posed by the desire of the North to preserve global climate stability and biodiversity and that of the South to secure a greater share of global resources and economic growth. Environmental problems plaguing the industrialized countries also pose equity issues, with domestic minority ethnic groups and the poor usually bearing the brunt of pollution. In the aftermath of environmental deterioration, national security systems are likely to be challenged by massive immigration to more favorably situated states.

If security analysts can be thoroughly informed about environmental problems, and if environmental analysts can come to understand the tools and experiences of the security community, there could be advances in ways to approach international environmental agreements. An example may help to clarify the nature of the problem. A critical environmental challenge of the day is limiting the emissions of carbon dioxide from the burning of fossil fuel. The lion's share of such emissions comes from the developed countries. But increasing numbers of people in the developing world are demanding improved standards of living, and that will lead to dramatically higher levels of combustion of fossil fuels. China's economic growth rate, for example, currently exceeds ten percent per year, and unless new energy technologies are introduced, this growth will rapidly raise the average level of carbon dioxide emissions from developing countries. Because Western standards of living have been built on inefficient uses of fossil fuels, it is likely that many developing countries will repeat that pattern as they industrialize. This will complicate North–South negotiations to attain environmentally sustainable development.

Equitable access to economic opportunity inhibits deadly conflict.

Experience from past international environmental and security negotiations may be found to guide the achievement of arrangements to control carbon dioxide emissions. The Montreal Protocols of 1987 limiting production of ozone-depleting chlorofluorocarbon compounds involved primarily the industrialized world. But when they were extended in the London agreements two years later, substantial interest on the part of the developing countries produced significant technical aid commitments from the industrialized countries.

Economists Sudhir Anand and Amartya Sen point out that the human development perspective translates readily into a critical recognition of the need for active international efforts to preserve the quality of the environment in which we live. They write:

Building an irrigation system in Indonesia.

"We have to see how the human developments we have achieved in the past, and what we are trying to achieve right now, can be sustained in the future—and further extended—rather than be threatened by pollution, exhaustion of natural resources and other deteriorations of local and global environments. But this safeguarding of future prospects has to be done without sacrificing current efforts towards rapid human development and the speedy elimination of widespread deprivation of basic human capabilities. This is partly a matter of cooperation across the frontiers, but the basis of that collaboration must take full note of the inequalities that exist now and the urgency of rapid human development in the more deprived parts of the world."[27]

Helping from Outside: Development Assistance

Promoting good governance has become the keynote of development assistance in the 1990s, along with the building of fundamental skills and local capacity for participation in the modern global economy. Compared with the overarching economic priorities of previous decades—reconstruction in the 1950s, development planning in the 1960s, meeting basic human needs in the 1970s, or structural adjustment in the 1980s—current policies of the major donors are more directly supportive of structural prevention. The new approach requires a state, at a minimum, to equip itself with a professional, accountable bureaucracy that is able to provide an enabling environment and handle macroeconomic management, sustained poverty reduction, education and training (including of women), and protection of the environment.

The Commission believes that more strenuous and sustained development assistance can also reduce the risk of regional conflicts when it is used to tie border groups in one or more states to their shared interests in land and water development, environmental improvement, and other mutual concerns. Nearly every region of the world has a major resource endowment that will require multiple states to cooperate to ensure that these resources are managed responsibly. In North America, the Rio Grande Valley and the Great Lakes region are prominent examples. In Russia and Central Asia, disputes over the Caspian Sea and the Fergana Valley have already proven this point. In the Middle East, no state is immune to a deep and abiding concern regarding the distribution of fresh water.

The emphasis on good governance has also encouraged a more robust and responsible private sector development in many countries. There is rising economic activity in the private sector around the world. Over the next ten years, the World Bank projects that developing economies will grow at over twice the rate of industrialized economies.[28]

Sustained growth requires investment in people, and careful programs must be crafted if deep, intergenerational poverty is not to become institutionalized. Foreign assistance to poor countries can include transitional budgetary support, especially for maintenance and to buffer the human cost of conversion to market economies. Extensive technical assistance, specialized training, and broad economic edu-

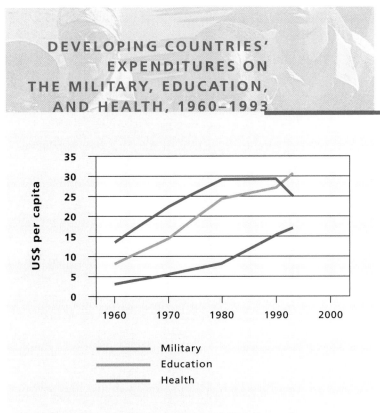

DEVELOPING COUNTRIES' EXPENDITURES ON THE MILITARY, EDUCATION, AND HEALTH, 1960–1993

Note: Values expressed in 1987 prices and in general converted to dollars at 1987 exchange rates.

Source: Ruth Leger Sivard, *World Military and Social Expenditures 1996* (Washington, DC: World Priorities, 1996), p. 44.

cation are all badly needed. So too is the building of indigenous institutions to sustain the vital knowledge and skills for development.

In sum, improving well-being requires a multifaceted approach. It means mobilizing and developing human capacities; broadening and diversifying the economic base; removing barriers to equal opportunity; and opening countries to participation in the global economy and the international community.

JUSTICE

When citizens are treated fairly and offered equal access to opportunities under the law, this, in turn, creates the political space necessary for people to fulfill their aspirations without the need to deprive others of the same opportunity. Based on the principles outlined in the UN Charter, governments should work to promulgate norms of behavior within and between states that strengthen and widen not only security and well-being, but also justice.

An understanding of and adherence to the rule of law is crucial to a healthy system of social organization, both nationally and internationally, and any effort to create and maintain such a system must itself rest on the rule of law. The rule of law is both a goal—it forms the basis for the just management of relations between and among people—and a means. A sound legal regime helps ensure the protection of fundamental human rights, political access through participatory governance, social accommodation of diverse groups, and equitable economic opportunity.

Justice in the International Community

States should develop ways to promote international law with particular emphasis in three main areas: human rights; humanitarian law, including the need to provide the legal underpinning for UN operations in the field; and nonviolent alternatives for dispute resolution, including more flexible intrastate mechanisms for mediation, arbitration, grievance recognition, and social reconciliation.

Human Rights

Norms that call for the protection of fundamental human rights are contained in the Universal Declaration of Human Rights.[29] The Universal Declaration bans all forms of discrimination, slavery, torture and other cruel, inhuman, or degrading treatment or punishment and guarantees every human's right to life, liberty, nationality, freedom of movement, religion, asylum, marriage, assembly, and many other fundamental rights and liberties. One hundred thirty states have become signatories to the Universal Declaration since its adoption by the General Assembly on December 10, 1948. The Universal Declaration is joined by the International Covenant on Economic, Social and Cultural Rights and the International Covenant on Civil and Political Rights with its two Optional Protocols to form the International Bill of Rights, the cornerstone of the United Nations "worldwide human rights movement" established in the Charter.[30]

Many regional organizations include the International Bill of Rights in their charters and proceedings; some even add additional human rights provisions. For example, the Helsinki Accords (the founding document of the Conference on Security and Cooperation in Europe [CSCE]) provide, as in the Universal Declaration, for freedom of thought, conscience, religion, and belief.[31] These human rights provisions were later expanded by the Charter of Paris, which undertook to protect the ethnic, cultural, linguistic, and religious identity of national minorities.[32]

States have only begun to use these criteria to shape their bilateral relations.[33] Despite the unprecedented range and volume of formal endorsements that states have given human rights since the founding of the United Nations, they have been reluctant to hold each other accountable for living up to these principles. Ensuring the protection of human rights requires active engagement by responsible governments. The guidelines, political will, and international capacity for such engagement are developing very slowly, however, in the

The International War Crimes Tribunal at The Hague.

absence of a clear consensus among states that efforts on behalf of human rights are in their national interest.

Yet, the original decision to enshrine a commitment to uphold human rights in the UN Charter reflected more than a humanitarian or idealist impulse of member governments. The founders of the UN were primarily interested in preventing another world war, and many had concluded that the terrible human rights abuses by the Nazis were the early warning signs of a potential aggressor. Had the international community acted to stop Hitler and his followers, World War II might have been prevented. On this much they agreed, but they could not agree on how to prevent wars. With the onset of the Cold War, prevention reverted to more traditional strategies of deterrence and balance of power. But in the 1990s, states face new problems of collective security that give human rights greater political salience.

As the UN's High Commissioner for Refugees so often reminds governments: "Today's human rights abuses are tomorrow's refugee movements."[34] Human rights, in this sense, are gaining significance not only as a moral imperative, but also as a tool of analysis and policy formation—with their violation an early warning of worse problems to come. Situations in which governments do not respect the rights of their own citizens could be a warning that refugee flows and other troubles might spiral into costly humanitarian emergencies. Human rights are thus becoming, properly, a rationale for preventive diplomacy and collective security.

Palestinians vote in Gaza City.

organ of the Council of Europe, was founded by the European Convention on Human Rights (1953) and has proven in recent years to be one of the most successful instruments of international law. The Inter-American Court, founded by the Organization of American States in 1979, has also become a powerful voice in human rights law, both regionally through its decisions and globally through its issuance of advisory opinions. The Court is mandated to promote respect for and to defend human rights—together with the Inter-American Commission, which determines the admissibility of petitions to the Court, engages in fact-finding missions, and attempts to arrange friendly settlements.[35]

One building block for promulgating humanitarian norms especially important to internal conflict is Article Three in each of the four Geneva Conventions. Common to all these conventions, it applies to all armed conflict of a "noninternational" character occurring in the territory of a signatory state. It calls for the humane treatment of noncombatants and others who do not take up arms, and prohibits violence of any type against these persons—including humiliating or degrading treatment, the taking of hostages, and all forms

Humanitarian Law

Several regional initiatives have been attempted in recent years to strengthen the value of human rights practices and other measures as essential factors for stability. The European Court of Human Rights and the Inter-American Court of Human Rights work within their respective regions to respond to intrastate and interstate oppression. The European Court, an

92   PREVENTING DEADLY CONFLICT

of extrajudicial punishment. Moreover, it requires that protections be accorded medical personnel and medical transport for the wounded and sick, and that arrangements for the dead be respectful.

But for societies wracked by years of conflict, overcoming years or even generations of violence, discrimination, and deprivation will not come easily. People must work to put the past behind them without creating a new basis for future violence. To do so, they often need the help of mediation or arbitration mechanisms.

Nonviolent Dispute Resolution

A wide array of approaches to mediation and arbitration exists to help broker disputes in nonviolent ways. Arbitration, the more limited of the two mechanisms, seems to work best under conditions of defined legal relationships such as international trade agreements. Arbitration clauses are often laid out in treaties and charters where members or signatories agree, in advance, to arbitrate disputes before a conflict escalates. This form of conflict resolution is limited by the fact that it takes place in a confrontational and defined framework within a judicial or quasi-judicial environment. The presence of appointed representatives and a decisive third-party role minimizes direct communication between the parties in conflict.[36] The Court of Conciliation and Arbitration, established by the Organization for Security and Cooperation in Europe (OSCE) in 1994, offered dispute resolution between consenting states in Europe and the former Soviet Union. Its rulings are legally binding on signatories to the Convention on Conciliation and Arbitra-

tion, and its conciliation procedures make it an attractive alternative for the settlement of disputes.[37]

Mediation, on the other hand, enjoys a higher rate of success in international application. It requires no advance commitment, allows conflicting parties to communicate directly, and has as its goal simply to settle the conflict to the satisfaction of all parties. Mediation has been used extensively as a tool for dealing with both interstate and internal conflicts. The civil wars in El Salvador and Mozambique and the dispute between Greece and the Former Yugoslav Republic of Macedonia were resolved through mediation.[38]

Less promising for the management and prevention of violent conflict is the International Court of Justice (ICJ). Its weak record on issues of conflict and peace is well documented. Over its life, it has decided about 100 cases, and only a handful have related to serious security issues. Controversies leading to deadly conflict are not often disputes about legal rights and obligations; they are political disputes involving perceived national interests, and countries have proven consistently unwilling to expose themselves to external adjudication. Many of the states that accept the Court's jurisdiction have reservations that exclude disputes involving national security and similar cases. The Court's relevance to intrastate conflict is severely limited by the fact that only states may be parties to cases brought before it. By their nature, the ICJ's legal proceedings intensify the confrontational and adversarial

Human rights are becoming, properly, a rationale for preventive diplomacy and collective security.

aspects of disputes, at least in the short run. Over the years, interesting suggestions have been made to strengthen the Court, e.g., in the appointment and functioning of judges and in greater use of advisory opinions. It remains to be seen whether the Court could become more effective in preventing deadly conflict.

Notwithstanding the limitations of the Court, the Commission believes that it has a role in helping to clarify contentious issues and legitimate norms of behavior among states. Governments should take steps to strengthen the Court for these purposes.

Justice within States

There is perhaps no more fundamental political right than the ability to have a say in how one is governed. Healthy political systems reflect a shared contract between the people and their government that, at its most basic, ensures the ability to survive free from fear or want. Beyond basic survival, however, participation by the people in the choice and replacement of their government—democracy—assures all citizens the opportunity to better their circumstances while managing the inevitable clashes that arise. Democracy achieves this goal by accommodating competing interests through regularized, widely accessible, transparent processes at many levels of government. Sustainable democratic systems also need a functioning and fair judicial system, a military that is under civilian control, and a police and civil service that are competent, honest, and accountable.[39]

There is perhaps no more fundamental political right than the ability to have a say in how one is governed.

Effective participatory government based on the rule of law reduces the need for people to take matters into their own hands and resolve their differences through violence. It is important that all groups within a society believe that they have real opportunities to influence the political process.[40] The institutions and processes to ensure widespread political participation can vary widely.

A state's internal political system influences its dealings with other states. It is now commonplace to note that democratic states tend not to fight one another. Despite some constraints and qualifications, this basic thesis stands up remarkably well to scrutiny.[41] Democratic states do not agree on everything, but their habits of negotiation and tolerance of domestic dissent tend to resolve conflicts well short of military action. In their dealings with each other, these states sometimes create new institutions and processes to meet new demands, such as the dispute resolution mechanisms in global economic organizations (some of which were discussed in chapter 3).

Transition to Democracy

Where the practice of democracy is lacking, how can it be created peacefully? This question is crucial for the many countries on several continents that are moving toward participatory government. Across Africa, arduous transitions are now under way in what UN Secretary-General Kofi Annan describes as a "Third Wave" of lasting peace based on democracy, human rights, and sustainable development. During five tumultuous decades, Africans first struggled with decolonization and apartheid, followed by a second wave of civil wars, the tyranny of military rule, and economic stagnation. But by the late 1990s difficult and diverse democratic transitions were under way in Benin, Eritrea, Ethiopia, Ghana, Malawi, Mozambique, Namibia, South Africa, Tanzania, Uganda, and elsewhere.

Engineering transitions to participatory governance, or restoring legitimate governance following conditions of anarchy, may require temporary power sharing. Many forms of power sharing are possible, but all provide for widespread participation in the reconstruction effort, sufficient resources to ensure broad-based access to educational, economic, and political opportunities, and the constructive involvement of outsiders (see Box 4.6).[42] Strong civil society has been important to the transition process in Eastern Europe. The transition to democracy in states with long or severe repression of civil society (e.g., Albania, Belarus, and Bulgaria) has been much more difficult than the transition in states where social cohesion and institutions of civil society have been stronger (e.g., the Czech Republic, Hungary, and Poland). In some extreme cases, Albania in 1997, for example, the transition to democracy may require temporary international intervention to reestablish law and order.

In transitions from military rule—in Argentina (1983), Chile (1989), Haiti (1995), and Turkey (1983)—the key to avoiding widespread bloodshed was a combination of a politically weakened core of military rulers and strong internal and external pressures. A military regime may be unable to deal simultaneously with dramatic political, institutional, and economic change (as was the case in Chile), or growing popular support for democracy combined with military overextension or failure (as

was the case in Argentina).[43] Other characteristics of transformation from military to civilian rule include growing uneasiness within the military about its own legitimacy in power, a failure to win over the public, the widespread disrepute of single-party regimes, and increased pressures from international financial institutions and the business community for greater openness. Also important are a willingness to expand political participation and constant public pressure supported by other governments, international organizations, and NGOs.[44]

In the aftermath of authoritarian regimes or civil wars characterized by atrocities, the legitimacy of the reconciliation mechanisms is paramount. At least three ways exist to bring perpetrators to justice and help move societies forward: aggressive and visible use of the existing judicial system; establishment of a special commission for truth and reconciliation; or reliance on international tribunals. For example, Germany, after unification, remanded those accused of criminal behavior to the existing systems of justice. In Argentina, Chile, El Salvador, and South Africa, truth and reconciliation commissions have proven essential for airing grievances and bringing criminals to justice (see Box 4.7).[45] Rwanda and the former Yugoslavia have relied on the establishment of an international tribunal.

International tribunals serve important accountability, reconciliation, and deterrence functions, inasmuch as they provide a credible forum to hear grievances and a legitimate process through which individuals rather than an entire nationality are held accountable for their transgressions. Notwithstanding a number of serious problems, the tribunals do, according to one scholar, challenge any notion leaders

Recognizing the need to support recent democratic transitions around the world, 14 governments founded the Stockholm-based International Institute for Democracy and Electoral Assistance (International IDEA) in 1995 to "work for the promotion and advancement of sustainable democracy worldwide and within this context improve and consolidate electoral processes."

International IDEA provides a central meeting place and information source for those working to promote democracy throughout the world. Its work program is divided into four parts: information gathering, dissemination, and promotion of democracy; developing rules and guidelines to implement electoral systems that reflect internationally acceptable standards; developing national and regional capacities for democracy; and conducting research on, and developing methods of addressing, deficiencies in electoral systems. Projects include forums around the world that bring together political authorities and representatives from civil society and international organizations, a study of political parties and their funding, and an evaluation of electoral dispute resolution mechanisms.

International IDEA membership is open to governments, international organizations, and international NGOs. Members include Australia, Barbados, Belgium, Botswana, Chile, Costa Rica, Denmark, Finland, India, Namibia, Netherlands, Norway, Portugal, South Africa, Spain, and Sweden. NGO members now include the Inter-American Institute of Human Rights, the International Federation of Journalists, the International Press Institute, and Parliamentarians for Global Action. A cooperative agreement has also been reached with the United Nations Development Program, the International Commission of Jurists, and the International Parliamentary Union.

Sources: "Agreement Establishing the International Institute for Democracy and Electoral Assistance," Founding Conference, February 27-28, 1995; Ministry of Foreign Affairs, *Free and Fair Elections and Beyond* (Stockholm, 1994);*The Newsletter of the International IDEA*, No. 1, March 1995; No. 2, October 1995; No. 7, April 1997.

may have that they can precipitate mass violence or genocide with impunity, and they have set important precedents on such key legal issues as competence and jurisdiction.[46] The Commission believes that the United Nations should move to establish an international criminal court, and it welcomes the secretary-general's proposal that an international conference be held in 1998 to finalize and adopt a treaty to establish such a court.[47]

Many institutions of civil society have a key role to play in reconciliation, including religious institutions, the media, community organizations, and educational institutions.

Though lacking the binding force of law, their efforts can be decisive. The following chapter discusses the role of these institutions in greater detail.

Proliferation of organized political parties demonstrates one way in which political participation can be expanded. A number of other elements are at least of equal importance to the democratizing process: a free and independent media through which citizens can communicate with each other and their government; equitable access to economic opportunities—including civil service and other state

Chile's 1989 presidential election brought an end to the 16-year rule of General Augusto Pinochet Ugarte, under whose authority widespread human rights abuses occurred. In May 1990, the newly elected president, Patricio Aylwin Azocar, established the National Commission for Truth and Reconciliation to investigate the most egregious of these violations—those that had resulted in the death or disappearance of individuals.

The president believed that "for the sake of the nation's moral conscience the truth had to be brought to light, for only on such a foundation...would it be possible to satisfy the most basic requirements of justice and create the necessary conditions for achieving true national reconciliation." The commission was charged with four tasks: 1) to establish the truth about the events of the past 16 years; 2) to gather evidence that would help to identify the victims and what had become of them; 3) to recommend measures of reparation; and 4) to recommend legal and administrative measures to prevent further serious human rights violations from being committed.

The eight-person commission benefited from, among other factors: participation by individuals from across the political spectrum; the support of nongovernmental organizations, who played an active role in providing information at the onset of the investigation; Chile's strong legal tradition which meant that detailed records of prosecutions could be gathered; and adequate staffing and funds to ensure that each case was thoroughly investigated.

Of the 3,400 cases brought to the commission, 2,920 were deemed within its mandate. The commission released its findings in February 1991. Nearly 2,000 pages in length, more than half of the report is devoted to a history of the repression of the Pinochet years, and the remaining pages include a chronological listing of individual human rights violations, proposals for reparations, and recommendations for the prevention of further human rights abuses.

Although the commission did not hold public hearings or assign responsibility for abuses, its work proved to be extremely effective in establishing an official record of the human rights abuses that were committed by the Pinochet regime, and many of the report's recommendations were implemented. As a follow-up to the commission's report, the government established a National Corporation for Reparation and Reconciliation to search for the remains of the "disappeared," resolve outstanding cases, and oversee reparations to victims, such as medical and education benefits and a pension for the survivors of the people who disappeared or were executed. The corporation concluded its work in December 1996.

Sources: Priscilla B. Hayner, "Fifteen Truth Commissions—1974 to 1994: A Comparative Study," in *Transitional Justice: How Emerging Democracies Reckon With Former Regimes*, vol. 1, ed. Neil J. Kritz (Washington, DC: U.S. Institute of Peace Press, 1995), pp. 235-237; Neil J. Kritz, ed., *Transitional Justice: How Emerging Democracies Reckon with Former Regimes*, vol. 3 (Washington, DC: U.S. Institute of Peace Press, 1995), pp. 101-104.

employment—fair and balanced taxation systems; an independent judiciary; constitutional or statutory national institutions to promote and protect human rights (see Box 4.8); equitable representation in high-level government positions; and uniform rules for conscription to military service to preserve the legitimacy of the official military arm of the state.[48]

In short, the right to a say in how one is governed is a fundamental human right and the foundation of a political framework within which disputes among groups or their members can be brokered in nonviolent ways. But merely giving people a say will not, of itself, ensure political accommodation. People must believe that their government will stay free of corruption, maintain law and order, provide for their basic needs, and safeguard their interests without compromising their core values.

Social Justice

While democratic political systems strive to treat people equally, this does not mean that they treat all people the same. Just as efforts are made to accommodate the special needs of the very old, the very young, the poor, and the disabled, it is usually necessary to acknowledge explicitly the differences that may exist among various groups within a society and accommodate to the greatest extent possible the particular needs these groups may have. Among the most important needs are the freedom to preserve important cultural practices, including the opportunity for education in a different language, and freedom of religion.

These issues are politically explosive, even in such open societies as Canada and the United States. The "English only" debate in the United States, for example, reveals the extent to which some people perceive that providing entitlements for one group—in this case most notably, Spanish-speaking Americans—would erode their own. In Canada, the Quebec separatist movement was put into a wider context, in part, by the prospect that the province itself might be subject to further division from native Indians and Inuit seeking their own cultural autonomy.[49]

One solution is to permit cultural and linguistic groups to operate private educational institutions. Another is to mandate dual-language instruction. In South Africa, for example, in an effort to ensure cultural self-determination of groups in the country, the new constitution recognizes 11 official languages, and students have the right to an education in the language of their choice. In India, where English is widely used, the constitution lists 18 official languages, all of which are indigenous to the country. Belgium has adopted many laws and practices to accommodate its linguistic communities—broad authority over cultural, educational, and linguistic matters has been granted to "communities" representing the Flemish, French, and German-speaking populations of the country.[50] Switzerland has successfully maintained national unity while protecting four distinct cultures and three linguistic groups within its boundaries. Canada enacted a policy of bilingualism and multiculturalism in 1971. In the United Kingdom, the Welsh Language Act of 1993 granted Welsh equal status with English in Wales.[51]

On the other hand, use of a single language can have a unifying effect in certain circumstances. In Tanzania, for example, notwithstanding many other problems the

The World Conference on Human Rights, held in Vienna in 1993, emphasized the important role that national institutions could play in the promotion and protection of human rights. While recognizing the right of each state to choose the framework that most suits its needs at the national level, the World Conference encouraged, in particular, the establishment and strengthening of national institutions based on the "Paris Principles" which had been elaborated at the first international meeting of national institutions in October 1991.

According to those principles, a national institution should have as broad a mandate as possible clearly set forth in a constitutional or legislative text specifying the institution's composition and sphere of competence. The responsibilities of such institutions should, inter alia, be:

- To submit recommendations, proposals, and reports on any matter relating to human rights (including legislative and administrative provisions and any situation of violation of human rights) to the government, parliament, and any other competent body
- To promote conformity of national laws and practices with international human rights standards
- To encourage ratification and implementation of international standards
- To contribute to the reporting procedure required under international instruments
- To assist in formulating and executing human rights teaching and research programs and to increase public awareness of human rights through information and education
- To cooperate with the United Nations, regional institutions, and national institutions of the countries

The principles also recognized that a number of national institutions have been given jurisdiction to receive and act on individual complaints of human rights violations. They stipulate that the functions of national institutions in this respect may include:

- Seeking an amicable settlement of the matter through conciliation, binding decision, or other means
- Informing the complainant of his or her rights and of available means of redress, and promoting access to such redress
- Hearing complaints or referring them to a competent authority
- Making recommendations to the competent authorities, including proposals for amending laws and regulations that obstruct the free exercise of human rights

The principles also include detailed guidelines on the composition of national institutions and the appointment of members; on guarantees of independence and pluralism; and on methods of operation, including the need to cooperate with other bodies responsible for protecting human rights, such as ombudsmen and nongovernmental organizations active in this field. The principles were endorsed by the United Nations Commission on Human Rights and by the General Assembly and annexed to resolutions adopted by these bodies in 1992 and 1993, respectively.

Source: Center for Human Rights, *National Human Rights Institutions: A Handbook on the Establishment and Strengthening of National Institutions for the Promotion and Protection of Human Rights*, Professional Training Series No. 4 (Geneva: United Nations, 1995).

Box 4.9
CONCEPTS OF POWER SHARING

A recent study has identified more than 200 ethnic and religious minority and oppressed majority groups throughout the world that are politically active—that is, engaged in an effort to secure or improve their legal or political rights. In many multiethnic societies, the procedures of majoritarian democracy have proven effective for managing group relations and maintaining social cohesion. However, in societies with deep ethnic divisions and little experience with democratic government and the rule of law, strict majoritarian democracy can be self-defeating. Where ethnic identities are strong and national identity is weak, populations may vote largely along ethnic lines. Domination by one ethnic group can lead to a tyranny of the majority, which often gives rise to hatred and sometimes open conflict. A preferable solution may be the adoption of mutually agreed upon power-sharing arrangements that encourage broad-based governing coalitions.

Forms of power sharing include: granting territorial autonomy; adopting proportional representation of groups in administrative appointments; implementing a policy of consensual decision making by the executive; establishing a proportional electoral system; developing a nonethnic federal structure; and encouraging cross-ethnic coalitions. At its root, however, power sharing involves broad-based access to power structures of all kinds in a society as a means to ensure equitable distribution of resources and opportunities.

Development of effective power-sharing arrangements is an extremely complex task; a delicate balance must be struck in satisfying the security needs of rival groups. Efforts to date have met both with notable success (e.g., Switzerland) and notable failure (e.g., Lebanon during the years of the civil war). A Commission-sponsored study identified several conditions under which power-sharing arrangements are most likely to be successful: 1) when they are embraced by a core group of moderate political leaders who are genuinely representative of the groups that they purport to lead; 2) when the practices are flexible and allow for equitable distribution of resources; 3) when the arrangements are developed locally and are region specific; and 4) when parties can gradually eliminate the extraordinary measures that some power-sharing arrangements entail and allow a more integrative and liberal form of democracy to emerge.

Sources: Timothy D. Sisk, *Power Sharing and International Mediation in Ethnic Conflicts* (Washington, DC: United States Institute of Peace Press and Carnegie Commission on Preventing Deadly Conflict, 1996); Ted Robert Gurr, *Minorities at Risk: A Geopolitical View of Ethnopolitical Conflicts* (Washington, DC: United States Institute of Peace Press, 1993), p. ix.

country faces, the dozens of ethnic groups now all speak Swahili—giving all of Tanzania's peoples a sense of national cohesion.

Scholars and policymakers alike are still trying to understand post-Communist rule in the former Soviet Union and Eastern Europe. Of particular importance, in addition to the role of leaders and social cohesion, has been the accommodation of minority groups (see Box 4.9), especially those with ethnic kin states bordering their host countries, such as ethnic Albanians, Armenians, Hungarians, Russians, and Serbs in Europe. One scholar, after a comprehensive examination of disadvantaged minority groups throughout the world, concludes: "The

Box 4.10
NAGORNO-KARABAKH
Impact of Kin Populations Abroad

Some states have inherited from the Soviet period a dangerous nationality situation in which ethnic groups span state borders. An ethnic minority that feels oppressed in one state may look to kin or co-religionists in another state for support. Conversely, the inhabitants of one state may see the existence of kin in another state as justification for involvement in the affairs of that state. The conflict in Nagorno-Karabakh highlights the potential of these connections to spawn mass violence and to involve outside parties.

Nagorno-Karabakh is largely peopled by Armenians, who are a minority within the surrounding Azerbaijan. In the late 1980s, believing independence to be unattainable, Karabakh Armenians began to call for union with the Soviet Republic of Armenia. Azeri nationalism grew, along with resentment against the pro-Armenian demonstrations led by Karabakh Armenians. Azeri riots directed at Armenian communities sparked retaliatory violence. Russia was unable to control the downward spiral in the 1990s.

The disintegration of the Soviet Union thrust the conflict between the Armenians and the Azeris onto the international stage and into a political vortex. Armenia supported the Karabakh Armenians but felt under pressure from Azerbaijan and Turkey. Turkey supported Azerbaijan, which in turn felt pressure from Russia. Russia believed Turkey sought to expand its sphere of influence at Russia's expense. The inability of the Armenians and Azeris to resolve their differences peacefully, combined with leaders seeing a chance to gain power and expand influence amid the break up of the Soviet Union, underpinned intense violence. The ability of a minority group to call on kin in another state, and the receptivity of that kin, amplified the voice of the Karabakh Armenians and helped mobilize kin populations around the world.

This situation illustrates a larger dilemma left in the wake of the Soviet breakup. The states emerging out of the Soviet Union have, in nearly every case, inherited dangerous nationality problems. These problems combine with the presence of valuable natural resources in many former republics and the complications associated with their extraction and economic exploitation.

Sources: John J. Maresca, "The International Community and the Conflict over Nagorno-Karabakh" in *Opportunities Missed, Opportunities Seized: Preventive Diplomacy in the Post-Cold War World*, ed. Bruce Jentleson (Lanham, MD: Rowman & Littlefield, forthcoming); Daniel Byman and Stephen Van Evera, "Contemporary Deadly Conflict: Causes and Future Prospects," paper prepared for the Carnegie Commission on Preventing Deadly Conflict, Washington, DC, 1997.

most important spillover effects in communal conflict occur among groups that straddle interstate boundaries" (see Box 4.10).[52] Circumstances of minorities abroad demand open channels of dialogue between capitals, channels that can also help keep tension between these states at a low level.

The ability of groups to engage in cultural or religious practices that differ from the majority of the population must also be preserved. Many states have created an environment in which people can demonstrate and benefit from mutual respect for different cultural and religious traditions. In Cyprus, to cite a small but instructive example, where Greek and Turkish Cypriot leaders remain unable to resolve their own differences, the small population of Maronite Christians is able to travel across the Green Line in Nicosia and practice its faith.

Simply put, vibrant, participatory systems require religious and cultural freedom. As Hans Küng noted: "The survival of humanity is at stake. . . . There will be no peace among the nations without peace among the religions."[53]

It is worth repeating the fundamental point of this chapter: security, well-being, and justice not only make people better off, they inhibit the tendency to resort to violence. But how are these conditions achieved? What are the roles of governments, international organizations, and civil society in improving security, well-being, and justice, and what are their roles in helping to prevent deadly conflict? The following chapter examines these questions.

"There will be no peace among the nations without peace among the religions."

U.S. Air Force personnel
unload equipment in
Saudi Arabia as part of
coalition enforcement of the
no-fly zone over southern Iraq
in 1996; Ronald Reagan with
Mikhail Gorbachev at
the White House in 1987;
Rwandan refugees in
Bujumbura attend a UNHCR-
funded primary school.

CHAPTER 5

PREVENTING DEADLY CONFLICT

The Responsibility of States, Leaders, and Civil Society

Widespread deadly conflict threatens global stability by eroding the rules and norms of behavior that states have sought to establish. Rampant human rights abuses are often the prelude to violence. They reflect a breakdown in the rule of law, and if they are allowed to continue unchecked, the result will be weakened confidence in states' commitment to the protection of human rights, democratic governance, and international treaties. Moreover, the lack of a response—particularly by states that have an obvious capacity to act—will encourage a climate of lawlessness in which disaffected peoples or opposing factions will increasingly take matters into their own hands. The effort to help avert deadly conflict is thus not only a matter of humanitarian obligation, but also of enlightened self-interest.

STATES AND THEIR LEADERS

Major preventive action remains the responsibility of states, and especially their leaders. States must decide whether they do nothing, act alone, act in cooperation with other governments, work through international organizations, or work with elements of the private sector. It should be an accepted principle that those with the greatest capacity to act have the greatest responsibility to act.

The Commission is of the strong view that the leaders, governments, and people closest to potentially violent situations bear the primary responsibility for taking preventive action. They stand to lose most, of course, if their efforts do not succeed. The Commission believes that the best approach to prevention is one that emphasizes local solutions to local problems where possible, and new divisions of labor—involving governments and the private sector—based on comparative advantage and augmented as necessary by help from outside. The array of those who have a useful preventive role to play should extend beyond governments and intergovernmental organizations to include the private sector with its vast expertise and resources. The Commission urges combining governmental and nongovernmental efforts.

Governments ignore violent conflict, wherever it occurs, at great risk. The bills for postconflict reconstruction and economic renewal inevitably come due, and there are only a limited number of states willing and able to pay them, mainly the industrialized democracies. The Commission believes that these states should engage more constructively and comprehensively to help prevent deadly conflict, guided by international standards and their common respect for human rights, the dignity of the individual, and the protection of minorities. They could, for example, act within the

> **Leaders, governments, and people closest to potentially violent situations bear the primary responsibility for taking preventive action.**

Box 5.1
THE ROLE OF STATES AS MEDIATORS
Sierra Leone's Civil War

Third-party mediation is a well-established practice to help resolve conflicts throughout the world. States of many types, both large and small, neighbors and those more remote, have helped to broker a conflict's end. While many efforts have ended in failure, others have made invaluable and unexpected contributions to the prevention and resolution of seemingly intractable conflicts. Côte d'Ivoire's role in mediating Sierra Leone's civil war provides a recent example of both the potential and the pitfalls of outside involvement in intrastate conflicts.

In the 1980s and early 1990s, the international community largely ignored Sierra Leone's long slide into chaos due to corruption and mismanagement by a succession of governments. Sierra Leone's brutal five-year civil war, begun in 1991, left upwards of 50,000 people dead and nearly half of its population displaced. The absence of any significant outside pressure allowed the disintegration to accelerate as little progress, or even contact, between leaders of the government and its opposition, the Revolutionary United Front (RUF), was evident throughout the course of the violence. Some observers argued that even limited pressure on the government for greater accountability and some sound rudimentary military discipline could have checked the rebellion.

Finally, and at the request of the Sierra Leonean government, Côte d'Ivoire stepped into the breach in February 1996. After a series of preliminary contacts, Côte d'Ivoire Foreign Minister Amara Essy arranged a clandestine meeting with RUF leader, Foday Sankoh. Essy persuaded the RUF to enter negotiations with the government by convincing Sankoh that by refusing he would be isolated from outside assistance, and that by joining the negotiations he could gain international legitimacy, recognition as a political force in the country, access to economic assistance for the areas under his control, and a political solution to the struggle.

On March 15, 1996, a democratically elected government under President Ahmad Tejan Kabbah replaced the military junta that had controlled the country. In the ensuing months a series of talks was held, presided over by Essy

UN system—together with other like-minded states—to establish and reinforce norms of fairness and nonviolent conflict resolution. As the previous chapter argued, democratic practice is linked to the prevention of deadly conflict.

The Commission recognizes that sometimes the industrialized democracies promote policies abroad that contradict their democratic values at home and thereby contribute to deadly conflict. Moreover, some democracies have been reluctant to meet their responsibilities in the United Nations and elsewhere, weakening a potentially powerful force for the international community in preventing mass violence.

At a minimum, these states must do what they can to ensure that their own development and economic expansion do not engender volatile circumstances elsewhere. Further, they should develop mechanisms to anticipate violent conflict and to formulate coordinated responses. For example, the agenda of any G-8 meeting should include a discussion of developing conflicts and ways members can help resolve them before they become violent.

and Côte d'Ivoire President Henri Konan Bédié. These talks led first to the declaration of a cease-fire and finally, on November 30, 1996, to a 28-point peace agreement between Sierra Leone's government and the RUF. In addition to the dedicated work of officials from Côte d'Ivoire, some measure of the mediation's success has been attributed to pressure applied by outsiders in support of the peace process. International donors withheld offers of relief funds while the fighting went on, and they pressured the government to reduce the role of mercenaries. The 15 members of the Economic Community of West African States (ECOWAS) supported a peaceful settlement by denying outside military assistance to either side, and Nigeria and Guinea deployed troops to Sierra Leone to help maintain the peace.

Unfortunately, despite the efforts of Sierra Leone's neighbors, peace has not been sustained. On May 25, 1997, President Kabbah was overthrown by a military coup. Coup leaders, calling themselves the Armed Forces Revolutionary Council (AFRC), claim that Kabbah's government did not deliver on the promises of the 1996 agreement and was instead promoting tribalism. In response to the coup, the Economic Community of West African States Monitoring Group deployed troops to Sierra Leone, and as of this writing, efforts to restore democracy continue. As in 1996, the active support of African and other states for a peaceful settlement will be essential to progress in restoring democracy in that strife-torn nation.

Sources: Howard W. French, "A Muscular Nigeria Proves a Flawed Peacekeeper," *New York Times*, June 26, 1997, p. A12; "Rebels Told To Give Up In West Africa," *New York Times*, June 5, 1997, p. A12; Howard W. French, "Sierra Leone a Triumph of Peacemaking by Africans," *New York Times*, December 2, 1996, p. A8; "Sierra Leone Web," *Sierra Leone Web - Sierra Leone Archives*. http://www.sierra-leone.org., updated September 23, 1997; "Sierra Leone Signs Pact to End 5-year Civil War," *Baltimore Sun*, December 1, 1996, p. 36A; "Sierra Leone: Peace, perhaps," *The Economist* (December 7, 1996), pp. 41-42.

Leaders should make prevention a high priority on the agenda of *every* head of state/government summit meeting and on the agenda of *all* foreign and defense ministerials. They should use all of their relevant meetings to discuss circumstances of incipient violence and to formulate strategies to link bilateral, regional, and UN efforts to prevent actual outbreaks. Their summit communiques should highlight leaders' awareness of and plans for dealing with the developing crises.

Sometimes those involved in conflict ask for outside help early, but all too often they wait until long after it has become clear that they cannot possibly sort out their problems or deal with the consequences on their own. As violence escalates, rational and moderate behavior becomes increasingly difficult. The parties become more and more reluctant to resort to nonviolent dispute resolution mechanisms. In such situations, those more remote from the conflict may help to convey a realistic picture of the advantages of peaceful solutions and the disadvantages of violence, and thus persuade the combatants at last to turn away from violence (see Box 5.1). This kind of help can come from other states, intergovernmental organizations, and the nongovernmental or private sectors. Governments should refine this capacity to identify and track circumstances of potential violence—to develop reliable links between the private sector, where warning is often most apparent, and senior government decision makers with the authority to act in the face of such warning, and, in turn, to international organizations for coordinated action.

Increasingly, many states—often not the major powers but smaller states that are also practiced in the art of what can be achieved through coalition building and selectively focused efforts—have begun to respond to the rising tide of worldwide violence. Certain countries—the Nordics, for example—have a distinguished record of deep commitment and action in helping moderate the effects of violence around the world. Norway has organized an innovative governmental–private sector approach to international crisis that can be mobilized in short order to great effect (see Box 5.2). This so-called Norwegian Model involves close cooperation between all relevant government departments and NGOs, and a well-informed and supportive public that can yield hundreds of volunteers on short notice to participate in international humanitarian and peace initiatives.[1] The Swedish Foreign Ministry instructs its missions to relay information on human rights practices, which can be used to assess the risk of conflict.[2] This information would be used not only to strengthen the ability of Swedish institutions to respond more rapidly and effectively to emerging conflicts, but also to aid in early warning and response efforts at the international level.

Canada, the Netherlands, and Ireland also have long traditions of humanitarian engagement. Canadian and Dutch studies have explored ways to make a rapid reaction capability available for the United Nations, and the results of these efforts have helped advance the debate over this issue beyond theoretical argument to practical organization (see pages 65–67 for further discussion).[3] Ireland has sent humanitarian aid workers throughout Africa, including to some of the most difficult and dangerous areas, such as Somalia, Ethiopia, and the Democratic Republic of Congo (Zaire).

In the United States, the Department of State established the Secretary's Preventive Action Initiative in 1994 as an internal mechanism to improve political and diplomatic anticipation of violence, and the Department of State's National Foreign Affairs Training Center has added conflict prevention training to its curriculum. The Department of Defense has for several years pursued a program of "preventive defense," tying military and nonmilitary programs together in an effort to coordinate and broaden American efforts to prevent deadly conflict.[4] In Great Britain, the Foreign and Commonwealth Office has taken steps to create a capacity to anticipate and respond to incipient violence. Australia played a conspicuous role in the Cambodian peace process, in advancing the Chemical Weapons Convention and the Comprehensive Test Ban Treaty, and—prominently through the Canberra Commission—in making the case for the ultimate elimination of nuclear weapons.

In addition to these examples, a number of governments are engaged in a major cooperative effort, as this report is written, to institute a worldwide ban on the production, stockpiling, distribution, and use of land mines. The Commission strongly endorses this effort.[5]

Box 5.2
THE NORWEGIAN EXAMPLE OF
GOVERNMENT–NGO RELATIONS

The so-called Norwegian Model provides an example of government–NGO cooperation to overcome the gap between warning and response in complex emergencies. The framework for Norwegian efforts is provided by the Norwegian Emergency Preparedness System (NOREPS) and the Norwegian Resource Bank for Democracy and Human Rights (NORDEM), which provide flexible standby arrangements and foster close cooperation between government, voluntary, private sector, and academic entities. This system has been used effectively in a number of recent crises.

NOREPS provides assistance by:

- Making rapidly available, carefully selected relief items and lifesaving equipment which have been prepositioned in disaster-prone areas
- Organizing a standby force of more than 400 professionals who are trained and prepared for deployment in the field within 72 hours
- Assembling "service packages" which combine the most suitable emergency equipment with professionals in areas such as water and sanitation, primary health care clinics, field hospitals, and demining

Since 1991, goods and services from the NOREPS system have been utilized in various parts of the world to an increasing extent by UN agencies and other international relief organizations. NORDEM is a resource bank of experts prepared to help the UN and others on short notice in areas such as human rights, electoral assistance, and other forms of democracy support. In recent years, the NOREPS and NORDEM systems have resulted in the deployment of hundreds of relief workers, human rights advisors, peace mediators, and observers to dozens of countries around the world.

There are many other consultation arrangements between the Norwegian government and Norwegian NGOs, including "Disaster Committees" composed of NGOs involved in relief and representatives from the ministries of Defense and Foreign Affairs.

Sources: Ian Smillie and Ian Filewod, "Norway," in *Non-Governmental Organisations and Governments: Stakeholders for Development*, eds. Ian Smillie and Henry Helmich (Paris: Organization for Economic Cooperation and Development, 1994), pp. 222-223; John Stremlau, *People in Peril: Human Rights, Humanitarian Action, and Preventing Deadly Conflict* (Washington, DC: Carnegie Commission on Preventing Deadly Conflict, May 1998).

As states and leaders become more attentive to prevention, new policies should build on such steps and combine more effectively governmental and nongovernmental efforts. The goal is a system of conflict prevention that takes into account the strengths, resources, and limitations of each component of the system.

PIVOTAL INSTITUTIONS OF CIVIL SOCIETY

The record of unprecedented slaughter in the twentieth century suggests that the traditional system, if it can be called a system, in which governments and intergovernmental organizations take an exclusive role in efforts to cope

Box 5.3
SOUTH AFRICA'S HIDDEN STRENGTH
Civil Society

Though opposition groups had been active for many decades in South Africa, the 1976 Soweto uprising and its aftermath marked the beginning of a period of explosive growth in civic organizations within the black and other nonwhite communities and among some white groups. From urban townships to rural hamlets, student associations, labor unions, church groups, women's groups, and liberation movements arose. Many of these organizations provided much needed social services, such as health clinics, housing assistance, and education services. Others worked to bring domestic and international pressure to bear on the ruling National Party for changes to the political system. The development of coalitions of like-minded organizations, such as the Congress of South African Trade Unions and the United Democratic Front, brought unity, national influence, and international attention to the struggle. As Archbishop Desmond Tutu has noted, international support for these organizations during their nascent stages was crucial to their success.

As the branches of civil society grew in number and sophistication, so did the ranks of their leadership. A number of these leaders played prominent roles in the negotiated transition to democracy, and many now occupy high-ranking positions in government and the private sector.

The South African government alone does not have the resources to overcome the poverty and social inequality that are the legacy of apartheid. If peace and democracy are to be lasting, it is of the utmost importance that South Africa's civil society remain a strong component of everyday life.

Sources: Marina Ottaway, *South Africa* (Washington, DC: The Brookings Institution, 1993); Desmond Tutu, "Building a Democracy in South Africa," *Washington Post*, August 19, 1996, p. A15; Mamphela Ramphele and Francis Wilson, *Uprooting Poverty: The South African Challenge*, report for the Second Carnegie Inquiry into Poverty and Development in Southern Africa (New York: W.W. Norton and Company, 1989); John Stremlau with Helen Zille, *A House No Longer Divided: Progress and Prospects for Democratic Peace in South Africa* (Washington, DC: Carnegie Commission on Preventing Deadly Conflict, July 1997).

with problems of conflict, mass violence, war, and peace, has not worked well. It is, therefore, necessary to look to relatively new groups to augment efforts in this vital task.

It bears repeating that governments—especially those closest to a conflict—have the greatest responsibility for preventive action. The following sections discuss the capacity for preventive action that resides in the private and nongovernmental sectors, and the following chapter discusses the preventive capacities of intergovernmental organizations. The Commission believes that much of what these various

agencies and organizations can do to help prevent deadly conflict will be aided or impeded by the actions of states.

How can the contributions of various elements of the private sector—NGOs, religious leaders and organizations, the educational and scientific communities, business, and the media—contribute to the prevention of conflict? How can these various groups be strengthened in societies where violence threatens? This latter question becomes especially important in circumstances where repressive regimes stifle civil society and undermine the development of local capacities for problem solving. It is important to identify elements of civil society that can be used to reduce hatred and violence and to encourage attitudes of concern, social responsibility, and mutual aid within and between groups. Labor unions, for example, have in many circumstances helped facilitate citizen participation in peaceful democratic change.[6] Indeed, in South Africa the broader role of civil society represents an example of how this can work on a nationwide scale (see Box 5.3).

Many elements in the private sector around the world are dedicated to helping prevent deadly conflict and have declared a public commitment to the well-being of humanity in their various activities. They have raised considerable sums of money on the basis of this commitment, bringing them many opportunities but also great responsibilities.

Nongovernmental Organizations

Virtually every conflict in the world today has had some form of international response and presence—whether humanitarian, diplomatic, or other—and much of that presence comes from the nongovernmental community. Performing a wide variety of humanitarian, medical, educational, and other relief and development functions, nongovernmental organizations are deeply engaged in the world's conflicts, and are now frequently significant participants in most efforts to manage and resolve deadly conflict. Indeed, NGO workers are often exposed to the same dangers and hardships as any uniformed soldier.

Nongovernmental organizations, an institutional expression of civil society, are important to the political health of virtually all countries, and their current and potential con-

tributions to the prevention of deadly conflict, especially mass violence within states, is rapidly becoming one of the hallmarks of the post–Cold War era.[7]

As pillars of any thriving society, NGOs at their best provide a vast array of human services unmatched by either government or the market, and are the self-designated advocates for action on virtually all matters of public concern.[8] The rapid spread of information technology, market-driven economic interdependence, and easier and less expensive ways of communicating within and among states have allowed many NGOs—through their worldwide operations—to become key global transmission belts for ideas, financial resources, and technical assistance. In difficult economic and political transitions, the organizations of civil society are of crucial importance in alleviating the dangers of mass violence.

Virtually every conflict in the world today has had some form of international response and presence.

NGOs vary in size and mandate. They range from large global organizations, such as Oxfam, that operate in scores of countries with budgets in the hundreds of millions of dollars, to much smaller NGOs, such as the Nairobi Peace Initiative in Kenya, that focus only on one country or on one type of problem (see Box 5.4).

An expanding array of NGOs work at the frontiers of building the political foundations and international arrangements for the long-term prevention of conflict. They work on problems of the environment, arms control, world health, and a host of other global issues. Three broad categories of NGOs offer especially important potential contributions to the

Box 5.4
MAJOR INTERNATIONAL HUMANITARIAN
AGENCIES

The United Nations

Various UN specialized agencies were founded in the post–World War II period to assist with problems arising from interstate conflicts and underdevelopment, with particular emphasis on refugees, food, children, and health. In recent years, the increasing number of internal conflicts, compounded by natural disasters and weak state structures, has resulted in complex humanitarian emergencies. Hence, rapid, coordinated action in emergency situations has become an increasingly important challenge for UN agencies, not initially established to deal with them. The UN agencies with primary responsibilities for humanitarian emergencies are the:

- UN High Commissioner for Refugees (UNHCR)
- World Food Program (WFP)
- UN Children's Fund (UNICEF)
- World Health Organization (WHO)
- UN Relief Works Agency for Palestine Refugees in the Near East (UNRWA)
- Department of Humanitarian Affairs (DHA)

Nongovernmental Organizations (NGOs)

The delivery of emergency relief is dominated by about 15 to 20 major international NGOs or federations of national NGOs, which have budgets of at least $75-100 million and work in eight to ten countries around the world. Major NGOs responding to multiple complex emergencies include:

- Action Internationale Contre le Faim (AICF)
- Adventist Development Relief Agency (ADRA)
- Caritas Internationalis (CI) (Catholic Organizations for Charitable and Social Action)
- Catholic Relief Services (CRS)
- Cooperative for Assistance and Relief Everywhere (CARE)
- Equilibre
- International Rescue Committee (IRC)
- Irish Concern
- Lutheran World Federation (LWF)
- Médecins Sans Frontières (MSF)
- Médecins du Monde (MDM)
- Mercy Corps International (MCI)
- Oxford Committee for Famine Relief (Oxfam)
- Save the Children Federation
- Solidarités
- World Vision

The International Red Cross and Red Crescent Movement

The International Committee of the Red Cross (ICRC) and the International Federation of Red Cross and Red Crescent Societies, together with 170 national Red Cross and Red Crescent societies,* form the International Red Cross and Red Crescent Movement. ICRC is the oldest international humanitarian organization and the largest outside the UN system—with operations in more than 50 countries as of 1995. The ICRC has been given unique missions under international humanitarian law—such as monitoring the treatment of POWs and detainees and promoting reunification of family members separated by conflict—that set it apart from other international organizations and NGOs.

*The national Red Cross/Red Crescent societies around the world provide assistance to victims of natural disasters and armed conflicts in their own countries. The societies serve as auxiliary humanitarian arms to governments in peacetime and provide backup military medical services in times of conflict.

Sources: International Committee of the Red Cross, *The Fundamental Principles of the Red Cross and Red Crescent Movement*, http://www.icrc.org/; International Federation of the Red Cross, *About the International Federation*, http://www.ifrc.org/

prevention of deadly conflict: human rights and other advocacy groups; humanitarian and development organizations; and the small but growing number of "Track Two" groups that help open the way to more formal internal or international peace processes.

Human rights, Track Two, and grassroots development organizations all provide early warning of rising local tension and help open or protect the necessary political space between groups and the government that can allow local leaders to settle differences peacefully. Nongovernmental humanitarian agencies have great flexibility and access in responding to the needs of victims (especially the internally displaced) during complex emergencies. Development and prodemocracy groups have become vital to effecting peaceful transitions from authoritarian rule to more open societies and, in circumstances of violent conflict, in helping to make peace processes irreversible during the difficult transitions to reconstruction and national reconciliation. The work of international NGOs and their connection to each other and to indigenous organizations throughout the world reinforce a sense of common interest and common purpose, as well as the political will to support collective measures for preventive action.

Many NGOs have deep knowledge of regional and local issues, cultures, and relationships, and an ability to function in adverse circumstances even, or perhaps especially, where governments cannot. Moreover, nongovernmental relief organizations often have legitimacy and operational access that do not raise concerns about sovereignty, as government activities sometimes do.

Some NGOs have an explicit focus on conflict prevention and resolution. They may: monitor conflicts and provide early warning and insight into a particular conflict; convene the adversarial parties (providing a neutral forum); pave the way for mediation and undertake mediation; carry out education and training for conflict resolution, building an indigenous capacity for coping with ongoing conflicts; help to strengthen institutions for conflict resolution; foster development of the rule of law; help to establish a free press with responsible reporting on conflict; assist in planning and implementing elections; and provide technical assistance on democratic arrangements that reduce the likelihood of violence in divided societies.

With conflicts raging in every part of the globe, the NGO community has become overstretched by incessant demands for engagement and resources.[9] To meet these demands, NGOs must improve coordination with other NGOs and with intergovernmental organizations and governments to reduce unnecessary redundancies among and within their own operations. Indeed, some of the global NGOs have begun to sharpen their focus on specific aspects of humanitarian relief. For example, Oxfam UK and Ireland focuses on water and sanitation, CARE on logistical operations, and Catholic Relief Services on food distribution.[10]

The leadership of the major global humanitarian NGOs should agree to meet regularly—at a minimum on an annual basis—to share information, reduce unnecessary redundancies, and promote shared norms of engagement in crises. This collaboration should lead directly to the wider nongovernmental commitment to network with indigenous NGOs in regions of potential crisis, human rights groups, humanitarian organizations, development organizations, and those involved in Track Two efforts to help prevent and resolve conflict.

Because they have had to work more closely with intergovernmental organizations and with governments—particularly with the military—in dangerous, uncertain circumstances, NGOs have had to broaden their dialogue with these partners to reduce the potential for dysfunctional relationships that can further complicate already extremely complex and difficult operations. One way in which the process of information sharing can be improved is through the establishment of conflict forums (e.g., the Great Lakes Policy Forum in the United States) to exchange information in a timely fashion and craft creative approaches to nonviolent problem solving. The Commission also recommends that the secretary-general of the UN follow through with his aim of strengthening NGO links to UN deliberation by establishing a means whereby NGOs and other agencies of civil society would bring relevant matters to the attention of competent organs of the United Nations. Other ideas to strengthen the UN for prevention are presented in chapter 6.

Unlike governments, NGOs cannot compel belligerents to respect human rights or cease violent attacks. Whatever their niche, NGOs must function with cultural and political sensitivity or risk accusations of paternalism, or worse, political partiality or corruption. To avoid any sense that they might become tools or pawns in the hands of conflicting factions, NGOs have been working to establish their own code of ethics.[11]

> The leadership of the major global humanitarian NGOs should meet regularly to share information, reduce unnecessary redundancies, and promote shared norms of engagement in crises.

The Commission strongly endorses the important role of NGOs in helping to prevent deadly conflict. NGOs have the flexibility, expertise, and commitment to respond rapidly to early signs of trouble. They witness and give voice to the unfolding drama, and they provide essential services and aid. Not least, they inform and educate the public both at the national level and worldwide on the horrors of deadly conflict and thus help mobilize opinion and action.

Religious Leaders and Institutions

Five factors give religious leaders and institutions from the grass roots to the transnational level a comparative advantage for dealing with conflict situations: 1) a clear message that resonates with their followers; 2) a long-standing and pervasive presence on the ground; 3) a well-developed infrastructure that often includes a sophisticated communications network connecting local, national, and international offices; 4) a legitimacy for speaking out on crisis issues; and 5) a traditional orientation to peace and goodwill. Because of these advantages, religious institutions have on occasion played a reconciling role by inhibiting violence, lessening tensions, and contributing decisively to the resolution of conflict (see Box 5.5).

A number of religious groups are deeply committed to building bridges between factions in conflict. Since 1965, the Corrymeela Community, one of a number of groups engaged in religious reconciliation in Northern Ireland, has attempted to provide forums for interaction in the communities to dispel ignorance, prejudice, and fear and to promote mutual respect, trust, and cooperation. In the

Box 5.5
THE CATHOLIC CHURCH AND
THE PHILIPPINE REVOLUTION

Corruption, human rights violations, and the assassination in 1983 of Benigno Aquino, former Philippine senator and opponent of President Ferdinand Marcos, unified opposition among powerful groups in Philippine society and led to the overthrow of Marcos in 1986. Among those who supported the revolution, the Roman Catholic Church was instrumental in encouraging dissent while promoting nonviolence.

By the time of the revolution, the Church was in a position to build upon its elevated moral and political status. Division existed between progressives working for social justice and conservatives who preferred concentrating on individual salvation and spirituality. But under the leadership of Cardinal Jaime Sin, both sides forged a working consensus on matters relating to peace and justice, and these were broadly accepted as worthy spiritual and political goals. The Church consolidated religious opposition to the regime after the imposition of martial law in September 1972 and then, increasingly through the 1980s, by providing support, resources, and leadership to the political parties in opposition to Marcos. It frequently issued pastoral letters focusing on sociopolitical matters and making concrete demands while resisting calls by extremists for violent responses to government repression.

Many Church members were active in the National Citizens' Movement for Free Elections (NAMFREL), and the Church itself pledged its support. Radio Veritas, a station owned by the Bishops Conference and run by the Archdiocese of Manila, became the voice of the opposition, and during the revolution it kept people informed, mobilized them into action, and gave them directions, telling them where to go and what to do. Church-run newspapers and magazines challenged the government's press accounts. After the "snap election" of February 7, 1986, the Church denounced the unfair nature of the election and declared that the regime had lost its mandate and its moral basis to govern.

The Church's opposition to the Marcos regime marked a significant departure from its traditional pattern of political participation. In the early years of the Marcos regime, the church abstained from political criticism. However, the events of 1972 helped opposition elements in the Church to coalesce and gradually become a moderate movement of dissent. Through criticism of those in power and by offering alternative goals and nonviolent means by which to reach them, the Church precluded extremist elements on both sides from escalating the issues at hand into outright violence. No other actor, given the Church's position as the only significant institution with moral legitimacy in Philippine society, could likely have played a comparable role.

Source: Henry Wooster, "Faith at the Ramparts: The Philippine Catholic Church and the 1986 Revolution," in *Religion, The Missing Dimension of Statecraft*, eds. Douglas Johnston and Cynthia Sampson (New York: Oxford University Press, 1994), pp. 153-166.

former Yugoslavia, a permanent Inter-Religious Council has been created by the leaders of four religious communities—Muslim, Jewish, Serb Orthodox, and Roman Catholic—to promote religious cooperation in Bosnia and Herzegovina by identifying and expressing their common concerns independent of politics.[12]

Religious advocacy is particularly effective when it is broadly inclusive of many

Friday prayers in Algiers.

faiths. A number of dialogues between religions already exist—the World Council of Churches as well as forums for Jewish/Christian dialogue, Christian/Muslim dialogue, and others—to provide opportunities for important interfaith exchanges on key public policy issues.

When a religious community is perceived as neutral and apolitical, it may qualify as an honest broker and neutral mediator. The good offices of religious groups, active in most settings through impressive works of charity and social relief, often lend legitimacy to negotiations. This role was officially recognized in the Ottoman Empire's millet system, for example, where the religious leaders of Judaism and several Christian churches were entrusted with arbitrating conflicts among their coreligionists.

The Community of Sant'Egidio played an essential role in brokering the settlement of the Mozambique civil war.[13] It also brokered an agreement on education in Serbia's Kosovo province between Belgrade and the local ethnic Albanian leadership. For more than a year, Sant'Egidio hosted secret peace talks in Rome for the warring factions in Burundi that led to the formal intergovernmental negotiations, known as the Arusha process, chaired by former Tanzanian President Julius Nyerere. The All Africa Conference of Churches has also become diplomatically active, notably in the 1997 conflict in the Democratic Republic of Congo, by advocating peaceful political change, and respect for the rule of law and human rights throughout Central Africa.[14]

Religious groups are simultaneously local, national, and international entities. They

Box 5.6
THE ROLE OF THE PROTESTANT CHURCHES
IN EAST GERMANY

Using a combination of protest and mediation, Protestant churches in the former German Democratic Republic (GDR) played a critical role in the peaceful revolution of the autumn of 1989 and during the subsequent period of transition to democracy in early 1990.

The East German revolution can be divided into two distinct phases: 1) development and protection of the protest movement; and 2) creation of a new order after the collapse of the old system. Religious institutions acted in both phases, sometimes facilitating protest and at other times facilitating conciliation. They became the providers of space for expression; empowerment for action; and models for strategic commitment to nonviolence. The values of these churches—reconciliation, dialogue, participation, and community—contrasted with those of a Marxist state that demanded conformity and collusion. The churches helped formulate the issues that fostered revolution: emigration, ecology, economy, and human rights. The churches' commitment to nonviolence had a direct impact on the peaceful nature of the protests.

During the revolution, or *die Wende* ("the turnaround"), of 1989, churches called for political change and demanded economic reforms, free press, free travel, and multiparty elections. They negotiated with the government over both political policies and the liberation of prisoners, and mediated disputes between the state and opposition groups, encouraging nonviolent resistance. From December 1989 to March 1990, they moderated roundtables throughout the GDR. These forums functioned as interim governments and were largely responsible for the peaceful transition to free elections on March 18, 1990. Religious leaders were critical in establishing a working accord between government representatives and those of the opposition.

At the conclusion of the revolution, there was immense popular support for religious institutions. Nineteen pastors and numerous lay persons were elected to the new parliament. A number of church leaders were appointed to high positions within the state, including prime minister, foreign minister, minister for defense and disarmament, and minister for developmental aid.

Source: David Steele, "East Germany's Churches Give Sanctuary and Succor to the Purveyors of Change," in *Religion, The Missing Dimension of Statecraft*, eds. Douglas Johnston and Cynthia Sampson (New York: Oxford University Press, 1994), pp. 119-152.

are on the ground, but also part of an extensive and constantly growing transnational network. Drawing on this distinctive advantage, some churches in the former Soviet Bloc kept national pride and religious consciousness alive during the Communist period by maintaining important links to the West through their ecclesiastical and ecumenical contacts. Churches in East Germany, for example, were probably cru- cial in averting mass violence in the transition away from dictatorial rule (see Box 5.6). Similar functions have been served during the past decade in South Africa (highlighted by the remarkable leadership of Desmond Tutu) and, as noted, the Philippines.

There is a need for increased interfaith dialogue, so that religious leaders can discover

Box 5.7
THE PRINCIPLES OF A GLOBAL ETHIC

No new global order without a new global ethic

- We all have a responsibility for a better global order.
- Our involvement for the sake of human rights, freedom, justice, peace, and the preservation of earth is absolutely necessary.
- Our different religious and cultural traditions must not prevent our common involvement in opposing all forms of inhumanity and working for greater humaneness.
- The principles expressed in this global ethic can be affirmed by all persons with ethical convictions, whether religiously grounded or not.

A fundamental demand: Every human being must be treated humanely

There is a principle which is found and has persisted in many religious and ethical traditions of humankind for thousands of years: What you do not wish done to yourself, do not do to others! Or in positive terms: What you wish done to yourself, do to others! This should be the irrevocable, unconditional norm for all areas of life, for families and communities, for races, nations, and religions.

Four irrevocable directives

- Commitment to a culture of nonviolence and respect for life
- Commitment to a culture of solidarity and a just economic order
- Commitment to a culture of tolerance and a life of truthfulness
- Commitment to a culture of equal rights and partnership between men and women

Source: Hans Küng, "The Principles of a Global Ethic" in *Yes to a Global Ethic*, ed. Hans Küng (New York: Continuum, 1996), pp. 12-26.

their common ground. The Commission believes that religious leaders and institutions should be called upon to undertake a worldwide effort to foster respect for diversity and to promote ways to avoid violence.[15] They should discuss as a priority matter, during any interfaith and intrafaith gathering, ways to play constructive and mutually supporting roles to help prevent the emergence of violence. They should also take more assertive measures to censure coreligionists who promote violence or give religious justification for violence. They can do so, in part, through worldwide promulgation of norms for tolerance to guide their faithful (see Box 5.7 for one prominent example).

The Scientific Community

One of the great challenges for scientists and the wider scholarly community in the coming decades will be to undertake a much broader and deeper effort to understand the nature and sources of human conflict, and above all to develop effective ways of resolving conflicts before they turn violent.

The scientific community is the closest approximation we now have to a truly international community, sharing certain fundamental interests, values, standards, and a spirit of inquiry about the nature of matter, life, behavior, and the universe. This shared quest for understanding has overcome the distorting effects of national boundaries, inherent prejudices, imposed ethnocentrism, and barriers to the free exchange of information and ideas.

Drawn together more than ever by recent advances in telecommunications, these attributes of the scientific community have been put to work in recent decades in efforts to prevent war and especially to reduce the nuclear danger. The community draws on a scientific base of accurate information, sound principles, and well-documented techniques. It acts flexibly, exploring novel or neglected paths toward conflict resolution, and it builds relationships among well-informed people who can make a difference in attitudes and in problem solving and who are taken seriously by governments.

The scientific community first and foremost provides understanding, insight, and stimulating ways of analyzing important problems. It can and must do so with regard to deadly conflict. Through their institutions and organizations, scientists can strengthen research in a variety of areas, for example, the biology and psychology of aggressive behavior, child development, intergroup relations, prejudice and ethnocentrism, the origins of wars and conditions under which they end, weapons development and arms control, and innovative pedagogical approaches to mutual accommodation and conflict resolution. Other research priorities include exploring ways to use the Internet and other communications innovations to defuse tensions, demystify adversaries, and convey information to strengthen moderate elements. The scientific community should also establish links among all sides of a conflict to determine whether any aspects of a crisis are amenable to technical solutions and to reduce the risk that these issues could provide flash points for violence.

During the decades of the Cold War, the scientific community sought ways to reduce the number of nuclear weapons and especially their capacity for a first strike. It also worked to decrease the chance of accidental or inadvertent nuclear war, to safeguard against unauthorized launch and serious miscalculation, and to improve the relations between the superpowers, partly through cooperative efforts in key fields bearing on the health and safety of humanity. One of the reasons that scientists were able to exercise influence in Cold War affairs certainly stemmed from their role in creating the technology of the nuclear age. For their part, scientists believed they had a heavy responsibility to think about the implications of the devastating weapons they had created.

A prominent example of international scientific cooperation during the Cold War was the Pugwash Conferences on Science and World Affairs, awarded the Nobel Peace Prize in 1995. In the mid-1950s, Albert Einstein and Bertrand Russell issued a manifesto calling on the world's scientists to devise ways to avert the disaster threatened by the products of their science (their first meeting took place in Pugwash, Nova Scotia, in 1957). At that meeting, the participants found in scientific objectivity and in their common humanity the possible basis for solutions to the nuclear problem that could transcend national differences. After the initial meeting, a continuing series of informal discussions among the world's scientists yielded many recommendations to world governments.[16]

The Cold War experience makes clear that there is an important role for the scientific and scholarly community in international conflict prevention. It has much to contribute, and governments and nongovernmental organizations, in turn, have much to learn.

Educational Institutions

All research-based knowledge of human conflict, the diversity of our species, and the paths to mutual accommodation are appropriate for education. Education is a force for reducing intergroup conflict by enlarging our social identifications beyond parochial ones in light of common human characteristics and superordinate goals—highly valued aspirations that can be achieved only by intergroup cooperation. We must seek a basis for fundamental human identification across a diversity of cultures in the face of manifest differences. We are a single, interdependent, meaningfully attached, worldwide species sharing a fragile planet. The give and take fostered within groups can be extended far beyond childhood, toward relations between adults and into larger units of organization, including international relations.

There is an extensive body of research on intergroup contact that bears on this question. For example, experiments have demonstrated that the extent of contact between groups that are negatively oriented toward one another is not the most important factor in achieving a more constructive orientation. What matters is whether the contact occurs under favorable conditions. If there is an aura of mutual suspicion, if the parties are highly competitive, if they are not supported by relevant authorities, or if contact occurs on the basis of very unequal status, then it is not likely to be helpful, whatever the amount of exposure. Contact under unfavorable conditions can stir up old tensions and reinforce stereotypes.

On the other hand, if there is friendly contact in the context of equal status, especially if such contact is supported by relevant authorities, if the contact is embedded in cooperative activity and fostered by a mutual aid ethic, then there is likely to be a strong positive outcome. Under these conditions, the more contact the better. Such contact is then associated with improved attitudes between previously suspicious or hostile groups, as well as with constructive changes in patterns of interaction between them.[17]

Pivotal educational institutions such as the family, schools, community-based organizations, and the media have the power to shape attitudes and skills toward decent human relations—or toward hatred and violence. Such organizations can utilize the findings from research on intergroup relations and conflict resolution.[18] Much of what schools can accomplish is similar to what parents can do—employ positive discipline practices, teach the capacity for responsible decision making, foster cooperative learning procedures, and guide children in prosocial behavior outside the schools as well as in them. They can convey the fascination of other cultures, making understanding and respect a core attribute of their outlook on the world—including the capacity to interact effectively in the emerging global economy, a potentially powerful motivation in the world of the next century. They can use this knowledge to foster sympathetic interest across cultures, recognition of shared and valued goals, as well as a mutual aid ethic.[19] The process of developing school curricula to introduce students to the values of diversity and to break down stereotypes should be accelerated.

Institutions such as the family, schools, community-based organizations, and the media have the power to shape attitudes and skills toward decent human relations—or toward hatred and violence.

The Media

With so many post–Cold War conflicts instigated by harshly nationalist and sectarian leaders, the media's role in disseminating erroneous information or inflammatory propaganda has become an issue of great significance. Because these wars often occur in remote areas and have complicated histories, the international view of them will depend to a large extent on how international journalists present and explain the conflict. On the other hand, some of the deadliest conflicts, as in Sierra Leone, receive little mention in the global media.

A number of examples in the 1990s suggest that the impact of media reporting may generate political action. In Somalia, vivid images of a dead American soldier being dragged through the streets of Mogadishu were broadcast around the world and played a role in the precipitous American withdrawal from that country. In Bosnia, while many episodes of violence occurred over four years, those that were widely covered by the media, such as the marketplace bombing in Sarajevo in 1994, directly influenced responses from the United States, the European Union, and the UN.[20]

If the linkage is as tight as these examples suggest, it raises the question of how the media should recast their own sense of responsibility when covering conflicts or crises. Whether or not the media can rightly be construed as independent entities, their influence as a whole is enormous, particularly in real time. Across the spectrum of activities, from worldwide broadcasts of violence and misery to the local hate radio that instigated killing in Rwanda and Bosnia, the media's interpretive representation of violent events has a wide and powerful impact. It is important to encourage the constructive use of the media to promote understanding, nonviolent problem solving, and decent intergroup relations, even though these issues often do not come under the heading of "breaking news."

A great challenge for the media is to report conflicts in ways that engender constructive public consideration of possibilities for avoiding violence. The media can stimulate new ideas and approaches to problems by involving independent experts in their presentations who can also help ensure factual, accurate reporting. The media should develop standards of conduct in crisis coverage that include giving adequate attention to serious efforts under way to defuse and resolve conflicts, even as they give full international exposure to the violence itself. An international press council, consisting largely of highly respected professional journalists, could be helpful in this regard, especially in monitoring and enforcing acceptable professional practices. The council could bring professional peer pressure on editors in conflict areas who might otherwise disseminate hate messages—especially if the council had a rapid reaction capability. There might be professional sanctions for promoting hate messages, such as cutting off access to international news programming and services. In addition, major networks should develop ways to expose publics to the circumstances and issues that could give rise to mass violence through regular public service programming that focuses on individual "hot spots." Such a service could be coproduced with international media collaborators and also made available to schools and other educational outlets. Models of professional standards for media in reporting on serious conflicts have recently been created and should be widely disseminated.[21]

Television and radio have an unfulfilled potential for reducing tensions between countries or other disputants, and they can be used to demystify the adversary and improve

A television cameraman at work in Sarajevo.

vidual and group efforts for peace. A core series of 24 documentary programs in several languages is adapted to the needs of specific audiences. It has included a lecture series on media and conflict prevention, a workbook for journalists reporting in emerging democracies, and broadcasting on conflict resolution. Activities have included journalist training in Angola and a daily radio show broadcast in the Kinyarwanda/Kirundi language aimed at Rwanda and Burundi.[22]

A Cold War example was provided by U.S.–Soviet "space bridge" programs—live, unedited discussion between citizens of the two countries made possible by communications satellites and simultaneous translation. Starting in 1983, U.S.–Soviet space bridges brought together American and Soviet citizens in an effort to overcome stereotypes, and they provided an opening to Gorbachev's policy of *glasnost*. Each space bridge program reached about 200 million people. Later, Internews's "Capital to Capital" program—broadcast simultaneously on U.S., Soviet, and East European television—linked members of Congress and the Supreme Soviet for uncensored debate on arms control, human rights, and the future of Europe.

understanding. For example, the Voice of America (VOA), part of the United States Information Service, launched a Conflict Resolution Project in 1995. The project develops and produces special programs to introduce its worldwide audience to the principles and practices of conflict resolution. For this series, journalists move beyond hard news toward production of stories that explore local efforts to resolve problems, social relations, and indi-

Independent, pluralistic media can promote democracy by clarifying issues and helping the public to understand candidates. International election monitors should therefore observe media practices, such as candidate access, as well as the voting process itself. Mass media reporting on the possibilities for conflict resolution, and on the willingness and capacity of the international community to help, could become a useful support for nonviolent problem solving. Conflict areas need independent television and radio news channels broadcasting throughout the region. Radio can reach virtually everyone, everywhere. Independent radio was particularly effective during the UN operation in Cambodia. Radio UNTAC, as the UN's network was known, broadcast a variety of news and civic education programs to all regions of the country. The broadcasts were a vital tool for educating Cambodians about the UN's activities—particularly the electoral process established and administered by UNTAC—and for countering anti-UN propaganda.[23]

The Business Community

International business has been criticized for insensitivity in matters of human rights, democracy, and conflict resolution. Yet the business community is beginning to recognize its interests and responsibilities in helping to prevent conditions that can lead to deadly conflict. Many businesses are in fact truly global in character, and violence or dangerously unstable circumstances will inevitably affect their interests (see Figure 5.1). Businesses should accelerate their work with local and national authorities in an effort to develop business practices that not only permit profitability but also contribute to community stability. This "risk reduction" approach to market development

To explain the theory and practice of democracy to Russian listeners, BBC created the *Democracy at First Hand* series through its Marshall Plan of the Mind (MPM) Trust. The MPM Trust was launched by the BBC World Service in 1992 to convey to Russians information about business, politics, and market economics.

Broadcast from November 1994 through May 1995, the 23-part series explained that democracies share fundamental traits—yet each is unique because of its political history and stage of development. Topics in the series included the building blocks of democracy, the structures of government, and policies and performance. To encourage regional political initiatives, four special programs in the series arranged for Russian listeners to question local and national political figures.

Produced from a Russian perspective, the series promoted understanding of democracy through features on Germany, Italy, Russia, Spain, the United Kingdom, and the United States, and interviews with politicians, political scientists, and citizens. Participants in the series included United States Supreme Court Justice Sandra Day O'Connor, former Spanish Communist Party leader Santiago Carillo, and politicians from the three main British parties.

Source: BBC International Press Office, "BBC Brings 'Democracy' to Russians," November 30, 1994.

will help sensitize businesses to any potentially destabilizing violent social effects that new ventures may have, as well as reduce the premiums businesses may have to pay to insure their operations against loss in volatile areas.

Multinational corporations are under increasing pressure from consumers and shareholders to work toward economic, political, and social justice, and they have responded by

Figure 5.1
THE STAKE OF THE BUSINESS COMMUNITY IN PEACE AND SECURITY
Companies in the top 25 of the *Fortune* Global 500 with operations in or near major armed conflicts of the 1990s

Russia
AT&T
British Petroleum
Daimler-Benz AG
Exxon
Ford
General Motors
Hitachi
IBM
Itochu
Mitsubishi
Mobil
Royal Dutch/Shell
   Group
Siemens AG
Sumitomo

India
British Petroleum
Daimler-Benz AG
Exxon
General Motors
Hitachi
IBM
Itochu
Mitsubishi
Royal Dutch/Shell
   Group
Siemens AG
Sumitomo
Toyota

Pakistan
Ford
IBM
Itochu
Mitsubishi
Royal Dutch/Shell
   Group
Siemens AG
Sumitomo
Toyota

Philippines
British Petroleum
Ford
Itochu
Mitsubishi
Royal Dutch/Shell
   Group
Siemens AG
Sumitomo
Toyota

Sri Lanka
Ford
IBM
Itochu
Mitsubishi
Royal Dutch/Shell
   Group
Sumitomo

Cambodia
Itochu

Tajikistan
IBM

Turkey
British Petroleum
Ford
General Motors
IBM
Itochu
Mitsubishi
Mitsui
Mobil
Royal Dutch/Shell
   Group
Siemens AG
Sumitomo
Toyota

Azerbaijan
British Petroleum
Exxon
Ford
Mobil
Sumitomo

Iraq
Sumitomo

Moldova
IBM

Croatia
Daimler-Benz AG
Ford
IBM
Siemens AG

Lebanon
Ford
IBM
Itochu
Sumitomo

Yugoslavia
Siemens AG

El Salvador
Exxon
Ford
IBM
Itochu
Mitsubishi
Royal Dutch/Shell
   Group
Sumitomo
Toyota

Algeria
British Petroleum
Ford
Itochu
Mitsubishi
Mobil
Sumitomo
Toyota

Guatemala
Ford
Hitachi
Itochu
Mitsubishi
Royal Dutch/Shell
   Group
Toyota

Colombia
British Petroleum
Exxon
GM
IBM
Itochu
Mitsui
Royal Dutch/Shell
   Group
Siemens AG
Sumitomo
Toyota

Peru
Exxon
Ford
Hitachi
IBM
Itochu
Mitsubishi
Mitsui
Mobil
Royal Dutch/Shell
   Group
Siemens AG
Sumitomo
Toyota

Sierra Leone
IBM
Mobil
Royal Dutch/Shell
   Group
Toyota

Nigeria
General Motors
Mobil
Royal Dutch/Shell
   Group
Toyota

**Dem. Rep. of
Congo**
Exxon
Ford
IBM
Itochu
Mitsubishi
Toyota

Liberia
IBM
Toyota

**Republic of
Congo**
Exxon
Toyota

Angola
British Petroleum
Exxon
IBM
Itochu
Mitsubishi
Mobil
Royal Dutch/Shell
   Group
Sumitomo
Toyota

Chad
Exxon
Royal Dutch/
   Shell Group

Sudan
Ford
IBM
Royal Dutch/Shell
   Group
Toyota

South Africa
British Petroleum
Chrysler
Daimler-Benz AG
General Motors
Hitachi
IBM
Itochu
Mitsubishi
Royal Dutch/Shell
   Group
Siemens AG
Sumitomo
Toyota

Uganda
Ford
IBM
Royal Dutch/Shell
   Group
Toyota

Rwanda
British Petroleum
IBM
Toyota

Burundi
Toyota

Gulf Region
British Petroleum
Chrysler
Daimler-Benz AG
Ford
Itochu
Mitsubishi
Mobil
Royal Dutch/Shell
   Group
Siemens AG
Toyota

Yemen
Exxon
Ford
Itochu
Mitsubishi
Royal Dutch/Shell
   Group
Sumitomo
Toyota

Indonesia
British Petroleum
General Motors
Hitachi
Itochu
Mitsubishi
Mobil
Nippon Tele-
   graph and
   Telephone
Siemens AG
Toyota
Wal-Mart

Map labels: Greenland, Moldova, Azerbaijan, Chechnya, Afghanistan, Croatia, Bosnia, Georgia, Tajikistan, Southeast Turkey, Lebanon, Kashmir, Algeria, Iraq, Persian Gulf War, Sindh, Chad, Sudan, Yemen, Haiti, Guatemala, El Salvador, Eritrea, Somalia, Tamil Uprising, Cambodia, Colombia, Sierra Leone, Ghana, Nigeria, Uganda, Rwanda, Burundi, Liberia, Republic of Congo, Democratic Republic of Congo (Zaire), Angola, Peru, South Africa

Source: Information compiled from corporate Internet sites, direct correspondence, and 1996 annual reports for the following companies: General Motors (Manufacturing and Assembly, excluding Delphi Automotive systems), Ford, Mitsui & Co., Mitsubishi Corporation, Itochu Corporation, Royal Dutch/Shell Group, Exxon, Sumitomo Corporation, Toyota, Wal-Mart, Nippon Telegraph and Telephone, IBM, Hitachi, AT&T Corporation, Mobil, Daimler-Benz AG, British Petroleum, Siemens AG, and the Chrysler Corporation. These companies were selected because they are among the 25 most profitable companies in the world, according to *Fortune* magazine's "Global 500."

developing codes of conduct for their business operations. These codes share several elements: 1) respect for human dignity and rights; 2) respect for the environment; 3) respect for stakeholders—customers, employees, shareholders, suppliers, and competitors; 4) respect for the communities in which businesses operate; and 5) maximizing value for the company. Among the corporations that have developed such codes are Levi Strauss & Company, Campbell Soup Company, and The Gap, Inc. Additionally, many companies now make corporate responsibility information available through their annual reports. The Body Shop, Ben & Jerry's, ARCO, and Ford Motor Company produce independent annual social and environmental progress reports.

The Commission believes that governments can make far greater use of business in conflict prevention. For example, governments might establish business advisory councils to draw more systematically on the knowledge of the business community and to receive their advice on the use of sanctions and inducements. With their understanding of countries in which they produce or sell their products, businesses can recognize early warning signs of danger and work with governments to reduce the likelihood of violent conflict. However, business engagement cannot be expected to substitute for governmental action.

The strength and influence of the business community give it the opportunity both to act independently and to put pressure on governments to seek an early resolution of emerging conflict (see Box 5.8). For this purpose it would be useful to reserve time at any major business gathering to discuss deadly conflict around the world and its consequences for international business.

The business community could also play a significant role in conflict prevention through industry's support of laboratory research in many parts of the world. The scientists and engineers who work in corporate laboratories have experience in cooperating with their peers across international boundaries, even in crisis situations. Their culture, like that of the scientific community in general, is one that relies heavily on international cooperation.

The People

Finally, what of ordinary people who may be the immediate victims of violence or citizens of countries that could prevent violence? Their choices are few and not easy to exercise. Those in conflict can, at considerable personal risk, refuse to support leaders bent on a violent course; those more removed can demand that their governments undertake preventive action and hold them accountable when they refuse. Their only real strength is in their numbers: in trade unions, community groups, and other organizations that make up civil society. The Solidarity movement in Poland is an example of this kind of citizen power (see Box 5.9). Women's movements are another potentially powerful force. Since the first International Women's Conference in Mexico City in 1995, women have been mobilizing internationally and pursuing their many shared interests throughout the world.[24]

Mass movements, particularly nonviolent movements, have changed the course of history, most notably in India where Mohandas

The strength and influence of the business community give it the opportunity both to act independently and to put pressure on governments to seek an early resolution of emerging conflict.

The Sullivan Principles, a series of guidelines developed by U.S. corporations in 1977 in response to growing opposition to the apartheid system, remain the primary example within the business community of voluntary implementation of a code of ethics for operating within a country.

Named after the Reverend Leon H. Sullivan, then a board member of General Motors Corporation, the principles obliged participating corporations to support the desegregation of all work facilities; provide equal pay for employees doing equal work; initiate and develop training programs to prepare blacks and other nonwhites for supervisory, administrative, and technical jobs; increase the number of blacks and other nonwhites in supervisory positions; and improve the quality of employees' housing, transportation, schooling, and health facilities. In subsequent years, the principles were modified and strengthened a number of times. To promote compliance, companies were required to subject their spending and programmatic activities to outside monitoring. A yearly "Report on the Signatory Companies to the Statement of Principles for South Africa," made available to the public, evaluated corporate progress in implementing the principles. By 1985, more than 180 corporations, together representing 75 percent of U.S. investment in South Africa, had agreed to support the Sullivan Principles. In the 17 years they were in effect, $350 million was spent on activities prescribed by the principles.

The principles were not without their critics. Those who favored complete divestment from South Africa argued that the policy of incremental change supported by the principles was too accommodating. As originally conceived, the principles did not address the broader issues of civil and political rights for nonwhites; not until late in 1983 were the principles amplified to require companies to actively oppose apartheid. Because of the business community's initial reluctance to speak out against the apartheid regime, many opposition groups were skeptical of their intentions. Critics also highlighted weaknesses in the design of the principles, which they believed were dollar-focused rather than goal-oriented and discounted local participation in program development. Most would agree, however, that the Sullivan Principles served as a powerful symbol of the international community's opposition to apartheid and provided much-needed support for black South Africans.

Sources: S. Prakesh Sethi, "Working with International Codes of Conduct: Experience of U.S. Companies Operating in South Africa under the Sullivan Principles," *Business & The Contemporary World* 1 (1996), pp. 129-150; Oliver F. Williams, "The Apartheid Struggle: Learning from the Interaction between Church Groups and Business," *Business & The Contemporary World* 1 (1996), pp. 151-167.

Gandhi led his countrymen in nonviolent resistance to British rule. Hundreds of millions were moved by the example of a simple man in homespun who preached tolerance and respect for the least powerful of India's peoples and full political participation for all. In South Africa, the support of the black majority for international sanctions and the broadly nonviolent movement to end apartheid helped bring the white government to the realization that the status quo could no longer be maintained. In the United States, the leadership of Martin Luther King, Jr., inspired whites and blacks in a massive movement for civil rights. The power of the people in the form of mass mobilization in the streets was critical in achieving the democratic revolution in the Philippines in 1986 and in Thailand in 1992.

Box 5.9
NONVIOLENT RESISTANCE IN POLAND

Polish resistance to the Communist system intermittently manifested itself in nonviolent actions and, particularly after 1970, through labor strikes. Following the repression of a series of strikes in 1976, the Worker's Defense Committee (KOR), originally formed to assist victims of the government crackdown, became the focal point of ongoing resistance. A strong emphasis was placed on the use of nonviolent actions, including the development of information networks, publishing activities, and self-education efforts.

A new round of strikes launched in the summer of 1980 combined calls for improved working conditions with demands for political freedoms. As the strikes spread, the government acquiesced in four major agreements: 1) wage increases; 2) a five-day work week; 3) legal limitations on censorship; and the 4) legalization of trade unions. Following these agreements, the trade union Solidarity was created. Under pressure from the Soviet Union, however, the Polish government quickly reversed course and blocked implementation of the agreements. In December 1981, the government declared martial law, established curfews, arrested and interned thousands of opposition leaders, and suppressed strikes with force.

With many of its leaders jailed or under close scrutiny, Solidarity was driven underground and forced to reorganize. At the local level, "underground societies" flourished. Journalists refused to write for Communist papers, intellectuals boycotted government-sponsored events, and many educators refused to follow official curricula. This pattern of resistance continued throughout the decade. As a result of Gorbachev's reform movement in the Soviet Union, recognition that Poland's poor economic performance could not be reversed without the support of Solidarity, and the threat of renewed strikes in 1988, the government opened roundtable discussions with the organization in early 1989. These talks provided the framework for a democratic transition that culminated in parliamentary elections in June 1989, which were won decisively by Solidarity candidates.

The decision to pursue nonviolent resistance in Poland was both a practical response to the overwhelming strength of government forces and a means of further delegitimating the Communist regime. Yet from this decision, Solidarity gained legitimacy and support from the international community for its nonviolent tactics. It is a vivid example of the role that labor unions can play in promoting democracy and preventing deadly conflict.

Sources: Peter Ackerman and Christopher Kruegler, *Strategic Nonviolent Conflict* (Westport, CT: Praeger Publishers, 1994), pp. 283-316; Adam Roberts, *Civil Resistance in the East European and Soviet Revolutions*, The Albert Einstein Institution, Monograph Series Number 4 (Cambridge, MA: The Albert Einstein Institution, 1991).

Is it possible to harness the energy of the masses to help avert the outbreak of violence? Is it possible to turn people's energies away from violence and toward more constructive resolution of conflict? Would this require more leaders like Gandhi or Mandela or King? Would it require a new commitment by parents and schools to educate our children in conflict prevention? Following a discussion of the role that international organizations can play, this report concludes with a chapter on the possibilities for building a worldwide culture of prevention.

Refugees sheltered by UNHCR.

CHAPTER 6

PREVENTING DEADLY CONFLICT

The Responsibility of the United Nations and Regional Arrangements

THE UNITED NATIONS

The UN is a unique, comprehensive forum for collective security and world dialogue. Serving not as a world government but as a clearinghouse for a worldwide network of human services on behalf of all people—the affluent as well as the desperately poor—the UN today is on the threshold of a new period in its history: no longer a hostage to Cold War bickering, it has moved to establish a fresh sense of its role and purpose.

The UN has already made considerable progress toward fulfillment of some of the aspirations of member states—greater security between states, decolonization, economic and social development, protection of human rights and fundamental freedoms, and, in general, cooperation among nations on common approaches to global problems. The UN has served to legitimize the engagement of member states in coping with crises, and, on occasion, has undertaken challenging responsibilities that member states cannot or will not shoulder individually.

The UN has, at times, however, appeared to be little more than a discordant association of sovereign states. Both in practical endeavors and in efforts to reform the organization, the UN has frequently come up against governments' concern to protect national sovereignty and a deep, if unexpressed, reluctance to countenance any development in the direction of supranationalism.

These two images of the UN—a successful, practical (indeed, necessary) organization or a group of quarreling states—again point up one of the fundamental conclusions of this report. The main responsibility for addressing global problems, including deadly conflict, rests on governments. Acting individually and collectively, they have the power to work toward solutions or to hinder the process. The UN, of course, is only as effective as its member states allow it to be.

The UN can be an an essential focal point for marshaling the resources of the international community to help prevent mass violence. No single government, however strong, and no nongovernmental organization can do all that needs doing—nor should they be expected to. To be sure, the involvement of the UN in conflict management in the post–Cold War period has brought it much criticism, both just and unjust.[1] In Rwanda, for example, as was discussed in the prologue to this report, the Security Council withdrew forces at perhaps the worst possible moment. But some of the failings of the UN reflect, among other things, the very real concerns of member states regarding unwanted intrusion into national sovereignty. These concerns have sometimes inhibited efforts to anticipate and respond to incipient vio-

The UN can be an essential focal point for marshaling the resources of the international community to help prevent mass violence.

lence, especially within states. In particular, these concerns have played a role in thwarting attempts so far to set up a standing rapid reaction force. One of the UN's greatest challenges is whether and how to adapt its mechanisms for managing interstate disputes to deal with intrastate violence. If it is to move in this direction, it must do so in a manner that commands the trust of the membership and their voluntary cooperation.

Strengths of the UN

As the sole global collective security organization, the UN's key goals include the promotion of international peace and security, sustainable economic and social development, and universal human rights. Each of these goals is relevant to the prevention of deadly conflict.

The global reach and intergovernmental character of the UN give it considerable influence, especially when it can speak with one voice. The Security Council has emerged as a highly developed yet flexible mechanism to help member states cope with a remarkable variety of problems. The Office of the Secretary-General has considerable prestige, convening power, and the capacity to reach into problems early when they may be inaccessible to governments or private organizations. Many of the UN's functional agencies, such as the United Nations High Commissioner for Refugees (UNHCR), the United Nations Children's Fund (UNICEF), the United Nations Development Program (UNDP), the World Food Program (WFP), the World Health Organization (WHO) and, for that matter, the Bretton Woods financial institutions—the International Bank for Reconstruction and Development (more commonly known as the World Bank) and the International Monetary Fund (IMF)—conduct effective programs of great complexity around the world.

The UN system is vital to any effort to help prevent the emergence of mass violence. Its long-term programs to reduce the global disparity between rich and poor and to develop the capacity of weak governments to function more effectively are of fundamental importance to its role.

Member states have often used the Security Council, and sometimes the General Assembly, to address rapidly unfolding crises. In the Middle East, Africa, Cyprus, South Asia, Cambodia, Central America, and elsewhere, the UN has developed a number of innovative practices—observer missions, peacekeeping, massive humanitarian actions, special representatives of the secretary-general, election organization and monitoring, and human rights support—to address a wide range of potentially deadly disputes. Partly as a result of these efforts, the UN has had important successes in averting crises, preventing the further deterioration of crises, and ending hostilities.[2]

The UN gives a voice to all member states, large and small, and provides a forum for their voices to be heard on a wide range of concerns. In addition, many critical issues—such as apartheid and Palestinian rights—have been kept alive and debated at the UN in the search for a solution.

Providing an open forum gives the UN an early awareness of incipient troubles, a possibility for warning that those troubles may be taking a turn for the worse, a means—through dialogue and information sharing—to clarify dangerous situations, and ways, through the Security Council, the General Assembly, the Office of the Secretary-General, and the various UN agencies, to develop effective responses. The UN has also proved valuable as an organization through which states could deal with many kinds of problems that transcend national and regional boundaries and that lay beyond the capacity of any single member to handle alone. In this way, the UN has addressed such global concerns as disarmament and arms control, the environment, population, health, illegal drugs, the plight of children, the inequality of women, and human rights. Global agreement in many of these fields has emerged from UN initiatives, and the UN remains heavily engaged in the ongoing work (see Box 6.1).[3]

In 1996, for example, UNICEF launched its "Anti-War Agenda" to lessen the suffering of children as a result of mass violence. The agenda's top priority is prevention with special emphasis on the protection of girls and women, rehabilitation of child soldiers, a ban on recruitment of children under 18 years of age, a ban on land mines, aggressive prosecution of war crimes, establishment of "zones of peace" to create humanitarian outposts in conflict, and a requirement that a "child impact statement" be drafted before sanctions are imposed. The agenda also stresses the need to prevent and treat the psychological trauma that children suffer as a result of war and the importance of education to promote tolerance and peaceful means of dispute resolution.[4]

The Office of the UN High Commissioner for Refugees was created in 1951 primarily to protect individuals forcibly displaced by World War II and the creation of the Iron Curtain. For its first 40 years, UNHCR operated essentially in countries of asylum, but by the mid-1980s it was increasingly being asked to assist internally displaced persons (IDPs), those in refugee-like situations who had not crossed an international frontier. These humanitarian crises, which averaged five per year until 1989, suddenly jumped to 20 in 1990 and to 26 in 1994. By the end of 1996, there were an estimated 20 million IDPs worldwide and about 16 million refugees, and UNHCR's budget over the past 20 years has increased twentyfold.[5]

UNHCR is under constant pressure by governments to do more. As its responsibilities have expanded, its traditional mission of protection has come under strain from the demands of providing relief and repatriation, as was painfully evident in the so-called safe havens in Bosnia and the terrorized Rwandan refugee camps of Eastern Zaire. High Commissioner Sadako Ogata has called on governments to strengthen the UN's capacity to protect and care for refugees and IDPs, including, where necessary, providing multilateral security forces to protect UN-mandated humanitarian operations—steps the Commission endorses.

Its intergovernmental character gives the UN real value and practical advantages for certain kinds of early preventive action—such as discreet, high-level diplomacy—that individual governments do not always have. Here, the Office of the Secretary-General has proven particularly valuable on a wide array of world problems in need of international attention. The secretary-general has brought to the attention of the Security Council early evidence of threats to peace, genocide, large flows of refugees threatening to destabilize neighboring countries, evidence of systematic and widespread human rights violations, attempts at the forcible overthrow of governments, and poten-

Box 6.1

INTERNATIONAL INSTRUMENTS
FOR HUMAN RIGHTS

Twenty-five international instruments, adopted by the United Nations, protect and promote human rights around the world:

- Slavery Convention of 1926 (1926)
- Convention on the Prevention and Punishment of the Crime of Genocide (1948)
- Convention for the Suppression of the Traffic in Persons and of the Exploitation or the Prostitution of Others (1949)
- Convention Relating to the Status of Refugees (1951)
- Convention on the Political Rights of Women (1952)
- 1953 Protocol Amending the Slavery Convention of 1926 (1953)
- Slavery Convention of 1926 as amended (1953)
- Convention Relating to the Status of Stateless Persons (1954)
- Supplementary Convention on the Abolition of Slavery, the Slave Trade, and Institutions and Practices Similar to Slavery (1956)
- Convention on the Nationality of Married Women (1957)
- Convention on the Reduction of Statelessness (1961)
- Convention on Consent to Marriage, Minimum Age for Marriage and Registration of Marriages (1962)
- International Convention on the Elimination of All Forms of Racial Discrimination (1965)
- International Covenant on Civil and Political Rights (1966)
- International Covenant on Economic, Social and Cultural Rights (1966)
- Optional Protocol to the International Covenant on Civil and Political Rights (1966)
- Protocol Relating to the Status of Refugees (1967)
- Convention on the Non-Applicability of Statutory Limitations to War Crimes and Crimes against Humanity (1968)
- International Convention on the Suppression and Punishment of the Crime of Apartheid (1973)
- Convention on the Elimination of All Forms of Discrimination against Women (1979)
- Convention against Torture and other Cruel, Inhuman or Degrading Treatment or Punishment (1984)
- International Convention against Apartheid in Sports (1985)
- Convention on the Rights of the Child (1989)
- Second Optional Protocol to the International Covenant on Civil and Political Rights (aims at the abolition of the death penalty) (1989)
- Convention on the Rights of Migrant Workers and the Members of their Families (1990)

Source: United Nations, *Human Rights: International Instruments*, Chart of Ratifications as of 30 June 1996, ST/HR/4/Rev.14 (New York, 1996).

tial or actual damage to the environment. The secretary-general has also helped forge consensus and secure an early response from the Security Council by deploying envoys or special representatives, assembling a group of "friends" to concentrate on a particular problem, and by speaking out on key issues such as weapons of mass destruction, environmental degradation, and the plight of the world's poor (see Box 6.2).[6]

Limitations of the UN

The features that give the UN its potential often come at a price. Its global reach often demands some sacrifice of efficiency and focus, and the UN is, of course, fully dependent on its membership for political legitimacy, operating funds, and personnel to staff its operations and carry out its mandates (see Box 6.3). Moreover, it is ironic that many states, while quick to turn to the UN to seek consensus for action in a crisis, are slow to provide resources for the action they demand and the missions they develop.

For its part, the Security Council can have a powerful voice in legitimizing or condemning state action. Yet, some aggressive states remain defiant, a situation that results from an erosion of the authority of the Security Council, and sometimes the consequences of ill-conceived, underfunded, underequipped, or poorly executed operations. This erosion of authority points to the need to reform the Security Council by making it more representative of the member states of the UN and worthy of their trust.

While member states seem in broad agreement that the UN should be concerned with a wide range of issues, there is far less agreement on what exactly the organization should do. Many countries, including some of the most powerful, use the UN as a fig leaf and a scapegoat, to blur unwanted focus, to defuse political pressure, or to dilute or escape their own responsibilities. States—again, even the most powerful—make commitments in the abstract, yet fail to honor them in practice. The 1993 resolution by the Security Council to protect several cities in Bosnia as "safe-areas" is a case in point. Against the advice of many experts and the warning of the secretary-general, the Security Council resolved to protect Gorazde, Sarajevo, Srebrenica, and several other cities and towns, and it authorized UNPROFOR under Chapter VII of the UN Charter to use "all measures necessary" to keep citizens secure. But it refused to provide the forces or the resources to carry out this mission, and the results were disastrous.[7] Assigning difficult missions but failing to provide adequate resources or authority for their implementation must not continue if the UN is to remain useful as an instrument of preventive action.[8]

Despite the lack of agreement on engagement in domestic conflicts by international organizations, the UN has been required to intervene in several. It shepherded the transition from war to peace in Cambodia, helped broker solutions to conflicts in new states such as Bosnia and Georgia, marshaled an unprecedented humanitarian relief effort in Somalia, and dealt with refugees from the mass slaughter in Rwanda.

Assigning difficult missions but failing to provide adequate resources or authority for their implementation must not continue if the UN is to remain useful as an instrument of preventive action.

Box 6.2

"FRIENDS" OF THE SECRETARY-GENERAL

Groups of "friends" of the UN secretary-general are composed of a small number of states of the United Nations, often three to six members, which consult and advise the secretary-general on specific issues usually related to a crisis. Originally conceived to aid the secretary-general in applying UN resources to help manage crises, their formation and coordination is ad hoc and informal. They have been used with varying success in such places as El Salvador (1989), Haiti (1993), Western Sahara (1993), and Guatemala (1994). They are an important tool to help ensure that international attention stays focused on a dispute and that belligerents know that the international community remains engaged.

Groups of friends of the secretary-general can apply pressure on the parties to a conflict to avoid violence, provide an interested but impartial element to the peace process, and help develop and implement peaceful resolutions to conflict. They prepare and provide support for Security Council and General Assembly resolutions. As the best informed and most engaged members on the issue, these groups of friends are instrumental in maintaining support for UN peacekeeping operations in the field. Through continued mediation and consultation, friends groups also permit the secretary-general to monitor the peace process in conflict areas even after the official UN withdrawal.

A number of conditions help facilitate the formation of friends groups: governments from both the region of conflict and outside, who are impartial and have the capacity to apply pressure or offer resources, must be willing to participate; members of the group must have the political will necessary to adopt an issue and the ability to maintain involvement; and consensus with one another and with the secretary-general is key.

For example, the group of friends formed to address the mounting crisis in Haiti in 1993—Canada, France, the United States, and Venezuela—quickly developed a strategy to restore democratic rule. Thanks to a broad consensus on the nature and goals of the policy, the friends group was successful in convincing the Security Council and the international community of the utility of sanctions and of ways to pursue more constructive engagement.

Groups of friends of the secretary-general are most successful when they maintain consensus, open communication, and a positive relationship with the secretary-general, other UN agencies, engaged governments, and major private sector enterprises. At a time when the Security Council is occupied with numerous global issues, a group of friends can gather information and prepare and implement a strategy to help resolve conflict and prevent the initiation of violence.

Source: Jean Krasno, "The Group of Friends of the Secretary-General: A Useful Diplomatic Tool," paper prepared for the Carnegie Commission on Preventing Deadly Conflict, December 1996 (available on the Commission's Web site: www.ccpdc.org).

Box 6.3
THE PRICE OF PEACE
How Expensive Is the UN?

As of February 28, 1997, member states collectively owed the UN more than $3 billion. This failure to meet financial obligations has hampered the organization's ability to take on all but the most pressing tasks. As a result, the UN's role in conflict prevention (through both long-term economic and social development programs, as well as short-term operational missions) is severely limited. A few comparisons help put the UN's budget in perspective:

- Americans spend approximately $5.6 billion a year at movie theaters—more than four times the UN's $1.3 billion budget for core functions.
- Americans spend approximately $5.3 billion a year on spectator sports; the UN and its specialized agencies spend $4.6 billion on economic and social development.
- The entire UN system (including related programs such as UNICEF and specialized agencies such as the WHO and IMF) employs 53,333 people—less than Disney World, Disneyland, and Euro Disney and only one-third the number of McDonald's employees.
- The UN's core budget—that is, for the Secretariat operations in New York, Geneva, Nairobi, Vienna, and the five regional commissions involving some 14,000 people—is $1.3 billion a year, about $1 billion less than the annual budget of Tokyo's fire department.

Sources: United Nations, "Setting the Record Straight: Some Facts About the United Nations," March 1997 Update, DPI/1753/Rev.12; United Nations, *Questions & Answers About the United Nations - Chapter Six/Who Works at the UN and What They Do There*, http://www.un.org/geninfo/ir/, updated June 1997; U.S. Department of State, Bureau of International Organizations, *International Organizations: Personnel Statistics* (as of December 31, 1996), unpublished report; Robert Farnighetti, ed., *The World Almanac and Book of Facts 1997* (New York: St. Martin's Press, 1997); Gareth Evans, "The UN at Fifty: Looking Back and Looking Forward," Statement to the Fiftieth General Assembly of the United Nations, New York, October 2, 1995.

With the increasing number of conflicts within states, the international community must develop a new concept of the relationship between national sovereignty and international responsibility. As former Secretary-General Boutros Boutros-Ghali has observed:

> Respect for [states'] fundamental sovereignty and integrity [is] crucial to any common international progress. The time of absolute and exclusive sovereignty, however, has passed; its theory was never matched by reality. It is the task of leaders of states today to understand this and to find a balance between the needs of good internal governance and the requirements of an ever more interdependent world.[9]

Echoing this theme, the Commission on Global Governance has noted:

> Where people are subjected to massive suffering and distress...there is a need to weigh a state's right to autonomy against its people's right to security. Recent history shows that extreme circumstances can arise within countries when the security of people is so extensively imperilled that external collective action under international law becomes justified.[10]

The Commission on Global Governance has proposed a specific UN Charter amendment to authorize such action. However, as we already noted, there has been some tacit willingness in recent years to rely on liberal interpretations of the Charter language of "threats to international security," reinforced by the concept of "human security" and placing particular emphasis on human rights responsibilities. Nonetheless, questions of sovereignty and the role of outsiders remain extremely sensitive and controversial in many countries. The existing language of Article 2 (7) of the UN Charter written 50 years ago, states an important principle:

> Nothing contained in the present Charter shall authorize the United Nations to intervene in matters which are essentially within the domestic jurisdiction of any state or shall require the Members to submit such matters to settlement under the present Charter; but this principle shall not prejudice the application of enforcement measures under Chapter VII.

This provision was one of the features of the Charter that made it possible for a wide range of governments to endorse it in 1945. While states at that time recognized the role that the most powerful among them might play to help prevent a third World War (hence the inclusion of Chapter VII provisions for "all means necessary"), they also recognized that weaker states needed a safeguard against encroachments by the strong. Now with the current waning of interstate conflict and the massive increase of intrastate violence, the demand for action has forced states to reinterpret, in practice at least, the meaning of this provision.

The contradiction between respecting national sovereignty and the moral and ethical imperative to stop slaughter within states is real and difficult to resolve. The UN Charter gives the Security Council a good deal of latitude in making such decisions, but it also lays out a number of broad principles to guide the application of these decisions. The responsibility for determining where one principle or the other is to prevail resides with the Security Council and the member states on a case-by-case basis. Again, it is precisely the sensitivity of such a responsibility that has led to the growing demand for reform of the Security Council in order to make it more representative of the membership and more legitimate in the discharge of its responsibilities.

Strengthening the UN for Prevention

The Commission believes that the UN can have a central, even indispensable, role to play in prevention to help governments cope with incipient violence and to organize the help of others. Its legitimating function and ability to focus world attention on key problems, combined with the considerable operational capacity of many of its operating agencies, make it an important asset in any prevention regime. Yet certain reforms are necessary to strengthen the UN for preventive purposes. In a major statement on reform, Secretary-General Kofi Annan acknowledged this key responsibility of the UN and the need for a comprehensive approach to adapting the organization to meet this responsibility.

The UN can have a central, even indispensable, role to play in prevention to help governments cope with incipient violence and to organize the help of others.

The international community can have a human face: the UN High Commissioner for Refugees, Sadako Ogata, meets a refugee baby.

The prevalence of intra-state warfare and multi-faceted crises in the present period has added new urgency to the need for a better understanding of their root causes. It is recognized that greater emphasis should be placed on timely and adequate preventive action. The United Nations of the twenty-first century must become increasingly a focus of preventive measures.[11]

He outlines a number of measures to strengthen the UN to assume this role, including, for example:

- Increased and improved contact between the Security Council and governments, regional organizations, NGOs, and academic institutions to improve its capacity to detect potential threats to international peace and security;

- Steps to enhance the UN's rapid reaction capability;

- Measures to integrate humanitarian assistance with other preventive measures such as early warning and human rights monitoring to ensure the constructive complementarity of these activities and to help ease the transition from crisis to long-term programs;

- A strengthened Office of the High Commissioner for Human Rights (UNHCHR) to enhance its early warning function and role in peacemaking, peace building, and humanitarian operations; and

Vote by the UN Security Council to oust Iraq from Kuwait with force.

● The establishment of a department for Disarmament and Arms Regulation to develop strategies and policies to prevent the proliferation of all types of weapons and to control the flow of conventional weapons to areas of conflict.[12]

More is necessary, however. The Commission believes that the secretary-general should play a more prominent role in preventing deadly conflict through several steps: more frequent use of Article 99 to bring potentially violent situations to the attention of the Security Council and, thereby, to the international community; greater use of good offices to help defuse developing crises; and more assertive use of the considerable convening power of the Office of the Secretary-General to assemble

"friends" groups to help coordinate the international response.

In addition, the Commission believes that:

● Member governments should be encouraged to make annual contributions to the Fund for Preventive Action established by the Norwegian government in 1996 for the use of the secretary-general for preventive purposes. The secretary-general should use the fund to expand the pool of suitable candidates who serve as envoys and special representatives and to provide the resources necessary to train and support their missions.

● The secretary-general should convene at least one meeting with the heads of the major regional organizations—as was done

PREVENTING DEADLY CONFLICT

in August 1994—during each term of office. These meetings can be used to discuss, among other topics, potential violence in the regions, possible preventive strategies, and ways to coordinate regional and UN efforts.

- The secretary-general should establish a private sector advisory committee to draw more systematically on the expertise and insights of civil society for preventive action.

- The secretary-general should establish an advisory committee on science and technology, broadly composed of representatives from across the spectrum of sciences, to offer advice and recommendations on a wide range of problems.

- The Security Council should call on the General Assembly to reconstitute the Collective Measures Committee to evaluate existing practices regarding the imposition and implementation of sanctions and to make recommendations regarding ways to improve their deterrent value. The Security Council should retain authority to decide when international norms have been violated and when and how the imposition of sanctions would be justified.

- UNICEF, UNDP, and UNHCR should integrate their new emphasis on prevention with a more activist UN High Commissioner for Human Rights to strengthen the UN's role in early warning, protection of human rights, and conflict prevention. The Office of the Secretary-General can play a key role in this integration.

SPECIAL REPRESENTATIVES AND PERSONAL ENVOYS OF THE UN SECRETARY-GENERAL

The UN Charter grants the secretary-general limited powers to pursue preventive diplomacy by dispatching personal envoys to assist in early warning, fact-finding, and third-party mediation when requested by the parties to a dispute. The secretary-general also recruits special representatives to oversee Security Council-mandated operations of peacekeeping and peace enforcement.

Demand for these missions has risen sharply since 1990, as the UN has been tasked to help resolve several long-standing regional conflicts and to deal with new threats of mass violence and a proliferation of complex emergencies. By the mid-1990s more than 20 representatives and envoys were deployed in trouble spots around the world, four times the number typically engaged a decade ago.

An assessment prepared by the Commission advocates a more activist approach to expand the pool of well-qualified persons to serve as special representatives and to increase the modest funding to support these operations under the aegis of the secretary-general. The Commission urges governments to provide sufficient resources under the UN's regular budget to strengthen the Secretariat's ability to undertake preventive diplomacy.

The Government of Norway has initiated a Fund for Preventive Action for voluntary contributions to meet this objective in the short term. The Commission also endorses efforts by various governments and nongovernmental agencies to assist in training, recruitment, and evaluation to improve the staffing and operations of UN personal envoys and special representatives.

Source: Cyrus R. Vance and David A. Hamburg, *Pathfinders for Peace: A Report to the UN Secretary-General on the Role of Special Representatives and Personal Envoys* (Washington, DC: Carnegie Commission on Preventing Deadly Conflict, September 1997).

Paper by the Chairman of the Open-Ended Working Group on the Question of Equitable Representation on and Increase in the Membership of the Security Council and Other Matters Related to the Security Council

The General Assembly,...

<u>Recognizing</u> the primary responsibility of the Security Council for the maintenance of international peace and security under the Charter of the United Nations,...

1. <u>Decides:</u>
   a) to increase the membership of the Security Council from fifteen to twenty-four by adding five permanent members and four non-permanent members;
   b) that the five new permanent members of the Security Council shall be elected according to the following pattern:
      (I)   One from the developing States of Africa;
      (ii)   One from the developing States of Asia;
      (iii) One from the developing States of Latin America and the Caribbean;
      (iv)   Two from the industrialized States;
   c) that the four new non-permanent members of the Security Council shall be elected according to the following pattern:
      (I)   One from African States;
      (ii)   One from Asian States;
      (iii) One from Eastern European States;
      (iv)   One from Latin American and Caribbean States;

2. <u>Invites</u> interested States to inform the members of the General Assembly that they are prepared to assume the function and responsibilities of permanent members of the Security Council;

3. <u>Decides</u> to proceed by a vote of two-thirds of the members of the General Assembly by 28 February 1998, to the designation of the States that will be elected to exercise the functions and responsibilities of the permanent members of the Security Council, according to the pattern described in paragraph 1b, it being understood that if the number of States having obtained the required majority falls short of the number of seats allocated for permanent membership, new rounds of balloting will be conducted for the remaining category(ies), until five States obtain the required majority to occupy the five seats;

4. <u>Recognizing</u> that an overwhelming number of Member States consider the use of veto in the Security Council anachronistic and undemocratic, and have called for its elimination, <u>decides:</u>
   a) to discourage use of the veto, by urging the original permanent members of the Security Council to limit the exercise of their veto power to actions taken under Chapter VII of the Charter;
   b) that the new permanent members of the Security Council shall have no provision of the veto power;

5. <u>Decides</u> that for peacekeeping assessments, all new and original permanent members of the Security Council shall pay the same percentage rate of premium surcharge over and above their regular budget rate of assessment.

Source: "Paper by the Chairman of the Open-Ended Working Group on the Question of Equitable Representation On and Increase In the Membership of the Security Council and Other Matters Related to the Security Council," submitted to the UN General Assembly by the Malaysian ambassador to the United Nations, Tan Sri Razali Ismail, as President of the UN General Assembly, New York, March 20, 1997. A similar proposal has been advanced by the Commission on Global Governance. See *Our Global Neighborhood* (New York: Oxford University Press, 1995).

UN peacekeepers amid the destruction of Mostar.

Such measures, together with those offered by the secretary-general and others contained in this report, would go a long way toward establishing a prevention orientation in the international community and laying the groundwork to develop standard practices that link UN actions with those of governments and NGOs.

Reform of the Security Council

There is a compelling need to enlarge and modernize the Security Council to ensure that its membership reflects the world of today rather than 1945.* There is almost universal agreement to that effect among the UN member states, but agreement about how precisely this objective might be accomplished has so far proved elusive for several reasons: the Security Council must not be unworkably large; there is no readily achievable consensus as to which major countries in Africa, Asia, and Latin America should have permanent membership status; and the existing five permanent members are not likely to abandon or dilute their present veto power. One promising proposal is that put forward by Malaysian Permanent Representative, Tan Sri Razali Ismail, during his term as president of the General Assembly (see Box 6.4). The Commission proposes to remove

---

* As noted in the prologue, Commission member Sahabzada Yaqub-Khan dissents from the Commission's view on Security Council reform. In his opinion, the additional permanent members would multiply, not diminish, the anomalies inherent in the structure of the Security Council. While the concept of regional rotation for additional permanent seats offers prospects of a compromise, it would be essential to have agreed global and regional criteria for rotation. In the absence of an international consensus on expansion in the permanent category, the expansion should be confined to nonpermanent members only.

the prohibition on election of any new nonpermanent members for successive terms from the Charter, enabling other major powers with aspirations to continuous or recurring membership to negotiate their reelection on a continuous or rotating basis.

On July 17, 1997, the Clinton administration joined the debate on Security Council reform by announcing a proposal to add five new permanent members—Germany and Japan plus three developing countries—to be selected by an unspecified process. As in the Razali proposal, none of the new members would be allowed a veto. The United States would, however, limit the size of the Council to no more than 20 or 21 seats, at least three less than the total recommended by Ambassador Razali.

In the Commission's view, the addition of new members should reflect not only the world's capacities but also the world's needs. The Commission believes that any arrangement should be subject to automatic review after ten years. The use of size, population, GDP, and level of international engagement (measured, for example, through such indices as participation in UN peacekeeping) might serve as criteria for permanent membership (see Table 6.1). The language of Article 23 of the UN Charter is worth recalling also, in its statement of appropriate criteria for any member of the Security Council, requiring that due regard be paid "for the contribution...to the maintenance of international peace and security and to the other purposes of the organization and also to equitable geographical distribution."

The Commission is under no illusion that any model will satisfy every member state. Despite the difficulties, it is crucial for agreement on reform to be reached quickly. Every year that the Security Council continues with its present structure, the UN suffers because the increasingly apparent lack of representativeness of the council membership diminishes its credibility and weakens its capacity for conflict prevention.

The UN's Role in Long-Term Prevention

The long-term role of the UN in helping to prevent deadly conflict resides in its central purposes of promoting peace and security, fostering sustainable development, inspiring widespread respect for human rights, and developing the regime of international law. Three major documents combine to form a working program for the UN to fulfill these roles: *An Agenda for Peace,* published in 1992; *An Agenda for Development,* published in 1995; and *An Agenda for Democratization,* published in 1996. Each report focuses on major tasks essential to help reduce the global epidemic of violence, preserve global peace and stability, prevent the spread of weapons of mass destruction, promote sustainable economic and social development, champion human rights and fundamental freedoms, and alleviate massive human suffering. Each is an important statement of the broad objectives of peace, development, and democracy, as well as a valuable road map to achieving those objectives. In combination, they suggest how states might use the UN more effectively over the long term to reduce the incidence and intensity of global violence.

The addition of new members to the Security Council should reflect not only the world's capacities but also the world's needs.

Table 6.1

CONSIDERING UN SECURITY COUNCIL MEMBERSHIP
Data on Selected Countries

Country	Population	Area (km²)	GDP (billions of US$)	INTERNATIONAL ENGAGEMENT UN Assessment (% of regular budget)	Overseas Development Assistance for 1995 (millions of US$)	Overseas Development Assistance for 1995 (% of GDP)	UN Peacekeeping[a] Assessment (US$)	Payment (US$)[b]	Personnel Contributions to UN Peacekeeping Operations for 1994 (man-months)[c]
Africa and Middle East									
Algeria	26,581,000	2,381,741	41	0.16	R[d]	0.0	616,521	303,252	0
Congo, Dem. Rep. (former Zaire)	36,672,000	2,344,885	6	0.01	R	0.0	99,507	9,342	0
Egypt	59,226,000	997,739	47	0.07	R	0.0	273,678	254,892	25,018
Ethiopia	56,677,100	1,133,380	5	0.01	R	0.0	27,636	35,000	4,019
Iran	59,778,000	1,648,000	105	0.47	R	0.0	5,294,713	2,227,448	0
Iraq	17,903,000	438,317	53[e]	0.14	R	0.0	1,506,522	0	0
Libya	4,899,000	1,775,500	25[e]	0.20	R	0.0	2,727,594	57,192	0
Nigeria	97,223,521	923,768	27	0.12	R	0.0	1,030,911	699,179	9,136
Saudi Arabia	16,929,294	2,240,000	126	0.72	R	0.0	3,088,647	6,147,374	1,512
South Africa	41,244,500	1,219,080	136	0.32	NA	NA	8,703,537	20,707,249	0
Australia and Asia									
Australia	17,843,268	7,682,300	349	0.48	1,194	0.34	27,500,802	25,079,082	2,896
China	1,211,210,000	9,571,300	698	0.74	R	0.0	16,845,586	30,148,785	754
India	913,200,000	3,287,263	324	0.31	R	0.0	1,259,351	1,178,341	61,312
Indonesia	194,440,500	1,904,443	198	0.14	R	0.0	1,433,912	1,083,715	1,457
Japan	125,761,000	377,829	5,109	15.44	14,489	0.28	263,936,434	167,669,618	638
Kazakstan	16,763,000	2,717,300	21	0.20	R	0.0	2,552,781	428,210	0
Malaysia	20,689,000	329,758	85	0.14	R	0.0	522,103	530,027	32,836
Pakistan	129,808,000	796,095	61	0.06	R	0.0	234,239	279,535	95,417
Europe									
France	58,143,000	543,965	1,536	6.41	8,443	0.55	143,759,355	143,075,956	74,398
Germany	81,538,603	356,978	2,416	9.04	7,524	0.31	167,025,966	164,974,151	2,728
Italy	57,268,578	301,323	1,087	5.2	1,623	0.15	88,906,233	79,091,768	9,795
Poland	38,609,400	312,685	118	0.34	R	0.0	5,048,163	4,520,535	23,308
Russian Federation	147,501,000	17,075,400	345	4.45	R	0.0	272,848,142	314,616,432	17,592
Turkey	62,697,000	779,452	165	0.38	R	0.0	2,979,676	3,646,780	10,389
Ukraine	51,639,000	603,700	80	1.14	R	0.0	83,877,983	5,582,762	11,795
United Kingdom	58,605,800	241,752	1,106	5.32	3,157	0.29	117,721,934	115,114,700	44,525
North America									
Canada	29,606,000	9,958,319	569	3.1	2,067	0.36	56,861,445	52,740,934	30,503
Mexico	90,487,000	1,958,201	250	0.79	R	0.0	3,196,736	3,591,339	417
United States	265,284,000	9,809,155	6,952	25.00	7,367	0.11	725,353,054	396,776,005	11,654
South America									
Argentina	34,768,455	2,780,400	281	0.48	R	0.0	2,378,152	4,154,753	16,895
Brazil	155,822,440	8,511,996	688	1.62	R	0.0	7,185,163	1,952,533	2,618
Colombia	37,422,791	1,141,748	76	0.1	R	0.0	448,087	989,242	523
Peru	23,088,000	1,280,000	57	0.06	R	0.0	681,503	51,386	0
Venezuela	21,644,000	912,050	75	0.34	R	0.0	4,955,655	461,715	220

Sources: *The Europa World Year Book 1997*, 2 vols. (London: Europa Publications Limited, 1997); The World Bank; The World Resources Institute, *World Resources 1996-97* (New York: Oxford University Press, 1996), pp. 166-67; The World Bank, *World Development Report 1997: The State of a Changing World* (Oxford: Oxford University Press, 1997), pp. 236-37; New Zealand Ministry of Foreign Affairs and Trade, *United Nations Handbook 1996* (Wellington: Ministry of Foreign Affairs and Trade, 1996), pp. 338-340; James H. Michel, *Development Co-operation* (Paris: Organisation for Economic Cooperation and Development, 1997), pp. A21- A22; United Nations Secretariat, "Status of Contributions as at 31 December 1996," Document ST/ADM/SER.B/505, 8 January 1997; United Nations Secretariat, Department of Peacekeeping Operations.

a. Please refer to Appendix 3 for a listing of personnel contributors by mission.

b. In some cases, payment exceeds assessment as a result of countries paying arrears.

c. 1994 was the peak year for the assignment of personnel to UN peacekeeping. A man-month is defined as the assignment of an individual to peacekeeping duty for one month.

d. "R" indicates that a country is a net ODA recipient.

e. The World Resources Institute, *World Resources 1996-97* (New York: Oxford University Press, 1996), pp. 166-67. Reliable current GDP data are not available for Iraq and Libya. Data for Libya are from 1989, and for Iraq from 1990.

A Bosnian child and a UN armored personnel carrier.

An Agenda for Peace and the *Supplement to An Agenda for Peace* (published in 1993) emphasize the need to identify at the earliest possible moment the circumstances that could produce serious conflict and to try through diplomacy to remove the sources of danger.[13] While putting a high priority on such early attention to and engagement in potential crises, the basic report also discusses the necessity of dealing at later stages with peacemaking, peacekeeping, or peace building for the long run. It also stresses the need to address the deepest causes of conflict: economic despair, social injustice, and political oppression. *An Agenda for Peace* and the *Supplement* point the way for states to apply their considerable experience in managing interstate conflict to the pressing demands of the increasing numbers of wars within states.

An Agenda for Development recognizes that accelerated economic growth and widespread economic opportunity help generate positive social and technological transformations.[14] Economic growth should be pursued to provide employment, educational opportunities, and improved living standards for ever wider segments of the population. Traditional approaches to development that have given little regard to the political systems of developing countries have fallen into disfavor, and experts now generally agree that political progress toward representative government and economic progress toward market mechanisms with provisions for a social safety net are inextricably linked. It is also best to consider emergency relief and development jointly. *An Agenda for Development* helps channel the now-considerable interest that exists in rethinking and strengthening the UN's role in facilitating sustainable development.

An Agenda for Democratization makes clear that the UN can, when called upon, play a useful role in helping states establish and solidify a hold on democracy.[15] The right of the governed to a say in how they are governed has gained greater currency around the world as states have shed totalitarian pasts and as existing democracies cope with the burgeoning— and perhaps previously disregarded—needs of *all* citizens. Many models of democracy exist as do many paths to that end. UN action to promote democratic practices rests on the principles outlined in three core documents; the UN Charter, the Universal Declaration of Human Rights, and the Declaration on the Granting of Independence to Colonial Countries and Peoples. Today, the UN, together with its member states, offers a wide range of assistance to help build the political culture necessary to sustain democratic practices.

THE INTERNATIONAL FINANCIAL INSTITUTIONS

Although many people may have forgotten it, the international financial institutions (IFIs) created at Bretton Woods—led by the World Bank and the International Monetary Fund (IMF)—are part of the UN system. These insti-

tutions remained aloof from the UN and its other agencies during the Cold War, but today, together with regional financial institutions, the Bank and the IMF have a major interest and role to play in helping to prevent or cope with mass violence. Peace agreements need to be strengthened with economic development, and the Bank and the IMF have begun to focus on reconstruction to help prevent violence from reemerging.

The leverage of the IFIs could be used even more widely to provide incentives for cooperation in tense regions. Investment may act as a restraint on the causes of violence, and conditional assistance might be used to show that loans and grants are available to those who cooperate with their neighbors. In fact, the IFIs have experimented as far back as the 1950s with programs to demonstrate that economic growth could be achieved only through intergroup or regional cooperation. Moreover, with large investments in many conflict-prone countries, the Bank and the IMF have become concerned with both the need for good governance and the dangers of instability and violence. In 1997, for example, the World Bank signaled a major shift in its willingness to address issues of governance by devoting its annual flagship publication, *World Development Report,* to the theme "The State in a Changing World." But before these organizations can be more truly effective, they must also become more sensitive to local conditions, acquire and develop the necessary staff for dealing with critical social and political issues, and be more responsible for the advice they give (see Box 6.5).[16]

Helping to prevent the recurrence of major international conflict by reducing economic instability was the principal motivation for establishing the World Bank and other international financial institutions of the UN system immediately following World War II. Their role has been to provide badly needed financial capital and technical assistance to help countries stabilize and restructure their economies in ways that promote rapid and sustainable economic growth. In so doing, the World Bank has contributed substantially to an unprecedented expansion of global economic activity and the transformation of centrally planned economies and their rapid integration into world markets. It has fostered degrees of cooperation—especially among former adversaries in Europe and in Asia—that make war almost unthinkable among the world's major powers.

Following the end of the Cold War, the needs and opportunities for the Bank to play a major role in the reconstruction of war-torn states have changed dramatically. These challenges are more diffuse, longer term, and more uncertain than those facing the Bank in Europe 40 years ago.

The clearest example of the new commitment to postconflict reconstruction is in the former Yugoslavia, where the World Bank is leading a $5.1 billion program funded by several multilateral and bilateral donors. The Bank intends to revitalize enterprise development and rehabilitate the social sectors in order to pave the way for economic recovery; strengthen and rebuild key institutions; and assist the transition to a market-based economy. Similar programs are currently under way in other war-torn societies, including Cambodia, Eritrea, Lebanon, Mozambique, and Rwanda. In addition, the Bank has funded mine clearing—a prerequisite in many countries for rebuilding roads and infrastructure—refugee resettlement, and agricultural development.

As one Bank official suggests, "Development institutions cannot resolve conflicts, but the transition to peace can be supported by a series of well-timed technical interventions that remove some of the core impediments of postconflict reconstruction and build a firmer base for sustainable development."

Sources: Paul Blustein, "A Loan Amid the Ruins," *Washington Post*, February 13, 1996, p. D1; James D. Wolfensohn, "Address to the Board of Governors of the World Bank Group," Washington, DC, October 1995; The World Bank, "Bosnia and Herzegovina: Priority Reconstruction Projects Update," September 1996; World Bank, "World Bank News," February 15, 1996. See also Robert J. Muscat, "Conflict and Reconstruction: Roles for the World Bank," Draft Manuscript, Washington, D.C., 1995.

The Commission believes that governments should encourage the World Bank and the IMF to establish better cooperation with the UN's political bodies so that economic inducements can play a more central role in early prevention and in postconflict reconstruction.[17]

REGIONAL ARRANGEMENTS

Every major regional arrangement, or organization, draws its legitimacy, in part, from the principles of the UN Charter.[18] Regional organizations are linked to the UN, not least because most UN member states are also members of regional organizations. Chapter VIII of the UN Charter urges regional solutions to regional problems, and nearly all of the major regional organizations cite the Charter in their own framing documents. These organizations vary in size, mandate, and effectiveness, but all represent ways in which states have tried to pool their strengths and share burdens.[19]

Regional organizations have important limitations. They may not be strong enough on their own to counter the intentions or actions of a dominant state. Even if they are strong enough, regional organizations may not always be the most appropriate forum through which states should engage in or mediate an incipient conflict because of the competing goals of their member states or the suspicions of those in conflict. Nonetheless, if these organizations are inert or powerless in the face of imminent conflict, their functions as regional forums for dialogue, confidence building, and economic coordination will also be eroded. The potential of regional mechanisms for conflict prevention deserves renewed attention in the next decade.

Regional organizations, in all their diversity, can be divided into three groups: 1) security organizations of varying degrees of formality, such as the North Atlantic Treaty Organization, the Organization of American States, the Organization of African Unity, the Western European Union, and the Association of Southeast Asian Nations Regional Forum; 2) economic organizations, again, of varying degrees of formality, such as the European Union, the Asia–Pacific Economic Cooperation group, the North American Free Trade Agreement, the Mercado Común del Sur (MERCO-SUR), and the Gulf Cooperation Council; and 3) general dialogue groups or political/cultural associations, such as the Commonwealth, La Francophonie, the Nonaligned Movement, the Organization of the Islamic Conference, and the Association of Southeast Asian Nations (Appendix 2 lists selected regional organizations with brief discussions of their conflict prevention activities).

Security Organizations

Regional security organizations have some distinct advantages.[20] They are well situated to maintain a careful watch on circumstances and respond early and discreetly when trouble threatens. The Organization for Security and Cooperation in Europe (OSCE), for example, has evolved increasingly active prevention mechanisms over the past several years (see Box 6.6). In Europe the Office of the High Commissioner on National Minorities has played an important role in resolving conflicts, often involving minority rights, before they turn violent.

Economic Organizations

The connections that underpin the global economy make regional economic organizations potentially important vehicles for harnessing states' prevention efforts. A number of examples in which the EU has become active have already been discussed. In addition, the April 1996 near-coup in Paraguay demonstrated that through creative preventive diplomacy, neighboring states can avert a downward spiral into violent conflict. When General Lino Oviedo tried to force President Juan Carlos Wasmosy to step down, Argentina and Brazil stepped in, threatening to expel Paraguay from MERCOSUR. Their dominant economic status in the region and influence on Paraguayan business gave Buenos Aires and Brasilia considerable leverage that they translated into immediate and effective preventive action.[21]

Box 6.6
ORGANIZATION FOR SECURITY AND COOPERATION IN EUROPE
Innovation and Adaptation

Originally designed as a process by which participating states could work to normalize relations between East and West, the Conference on Security and Cooperation in Europe (CSCE, now the Organization for Security and Cooperation in Europe, or OSCE) was established by the Helsinki Final Act in 1975. Twenty years after its founding, the OSCE has emerged with permanent institutions and regular meetings—including summits—to advance the common agenda of member states. With 54 members, the OSCE has adopted a number of innovations specifically designed to help anticipate and manage incipient conflict. Among these innovations are:

- The Permanent Council: An important forum for early identification and discussion of developing disputes and grievances, the council meets weekly and is composed of permanent representatives of participating states.

- The Chairman-in-Office: With the chairmanship rotating among the member states, the chairman-in-office works with the Permanent Council to develop and implement strategies to support dialogue and consultation. The chairman-in-office has a number of mechanisms available for this purpose: personal envoys and representatives, ad hoc steering committees to assist in fact-finding and mediation, and the ability to offer good offices in negotiations.

- The High Commissioner on National Minorities: A powerful asset for preventive diplomacy, this office conducts fact-finding missions, issues early warning notices to the Permanent Council, and implements early action to help prevent the escalation of conflicts. The High Commissioner carries out his duties through extensive on-site visits, consultations, direct mediation and negotiation, or, when necessary, proximity talks. Already active in over one dozen disputes, the High Commissioner's operations are characterized by discreet diplomacy and cultivation of trust and confidence of the parties.

- Long-Term Missions: Designed to aid the chairman-in-office and the Permanent Council in fact-finding, these missions consist of small, flexible teams of regional experts who typically spend more than six months gathering information on incipient or ongoing disputes. They have evolved a special utility in support of the efforts of the High Commissioner on National Minorities and have proven valuable aids to the decision-making process within the OSCE.

- The Office for Democratic Institutions and Human Rights (ODIHR): Established in 1990 to assist participating OSCE states in building democratic institutions and implementing human rights agreements, ODIHR focuses on supporting elections in accordance with OSCE standards and building civil society and democratic social structures. As of this writing, ODIHR has observed elections in 16 countries.

Sources: Diana Chigas, with Elizabeth McClintock and Christophe Kamp, "Preventive Diplomacy and the Organization for Security and Cooperation in Europe: Creating Incentives for Dialogue and Cooperation," in *Preventing Conflict in the Post-Communist World*, eds. Abram Chayes and Antonia Handler Chayes (Washington, DC: The Brookings Institution, 1996), pp. 25-98; Connie Peck, *Sustainable Peace: The Role of the UN and Regional Organizations in Preventing Conflict* (Lanham, MD: Rowman & Littlefield, 1997); Office for Democratic Institutions and Human Rights, Organization for Security and Cooperation in Europe, *OSCE ODIHR Annual Report for 1996* (Warsaw: OSCE, 1996); Organzation for Security and Cooperation in Europe, *OSCE Provisions Related to the Office for Democratic Institutions and Human Rights (ODIHR)* (Warsaw: OSCE, 1995).

Dialogue and Cooperation Groups

There are, of course, other regional and subregional organizations and partnerships through which states pursue common interests—in addition to the OSCE, the Organization of the Islamic Conference (OIC), the Gulf Cooperation Council, the Black Sea Economic Cooperation zone, and the Southern African Development Community (SADC) are examples of the increasing tendency of states to pursue common interests regionally in ways that complement their bilateral strategies.

Such efforts to promote cooperation, dialogue, and confidence building are, in many cases, still in the early stages. The histories of these organizations reflect a continual process of adapting to regional and global exigencies. Today, the greatest of these exigencies is violent conflict within the borders of states. No region is unaffected by this phenomenon. If regional organizations are to be helpful in coping with these changing circumstances, member states must be prepared to commit the resources and demonstrate the political will necessary to ensure that the regional efforts succeed.

The Commission believes that regional arrangements can be greatly strengthened for preventive purposes. They should establish means, linked to the UN, to monitor circumstances of incipient violence within the regions. They should develop a repertoire of diplomatic, political, and economic measures for regional use to help prevent dangerous circumstances from coalescing and exploding into violence. Such a repertoire would include developing ways to provide advance warning to organization members and marshaling regional support, including the necessary logistics, command and control, and other support functions for more assertive efforts authorized by the UN.

Girls attend school in Mexico.

CHAPTER 7

TOWARD A CULTURE
OF PREVENTION

This report emphasizes that any successful regime of conflict prevention must be multifaceted and designed for the long term. To deal with imminent violence, we need better warning and more ways of responding with preventive diplomacy, sanctions, inducements, or the use of force. To deal with the root causes of violence, we need structural approaches that ensure security, well-being, and justice for the almost six billion people on the planet. Civil society in its broadest sense—including nongovernmental organizations, religious leaders and institutions, the educational and scientific communities, the media, and the business community—must play an important role in the regime. The United Nations and regional organizations are essential for marshaling the resources of the international community.

The urgency of the task should be clear. This report describes the many forces that are pushing groups into conflict: for example, irresponsible leaders, historic intergroup tensions, population growth, increasing crowding in cities, economic deterioration, environmental degradation, repressive or discriminating policies, corrupt or incompetent governance, and technological development that increases the gap between rich and poor. In the vast majority of cases, however, these forces need not lead inevitably to violence.

The inescapable fact is that the decision to use violence is made by leaders to incite susceptible groups. The Commission believes that leaders and groups can be influenced to avoid violence. Leaders can be persuaded or coerced to use peaceful measures of conflict resolution, and structural approaches can reduce the susceptibility of groups to arguments for violence.

Beyond persuasion and coercion, however, we must begin to create a culture of prevention. Taught in secular and religious schools, emphasized by the media, pursued vigorously by the UN and other international organizations, the prevention of deadly conflict must become a commonplace of daily life and part of a global cultural heritage passed down from generation to generation. Leaders must exemplify the culture of prevention. The vision, courage, and skills to prevent deadly conflict—and the ability to communicate the need for prevention—must be required qualifications for leaders in the twenty-first century.

In our world of unprecedented levels of destructive weaponry and increased geographic and social proximity, competition between groups has become extremely dangerous. In the century to come, human survival may well depend on our ability to learn a new form of adaptation, one in which intergroup competition is largely replaced by mutual understanding and human cooperation. Curiously, a vital part of human experience—learning to live together—has been badly neglected throughout the world.

The work of international NGOs: Afghan refugee children attend an International Rescue Committee school in Pakistan.

It is not too late for us to develop a radically new outlook on human relations. Perhaps it is something akin to learning that the Earth is not flat. Through concerted educational efforts, such a shift in perspective throughout the world might at long last make it possible for human groups to learn to live together in peace and mutual benefit.

THE CHALLENGE TO EDUCATE

There is a very long evolutionary connection between human groups and their survival.[1] This basic fact has implications for conflict resolution and intergroup accommodation. During the past few decades, valuable insights have emerged from both field studies and experimental research on intergroup behavior. Among the most striking is the finding that the propensity to distinguish between in-groups and out-groups and to make harsh, invidious distinctions between "us" and "them" is a pervasive human attribute. Although these easily learned

responses may have had adaptive functions beneficial to human survival, they have also been a major source of conflict and human suffering.

Is it possible for groups to achieve internal cohesion and self-respect and sustain legitimate and effective political communities without promoting hatred and violence in the process? The immense human capacity for adaptation should make it possible for us to learn to minimize harsh and hateful distinctions. A great deal of laboratory and field research tells us that we can indeed learn new habits of mind, in spite of our evolutionary legacy.

There are countless examples of human tolerance and cooperation. What are the conditions under which group relations can go one way or another? If we could answer such questions better, perhaps we could learn to tilt the balance toward cultures of peace.

We might begin by strengthening research on child development, to better understand the causes of prejudice and the dynamics of intergroup relations. This sort of inquiry can help achieve a deeper understanding of human behavior that bears upon the ultimate problems of war and peace.

Current research is exploring practices within schools that can create a positive atmosphere of mutual respect and cooperative interactions among peers, as well as between students and teachers. In chapter 5, the valuable potential of educational institutions for preventing deadly conflict is emphasized. Teaching children the values of cooperation and toleration of cultural differences helps to overcome prejudicial stereotypes that opportunistic leaders routinely use for their own destructive ends. Tapping education's potential for toleration is an important and long-term task. It is necessary not only to strengthen the relevant curricula in schools and universities, but also to use the educational potential of popular media.

The Mass Media

A strong emphasis must be placed on freedom of the press—or the media in the broadest sense—with fair access for all parties, particularly for minority groups, and full freedom of political and cultural expression. This freedom also includes the opportunity to investigate governmental activities and to criticize all parties, even though the harshness of such criticism is often unpleasant and sometimes quite unfair.

How can the international community foster a mass media that is devoted to combating intergroup prejudice and ethnocentrism, as well as communicating the values and skills of conflict resolution? We are by now all too familiar with political entrepreneurs who use the media to exploit intergroup tensions—actions which often make their own constituencies as vulnerable as the groups that they target. Can these publics be reached by independent media? Radio is a relatively low-cost and widely accessible medium. As discussed in chapter 5, the international community should support radio and other independent media that combat divisive mythmaking by providing accurate information about current events, intergroup relations, and actual instances of conflict prevention.

Religious Institutions

Despite the fact that a belief in peace and brotherhood is professed by a wide variety of faiths, religious leaders frequently support and even incite intergroup violence. Today, we note with deep concern a growing fringe in many religions that is characterized by self-glorification on the one hand, and a bigoted, often fanatical, deprecation of "outsider" groups on the other. While clearly dangerous, such extremist orientations are seldom dominant. Indeed, both historically and today, the core creed of most religions tends to support social tolerance, respect for others, concern for the vulnerable, and the peaceful resolution of disputes. Moreover, as noted earlier, religious leaders throughout the world enjoy extensive popular confidence and influence in educational institutions.

Religious education has tended to focus narrowly on indoctrination in the history and theology of the faith. Typically, however, there also has been an ethical content that could serve as the basis for expanded efforts to address the moral and practical necessity for groups to learn to live together amicably. The international community should challenge religious leaders and institutions to examine these issues in their own way—in their schools, from their pulpits, and in their organizations.

The United Nations

Education for the peaceful management of conflict must not be confined by national boundaries. Here, the international community can play a decisive role in broadening public education on a whole range of problems associated with intergroup violence.

Eritrean women participate in civic education.

ambitious and unprecedented, but not entirely fanciful, for the UN to sponsor, for example, leadership seminars in cooperation with major universities or research institutes to which would be invited new heads of state, new foreign ministers, new defense ministers, and parliamentarians of varying groups and parties. On an on-going basis, such seminars could educate leaders about how the UN and other international organizations can help them establish more effective and inclusive institutions for addressing disputes. Given the contemporary climate, it is singularly important that such seminars deal with the problems of nationalism, ethnocentrism, and violence, and that they do so in a way that takes account of all available knowledge about conflict prevention.

Through these seminars, as well as through its publications program and the wider media, the UN can make more accessible the world's accumulated experience with conflict and conflict prevention. In particular, the UN could serve as a storehouse of information about specific conflicts; the responsible handling of weapons of mass destruction; the likely consequences of unregulated weapons buildups;

The UN is already the world's premiere institution for conflict resolution and is likely to become even more active in the decades ahead. Various UN organizations can provide invaluable leadership in educating policymakers and the general public about resolving conflicts without violence. It would be

PREVENTING DEADLY CONFLICT

the skills, knowledge base, and prestige properly associated with successful conflict resolution; effective strategies for economic development, including innovative uses of science and technology for development; and lessons from cooperative behavior in the world community, including the peaceful management of disputes at the international level.

The UN system can make these resources and skills accessible to the world by creating a comprehensive information program in which important knowledge is provided to key policymakers on a regular basis. In the same vein, the UN can build an information network among community groups, nongovernmental organizations, academic institutions, and the corporate sector. In this way, accurate and credible information can be provided on both intergroup and interstate conflicts as well as on ways of managing them constructively.

One illustration of the potential for educational innovation is an initiative launched by UNESCO in May 1996 to promote tolerance, cooperation, and conflict prevention and resolution in schools.[2] The "Culture of Peace" has developed a conceptual framework that participating educational institutions in countries around the world will use to design their own education strategies. In addition to educational materials, curricula guides, and teacher training, the project emphasizes the importance of the values, attitudes, and behaviors of a culture of peace by ensuring that they are built into the social relations of the learning process itself. Pilot activities are focused on peaceful conflict resolution in schools serving communities where children live in violence-prone conditions. This effort could serve as a model for more widespread international initiatives. There is an urgent need for local, national, and international ingenuity in this field.

The international community can expand the range of favorable contacts between people of different groups and countries. A greater comprehension of other, often unfamiliar, cultures is essential to the reduction of negative preconceptions. To this end, educational, cultural, and scientific exchanges can have lasting value and should be encouraged. Likewise, the international community should seek to develop joint projects that allow more sustained cooperation across political and cultural borders. If only on a small scale, such endeavors offer the practical experience of working together in the pursuit of a superordinate, commonly beneficial goal. There are a number of ways to overcome antagonistic attitudes between groups and, preferably, to prevent them from arising in the first place. Thus far, however, societies have been remarkably inattentive to these possibilities.

Those who have a deep sense of belonging to groups that cut across ethnic, national, or sectarian lines may serve as bridges between different groups and help to move them toward a wider, more inclusive social identity. Building such bridges will require many people interacting across traditional barriers on a basis of mutual respect. Developing a personal identification with people beyond one's primary group has never been easy. Yet, broader identities are possible, and in the next century it will be necessary to encourage them on a larger scale than ever before.

THE CHALLENGE TO LEAD

Time and again, the Commission has returned to the indispensability of leadership. Without effective and responsible leadership, it would not be possible to implement the strategies and use the practical tools for preventing deadly conflict.

Mikhail Gorbachev, former president of the Soviet Union, reflected on his years of intense interaction with political leaders all over the world.[3] One of his more noteworthy observations was the pervasive tendency among leaders to view "brute force" as their ultimate source of validation. Gorbachev highlights the continuation of a long-standing—and

tional, chemical, and biological weapons, he was wise enough not to interpret his own authority in terms of "brute force." Gradually, Gorbachev, as had then-U.S. President Ronald Reagan, took a great step forward by replacing the old security concept of nuclear superiority with an explicit endorsement of the principle that nuclear war can never be won and must never be fought.

It will take unprecedented leadership skills to move the world toward the elimination

Five thousand women march for their rights in Goma, Democratic Republic of Congo.

historically deadly—inclination of leaders to reduce the art of leadership to being tough, aggressive, and even violent. Indeed, for all too many leaders, projecting an image of physical strength is still the essence of leadership. Although Gorbachev controlled a vast nuclear arsenal, as well as immense power in conven-

of nuclear weapons. We still must confront the fact that a misjudgment or miscalculation brought about by the interplay of personal and mechanical foibles could lead to a nuclear disaster. As long as these weapons exist, so does this threat.

Although the prevention of deadly conflict requires many tools and strategies, bold leadership and an active constituency for prevention are essential for these tools and strategies to be effective. One of the central objectives of this Commission has been to help leaders to become better informed about the problems at hand and to suggest useful ways to respond to them. However, we recognize that raising leaders' awareness, although necessary, is not sufficient. We have also sought to offer practical measures by which leaders can be motivated, encouraged, and assisted to adopt a preventive orientation that is supported by the best knowledge and skills available.

We believe that lessons learned in other contexts can be usefully applied to the prevention of deadly conflict. In the sphere of public health, the application of the concept of prevention is familiar. We believe this view of the prevention process offers a useful practical analogy. In much the same way that sustained medical research and conscientious public health practices have eliminated many deadly epidemics, we believe that the security and well-being of millions of people could be improved where knowledge, skill, and dedication are placed in the service of preventing deadly conflict.

We urge leaders to develop an explicit focus on prevention, not only elected officials, but also leaders in business, media, religion, and other influential communities. By virtue of both their power and public prominence, these leaders bear a serious responsibility for utilizing their public influence for constructive purposes. In both word and deed, they can shape an agenda for cooperation, caring, and decent human relations.

What kind of leadership are we talking about? While leadership for preventing deadly conflict is the specific focus of this report, we also have in mind a broader notion of leadership that encompasses effective, democratic governance, humanitarian values, and justice.

Lessons of World War II

In this century, we have witnessed abundant examples of leadership that was brutal and effective, as well as leadership that was decent but ineffective. The events leading to the carnage of World War II serve well to illustrate both of these variants of maladaptive leadership.

In the early 1930s, there were unmistakable signs that there would be a reign of terror if the National Socialists came to power in Germany. Adolf Hitler did not hide his brutality. He elaborated his foreign policy views in speeches and made his view on war especially clear in *Mein Kampf* in 1924. There were moments during Hitler's rise to power and in the years following when the international community could have taken preventive action. The atrocities of Hitler's storm troopers in his first months in office should have been a powerful warning: a regime that massively violates domestic law and egregiously violates human rights will create a similarly lawless foreign policy.

Why, then, in light of all these warnings, did leaders and publics around the world miscalculate, tolerate, and fatally fail to react to the danger posed by Hitler's rise to power in 1933? Why did the representatives of the leading democracies not make the connection between Hitler's brutal domestic and foreign policies? Why were they unwilling to confront

We urge leaders to develop an explicit focus on prevention, not only elected officials, but also leaders in business, media, religion, and other influential communities.

the formidable danger posed by Hitler, despite his explicit threats and overt actions?

In part, the democracies did not react quickly to the early aggressive acts of totalitarian states because of their preoccupation with the Depression and the severe domestic hardships it created. The massive loss of life in World War I made leaders, especially of the established democracies, particularly anxious to avoid another war at almost any cost. Leaders readily invented excuses for acts of international lawlessness as well as for their own aversion to taking action to stop them. They deluded themselves with the idea that Hitler simply desired a revision of the Versailles Treaty and the restoration of Germany's 1914 boundaries. Once these terms were met, they hoped that Hitler would become a law-abiding citizen or that he would be a short-lived political phenomenon. Some thought he was capable of fomenting ill-will but not of ruling and that he would be replaced by more moderate power groups once the economic and political crisis in Germany was overcome. Citizens in democracies did not want to be burdened with additional problems, and they largely supported their leaders' passivity or appeasement.

Overall, world leaders blinded themselves to the acts of aggression, thereby actually enhancing the probability of another world war. There is a powerful lesson in the ubiquitous human capacity for wishful thinking in the face of danger. Tragically, such thinking led the world to neglect numerous opportunities to prevent the horrific catastrophes of genocide and war that followed.

The grim lessons of prewar diplomacy alert us to the profoundly important and sometimes negative role played by the responses of leaders to early warning. Fanatical, ruthless, and otherwise highly dangerous leaders must be checked before they become so powerful that stopping them requires massive armed intervention. With strong responses to Hitler's aggression, World War II and the Holocaust could have been prevented.

The Vision of Nelson Mandela

Yet there are many leaders who are capable of learning, of acting creatively and effectively in the face of new dangers and new opportunities, and of accommodating the legitimate concerns of rival groups.[4] There is perhaps no better example of this kind of courageous and visionary leader than Nelson Mandela.

During his many years as a political prisoner, Mandela experienced firsthand what it meant to have legitimate aspirations constantly frustrated by arbitrary power. He had ample reason for anger and a tempting motive for retaliation. Indeed, he could have pursued his political aims through violent means. Instead, reflection led him to a different conclusion: while violent struggle might indeed destroy his adversaries, in the process it might also destroy his own people—physically as well as morally. As we noted in chapter 2, Mandela thus came to embrace reconciliation, negotiated solutions to political differences, and the joint creation of mutually beneficial arrangements. From a different starting point, F.W. de Klerk underwent a transformation of his own. Together, the two men were able to generate a process of peaceful regime change in South Africa that avoided massive violence, despite the social and political tensions that apartheid had created.

The same kind of leadership was responsible for the peaceful conclusion of the Cold War. The evolution of relations between

Reagan and Gorbachev was similar to that of Mandela and de Klerk. During the course of their complicated—and often uneasy—negotiations, they too moved to embrace mutually supportive positions. Both of these examples are highly suggestive of the decisive role that bold and enlightened leadership can play in avoiding catastrophe and building better relations, both between and within states.

Especially at a time when many countries are struggling with the new and uncertain challenges of democratization, the international community must champion the norm of responsible leadership and support opportunities for leaders to engage in negotiated, equitable solutions to intergroup disputes. Leaders who demonstrate good-will and who engage in these practices should be recognized and rewarded. By the same token, conditions should be fostered that would allow electorates to hold their leaders accountable when and where they depart from democratic norms of peaceful conflict resolution. The international community must expand efforts to educate publics everywhere that preventing deadly conflict is both necessary and possible. To miss the opportunity for preventive action is a failure of leadership.

A Rwandan refugee child stands near bodies of people killed by cholera and other waterborne diseases, July 1994.

Both the complexity and risk of taking action in many dangerous situations today highlight the need to *share burdens* and *pool strengths*. The task can be made more feasible by strengthening institutional arrangements to improve decision-making processes.

Emulating the armed men, Mogadishu children play with toy guns.

Toward Wiser Decision Making

In the search for sound and meaningful policies, certain trade-offs are inevitable. There are two competing constraints in particular that impinge on leadership choices and that very often create insoluble policy dilemmas. To be effective, leaders must be sensitive to these constraints and use careful judgment. The first constraint is the need to create and sustain a modicum of policy consensus, both within the various branches of government and among the public at large. A second constraint stems from the finite nature of policymaking resources, both tangible financial and personnel resources and more intangible resources such as time and clear mandate. The careful, systematic search for a comprehensive policy should not preclude

a timely decision; an unduly protracted search could reduce the likelihood of a successful outcome. Likewise, any investment of time and policymaking resources in support of one policy may interfere with the implementation of other, often equally important, measures.

Organizational, procedural, and staff arrangements that support decision making can be institutionalized in ways that foster these problem-solving processes. The many recommendations emerging from studies of effective policymaking apply to efforts to prevent deadly conflict.[5] These studies suggest there are ways to ensure that leaders receive high-quality information, analysis, and advice, and avoid omissions in surveying objectives and alternatives.

There are five tasks that must be well executed within a policymaking system if the leader is to receive information, analysis, and advice of high quality.[6] These procedures do not guarantee high-quality decisions, but they increase their probability. The first task is to ensure that sufficient information about the current situation is obtained and analyzed adequately. Second, the policymaking process must facilitate consideration of all the major values and interests affected by the policy issue at hand. Third, the process should ensure a search for a relatively wide range of options and a reasonably thorough evaluation of the expected consequences of each. Fourth, the policymaking process should carefully consider the problems that might arise in implementing the options under consideration. Finally, the process should remain receptive to indications that current policies are not working: it is important to retain the capacity to learn rapidly from experience.

In crisis situations requiring operational prevention, where decisions must be made quickly in response to unanticipated threats, decision-making hazards are often amplified. Crisis decision making normally encounters a variety of additional constraints, including the moral complexity of making life-or-death choices and the psychological stress of working with incomplete information in changing and uncertain conditions, where time and viable options are scarce. Very often, the gravity of the crisis means that long-term consequences are discounted in favor of short-term objectives.

To overcome these obstacles, leaders should seek to mobilize the best available information by relying on well-informed advisers with different perspectives and encouraging an atmosphere of candid expression. In this way, they can ease the difficulties of differentiating between possible and probable courses of action, of appraising the costs and benefits of alternative policies, and of distinguishing relevant from irrelevant information. Thus, decision makers can be better equipped to cope with ambiguity, to refrain from impulsive action, and to respond flexibly to new developments.

It is important for leaders to take into account the powerful phenomenon of wishful thinking, in which individuals hear what they want to hear because they deeply wish it were true. Crisis situations are almost always complex and ambiguous. This ambiguity can be read in wishfully inaccurate ways and with wildly disappointing results. World War I, for example, began with an anticipation on both sides of quick and glorious victories, only to end several years later in the unprecedented destruction of Europe.

Naturally, in deciding whether and how to participate in preventive efforts, leaders must consider national interests. Traditionally, national interests have been narrowly conceived in terms of vital geopolitical or military advantage and have been invoked to defend against clear and present military or economic threats.

The Commission believes that, on the eve of the twenty-first century, there is a need for a broader conception of national interests, one which encompasses both enlightened self-

On the eve of the twenty-first century, there is a need for a broader conception of national interests, one which encompasses both enlightened self-interest and a realistic appraisal of the contemporary world.

interest and a realistic appraisal of the contemporary world. When every violent conflict is dismissed as distant and inconsequential, we run the risk of allowing a series of conflict episodes to undermine the vitality of hard-won international norms. In a world of increased economic and political interdependence, in which national well-being increasingly depends on the security and prosperity of other states and peoples, indifference of this sort could have corrosive and consequential effects for everyone. Rather than rely on obsolete notions of national interest, leaders must develop formulations that reflect this new reality.

Preventing deadly conflict serves the most vital human interest—that of survival.

We have noted earlier the risks of mass violence growing out of degraded conditions: the fostering of hatred and terrorism, of infectious pandemics, of massive refugee flows, of dangerous environmental effects. All these risks must be taken into account in a world of unprecedented proximity and interdependence. They will have a bearing on realistic appraisals of national interest and the interest of the international community in the next century.

From this perspective, the Commission strongly believes that preventing deadly conflict serves the most vital human interest—that of survival. Clearly, any effort to promote the norms of tolerance, mutual assistance, responsible leadership, and social equity is valuable in its own right. But the prevention of deadly conflict has a practical as well as a moral value: where peace and cooperation prevail, so do security and prosperity. Witness the steps taken after World War II, which laid the groundwork for today's flourishing European Union. Leaders such as Jean Monnet and George Marshall looked beyond both the wartime devastation and the enmities that had caused it, and envisioned a Europe in which regional cooperation would transcend adversarial boundaries and traditional rivalries. Correctly, they foresaw that large-scale economic cooperation would facilitate not only the postwar recovery but also the long-term prosperity which has helped Europe to achieve a degree of peace and security once thought unattainable. Postwar reconstruction is an excellent example of building structural prevention by creating conditions that favor social and economic development and peaceful interaction. A long-range vision and a broad view of regional opportunities can be exceedingly constructive.

Realizing this vision was not easy. It required constant and creative efforts to educate the public, mobilize key constituencies, and persuade reluctant partners. Moreover, maintaining this support required the prudent use of scarce political and social capital. To take just one example, the Marshall Plan initially enjoyed very little support among the American public. Had it not been for the determination and skill of President Harry Truman, the program that made the single most important contribution to Europe's postwar reconstruction and development would probably never have been implemented. The Marshall Plan is a model of what sustained international cooperation can accomplish; no less, it is an extraordinary illustration of the decisive importance of visionary and courageous leadership.

THE CHALLENGE TO COMMUNICATE

One of the greatest obstacles to the creation of an enduring framework for preventive action is the human aversion to risk. Indeed, as with

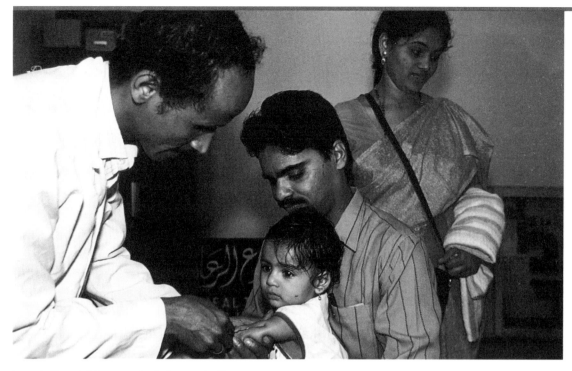

Inoculating children against disease in Yemen.

every new policy initiative, the prevention of conflict involves uncertainty and risk. Even the most well-designed and carefully coordinated preventive action can fail to achieve every objective. Very often, the results of prevention may be difficult to measure or may take considerable time to materialize. This means that leaders who bear the risk of undertaking new initiatives may no longer be in power when the time comes to claim the rewards of their success. Especially in pluralistic polities, leaders must in the meantime confront accusations that preventive missions waste resources or place military personnel in conditions of unnecessary risk, while achieving little. In view of all these hazards, how can leaders summon the determination and maintain the political will to act preventively?

One way is for leaders to focus on generating a broad constituency for prevention. With a public that is aware of the value of prevention and informed of the availability of constructive alternatives, the political risks of

sustaining preemptive engagement in the world are reduced. In practical terms, an enduring constituency for prevention could be fostered through measures that: identify latent popular inclinations toward prevention; reinforce these impulses with substantive explanations of rationales, approaches, and successful examples; make the message clearer by developing analogies from familiar contexts such as the home and community; and demonstrate the linkage between preventing deadly conflict and vital public interests. Such efforts are more likely to succeed if leaders can mobilize the media, the business community, and other influential and active groups in civil society.

Among the general public, there are already a range of dispositions, interests, and organizations that can be tapped for support. For example, as mentioned earlier, in a variety of democratic countries, a strong constituency for prevention in medicine and public health has emerged over the last several decades. Public awareness campaigns and the provision of information about health risks and preventive behavior have led to remarkable improvements in public health. Concepts like "an ounce of prevention is worth a pound of cure" have taken hold in the public imagination and are reflected positively in improved rates of immunization, better diet and exercise practices, and reduced cigarette smoking. In short, sustained public efforts at disease prevention have proven highly effective. This model of dedicated leadership and public education can be usefully applied to the prevention of deadly conflict. Earlier in this century, for example, U.S. President Franklin D. Roosevelt employed a similar approach, utilizing familiar examples, to make the imperative of international cooperative security during and after World War II meaningful for the American people. This strategy helped the United States to overcome domestic isolationist sentiments.

Community fire prevention provides another useful analogy. To put out fires early, one needs operational tools like fire alarms, reliable telephones, adequate supplies of water and firefighting equipment, and well-trained professionals. When it comes to the structural conditions under which fires are likely to occur, still other tools are needed—for example, specialized knowledge about hazardous substances and the skills to dispose of them safely, and public education about the perils of high-risk behavior. In short, effective firefighting requires both a ready stock of skills and tools as well as a long-term culture of prevention. The Commission is interested in putting out the fires of deadly conflict when they are small, before they get out of hand. But we are also concerned with eliminating conditions that make these fires likely in the first place.

In the past few years, there has been some concern about the United States reverting to the isolationist posture of the post–World War I era and forsaking the active internationalist role that it has performed so successfully since World War II, when U.S. leadership was instrumental in the creation of the UN, the World Bank, the International Monetary Fund, and NATO. Yet, careful analysis of recent survey research shows that popular opinion does not warrant this conclusion.[7] As in a number of other countries, the public is deeply aware of the wider world and is urging the government to assume greater international responsibilities.

Survey research indicates that the American public is not becoming parochial and isolationist in the post–Cold War era—a large majority of Americans continues to support U.S. involvement in international affairs.[8] But the American public does not support the idea of America acting as the "world's policeman" or global hegemon. Americans would prefer to see a revival of the kind of cooperative leadership and collective security that the United States demonstrated in supporting the creation of the UN.

Americans also support the development of the United Nations as the primary vehicle for international action.[9] They believe that the protection of human rights and the maintenance of global security are best achieved through collective efforts. Indeed, most Americans wish to see the United States assume a shared leadership role in multilateral organizations, including, where needed, participating in multilateral military interventions. Polls also show that Americans support foreign aid, particularly when it is used for humanitarian purposes.[10]

In the United States, as in many other countries, a nascent constituency for preventing deadly conflict already exists. To develop this constituency, leaders and their publics need an improved understanding of both the problems and the range of available solutions addressed by this Commission. These solutions—it bears repeating—call for the pooling of each country's respective strengths and an equitable sharing of burdens.

Consideration of contemporary public attitudes in the U.S. has led one scholar to elaborate a practical strategy for constituency building.[11] The key component of this strategy is the creation of an educational program that expressly addresses popular concerns about international involvement. As with people everywhere, most people in the industrialized democracies are concerned with the economic and social problems of daily life. They are perplexed by the rapid changes in the global economy and fearful of the potential for greater unemployment and a widened gap between rich and poor. They also tend to be suspicious of leadership priorities, believing that leaders are often more interested in advancing their own political careers than in promoting public interests. Many people are uneasy about international commitments because of concerns that the costs may be too high and the problems too difficult. Thus, leaders must work to clarify the links between the prevention of deadly conflict and domestic well-being. They must demonstrate to the public that preventive action, whether operational or structural in focus, is both cost-effective and able to generate desired results.

THE PROMISE OF PREVENTION

The twentieth century has witnessed some of the bloodiest, most destructive wars in recorded history. As the world approaches the eve of the third millennium, many unresolved intergroup and interstate conflicts continue to fester and to claim a massive toll in human lives and resources. For too long now, we have deluded ourselves with the complacent belief that the events in faraway lands are not our concern, that the problems of other peoples do not have consequences for us all. This short-sighted view has left us ill prepared to deal with conflicts when they occur. It has condemned us to muddle through from crisis to crisis, applying emergency first aid where what is most urgently needed are more fundamental solutions. This report has endeavored to show that we can indeed prevent deadly conflict—perhaps not easily, perhaps not quickly, but the capacity is within our grasp.

The record of this century also provides a compelling basis for hope. The decline of tyranny and the expansion of representative and responsive government, the protection of human rights, and the promotion of social justice and economic well-being—imperfect and incomplete though they are— suggest what human ingenuity can accomplish. If we are to lessen the destructiveness of humankind, we must pool our strengths to extend these achievements in the century to come. By placing the promise of prevention squarely at the forefront of the world's agenda, it is the hope of this Commission that leaders and publics will take up the challenges of education, leadership, and communication. Perhaps then we can achieve together the peace that has so far eluded us separately.

The prevention of deadly conflict has a practical as well as a moral value: where peace and cooperation prevail, so do security and prosperity.

ACRONYMS

ABACC	Argentinean–Brazilian Agency for Accounting and Control of Nuclear Materials
ADFL	Alliance of Democratic Forces for the Liberation of Congo-Zaire
ADRA	Adventist Development Relief Agency
AFRC	Armed Forces Revolutionary Council
AICF	Action Internationale Contre le Faim
ANC	African National Congress
APEC	Asia–Pacific Economic Cooperation
ARF	ASEAN Regional Forum
ASEAN	Association of Southeast Asian Nations
BASIC	British American Security Information Council
BBC	British Broadcasting Corporation
BWC	Biological Weapons Convention
CARE	Cooperative for Assistance and Relief Everywhere
CI	Caritas Internationalis (Catholic Organizations for Charitable and Social Action)
CBW	Chemical and Biological Weapons
CFE	Treaty on Conventional Armed Forces in Europe
CIS	Commonwealth of Independent States
COCOM	Coordinating Committee on Multilateral Export Controls (NATO)
CRS	Catholic Relief Services
CSCE	Conference on Security and Cooperation in Europe
CTBT	Comprehensive Test Ban Treaty
CTR	Cooperative Threat Reduction Program
CWC	Chemical Weapons Convention

DHA	Department of Humanitarian Affairs (UN)
DPKO	Department of Peacekeeping Operations (UN)
ECOMOG	ECOWAS Monitoring Group
ECOSOC	Economic and Social Council of the United Nations
ECOWAS	Economic Community of West African States
EU	European Union
FAO	Food and Agriculture Organization (UN)
FSU	Former Soviet Union
GDP	Gross Domestic Product
GDR	German Democratic Republic
IAEA	International Atomic Energy Agency
IBRD	International Bank for Reconstruction and Development
ICBM	Intercontinental Ballistic Missile
ICJ	International Court of Justice
ICRC	International Committee of the Red Cross
IDEA	Institute for Democracy and Electoral Assistance
IDP	Internally displaced person
IFI	International financial institution
IFOR	Implementation Force (NATO)
IMF	International Monetary Fund
IOM	International Organization for Migration
IRC	International Rescue Committee
MCI	Mercy Corps International
MCPMR	Mechanism for Conflict Prevention, Management, and Resolution (OAU)
MDM	Médecins du Monde
MERCOSUR	Mercado Común del Sur
MSF	Médecins Sans Frontières

NAFTA	North American Free Trade Agreement		SCF	Save the Children Federation
NAM	Nonaligned Movement		SFOR	Stabilization Force (NATO)
NAMFREL	National Citizens' Movement for Free Elections		SIPRI	Stockholm International Peace Research Institute
NATO	North Atlantic Treaty Organization		START	Strategic Arms Reduction Treaty
NGO	Nongovernmental organization		UN	United Nations
NORDEM	Norwegian Resource Bank for Democracy and Human Rights		UNAMIR	United Nations Assistance Mission for Rwanda
NOREPS	Norwegian Emergency Preparedness System		UNCIVPOL	United Nations Civilian Police
NP	National Party (South Africa)		UNDP	United Nations Development Program
NPT	Non-Proliferation Treaty		UNESCO	United Nations Educational, Scientific and Cultural Organization
OAS	Organization of American States		UNFICYP	United Nations Peacekeeping Force in Cyprus
OAU	Organization of African Unity		UNHCR	United Nations High Commissioner for Refugees
ODIHR	Office for Democratic Institutions and Human Rights (OSCE)		UNICEF	United Nations Children's Fund
OECD	Organization for Economic Cooperation and Development		UNMIH	United Nations Mission in Haiti
			UNMO	United Nations Military Observer
OIC	Organization of the Islamic Conference		UNPREDEP	United Nations Preventive Deployment Force (Former Yugoslav Republic of Macedonia)
OSCE	Organization for Security and Cooperation in Europe (formerly CSCE)		UNPROFOR	United Nations Protection Force
			UNRWA	United Nations Relief Works Agency for Palestine Refugees in the Near East
Oxfam	Oxford Committee for Famine Relief			
PER	Project on Ethnic Relations			
PFP	Partnership for Peace Program (NATO)		UNTAC	United Nations Transitional Authority in Cambodia
PKK	Kurdistan Workers' Party		UNTAG	United Nations Transition Assistance Group (Namibia)
PRC	People's Republic of China			
RPF	Rwandan Patriotic Front		UPD	Unit for the Promotion of Democracy (OAS)
RUF	Revolutionary United Front (Sierra Leone)		USAID	United States Agency for International Development
SAARC	South Asian Association for Regional Cooperation		USIA	United States Information Agency
SADC	Southern African Development Community		VOA	Voice of America
			WEU	Western European Union
SADCC	Southern African Development Coordination Conference		WFP	World Food Program
			WHO	World Health Organization
SAM	Sanctions Assistance Monitoring Team		WTO	World Trade Organization
SCCC	Common System of Accounting and Control of Nuclear Materials			

REGIONAL ARRANGEMENTS

When local parties to a dispute are unable to resolve their differences peacefully, regional arrangements are increasingly willing and able to take preventive action. This trend toward finding creative regional solutions for regional problems is being reinforced by the UN under Chapter VIII provisions of its Charter. The following examples of regional arrangements illustrate their growing capacity for conflict prevention. While this is not a definitive list, it suggests the capacities of the arrangements to bring together member states to discuss common problems and craft joint solutions. Whether designed primarily as security, economic, or dialogue groups, these arrangements can make contributions to conflict prevention in peaceful settlement of disputes, advancement of democracy, and protection of human rights.[1]

SECURITY ORGANIZATIONS

North Atlantic Treaty Organization (NATO).

NATO's current challenge is to find ways to adapt its sophisticated decision-making and operational capacities to the security problems faced by member states. This means not only developing prudent ways to react to destabilizing situations in the former Soviet Union, such as Chechnya, but also engaging in out-of-area activities, such as in the former Yugoslavia. NATO's deployment in Bosnia represents dramatic use of a defensive alliance to encourage the parties to a dispute to settle their differences peacefully. In its deployment in Bosnia, NATO's Stabilization Force (SFOR) has had to consider whether its role should expand to promote reconciliation by bringing to

justice people indicted by the International War Crimes Tribunal for the former Yugoslavia. NATO's Partnership for Peace is designed to help states of the former Warsaw Pact and newly independent states adapt to democratic governance and to build among the partnership countries a capacity to respond with military resources, when necessary, to a range of situations that may threaten peace. NATO's military-to-military programs advance civilian control of the military and promote democracy in the former Warsaw Pact countries. In addition, NATO is expanding to include countries in Central and Eastern Europe to further reduce risk and to build confidence among all the states of Europe.

Organization of American States (OAS).

The OAS has emphasized the need for member states to take an active role in the preservation of regional peace and stability. In the 1980s, President Oscar Arias Sánchez of Costa Rica and other leaders in Central and South America began to combine their efforts in a concerted approach to revitalize the role of the OAS in helping to end the violence that plagued many Latin American states. In 1987, Arias was awarded the Nobel Peace Prize for his efforts. The 1994 Miami Summit of the Americas served, in part, to confirm the progress of the OAS in this regard and its continuing role in preserving and strengthening democratic movements, protecting human rights, and eliminating poverty in the region.

In recent years, the OAS has been very active in promoting democracy. Passage of the Santiago Commitment in 1991 obligated signatories to act against violations of democratic norms in the hemisphere and indicated OAS states' willingness to intervene in each other's internal affairs, should the need arise. The OAS has used this procedure, also known as General Assembly Resolution 1080, four times to bolster democracy in Guatemala, Haiti, Paraguay, and Peru. The 1992 Protocol of Washington, which came into force September 25, 1997, adds a new article allowing the suspension of a member whose democratically elected government is overthrown by force.

In the Office of the Secretary General, the Unit for the Promotion of Democracy (UPD) was established to assist in democratic institution building, to encourage dialogue and information exchange, and to provide electoral assistance and other special programs. In 1995, the UPD initiated a Program for the Prevention and Resolution of Community-Level Conflicts in Guatemala and has spent considerable effort in researching root causes and aggravating factors of this conflict. It has also provided conflict resolution and mediation training for governmental and nongovernmental actors at local, regional, and national levels. The OAS has teamed up with the UN in conflict resolution operations in El Salvador, Guatemala, Nicaragua, and other countries.

The OAS has partner organizations that support human rights. The Inter-American Commission on Human Rights acts as a consultative organ of the OAS, while the Inter-American Court of Human Rights, an autonomous juridical institution of the OAS, interprets and applies the American Convention on Human Rights.

Organization of African Unity (OAU). The OAU was established in 1963 to promote respect for the territorial integrity and sovereign equality of newly independent African states in the postcolonial period. Its charter precludes interference in the internal affairs of member states, and this feature both reflects and reinforces member states' sensitivities to questions of sovereignty and unwanted interventions. As a consequence, the OAU has historically been reluctant to become involved in the internal disputes of member states. Over the years, however, the OAU has set up ad hoc commissions on regional issues such as the Western Sahara, Chad/Libya, and Mauritania/Senegal.[2] During 1991 and 1992, the OAU extended "good offices" to seven countries.[3] In recent years, the OAU has

devised more formal policy instruments for dispute resolution, and member states have worked to strengthen its ability to deal not only with ongoing violence, but with imminent violence as well. There has been a particular emphasis on early warning and information gathering. In 1993, the OAU established the OAU Mechanism for Conflict Prevention, Management, and Resolution (MCPMR) to help provide assistance to states beset by war; it has also strengthened the position of its secretary general for this purpose. The OAU created the African Peace Fund as a means to help finance the MCPMR and contributes five percent of its annual budget to the fund.

The OAU has developed an "African Charter on Human and Peoples' Rights" that came into force in 1986. The charter includes the principles of equality before the law, respect for life, prohibition of slavery and torture, freedom of conscience and assembly, equal pay for equal work, and the right to an education.[4]

Organization for Security and Cooperation in Europe (OSCE). The OSCE has long been involved in efforts to support the peaceful resolution of disputes. When still called the CSCE, it undertook preventive diplomacy missions of long duration in Chechnya, Estonia, Ukraine, Tajikistan, the former Yugoslavia, and other conflicts. Following the 1994 summit in Budapest, the OSCE broadened its approach to conflict management, formally establishing the Center for Preventive Action. The OSCE also has established a Court of Conciliation and Arbitration to offer members peaceful means to resolve disputes.[5] The OSCE's Office of the High Commissioner on National Minorities has taken on an important role in helping to broker peaceful solutions for the many groups that now find themselves in minority status in newly independent states. The OSCE has also assumed a broader role in promoting the transition to democracy and market economies of former Soviet bloc countries and newly independent states. The human rights agenda has been a pillar of the OSCE's activities since the signing of the Helsinki Final Act, which emphasized broad-based societal contacts (including among religious organizations), educational exchanges, and cultural cooperation.

Western European Union (WEU). The WEU was founded in 1948 as a collective defense mechanism, but quickly became overshadowed by NATO. In 1994, members revived the WEU as a defense component of the European Union (EU) and the European pillar within NATO. An example of its recent work on peaceful dispute settlement is the WEU's police element within the EU administration in the town of Mostar in Bosnia. This type of activity follows from the June 1992 Petersberg Declaration in which WEU foreign and defense ministers outlined a basis for preventive missions, including refugee and humanitarian assistance, peacekeeping, and peace enforcement operations. The ministers stated that the WEU could act on its own initiative in crises and at the request of the EU. Bulgaria, the Czech Republic, Estonia, Hungary, Latvia, Lithuania, Poland, Romania, and Slovakia have been admitted as associate partners, creating prospects for additional military cooperation.

ECONOMIC ORGANIZATIONS

Asia-Pacific Economic Cooperation (APEC) group. APEC was established in 1989 and has become an important forum for promoting economic growth and reducing trade barriers among its members. APEC countries have considered creating a regional dispute settlement mechanism to supplement that of the World Trade Organization. APEC's regular summit meetings provide opportunities for leaders to broaden their dialogue beyond economic matters to discuss a wide range of issues of mutual concern.

Economic Community of West African States (ECOWAS). The Treaty of Lagos created ECOWAS in 1975 to promote trade, cooperation, and self-reliance among 15 developing West African countries. In 1993, member states reformed the body to focus on measures to improve the free movement of goods and people. The new treaty also assigned ECOWAS the responsibility of preventing and settling regional conflicts, a step that added weight to the experimental peacekeeping effort that ECOWAS had under way in Liberia. ECOWAS has been a regional leader in dispute resolution. In 1990, for the first time, an all-African peacekeeping force, the ECOWAS Monitoring Group (ECOMOG), was deployed by an African multilateral organization to help restore order and prevent further conflict in a troubled African state. Four thousand troops from the Gambia, Ghana, Guinea, Nigeria, and Sierra Leone were deployed to Liberia. The force grew to 12,000 and was sustained with strong financial and political backing by Nigeria until Liberia finally held national elections in July 1997. A 1997 military coup in Monrovia also engaged ECOMOG forces in an effort to restore civilian government. ECOWAS has been active in supporting democracy, placing a trade embargo on Sierra Leone after a junta seized power from a democratically elected government.

European Union (EU). Although the EU traces its origin to an economic body, the European Coal and Steel Community, it has always had an underlying strategic purpose. The Coal and Steel Community brought together former adversaries France and Germany in a framework to manage resources that had been a source of conflict. The changing landscape of Europe has prompted the EU to take on a larger role in anticipating and managing conflicts even beyond the borders of member states. The Stability Pact developed by Edouard Balladur in 1994, for example, was designed to establish a means by which minority disputes in Central and Eastern Europe might be defused.[6]

Although the EU has focused on the strengthening and deepening of economic cooperation among its members, it has also taken steps to broaden its agenda by defining a common foreign and security policy and coordinating joint action. The European Parliament has taken several modest steps to become engaged more substantially in conflict prevention. A number of members have formed the Forum of the European Parliament for the Active Prevention of Conflicts—a loosely organized effort that seeks to investigate circumstances of incipient conflict and lobby for more active engagement. In addition, the EU's 1996 report on human rights urged the creation of a Center for Active Crisis Prevention and the establishment of a European Civil Corps to help EU member states deal more systematically and practically with potential conflict in Europe. This same report also called for the creation of a code of conduct for European businesses operating worldwide that would oblige them to abide by international agreements protecting fundamental human rights.[7]

Mercado Común del Sur (MERCOSUR). MERCOSUR was founded in 1991 by the Treaty of Asunción between Argentina, Brazil, Paraguay, and Uruguay. It has a formal dispute resolution mechanism, the Controversy Settling System, for commercial disputes. Beyond its formal structure, however, as the 1996 events in Paraguay demonstrated (discussed in chapter 6), the very existence of MERCOSUR combines the economic clout of its members and makes it a useful source of influence within the region in noneconomic matters as well.

Southern African Development Community (SADC). The first Southern African Development Coordination Conference (SADCC) was held in 1979 to harmonize development plans and promote collective security by reducing the economic dependence of ten southern African countries on South Africa. In 1992, in anticipation of the end of apartheid, a treaty was signed that transformed SADCC into SADC and included a commitment to achieve a fully developed common market. A tribunal has been established to arbitrate disputes between member states arising from the treaty. In 1994, SADC ministers of defense approved the establishment of a regional rapid deployment peacekeeping force to help contain regional conflicts or civil unrest in member states.

DIALOGUE ORGANIZATIONS

Association of Southeast Asian Nations (ASEAN). The original objective of ASEAN was to promote economic cooperation and development, but in recent years the organization has begun to explore how the shared interests of its members might enable it to take on additional tasks. ASEAN has developed mechanisms that could support dispute resolution. The ASEAN framework includes a ministerial-level High Council to help resolve disputes between members. The council offers good offices, and if parties agree, serves as a committee of mediation, inquiry, or concili-

ation. ASEAN together with its traditional dialogue partners has created a new, broader group, the ASEAN Regional Forum (ARF), to promote confidence-building mechanisms between states and preventive measures to anticipate and prevent potential conflicts. The ARF expands the links of ASEAN membership to other dialogue partner states primarily in the Asia/Pacific region, and has permitted still others to associate themselves with ARF deliberations through observer status. While ASEAN does not have specific instruments for promoting democracy or human rights, ASEAN representatives went to Cambodia following the July 1997 coup to help negotiate a settlement between Hun Sen and Prince Norodom Ranariddh. Although their overtures were rebuffed, this effort demonstrates the kind and level of effort ASEAN is prepared to take on behalf of its members.

The Commonwealth. Composed of the United Kingdom and most of its former colonies, the Commonwealth has evolved into a network of intergovernmental and nongovernmental organizations whose 54 member states account for 1.6 billion people, or over one quarter of the world's population. The heads of government meet biennially, and there are regular ministerial level meetings. Many of the 300 Commonwealth NGOs meet in an NGO Forum every two years under the auspices of the Commonwealth Foundation. The Commonwealth works to advance democracy within its member states and uses election observer groups, fact-finding missions, and suspension of members to advance these goals. The Commonwealth was a leader in the international anti-apartheid movement and forced South Africa to withdraw from membership in 1961. The organization imposed sanctions on Rhodesia after the Unilateral Declaration of Independence in 1965. The Commonwealth Ministerial Action Group (CMAG) was created in November 1995 to address breaches of the 1991 Harare Declaration, in which the members committed themselves to democracy, good governance, human rights, and the rule of law. Nigeria was the first case in which the CMAG was deployed following the suspension of Nigeria's membership in 1995 by the Commonwealth heads of government. The

CMAG has held discussions with the Nigerian government since then in an effort to restore democracy and reestablish normal relations between Abuja and the other Commonwealth members. In 1997, the Commonwealth withdrew recognition of the current regime in Sierra Leone after the army overthrew the elected government.

Nonaligned Movement (NAM). The NAM was formed in 1955 when a group of 29 predominantly newly independent states met in Bandung, Indonesia, to discuss colonialism, economic development, and the maintenance of peace. By 1961, Egypt, India, and Yugoslavia had taken the lead in establishing the NAM as a form of collective resistance to the two superpowers, with the ostensible goal of preventing deadly conflict between East and West. Today, the NAM has grown from 29 to over 100 members in a very loose and diverse coalition of states that operates by consensus; it has no means of enforcing its decisions. The NAM does not have a formal dispute resolution mechanism, nor does it promote democracy or human rights within member states. However, it does provide a voice for smaller states. Today, when the NAM meets, economic issues dominate the agenda. Indonesia has sought to promote a pragmatic role for the NAM that would emphasize research, training, and cooperation in science and technology for development as well as ways to improve the competitiveness of developing countries.

South Asian Association for Regional Cooperation (SAARC). Founded in 1985, the SAARC framework offers member states the opportunity to meet once a year to consider a wide range of issues. The organization has developed a facility for arbitration in commercial and industrial problems between members. SAARC has concentrated on a growing array of confidence-building programs to protect and educate children, provide adequate housing, protect the environment, and improve the living standards of the poor. SAARC has also conducted regional conventions that deal with illegal drugs, terrorism, and food security.

COUNTRIES CONTRIBUTING PERSONNEL TO UN PEACEKEEPING OPERATIONS

	UNTSO	UNMOGIP	UNEF I	UNOGIL	ONUC	UNSF	UNYOM	UNFICYP	DOMREP	UNIPOM	UNEF II	UNDOF	UNIFIL	UNGOMAP	UNIMOG	UNAVEM I	UNTAG	ONUCA	MINURSO	UNIKOM	UNAVEM II	ONUSAL	UNAMIC	UNPROFOR	UNTAC	UNOSOM I	ONUMOZ	UNOSOM II	UNOMUR	UNOMIG	UNOMIL	UNMIH	UNAMIR	UNASOG	UNMOT	UNAVEM III	UNCRO	UNPREDEP	UNMIBH	UNTAES	UNMOP	MONUA	UNTMIH
Afghanistan				X																																							
Albania																														X													
Algeria																X					X		X	X								X				X							
Antigua and Barbuda																																X											
Argentina	X		X	X			X							X	X		X	X	X	X	X	X		X		X				X	X					X	X	X	X	X	X		
Australia	X	X					X	X			X	X			X		X		X					X	X	X	X	X		X													
Austria	X			X			X				X	X		X	X		X		X	X				X	X	X				X		X	X			X					X		
Bahamas																																X											
Bangladesh														X			X			X	X			X	X	X	X	X	X	X	X	X	X	X	X	X	X	X	X	X	X	X	X
Barbados									X																							X											
Belgium	X	X						X									X			X				X	X			X		X		X				X	X		X	X			
Belize																																X											
Benin																																X											X
Bolivia																											X																
Botswana																											X	X	X														
Brazil			X		X	X				X	X						X		X		X	X		X		X				X	X		X			X	X	X			X	X	X
Brunei																									X																		
Bulgaria																									X											X	X		X			X	
Burma	X		X	X						X																																	
Cameroon																								X																			
Canada	X	X	X	X	X	X	X	X	X	X	X	X	X	X	X	X	X	X	X	X	X	X	X	X	X	X	X	X		X	X					X	X			X	X		X
Cape Verde																										X																	
Chad																																				X							
Chile	X	X		X				X											X	X				X																			
China	X																		X	X	X			X				X			X												
Colombia		X																	X			X	X		X																		
Congo																X	X							X						X			X			X						X	
Costa Rica																		X																									
Cuba																														X													
Czech Republic																												X		X		X	X				X	X			X	X	
Czechoslovakia														X	X		X							X	X	X																	
Denmark	X	X	X	X	X		X	X			X			X	X		X			X				X						X					X				X	X	X	X	
Djibouti																																		X	X								
Ecuador		X		X				X											X			X																					
Egypt														X					X		X			X	X	X	X			X		X				X	X		X	X	X	X	
El Salvador																			X																								

	UNTSO	UNMOGIP	UNEF I	UNOGIL	ONUC	UNSF	UNYOM	UNFICYP	DOMREP	UNIPOM	UNEF II	UNDOF	UNIFIL	UNGOMAP	UNIIMOG	UNAVEM I	UNTAG	ONUCA	MINURSO	UNIKOM	UNAVEM II	ONUSAL	UNAMIC	UNPROFOR	UNTAC	UNOSOM I	ONUMOZ	UNOSOM II	UNOMUR	UNOMIG	UNOMIL	UNMIH	UNAMIR	UNASOG	UNMOT	UNAVEM III	UNCRO	UNPREDEP	UNMIBH	UNTAES	UNMOP	MONUA	UNTMIH
Estonia																																					X		X				
Ethiopia					X					X																							X										
Fiji														X	X		X			X			X	X									X		X						X	X	
Finland	X	X	X	X				X			X	X	X	X	X	X	X			X	X			X			X	X								X	X	X	X	X			
France	X												X			X		X	X			X	X	X			X			X			X			X	X	X	X	X	X	X	X
Germany (GDR)																	X																										
Germany (FRG)														X	X	X	X			X	X	X		X			X						X			X	X						
Ghana					X		X			X			X	X	X	X	X			X	X	X		X	X		X	X					X	X		X	X	X	X	X			
Greece														X		X	X										X						X										
Guatemala																																X											
Guinea					X																												X										
Guinea-Bissau																					X			X					X	X	X		X							X			
Guyana																		X			X			X									X	X									
Honduras																			X														X		X								
Hungary								X					X		X	X	X	X		X				X			X	X	X				X	X			X			X			
India		X	X	X	X	X	X							X	X	X	X		X	X	X	X	X	X			X	X		X	X	X	X				X					X	X
Indonesia			X	X	X				X				X		X				X			X	X	X	X			X								X	X	X	X	X			
Iran					X						X	X																															
Ireland	X			X	X	X		X			X	X		X	X	X			X	X	X	X	X	X			X	X			X					X	X	X	X	X			
Italy	X	X		X	X		X			X			X		X		X		X	X				X			X	X					X										
Jamaica																			X													X											
Japan												X							X						X	X																	
Jordan														X						X			X	X	X			X	X	X	X		X	X	X	X	X	X	X	X	X	X	X
Kenya													X		X			X	X					X	X			X			X		X	X	X	X	X	X	X	X	X	X	X
Korea, Republic of		X																	X								X	X					X							X			
Kuwait																																	X										
Liberia					X																																						
Lithuania																								X													X						
Luxembourg																								X																			
Malawi																																	X										
Malaysia					X								X		X		X		X	X	X			X	X	X		X		X			X		X	X	X	X			X		
Mali					X																									X	X		X									X	X
Mexico		X																								X																	
Morocco					X																X			X	X		X						X										
Namibia																											X						X									X	
Nepal			X					X	X		X	X								X				X	X			X	X				X				X	X	X	X	X		
Netherlands	X			X	X		X			X			X			X				X			X	X	X			X	X	X		X				X	X	X	X	X		X	
New Zealand	X	X		X			X		X				X			X			X	X	X	X		X				X					X			X	X	X			X	X	X
Niger																																	X										
Nigeria				X	X					X			X		X		X			X	X			X	X			X					X	X			X	X			X	X	X
Norway	X	X	X	X	X		X			X			X			X	X	X		X	X	X	X		X	X	X	X								X	X	X	X	X	X	X	

	UNTSO	UNMOGIP	UNEF I	UNOGIL	ONUC	UNSF	UNYOM	UNFICYP	DOMREP	UNIPOM	UNEF II	UNDOF	UNIFIL	UNGOMAP	UNIIMOG	UNAVEM I	UNTAG	ONUCA	MINURSO	UNIKOM	UNAVEM II	ONUSAL	UNAMIC	UNPROFOR	UNTAC	UNOSOM I	ONUMOZ	UNOSOM II	UNOMUR	UNOMIG	UNOMIL	UNMIH	UNAMIR	UNASOG	UNMOT	UNAVEM III	UNCRO	UNPREDEP	UNMIBH	UNTAES	UNMOP	MONUA	UNTMIH
Pakistan					X	X	X										X		X	X			X	X	X	X	X			X	X	X	X			X	X	X	X	X	X	X	X
Panama										X							X																										
Peru				X							X	X			X		X		X																								
Philippines					X																			X				X							X								
Poland											X	X	X	X	X		X		X	X			X	X	X				X	X			X			X	X	X	X	X	X	X	X
Portugal				X													X			X				X													X	X	X	X	X	X	X
Romania																				X								X					X									X	
Russian Federation	X																		X	X			X	X	X			X	X	X	X	X				X	X	X	X	X	X	X	
Saint Kitts and Nevis																																X											
Saint Lucia																																X											
Saudi Arabia																										X																	
Senegal											X		X		X				X	X			X	X	X				X				X			X	X	X	X		X		
Sierra Leone				X																																							
Singapore															X						X	X			X																		
Slovak Republic																				X		X							X		X					X	X		X		X		
Soviet Union																	X				X	X		X																			
Spain														X	X	X				X	X			X				X					X			X	X	X					
Sri Lanka		X		X	X					X																		X															
Sudan					X												X																										
Suriname																																X											
Sweden	X	X	X		X	X	X	X			X	X		X	X	X	X	X		X	X	X		X	X	X	X		X	X						X	X	X	X	X	X	X	
Switzerland	X																X			X	X			X				X			X				X	X	X	X	X	X			
Tanzania	X																																			X				X			
Thailand				X													X			X			X	X	X																		
Togo																	X			X							X		X	X													X
Trinidad and Tobago																	X															X											
Tunisia				X													X			X			X	X	X			X			X	X				X					X	X	
Turkey										X										X				X				X								X					X	X	
Ukraine																								X												X	X	X	X	X	X	X	X
United Arab Emirates																										X																	
United Kingdom							X										X			X	X		X	X	X			X			X					X	X	X			X	X	
United Arab Republic					X																																						
United States	X	X			X														X	X			X	X	X	X	X				X					X	X	X					X
Uruguay		X															X		X	X			X				X			X	X		X			X	X					X	
Venezuela										X						X	X	X	X																								
Yugoslavia			X		X		X									X	X	X		X																							
Zambia																	X									X	X						X		X							X	
Zimbabwe																X							X				X	X					X									X	

Sources: United Nations, *The Blue Helmets: A Review of United Nations Peace-keeping*, 3rd ed. (New York: United Nations Department of Public Information, 1996); United Nations Secretariat, Department of Peacekeeping Operations, Sept. 30, 1997.

PEACEKEEPING OPERATIONS

UNTSO
United Nations Truce Supervision Organization
Egypt, Gaza, Golan Heights, Israel, Jordan, Lebanon,
Syria, and the West Bank
June 1948 to present

UNMOGIP
United Nations Military Observer Group in India and
Pakistan
January 1949 to present

UNEF I
First United Nations Emergency Force
Egypt, Gaza, and Israel
November 1956 to June 1967

UNOGIL
United Nations Observer Group in Lebanon
June 1958 to December 1958

ONUC
United Nations Operations in the Congo
July 1960 to June 1964

UNSF
United Nations Security Force in West New Guinea
(West Irian)
October 1962 to April 1963

UNYOM
United Nations Yemen Observation Mission
Yemen and Saudi Arabia
July 1963 to September 1964

UNFICYP
United Nations Peacekeeping Force in Cyprus
March 1964 to present

DOMREP
Mission of the Representative of the Secretary-General
in the Dominican Republic
May 1965 to October 1966

UNIPOM
United Nations India-Pakistan Observation Mission
September 1965 to March 1966

UNEF II
Second United Nations Emergency Force
Sinai
October 1973 to July 1979

UNDOF
United Nations Disengagement Observer Force
Golan Heights
June 1974 to present

UNIFIL
United Nations Interim Force in Lebanon
March 1978 to present

UNGOMAP
United Nations Good Offices Mission in Afghanistan
and Pakistan
May 1988 to March 1990

UNIIMOG
United Nations Iran-Iraq Military Observer Group
August 1988 to February 1991

UNAVEM I
United Nations Angola Verification Mission I
January 1989 to May 1991

UNTAG
United Nations Transition Assistance Group
Namibia
April 1989 to March 1990

ONUCA
United Nations Observer Group in Central America
Costa Rica, El Salvador, Guatemala, Honduras, and
Nicaragua
November 1989 to January 1992

MINURSO
United Nations Mission for the Referendum in Western
Sahara
April 1991 to present

UNIKOM
United Nations Iraq-Kuwait Observation Mission
April 1991 to present

UNAVEM II
United Nations Angola Verification Mission II
May 1991 to February 1995

ONUSAL
United Nations Observer Mission in El Salvador
July 1991 to April 1995

UNAMIC
United Nations Advance Mission in Cambodia
October 1991 to March 1992

UNPROFOR
United Nations Protection Force
Bosnia and Herzegovina, Croatia, and the Former
Yugoslav Republic of Macedonia
March 1992 to December 1995

UNTAC
United Nations Transitional Authority in Cambodia
March 1992 to September 1993

UNOSOM I
United Nations Operation in Somalia I
April 1992 to March 1993

ONUMOZ
United Nations Operation in Mozambique
December 1992 to December 1994

UNOSOM II
United Nations Operation in Somalia II
March 1993 to March 1995

UNOMUR
United Nations Observer Mission Uganda-Rwanda
June 1993 to September 1994

UNOMIG
United Nations Observer Mission in Georgia
August 1993 to present

UNOMIL
United Nations Observer Mission in Liberia
September 1993 to present

UNMIH
United Nations Mission in Haiti
September 1993 to June 1996

UNAMIR
United Nations Assistance Mission for Rwanda
October 1993 to March 1996

UNASOG
United Nations Auozou Strip Observer Group
Chad and Libya
May 1994 to June 1994

UNMOT
United Nations Mission of Observers in Tajikistan
December 1994 to present

UNAVEM III
United Nations Angola Verification Mission III
February 1995 to June 1997

UNCRO
United Nations Confidence Restoration Operation in
Croatia
March 1995 to January 1996

UNPREDEP
United Nations Preventive Deployment Force
Former Yugoslav Republic of Macedonia
March 1995 to present

UNMIBH
United Nations Mission in Bosnia and Herzegovina
December 1995 to present

UNTAES
United Nations Transitional Administration for Eastern
Slavonia, Baranja, and Western Sirmium
Croatia
January 1996 to present

UNMOP

United Nations Mission of Observers in Prevlaka

Croatia

January 1996 to present

MONUA

United Nations Observer Mission in Angola

July 1997 to present

UNTMIH

United Nations Transition Mission in Haiti

August 1997 to present

COMMISSION
PUBLICATIONS

REPORTS

- Graham T. Allison and Hisashi Owada, *The Responsibilities of Democracies in Preventing Deadly Conflict: Reflections and Recommendations,* forthcoming.
- *Comprehensive Disclosure of Fissionable Materials: A Suggested Initiative,* June 1995.
- Larry Diamond, *Promoting Democracy in the 1990s: Actors and Instruments, Issues and Imperatives,* December 1995.
- *Emerging Principles for the Use of Force in the Post–Cold War Era,* forthcoming.
- *Essays on Leadership* (by Boutros Boutros-Ghali, George Bush, Jimmy Carter, Mikhail Gorbachev, and Desmond Tutu), *December 1998.*
- Anthony Fainberg and Alan Shaw, *Nonlethal Technologies and the Prevention of Deadly Conflict,* forthcoming.
- Scott R. Feil, *Preventing Genocide: How the Early Use of Force Might Have Succeeded in Rwanda,* April 1998.
- Alexander L. George and Jane E. Holl, *The Warning–Response Problem and Missed Opportunities in Preventive Diplomacy,* May 1997.
- Tom Gjelten, *Professionalism in War Reporting: A Correspondent's View,* June 1998.
- Andrew J. Goodpaster, *When Diplomacy Is Not Enough: Managing Multinational Military Interventions,* July 1996.
- Nik Gowing, *Media Coverage: Help or Hindrance in Conflict Prevention?,* September 1997.
- David A. Hamburg, *Education for Conflict Resolution,* April 1995.
- David A. Hamburg, *Preventing Contemporary Intergroup Violence,* April 1994.
- Bruce Hoffman and Paul Wilkinson, with Suzanne M. Neilson, *A Violent Trajectory: How Terrorist Campaigns Evolve into Insurgencies,* forthcoming.
- Jane E. Holl, *Political Will,* forthcoming.
- George A. Joulwan and Christopher C. Shoemaker, *Civilian–Military Cooperation in the Prevention of Deadly Conflict: Implementing Agreements in Bosnia and Beyond,* December 1998.
- Donald M. Kennedy, *Environmental Quality and Regional Conflict,* December 1998.
- Gail W. Lapidus with Svetlana Tsalik, eds., *Preventing Deadly Conflict: Strategies and Institutions,* Proceedings of a Conference in Moscow, Russian Federation, April 1998.
- Edward J. Laurance, *Light Weapons and Intrastate Conflict: Early Warning Factors and Preventive Action,* July 1998.
- Douglas E. Lute, *Improving National Capacity to Respond to Complex Emergencies: The U.S. Experience,* April 1998.
- Francisco R. Sagasti with Elsa Bardalez, *Development for Conflict Prevention,* forthcoming.
- Timothy D. Sisk, *Power Sharing and International Mediation in Ethnic Conflicts,* June 1996 (copublished with the United States Institute of Peace Press).
- John Stremlau, *Sharpening International Sanctions: Toward a Stronger Role for the United Nations,* November 1996.
- John Stremlau with Helen Zille, *A House No Longer Divided: Progress and Prospects for Democratic Peace in South Africa,* July 1997.
- John Stremlau, *People in Peril: Human Rights, Humanitarian Action, and Preventing Deadly Conflict,* May 1998.
- John Stremlau and Francisco R. Sagasti, *Preventing Deadly Conflict: Does the World Bank Have a Role?,* June 1998.
- Symeon Tsomokos, *Business Diplomacy and Conflict Prevention: The Greek-Turkish Case,* forthcoming.
- Arturo Valenzuela, *The Collective Defense of Democracy: Lessons from the Paraguayan Crisis,* forthcoming.
- Cyrus R. Vance and David A. Hamburg, *Pathfinders for Peace: A Report to the UN Secretary-General on the Role of Special Representatives and Personal Envoys,* September 1997.
- M. James Wilkinson, *Resolving Greek–Turkish Hostility: From Conflict Prevention to Reconciliation,* forthcoming.

BOOKS*

- R. Scott Appleby, *The Ambivalence of the Sacred: Religion, Violence, and Reconciliation,* forthcoming.
- Henri J. Barkey and Graham E. Fuller, *Turkey's Kurdish Question,* 1998.
- Jeffrey Boutwell and Michael T. Klare, eds., *Light Weapons and Civil Conflict: Controlling the Tools of Violence,* forthcoming.
- Michael E. Brown and Richard N. Rosecrance, eds., *The Costs of Conflict: Prevention and Cure in the Global Arena,* 1999.
- Allison L.C. de Cerreño and Alexander Keynan, eds., *Scientific Cooperation, State Conflict: The Roles of Scientists in Mitigating International Discord.* New York Academy of Sciences, 1998.
- David Cortright, ed., *The Price of Peace: Incentives and International Conflict Prevention,* 1997.
- Shai Feldman and Abdullah Toukan, *Bridging the Gap: A Future Security Architecture for the Middle East,* 1997.
- Melanie Greenberg, John Barton, and Margaret McGuinness, eds., *Mediation and Arbitration to Prevent Deadly Conflict,* forthcoming.
- Bruce W. Jentleson, ed., *Opportunities Missed, Opportunities Seized: Preventive Diplomacy in the Post–Cold War World,* forthcoming.
- Robert B. Oakley, Michael J. Dziedzic, and Eliot M. Goldberg, eds., *Policing the New World Disorder.* National Defense University, 1998.
- Connie Peck, *Sustainable Peace: The Role of the UN and Regional Organizations in Preventing Conflict,* 1998.
- I. William Zartman, ed., *Negotiating to Prevent Escalation and Violence,* forthcoming.

SELECTED PUBLICATIONS OF CARNEGIE CORPORATION'S PROGRAM ON PREVENTING DEADLY CONFLICT

- Graham T. Allison, Owen R. Coté, Jr., Richard R. Falkenrath, and Steven E. Miller, *Avoiding Nuclear Anarchy: Containing the Threat of Loose Russian Nuclear Weapons and Fissile Material* (Cambridge, MA: MIT Press, 1996).
- Alexei Arbatov, Abram Chayes, Antonia Handler Chayes, and Lara Olson, eds., *Managing Conflict in the Former Soviet Union: Russian and American Perspectives* (Cambridge, MA: MIT Press, 1997).
- Michael E. Brown, Owen R. Coté, Jr., Sean M. Lynn-Jones, and Steven E. Miller, eds., *Nationalism and Ethnic Conflict* (Cambridge, MA: MIT Press, 1997).
- Michael E. Brown, Sean M. Lynn-Jones, and Steven E. Miller, eds., *Debating the Democratic Peace* (Cambridge, MA: MIT Press, 1996).
- Michael E. Brown, ed., *The International Dimensions of Internal Conflict* (Cambridge MA: MIT Press, 1996).
- Abram Chayes and Antonia Handler Chayes, eds., *Preventing Conflict in the Post-Communist World: Mobilizing International and Regional Organizations* (Washington, DC: Brookings, 1996).
- Antonia Handler Chayes, Abram Chayes, and George Raach, *Beyond Reform: Restructuring for More Effective Conflict Intervention* (Cambridge, MA: Conflict Management Group, 1996).
- Committee on International Security and Arms Control, *Managing and Disposition of Excess Weapons Plutonium: Reactor-related Options* (Washington, DC: National Academy of Sciences, 1995).
- Larry Diamond and Marc F. Plattner, eds., *Civil–Military Relations and Democracy* (Baltimore, MD: Johns Hopkins University Press, 1996).
- Maria Drohobycky, ed., *Crimea: Dynamics, Challenges, and Prospects* (Lanham, MD: Rowman & Littlefield, 1995).
- Maria Drohobycky, ed., *Managing Ethnic Tension in the Post-Soviet Space: The Examples of Kazakhstan and Ukraine* (Washington, DC: American Association for the Advancement of Science, 1995).
- Miriam Elman, ed., *Paths to Peace: Is Democracy the Answer?* (Cambridge, MA: MIT Press, 1997).
- Richard N. Haass and Gideon Rose, *A New U.S. Policy toward India and Pakistan* (New York: Council on Foreign Relations, 1997).
- John Marks and Eran Fraenkel, "Working To Prevent Conflict in the New Nation of Macedonia," *Harvard Negotiation Journal* 13, No. 3, July 1997.
- Charles William Maynes and Richard S. Williamson, eds., *U.S. Foreign Policy and the United Nations System* (New York: W.W. Norton & Co., 1996).
- Roald Z. Sagdeev and Susan Eisenhower, *Central Asia: Conflict, Resolution, and Change* (Chevy Chase, MD: CPSS Press, 1995).
- Augusto Varas, James A. Schear, and Lisa Owens, eds., *Confidence-Building Measures in Latin America, Central America and the Southern Cone* (Washington, DC: Stimson Center; Chile: LASCO–Chile, 1995).

*Books are published by Rowman & Littlefield unless otherwise indicated. They can be ordered by phone (1-800-462-6420), fax (1-800-338-4550), or mail: 15200 NBN Way, P.O. Box 191, Blue Ridge Summit, PA 17214, USA.

ABOUT THE
COMMISSIONERS

DAVID A. HAMBURG, cochair of the Commission, is president emeritus of Carnegie Corporation of New York, having served as president of the Corporation from 1983 to 1997. In addition to holding academic posts at Stanford and Harvard universities, he has been president of the Institute of Medicine, National Academy of Sciences. He has also been president and chairman of the board of the American Association for the Advancement of Science. Dr. Hamburg has served on the Chief of Naval Operations Executive Panel and currently serves on the Defense Policy Board of the U.S. Department of Defense. He is also a member of the President's Committee of Advisors on Science and Technology. He has long been concerned with the problems of human aggression and violence, especially with violence prevention and conflict resolution, and he is the author or coauthor of numerous publications on these subjects.

CYRUS R. VANCE, cochair of the Commission, is a partner in the New York law firm of Simpson Thacher & Bartlett. Mr. Vance was U.S. secretary of state from 1977 to 1980 during the Carter administration. He was secretary of the army from 1962 to 1964 and deputy secretary of defense from 1964 to 1967. From 1991 to 1993 Mr. Vance served as personal envoy of the secretary-general of the United Nations in the Yugoslavia crisis and as UN cochairman of the International Conference on the Former Yugoslavia (Lord Owen was the European Union cochairman of the conference). Mr. Vance was also personal envoy of the secretary-general in Nagorno-Karabakh and South Africa in 1992. He has been the secretary-general's personal envoy in the negotiations between Greece and the Former Yugoslav Republic of Macedonia (FYROM) from 1993 to the present. He has served as special representative of the U.S. president in civil disturbances in Detroit (1967), in the Cyprus crisis (1967),

and in Korea (1968), and he was one of two U.S. negotiators at the Paris Peace Conference on Vietnam (1968-1969).

GRO HARLEM BRUNDTLAND was the first woman prime minister of Norway, serving in that position three times: in 1981, from 1986 to 1989, and from 1990 to 1997. She has been a member of the Storting (parliament) since 1977 and was minister of the environment from 1974 to 1979. Mrs. Brundtland was leader of the Norwegian Labour Party from 1981 to 1992. She is first vice president of the Socialist International and was a member of the Independent Commission on Disarmament and Security Issues (the Palme Commission). From 1983 to 1987, she chaired the World Commission on Environment and Development, which produced the influential report, *Our Common Future*. She is currently director-general of the World Health Organization.

VIRENDRA DAYAL joined the Office of the United Nations High Commissioner for Refugees (UNHCR) in 1965, and for the next 14 years he was involved in the management of operations to protect and assist refugees in Africa, Asia, the Americas, and the Middle East. In 1979 he was appointed director of the Office of Special Political Affairs in the offices of the secretary-general, and in 1982 Secretary-General Pérez de Cuéllar asked him to serve as his chef de cabinet, with the rank of under-secretary-general. He continued to serve in this capacity with both Pérez de Cuéllar and Secretary-General Boutros-Ghali until March 1992, when he retired. After his retirement, he assisted Boutros-Ghali in writing *An Agenda for Peace*, and in September 1992 the secretary-general sent him to South Africa as his personal envoy. Since October 1993, Mr. Dayal has been serving as a member of the National Human Rights Commission of India.

GARETH EVANS is deputy leader of the opposition in the Australian Parliament. He was a minister for all 13 years of the Labour Government, most notably serving as Australian foreign minister from 1988 until the government's electoral defeat in March 1996. In 1989 Mr. Evans chaired the inaugural ministerial meeting to establish APEC (Asia–Pacific Economic Cooperation), and from 1989 to 1991 he played a leading role in developing the UN peace plan for Cambodia. Mr. Evans also led the Australian government's Chemical Weapons Convention initiatives, and in 1995 was instrumental in establishing the Canberra Commission on the Elimination of Nuclear Weapons. Among his publications is the 1993 book, *Cooperating for Peace*, and the 1994 *Foreign Policy* article, "Cooperative Security and Intrastate Conflict," for which he won the 1995 Grawemeyer Prize for Ideas Improving World Order.

ALEXANDER L. GEORGE is Graham H. Stuart Professor Emeritus of International Relations at Stanford University. A leading academic specialist on deterrence, crisis prevention and management, and coercive diplomacy, Dr. George came to Stanford in 1968 after 20 years at the Rand Corporation, where he had been head of the social science department. The most recent of his many scholarly publications are *Limits of Coercive Diplomacy* (1994) and *Bridging the Gap: Theory and Practice of Foreign Policy* (1993). *Deterrence in American Foreign Policy*, which he coauthored with Richard Smoke, won the Bancroft Prize in 1975. In 1983 he was the recipient of a MacArthur Foundation Five-Year Prize Award.

FLORA MacDONALD, a former foreign minister of Canada, is a native of Nova Scotia. She served from 1972 to 1988 as member of parliament for Kingston and the Islands (Ontario), during which time she held three cabinet positions: secretary of state for external affairs, minister of employment and immigration, and minister of communications. In 1989 the secretary-general of the United Nations appointed her to the Eminent Persons' Group to study transnational corporations in South Africa. She was the chairperson of the International Development Research Center from 1992 to 1997. In 1993 Miss MacDonald was named an Officer of the Order of Canada.

DONALD F. McHENRY is Distinguished Professor in the Practice of Diplomacy at Georgetown University. As U.S. permanent representative to the United Nations from 1979 to 1981, Ambassador McHenry was a member of President Jimmy Carter's cabinet. He had served as U.S. deputy representative to the UN Security Council from 1977 to 1979. He has represented the United States in a number of other international forums and was the U.S. negotiator on the question of Namibia. After ten years at the Department of State, he joined the Carnegie Endowment for International Peace in 1973 as a project director in Humanitarian Policy Studies. He has taught at Southern Illinois, Howard, American, and Georgetown universities.

OLARA A. OTUNNU is UN Special Representative on Children and Armed Conflict and president of the International Peace Academy, an independent, international institution affiliated with the United Nations and devoted to promoting peacemaking, preventive action, and peacekeeping in international and internal conflicts. Mr. Otunnu practiced and taught law before serving successively as a member of the Uganda Consultative Council (interim parliament), Uganda's permanent representative to the United Nations, and minister of foreign affairs. During his tenure at the UN, Mr. Otunnu served in various capacities, including president of the Security Council, chairman of the UN Commission on Human Rights, chairman of the Contact Group on Global Negotiations, and vice president of the UN General Assembly. After the period in diplomacy and government, Mr. Otunnu returned to academia, conducting research and teaching in Paris, before assuming his present position. He is currently a member of the UN Study on the Impact of Armed Conflict on Children and the Commission on Global Governance.

DAVID OWEN is a member of the House of Lords in the United Kingdom, chancellor of Liverpool University, and chairman of Humanitas, a charitable organization that builds on the work of the Independent Commission on International Humanitarian Issues, of which he was a member from 1983 to 1986. From August 1992 to June 1995, he was the European Union cochairman of the International Conference on the Former Yugoslavia (Cyrus Vance was the UN cochairman until 1993). Lord Owen was a member of the House of Commons from 1966 to 1992. During that time, under Labour governments, he served as Navy Minister, Health Minister, and Secretary of State for Foreign and Commonwealth Affairs. He cofounded the Social Democratic Party which he led from 1983 to 1990. He was a member of the Palme Commission from 1980 to 1989.

SHRIDATH RAMPHAL, a former foreign minister of Guyana, was secretary general of the Commonwealth from 1975 to 1990. He is cochairman of the Commission on Global Governance, whose report, *Our Global Neighborhood*, was published in January 1995. He chairs the board of the International Institute for Democracy and Electoral Assistance in Stockholm and the international steering committee of LEAD, the Leadership for Environment and Development program. Sir Shridath is a member of the council of the International Negotiation Network set up by former U.S. president Jimmy Carter and of the board of Canada's International Development Research Center. He is also chancellor of the University of the West Indies and of the University of Warwick in England. In 1991 he was a special advisor to the secretary-general of the UN Conference on Environment and Development—the Earth Summit—for which he wrote the book, *Our Country the Planet: Forging a Partnership for Survival*.

ROALD Z. SAGDEEV is Distinguished Professor in the department of physics at the University of Maryland and director of the East–West Space Science Center. Professor Sagdeev, whose area of special interest is nonlinear physics and plasmas, is one of the world's leading physicists. He was director of the Space Research Institute of the USSR Academy of Sciences for 15 years and was former president Gorbachev's science advisor. In 1987–1988 he was chairman of the Committee of Soviet Scientists for Global Security. Professor Sagdeev was a people's deputy of the USSR Congress, roughly the equivalent of a delegate to the U.S. Constitutional Convention. He has long been a strong and effective advocate of building bridges of understanding between the superpowers.

JOHN D. STEINBRUNER is a senior fellow at the Brookings Institution. From 1978 to 1997 he was the director of the Foreign Policy Studies program there. His research has focused on problems of international security. Before joining Brookings, he held academic positions at Yale University, the John F. Kennedy School of Government at Harvard University, and the Massachusetts Institute of Technology. Among the most recent of his many books and monographs is *A New Concept of Cooperative Security* (1992); he is also a major contributor to *Global Engagement: Cooperation and Security in the 21st Century* (1994), which was edited by Janne E. Nolan, and he wrote on international security conditions in *U.S.–Israeli Relations at the Crossroads* (1996), edited by Gabriel Sheffer. His articles have appeared in such journals as *Arms Control Today*, *Foreign Affairs*, *Politique Internationale*, *Soviet Economy*, *Daedalus*, and *Scientific American*.

BRIAN URQUHART was scholar-in-residence in the Ford Foundation's International Affairs Program from 1986 to 1996. From 1939 to 1945 Sir Brian served in the British army in infantry and airborne units in North Africa and Europe. His UN career began with the birth of the institution itself—from 1945 to 1946 he was personal assistant to Gladwyn Jebb, the executive secretary of the Preparatory Commission of the United Nations in London. He held many posts in his 40 years with the UN: he was personal assistant to Trygve Lie, the first secretary-general, for three and a half years, and from 1954 to 1971, during the tenure of Ralph J. Bunche, he served in various capacities in the Office of the Under-Secretary-General for Special Political Affairs, which dealt with peacekeeping and conflict control. In 1974 Sir Brian was appointed under-secretary-general for Special Political Affairs, a post he held until his retirement. As under-secretary-general, among his responsibilities was the direction of peacekeeping operations and negotiations in Cyprus, the Middle East, Namibia, and other conflict areas. The most recent of his many books are *Ralph Bunche: An American Life* (1993) and (with Erskine Childers) *Renewing the United Nations System* (1994) and *A World in Need of Leadership* (1996).

JOHN C. WHITEHEAD is chairman of AEA Investors Inc., a special situation investment company. During the Reagan administration, Mr. Whitehead was U.S. deputy secretary of state, under George Shultz, from 1985 to 1989. Among his areas of special interest were relations with Eastern Europe and the United Nations. After service in the navy, he began his professional career in 1947 at Goldman Sachs & Co., where he remained for 38 years, becoming senior partner and cochairman in 1976; he retired from Goldman Sachs in late 1984. He is chairman of the board of many institutions, including the Federal Reserve Bank of New York, the United Nations Association of the U.S.A., and the International Rescue Committee, and he is a former chairman of the Harvard Board of Overseers, the Asia Society, and the Brookings Institution.

SAHABZADA YAQUB-KHAN is the chairman of the board of trustees of the Aga Khan University and Hospital in Karachi, Pakistan. He retired from the Pakistan Army in 1971 after a long and distinguished career that began even before the establishment of Pakistan as an independent state. General Yaqub-Khan served as vice chief of the General Staff, commander Armoured Division, commandant of the Command and Staff College, and chief of the General Staff. He was promoted to the rank of lieutenant general as corps commander and commander, Eastern Zone, and governor of East Pakistan. After his retirement, he embarked on a career as a diplomat, first as ambassador to France (1972–1973 and 1980–1982), the United States (1973–1979), and the Soviet Union (1979–1980), and then as foreign minister for nearly nine years between 1982 and 1991, and again in 1996–1997, a post that he held under seven different governments. His career then shifted to the United Nations, where he was the special representative of the United Nations secretary-general for the Western Sahara from 1992 to 1997.

SPECIAL ADVISORS TO THE COMMISSION

ARNE OLAV BRUNDTLAND served for many years as senior research fellow and director of Studies in Foreign and Security Policy at the Norwegian Institute of International Affairs (NUPI) in Oslo. He was editor-in-chief of the institute's scholarly journal, *Internasjonal Politikk*, wrote a syndicated newspaper column on foreign policy for 15 years, and was professor of international affairs and government at the International Summer School of the University of Oslo. He is widely published and has been a visiting scholar at research institutions in the United States, Russia, and the Nordic states. He specialized in East-West affairs and Nordic security ("The Nordic Balance"). Mr. Brundtland is a member of the advisory council for arms control and disarmament of the Norwegian Ministry of Foreign Affairs and the International Institute for Strategic Studies. He received his Magister Artium degree in political science from the University of Oslo and began his specialization in arms control as a visiting scholar at Harvard University. He is currently associated with the World Trade Organization.

HERBERT S. OKUN is the U.S. member of the United Nations International Narcotics Control Board. He is a visiting lecturer on international law at Yale Law School. A career officer in the U.S. Foreign Service from 1955 to 1991, he served as ambassador to the German Democratic Republic and to the United Nations. From 1991 to 1993 he served as deputy cochairman of the International Conference on the Former Yugoslavia, and from 1993 to 1997 he was a mediator of the dispute between Greece and the Former Yugoslav Republic of Macedonia.

MEMBERS OF THE
ADVISORY COUNCIL

Morton Abramowitz
Former President
Carnegie Endowment for International Peace

Ali Abdullah Alatas
Minister of Foreign Affairs
Republic of Indonesia

Graham T. Allison
Director
Belfer Center for Science and
    International Affairs
Harvard University

Robert Badinter
Senator of Hauts de Seine, Senat

Carol Bellamy
Executive Director
UNICEF

Harold Brown
Counselor
Center for Strategic and International Studies

McGeorge Bundy*
Scholar-in-Residence
Carnegie Corporation of New York

Jimmy Carter
Chairman
The Carter Center

Lori Damrosch
Professor of Law
Columbia University School of Law

Francis M. Deng
Senior Fellow
Foreign Policy Studies Program
The Brookings Institution

Sidney D. Drell
Professor and Deputy Director
Stanford Linear Accelerator Center
Stanford University

Lawrence S. Eagleburger
Senior Foreign Policy Advisor
Baker Donelson Bearman and Caldwell

Leslie H. Gelb
President
Council on Foreign Relations

David Gompert
Vice President
National Security Research
RAND

Andrew J. Goodpaster
Chairman
The Atlantic Council of the United States

Mikhail Gorbachev
The Gorbachev Foundation

James P. Grant**
Executive Director
UNICEF

Lee H. Hamilton
United States House of Representatives

Theodore M. Hesburgh
President Emeritus
University of Notre Dame

_____

*Deceased September 1996
**Deceased February 1995

PREVENTING DEADLY CONFLICT

ACKNOWLEDGMENTS

A report of this size and complexity and, indeed, the entire corpus of Commission work would not have been possible without the assistance and advice of many people. They shared enthusiastically of their time and talent to help develop the Commission's ideas and the preparation of this report. The Commission gratefully acknowledges their assistance.

Yasushi Akashi, Airat Aklaev, Carl Alexandre, Ekua Annan, Margaret Anstee, Mark Anstey, R. Scott Appleby, Patricia Aquino-Macri, Alexei Arbatov, Karen Armstrong, Deana Arsenian, Paul Arthur, Sergei Arutiunov, Kader Asmal, Anatole Ayissi, J. Martin Bailey, Michael Bailey, Andy Bair, Nicole Ball, Karen Ballentine, Henri Barkey, Harry G. Barnes, Jr., Andrea Bartoli, John H. Barton, David Bayley, Ruth Beitler, Peter D. Bell, William J. Bien, Nils Gunnar Billinger, Anne-Marie Blackman, Michael Blakley, Barry Blechman, Landrum Bolling, Peter Bouckaert, Boutros Boutros-Ghali, Jeffrey Boutwell, James M. Brasher III, Thorstein Bratteland, David Bridgman, James Bright, Harry Broer, Michael Brown, Michael Bryans, Colin Bundy, James Burger, David Burrell, Brian X. Bush, George Bush, David Byman, Azar Cachalia, Charles T. Call, Ingvar Carlsson, William D. Carmichael, Burgess Carr, Rosalynn Carter, Bernadette Crasto, Carey Cavanaugh, Antonia H. Chayes, Abram Chayes, Frank Chikane, Sukyong Choi, Tyrus W. Cobb, Paul Conlon, Frances Cook, Richard E. Coombs, David Cortright, Theodore Couloumbis, Jeanne D'Onofrio, Romeo Dallaire, Mvume Dandala, Natasha Davids, Lynne Davidson, Robert Davies, Alvaro de Soto, Larry Diamond, Lynn DiMartino, Leokadia Drobizheva, Annette Dyer, Michael Dziedzic, Colin Eglin, Espen Barth Eide, Vigleik Eide, Luigi Einaudi, Mark S. Ellis, Michael Emery, Charles English, Ken Eyre, Maxime Faille, Anthony Fainberg, Karl Farris, Scott R. Feil, Shai Feldman, Barbara Finberg, Michèle A. Flournoy, David W. Foley, Virginia I. Foran, Shepard Forman, Jason W. Forrester, J. Wayne Fredericks, Jordana Friedman, Julie L. Fuerth, Graham Fuller, Robert L. Gallucci, John R. Galvin, Mahmut Gareev, Louis Geiger, Leslie H. Gelb, Thomas Gjelten, Eliot M. Goldberg, Richard J. Goldstone, James E. Goodby, Pravin Gordhan, Uri Gordon, Diana Gordon, Xavier Gorostiaga, Nik Gowing, Anthony Gray, W.C. Gregson, Melanie Greenberg, Fen Osler Hampson, Alan Hanson, Peter Hansen, Anton Harber, John Hardeman, Anne Harringer, Amy Harris, Elaine Hart, Jeffrey Herbst, Kate Heyl, Bruce Hoffman, David Holloway, P. Terrence Hopmann, Jonathan T. Howe, Edmund J. Hull, Heather Hurlburt, Bruce Jentleson, Douglas Johnston, Bruce Jones, Eason Jordan, Mark Juergensmeyer, Donald Kagan, Arnold Kanter, Daniel J. Kaufman, Colin Keating, Richard Kedzior, Michael J. Kelly, Donald Kennedy, Kevin Kennedy, Paul Kennedy, Alex Keynan, Arthur Khachikian, Irene Khan, Kevin King, John Kirton, Leonid Kishkovsky, Michael Klare, Robin Kline, Andre Kokoshin, Andrei Kortunov, Martin Kramer, Jean E. Krasno, Victor Kremenyuk, Winfried Lang, Gail Lapidus, Mark Laudy, Edward J. Laurance, Michèle Ledgerwood, John Ledlie, Marcel J. Lettre II, Tali Levy, Sol M. Linowitz, Tom Lodge, William J. Long, Robert Loosle, R.F.M. Lubbers, Vladimir Lukin, Michael Lund, Douglas E.

Lute, Princeton Lyman, Vladimir Lysenko, John Arch MacInnis, Robert Maguire, Clovis Maksoud, Robert Karl Manoff, Maxwell Manwaring, David Mares, John Maresca, Jessica T. Mathews, Amitabh Mattoo, Michael Mazarr, Mary McCarthy, Eileen McCormick-Place, Margaret McGuinness, Heather McKay, Kenneth Menkhaus, Barbara Messing, Elliott Milhollin, Eric E. Morris, Alex Morrison, Elva Murphy, Willam Nash, Andrew Natsios, Nicoli Nattrass, Beyers Naude, Nafez Nazzal, Richard Nelson, Joyce Neu, Kathleen Newland, Nancy Nielsen, Suzanne Nielson, Matthew Nimetz, Crystal Nix, Trygve Nordby, Kjell Åke Nordquist, Stefan Noreen, Joseph Nye, Brian O'Connell, Claus Offe, J. O'Neil Pouliot, Robert B. Oakley, Louis L. Ortmayer, Arnstein Overkil, Hisashi Owada, Dileep Padgaonkar, Harold Pakendorf, Ebrahim Patel, David L. Patton, Emil Payin, Connie Peck, Elizabeth Pelletreau, Robert Perito, William J. Perry, James Daniel Phillips, Barry Posen, William Potter, Sharon Poulson, Om Prakash Rathor, Jeremy Pressman, Moeen Qureshi, Mamphela Ramphele, Vicki J. Rast, Aviezer Ravitsky, Jairam Reddy, Jack Reed, James W. Reed, Wolfgang Reinicke, Lillian E. Rice, Iqbal Riza, Adam Roberts, David Robinson, Matt L. Rodriguez, Eric Roethlisberger, Alan Romberg, Victor Ronneberg, Michael Rose, Richard Rosecrance, Patricia L. Rosenfield, Caleb S. Rossiter, Barnett Rubin, Avery Russell, Abdulaziz Sachedina, Francisco Sagasti, Cynthia Sampson, John Samuel, Mary Lou Sandwick, Chris Saunders, James A. Schear, Erwin A. Schmidl, Enid C.B. Schoettle, Sarah Sewell, Duygu Sezer, Mintimer Shaimiyev, Alan Shaw, Tricia Shepherd, Susan Shin, Ints Silins, Aleksandr Sirotkin, Timothy Sisk, Gunnar Sjöstedt, Maggie Smart, Judy Smith, Scott Snyder, Steve Spataro, Bertram Spector, Leonard S. Spector, David C. Speedie, Alisa M. Stack, William Stanley, C.P. Steenkamp, Joel Stettenheimer, Vivien Stewart, Thomas Stransky, Jan Stromsen, Astri Suhrke, Charles L. Sykes, Strobe Talbott, Andrea Talentino, Rock Tang, Alexander Tchoubarian, Geoffrey Thale, Lynn Thomas, Frans Timmermans, Valery Tishkov, Abdullah Toukan, Greg Treverton, Holly Trotter, Svetlana Tsalik, Symeon Tsomokos, Astrid S. Tuminez, Arturo Valenzuela, Stephen Van Evera, John Van Oudenaren, Raimo Väyrynen, John W. Vessey, Sergio Vieira de Mello, Katharina R. Vogeli, Rudy von Bernuth, Molly Warlow, James Warner, Robert Wasserman, James D. Watkins, Todd Webb, Erika Weinthal, Joshua N. Weiss, Morten Wetland, Håkan Wiberg, Milton J. Wilkinson, Moegslen Williams, Molly Williamson, Francis Wilson, John F. Wolff, Suzanne Wood, James Woods, Susan L. Woodward, Robin Wright, Andrew Yarrow, Casimir Yost, I. William Zartman, and Helen Zille.

COMMISSION STAFF

Jane E. Holl
Executive Director

Esther Brimmer
Senior Associate

Thomas J. Leney
Senior Associate

Robert E. Lande
Managing Editor

Jeannette Aspden
Consulting Editor

Cornella Carter-Taylor
Office Administrator

Katherine M. Veit
Assistant to the Executive Director

Wanda M. Ellison
Administrative Assistant

Geneve Mantri
Information Systems/Research Assistant

Anita Sharma
Assistant Editor/Research Coordinator

Traci Swanson
Administrative/Research Assistant

Nancy L. Ward
Conference Coordinator

Kristin L. Wheeler
Administrative/Research Assistant

Former Staff Members

Katharine Beckman, Gabrielle Bowdoin, Marilyn O. Butler-Norris, Rachel A. Epstein, Brian J. George, Jenifer Hartnett, Timothy J. McGourthy, Jeffrey R. Pass, Heather A. Podlich, Yvonne E. Schilz, Linda Schoff, John J. Stremlau.

PROLOGUE

1. Berto Jongman, "War and Political Violence," in *Jaarboek Vrede en Veilegheid 1996* (Yearbook Peace and Security) (Nijmegen: Dutch Peace Research Center, 1996), p. 148. See also European Conference on Conflict Prevention, *From Early Warning to Early Action*, A Report on the European Conference on Conflict Prevention (Amsterdam: European Conference on Conflict Prevention, 1996), pp. 11, 15; United Nations High Commissioner for Refugees and International Peace Academy, *Healing the Wounds: Refugees, Reconstruction, and Reconciliation,* Report of the Second Conference Sponsored Jointly by the United Nations High Commissioner for Refugees and the International Peace Academy, June 30–July 1, 1996, p. 1. See also, Francis M. Deng, *Protecting the Dispossessed: A Challenge for the International Community* (Washington, DC: The Brookings Institution, 1993), p. v.

2. See U.S. Committee for Refugees, *World Refugee Survey 1997* (Washington, DC: Immigration and Refugee Services of America, 1997), p. 84.

3. Federation Internationale des Droits de l'Homme, Africa Watch, Union Interafricaine des Droits de l'Homme et des Peuples, Centre International des Droits de la Personne et du Developpement Democratique, *Rapport de la Commission Internationale d'Enquete sur les Violations des Droits de l'Homme au Rwanda Depuis le 1er October 1990* (New York: Africa Watch, 1993), pp. 62–66; Charles Trueheart, "U.N. Alerted to Plans for Rwanda Bloodbath," *Washington Post*, September 25, 1997, p. A1.

4. See, for example: *Humanitarian Aid and Effects,* The International Response to Conflict and Genocide: Lessons from the Rwanda Experience, Study 3 (Copenhagen: Steering Committee on the Joint Evaluation of Emergency Assistance to Rwanda, 1996), p. 52; Barbara Crossette, "Agencies Say U.N. Ignored Pleas on Hutu," *New York Times,* May 28, 1997, p. A3; "Open Wounds in Rwanda," *New York Times,* April 25, 1995, p. A22; John Pomfret, "Aid Dilemma: Keeping It from Oppressor," *Washington Post*, September 23, 1997, p. A1.

5. Eleanor Bedford, "Site Visit to Eastern Congo/Zaire: Analysis of Humanitarian and Political Issues," *USCR Site Visit Notes* (Washington, DC: U.S. Committee for Refugees, 1997), pp. 4–7.

6. The question of whether a rapidly deployed UN force could have dramatically reduced the level of violence in Rwanda was the focus of a conference, "Rwanda Retrospective," cosponsored by the Carnegie Commission on Preventing Deadly Conflict, the Institute for the Study of Diplomacy, Georgetown University, and the U.S. Army, January 23, 1997. For a brief review of the conference, see Scott R. Feil, "Could 5,000 Peacekeepers Have Saved 500,000 Rwandans?: Early Intervention Reconsidered," *ISD Reports* III, No. 2, Institute for the Study of Diplomacy, Georgetown University, Washington, DC, April 1997. See also the full conference report, Scott R. Feil, *Preventing Genocide: How the Early Use of Force Might Have Succeeded in Rwanda* (Washington, DC: Carnegie Commission on Preventing Deadly Conflict, April 1998). Former UNAMIR commander Major General Romeo Dallaire asserted, "I came to the

United Nations from commanding a mechanized brigade group of 5,000 soldiers. If I had had that brigade group in Rwanda, there would be hundreds of thousands of lives spared today." See "Rwanda: U.N. Commander Says More Troops May Have Saved Lives," *Inter Press Service*, September 7, 1994. Others have also made this point. See Brian Urquhart, "For a UN Volunteer Military Force," *New York Review of Books*, June 10, 1993.

7. The costs of relief and reconstruction are drawn from *Rebuilding Post-War Rwanda*, The International Response to Conflict and Genocide: Lessons from the Rwanda Experience, Study 4 (Copenhagen: Steering Committee of the Joint Evaluation of Emergency Assistance to Rwanda, March 1996), p. 32. Costs of prevention are estimated in Michael E. Brown and Richard N. Rosecrance, eds., *The Costs of Conflict: Prevention and Cure in the Global Arena* (Lanham, MD: Rowman & Littlefield, 1999).

8. The Commission's view is spelled out in chapter 6. Commission member Sahabzada Yaqub-Khan dissents from the Commission's view on Security Council reform. In his opinion, the addition of permanent members would multiply, not diminish, the anomalies inherent in the structure of the Security Council. While the concept of regional rotation for additional permanent seats offers prospects of a compromise, it would be essential to have agreed global and regional criteria for rotation. In the absence of an international consensus on expansion in the permanent category, the expansion should be confined to nonpermanent members only.

9. The rotating members of the Security Council would retain their contribution for at least one year after their period on the Council so as to cover political commitments entered into while a member.

10. Brian Urquhart, *Ralph Bunche: An American Life* (New York: W.W. Norton & Company, 1993), pp. 427–429, 474. The dispute over Bahrain's future—then a British protectorate—became increasingly virulent in the late 1960s, threatening the delicate peace in the region. In 1969, British and Iranian officials asked United Nations Secretary-General U Thant for UN mediation to determine a mechanism to resolve the issue of Bahrain's sovereignty in accordance with Bahraini views. Representing the UN's good offices, Ralph Bunche engaged the parties in discreet and unpublicized negotiations that enabled the sensitive talks to progress. In 1970, their agreement on Bahrain's independence was approved by the UN Security Council. For further information on the Bahraini negotiations or Ralph Bunche, see Brian Urquhart, "The Higher Education of Ralph Bunche," in *Journal of Black Higher Education* (Summer 1994), pp. 78–85. See also Husain al-Baharna, "The Fact-Finding Mission of the United Nations Secretary-General and the Settlement of the Bahrain-Iran Dispute, May 1970," *International and Comparative Law Quarterly 22* (1973), pp. 541–553.

CHAPTER 1

1. United Nations Children's Fund, *The State of the World's Children 1996* (New York: Oxford University Press, 1997), p. 13; Ruth Leger Sivard, *World Military and Social Expenditures 1996* (Washington, DC: World Priorities, 1996), pp. 7, 18–19; R.J. Rummell, *Death by Government* (New Brunswick, NJ: Transaction Publishers, 1994), p. 4.

2. Stockholm International Peace Research Institute, *SIPRI Yearbook 1997: Armaments, Disarmament and International Security* (New York: Oxford University Press, 1997), pp. 17–30.

3. Christer Ahlström, *Casualties of Conflict* (Uppsala: Department of Peace and Conflict Research, 1991), pp. 8, 19; United Nations Development Program, *Human Development Report 1997* (New York: Oxford University Press, 1997), p. 65.

4. United States Committee for Refugees, *World Refugee Survey 1997* (Washington, DC: Immigration and Refugee Services of America, 1997), p. 84.

5. Sena Eken et al., *Economic Dislocation and Recovery in Lebanon*, Occasional Paper 120, International Monetary Fund, Washington, DC, February 1995, p. 4.

6. The Carter Center, *State of World Conflict Report 1994–1995* (Atlanta, GA: The Carter Center, 1995), p. 2. For a broader discussion of the links between conflict, government policies, and food supply, see Joseph Collins, "World Hunger: A Scarcity of Food or a Scarcity of Democracy," in *World Security: Challenges for a New Century*, eds. Michael T. Klare and Daniel C. Thomas (New York: St. Martin's Press, 1994), p. 360; Amartya Sen, "Freedoms and Needs: An Argument for the Primacy of Political Rights," *The New Republic*, January 10 –17, 1994, pp. 31–33.

7. United States Mission to the United Nations, *Global Humanitarian Emergencies 1996* (New York: United States Mission to the United Nations, 1996), p. 6; United Nations Food and Agriculture Organization, *FAOSTAT Database,* Agriculture Data - Population: Crops Primary, http://www.fao.org.

8. United Nations Department for Economic and Social Information and Policy Analysis, *World Population Prospects: The 1996 Revision* (New York: United Nations Department for Economic and Social Information and Policy Analysis, Population Division, 1997). Estimate based on medium-variant projections.

9. Kevin Watkins, *The Oxfam Poverty Report* (Oxford: Oxfam UK & Ireland, 1995), p. 3. See also United Nations Development Program, *Human Development Report 1997* (New York: Oxford University Press, 1997), p. 9.

10. United Nations Development Program, *Human Development Report 1996* (New York: Oxford University Press, 1996), p. 13.

11. United Nations Development Program, *Human Development Report 1995* (New York: Oxford University Press, 1995), p. iii.

12. William F. Martin, Ryukichi Imai, and Helga Steeg, *Maintaining Energy Security in a Global Context,* The Triangle Papers 48 (New York: The Trilateral Commission, September 1996), p. 50; Energy and Atmosphere Program, Sustainable Energy and Environment Division, Bureau for Policy and Program Support, United Nations Development Program, *UNDP Initiative for Sustainable Energy 1996,* United Nations Development Program, New York, 1996, p. 1.

13. Nikos Alexandratos, ed., *World Agriculture: Towards 2010, An FAO Study* (Chichester, England: Food and Agriculture Organization of the United Nations and John Wiley and Sons, 1996), p. 86.

14. World Resources Institute, United Nations Environment Program, United Nations Development Program, and the World Bank, *World Resources 1996–97* (New York: Oxford University Press, 1996), p. 14, 35–37.

15. For example, see Gary Gardner, "Preserving Global Crop Land," in *State of the World 1997,* ed. Linda Starke (Washington: Worldwatch Institute, 1997), pp. 42-59; Congressional Budget Office, *Enhancing U.S. Security Through Foreign Aid* (Washington, DC: Congressional Budget Office, 1994), p. 11.

16. John D. Steinbruner, "Reluctant Strategic Realignment: The Need for a New View of National Security," *The Brookings Review* (Winter 1995), p. 6.

17. Lee Frederikson, "The Internet or Infomercial: Which Will Turn Your Audience On?" *Marketing News*, January 20, 1997, p. 15.

18. United Nations Development Program, *Human Development Report 1996* (New York: Oxford University Press, 1996), p. 8; John Stremlau, "Dateline Bangalore: Third World Technopolis," *Foreign Policy*, No. 102 (Spring 1996), p. 161.

19. Suzanne Berger and Ronald Dore, eds., *National Diversity and Global Capitalism* (Ithaca, NY: Cornell University Press, 1996).

20. In spite of an increased level of international cooperation on environmental issues, environmental destruction continues at a rapid pace. For a discussion of environmental degradation and its consequences, see Lester R. Brown, "The Acceleration of History," in *State of the World 1996,* ed. Linda Starke (New York: W.W. Norton & Company, 1996), p. 4; World Commission on Environment and Development, *Our Common Future* (Oxford: Oxford University Press, 1987), pp. 2-3; World Resources Institute,

United Nations Environment Program, United Nations Development Program, and the World Bank, *World Resources 1996-97* (New York: Oxford University Press, 1996), pp. xi-xiv; Commission on Developing Countries and Global Change, *For Earth's Sake* (Ottawa: International Development Research Centre, 1992), pp. 16-18. For a discussion of environmental degradation and its potential to generate conflict, see Thomas F. Homer-Dixon, "Environmental Scarcities and Violent Conflict: Evidence from Cases," *International Security* 19, No. 1 (Summer 1994), pp. 5-40; Thomas F. Homer-Dixon and Valerie Percival, *Environmental Scarcity and Violent Conflict: Briefing Book* (Toronto: University of Toronto, 1996); Donald M. Kennedy, *Environmental Quality and Regional Conflict* (Washington, DC: Carnegie Commission on Preventing Deadly Conflict, December 1998).

21. Peter Stalker, ed., *States of Disarray: The Social Effects of Globalization* (London: United Nations Research Institute for Social Development, 1995), p. 113.

22. United Nations, General Assembly, 49th Session, *Assistance in Mine Clearance: Report of the Secretary-General*, Document A/49/357, United Nations, New York, September 6, 1994, p. 7.

23. United Nations Development Program, *Human Development Report 1997* (New York: Oxford University Press 1997), p. 215.

24. This sect was also found to have considerable biological weapons capability. "Nerve Gas Attack on Tokyo Subway Kills 10; Police Raid Religious Sect's Offices, Seize Chemicals," *Facts on File: World News Digest with Index* 55, No. 2834 (March 23, 1995), p. 205.

25. Ron Purver, "The Threat of Chemical and Biological Terrorism," *The Monitor: Non-Proliferation, Demilitarization and Arms Control* 3, No. 2 (Spring 1997), p. 5. See also Neil C. Livingstone and Joseph D. Douglass, Jr., *CBW: The Poor Man's Atomic Bomb* (Cambridge, MA: Institute for Foreign Policy Analysis, 1984).

26. Nicole Ball, "The Challenge of Rebuilding War-Torn Societies," in *Managing Global Chaos*, eds. Chester A. Crocker and Fen Osler Hampson with Pamela Aall (Washington, DC: United States Institute of Peace Press, 1996), pp. 607-622. Also see Michael E. Brown and Richard N. Rosecrance, eds., *The Costs of Conflict: Prevention and Cure in the Global Arena*, (Lanham, MD: Rowman & Littlefield, 1999).

27. Francois Jean, ed., *Populations in Danger 1995* (London: Médecins Sans Frontières, 1995); Graça Machel, *Impact of Armed Conflict on Children* (New York: UN Department of Public Information, 1996).

28. Gregory Quinn, "The Iraq Conflict," in *The True Cost of Conflict,* ed. Michael Cranna (New York: The New Press, 1994), pp. 25-54.

29. United Nations High Commissioner for Refugees, *The State of the World's Refugees 1995* (New York: Oxford University Press, 1995), p. 255; United Nations High Commissioner for Refugees, *Report of the United Nations High Commissioner for Refugees*, Economic and Social Council, E/1996/52, United Nations, New York, May 13, 1996.

30. James H. Michel, *Development Cooperation*, Development Assistance Committee 1995 Report, Organization for Economic Co-operation and Development (OECD), 1996, pp. A8, 98.

31. International Committee of the Red Cross, *ICRC Annual Report 1996* (Geneva: International Committee of the Red Cross, 1997), p. 323.

32. Médecins Sans Frontières, *Médecins Sans Frontières Activity Report, July 95-July 96* (Brussels: Médecins Sans Frontières, 1996), p. 86; CARE, *CARE International 1995 and 1996* (Brussels: CARE, 1996).

33. "The Philanthropy 400," *The Chronicle of Philanthropy* 4, No. 2 (October 31, 1996), pp. 41-47.

CHAPTER 2

1. See, for example, Edward E. Azar and John W. Burton, eds., *International Conflict Resolution: Theory and Practice* (Sussex: Wheatsheaf Books, 1986); Robert O. Matthews, Arthur G.

Rubinoff, and Janice Gross Stein, eds., *International Conflict and Conflict Management: Readings in World Politics* (Scarborough, Ontario: Prentice-Hall Canada, Inc., 1989); John W. McDonald, Jr., and Diane B. Bendahmane, eds., *Conflict Resolution: Track Two Diplomacy* (Washington, DC: U.S. Government Printing Office, 1987); Joseph V. Montville, ed., *Conflict and Peacemaking in Multiethnic Societies* (Lexington, MA: Lexington Books, 1990); Jack Nusan Porter, *Conflict and Conflict Resolution: A Historical Bibliography* (New York: Garland Publishing, Inc., 1982); Leif Ohlsson, ed., *Case Studies of Regional Conflicts and Conflict Resolution* (Gothenburg, Sweden: Padrigu Papers, 1989); Ramesh Thakur, ed., *International Conflict Resolution* (Boulder, CO: Westview Press, 1988).

2. Robert Gilpin, *War and Change in World Politics* (New York: Cambridge University Press, 1981); George F. Kennan, *Realities of American Foreign Policy* (Princeton, NJ: Princeton University Press, 1954); Henry A. Kissinger, *A World Restored* (New York: Grosset and Dunlap, 1964); Hans J. Morgenthau, *Politics Among Nations* (New York: Knopf, 1948); Kenneth N. Waltz, *Theory of International Politics* (Reading, MA: Addison-Wesley Publishing Company, 1979); Mohammed Ayoob, "The New-Old Disorder in the Third World," in *The United Nations and Civil Wars*, ed. Thomas G. Weiss (Boulder, CO: Lynne Rienner, 1995), pp. 13-30.

3. Mark Katz, "Collapsed Empires," in *Managing Global Chaos*, eds., Chester A. Crocker and Fen Osler Hampson, with Pamela Aall (Washington, DC: United States Institute of Peace Press, 1996), pp. 25-35.

4. These countries moved toward democratic rule through transitional elections. See Roger Kaplan, *Freedom in the World* (New York: Freedom House, 1996), pp. 105-107.

5. Edward D. Mansfield and Jack Snyder are among those who argue that states in transition to democracy are prone to conflict. Edward D. Mansfield and Jack Snyder, "Democratization and the Danger of War," *International Security* 20, No. 1 (Summer 1995), pp. 5-38. For criticisms of their argument, see "Correspondence," *International Security* 20, No. 4 (Spring 1996), pp. 176-207. The scholarly debate over the democratic peace proposition is captured in a selection of essays presenting both sides of the issue; see Michael E. Brown, Sean M. Lynn-Jones, and Steven E. Miller, eds., *Debating the Democratic Peace* (Cambridge, MA: MIT Press, 1996). See also the discussion of this subject in chapter 4.

6. Richard E. Bissell, "The Resource Dimension of International Conflict," in *Managing Global Chaos*, eds., Chester A. Crocker and Fen Osler Hampson, with Pamela Aall (Washington, DC: United States Institute of Peace Press, 1996), pp. 141-153; Naomi Chazan and Donald Rothchild, "The Political Repercussions of Economic Malaise," in *Hemmed In: Responses to Africa's Economic Decline*, eds., Thomas M. Callaghy and John Ravenhill (New York: Columbia University Press, 1993), pp. 180-214; Gareth Porter, "Environmental Security as a National Security Issue," *Current History* 94, No. 592 (May 1995), pp. 218-222; David A. Lake and Donald Rothchild, "Ethnic Fears and Global Engagement: The International Spread and Management of Ethnic Conflict," Policy Paper #20, Institute on Global Conflict and Cooperation, San Diego, CA, January 1996.

7. Articles from regional newspapers illustrate the concern of states with internal strife that outside actors are attempting to influence the outcome of events. Turkish president Suleyman Demirel has accused Syria of supporting the Kurdistan Workers' Party (PKK): "Syria's support for the PKK is clearly evident...it not only supports the PKK, but actively supports all the other organizations that want to change the regime in Turkey." (Makram Muhammad Ahmad, "Turkey: Demirel on Ties With Syria, Terrorism," *Al-Musawwar*, July 26, 1996, pp. 18-21, 82-83.) Typical of many states of the former Soviet Union, Georgian denunciation of Russian aid and support for the Abkhaz rebels reflects anger over Moscow's perceived double standard

Table N.1

THE UNDERLYING AND PROXIMATE CAUSES OF INTERNAL CONFLICT

UNDERLYING CAUSES	PROXIMATE CAUSES
Structural Factors	**Structural Factors**
Weak states	Collapsing states
Intrastate security concerns	Changing intrastate military balances
Ethnic geography	Changing demographic patterns
Political Factors	**Political Factors**
Discriminatory political institutions	Political transitions
Exclusionary national ideologies	Increasingly influential exclusionary ideologies
Intergroup politics	Growing intergroup competitions
Elite politics	Intensifying leadership struggles
Economic/Social Factors	**Economic/Social Factors**
Economic problems	Mounting economic problems
Discriminatory economic systems	Growing economic inequities
Economic development and modernization	Fast-paced development and modernization
Cultural/Perceptual Factors	**Cultural/Perceptual Factors**
Patterns of cultural discrimination	Intensifying patterns of cultural discrimination
Problematic group histories	Ethnic bashing and propagandizing

Source: Michael E. Brown, "The Causes and Regional Dimensions of Internal Conflict," in *The International Dimensions of Internal Conflict,* ed. Michael E. Brown (Cambridge, MA: MIT Press, 1996), p. 577.

policy for its "near abroad." ("Anti-Russian 'Hysteria' Over Abkhazia in Georgia," *Pravda,* July 13, 1995, p. 1.)

8. The development of conflict indicators for crises within states is a new field with much experimentation. For example, Pauline Baker and John Ausink identify the following indicators of potential internal strife: demographic pressures, massive refugee movements, uneven economic development along ethnic lines, a legacy of vengeance-seeking behavior, criminalization, and suspension of the rule of law. Pauline H. Baker and John A. Ausink, "State Collapse and Ethnic Violence: Toward a Predictive Model," *Parameters* 26, No. 1 (Spring 1996), pp. 19-31. A study by Michael Brown identifies both underlying and proximate causes of internal conflict (see Table N.1). Additionally, the Organiza-

tion of African Unity (OAU) is developing a Conflict Management Division and an extensive list of early warning indicators.

9. Personal communication, Irene Khan, Chief of Mission, United Nations High Commissioner for Refugees—New Delhi, April 17, 1995.

10. Jack S. Levy, "Prospect Theory and International Relations: Theoretical Applications and Analytical Problems," in *Avoiding Losses/Taking Risks: Prospect Theory and International Conflict,* ed. Barbara Farnham (Ann Arbor: University of Michigan Press, 1994), pp. 119-145.

11. "Susceptibility" here does not mean being unwitting, but rather "open" or disposed (for many reasons) to follow leadership in this direction. In fact, whole societies or groups do not have to go along, only some critical part— armies or some groups of those willing to fight. Conversely, various factors can inhibit the will-

ingness of a group to be led to initiate conflict, such as physical dispersion, widespread prosperity or even pervasive poverty, war weariness, or indifference to the issues said to be at stake. This analysis builds on the work of Dean G. Pruitt and Jeffrey Z. Rubin, *Social Conflict: Escalation, Stalemate, and Settlement* (New York: Random House, 1986).

12. Other examples include Benin, Eritrea, Zambia, Zimbabwe, and the breakup of Czechoslovakia into the Czech Republic and Slovakia.

13. As disclosures now bring to light, even the highest levels of Afrikaner leadership may have been actively engaged in the violent, clandestine counterinsurgency efforts aimed at breaking resistance to the apartheid regime. "'Prime Evil' de Kock Names Ex-President Botha, Cabinet Ministers, Police Generals in 'Dirty War,'" *Southern Africa Report* 14, No. 38 (September 20, 1996). For an in-depth treatment of the earliest meetings between National Party officials and opposition leaders, see Allister Sparks, *Tomorrow Is Another Country: The Inside Story of South Africa's Road to Change* (New York: Hill and Wang, 1995).

14. Jack Reed, "De Klerk Lifts ANC Ban, Says Mandela Will be Freed Soon," United Press International, February 2, 1990; Timothy D. Sisk, *Democratization in South Africa: The Elusive Social Contract* (Princeton, NJ: Princeton University Press, 1995), pp. 83-84.

15. In 1986, a privately funded study commission on U.S. policy toward South Africa, chaired by Franklin A. Thomas, facilitated initial contacts between ANC leaders and prominent Afrikaners with close ties to the apartheid government. These contacts helped open the way for the crucial political dialogue which followed. Allister Sparks, *Tomorrow Is Another Country: The Inside Story of South Africa's Road to Change* (New York: Hill and Wang, 1995), pp. 72-73.

16. For detailed discussions of South Africa's transition, see David Ottaway, *Chained Together* (New York: Times Books, 1993); Marina Ottaway, *South Africa* (Washington, DC: The Brookings Institution, 1993); Timothy D. Sisk,

Democratization in South Africa: The Elusive Social Contract (Princeton, NJ: Princeton University Press, 1995); Patti Waldmeir, *Anatomy of a Miracle: The End of Apartheid and the Birth of the New South Africa* (New York: W.W. Norton & Co., 1997). See also John Stremlau with Helen Zille, *A House No Longer Divided: Progress and Prospects for Democratic Peace in South Africa,* (Washington, DC: Carnegie Commission on Preventing Deadly Conflict, July 1997).

17. Some analysts argue that although the term "perestroika" was used in 1985, real reform did not begin until 1986. Others, however, assert that Gorbachev's 1985 personnel changes, which moved reformers into positions of power, constitute the beginnings of reform. Gorbachev sets the beginning of reform as early as 1985; in *Perestroika*, he states that reform had been under way for two and one-half years. Mikhail Gorbachev, *Perestroika: New Thinking for Our Country and the World* (New York: Harper and Row, 1987), p. 60; Seweryn Bialer, "The Changing Soviet Political System: The Nineteenth Party Conference and After" in *Politics, Society and Nationality Inside Gorbachev's Russia,* ed. Seweryn Bialer (Boulder: Westview Press, 1989), pp. 193-241. See also Jack F. Matlock, Jr., *Autopsy on an Empire: The American Ambassador's Account of the Collapse of the Soviet Union* (New York: Random House, 1995), pp. 52-67.

18. The West's negotiation strategy in concluding the November 1990 Two + Four Agreement, which laid the framework for German reunification, was instrumental in assuaging Russian security fears. For further reading, see Michael Beschloss and Strobe Talbott, *At the Highest Levels: The Inside Story of the End of the Cold War* (Boston: Little, Brown & Company, 1993), pp. 184-190; Mikhail Gorbachev, *Memoirs* (New York: Doubleday, 1996), especially pp. 527-535; Philip Zelikow and Condoleezza Rice, *Germany Unified and Europe Transformed: A Study in Statecraft* (Cambridge, MA: Harvard University Press, 1995), pp. 149-197, 328-352.

CHAPTER 3

1. For an assessment of missed opportunities in Rwanda, see Astri Suhrke and Bruce Jones, "Preventive Diplomacy in Rwanda: Failure to Act, or Failure of Actions?," in *Opportunities Missed, Opportunities Seized: Preventive Diplomacy in the Post–Cold War World*, ed. Bruce Jentleson (Lanham, MD: Rowman & Littlefield, forthcoming). Major General Romeo Dallaire stated that with a force of 5,000 trained troops and an appropriate mandate he could have prevented thousands of deaths. "Rwanda: UN Commander Says More Troops May Have Saved Lives," Inter Press Service, September 7, 1994, p. 2.

2. United Nations Security Council Resolution 795 (1992), adopted on December 11, 1992.

3. Almost immediately following Serrano's suspension of the constitution, judiciary, and legislature, a broad-based civilian movement began to mobilize. Three major democratic institutions—the Supreme Electoral Tribunal, the Court of Constitutionality, and the Office of the Human Rights Ombudsman—refused to accept the self-coup (*autogolpe*) and actively defied Serrano. Most of the military would not support Serrano's actions, and the media was vocal in its denunciations. Members of civil society united under the Instancia Nacional de Consenso—a representative forum which was instrumental in reversing the coup after only two weeks. Internationally, the Organization of American States offered its support to the opposition, and dispatched fact-finding missions to investigate the situation. Secretary-General João Baena Soares met with representatives of civil society—including business, religious, and human rights leaders—and warned of severe international repercussions. For more information, see Francisco Villagrán de León, "Thwarting the Guatemalan Coup," *Journal of Democracy* 4, No. 4, October 1993, pp. 117-124; Rachel M. McCleary, "Guatemala's Postwar Prospects," *Journal of Democracy* 8, No. 2, April 1997, pp. 129-143; "OAS Starts Probe of Guatemala Leader's Use of Emergency Rule," *Chicago Tri-bune*, May 31, 1993, p.7; Michael Lund, *Preventing Violent Conflicts: A Strategy for Preventive Diplomacy* (Washington, DC: United States Institute of Peace Press, 1996), pp. 77-78.

4. Following Congo's first-ever democratic elections in 1992, tensions simmered between supporters of President Pascal Lissouba and opposition groups. Local conflict resolution initiatives failed to secure a peaceful settlement. After legislative elections in early 1993, violent acts increased and threatened to escalate into open conflict. At this critical juncture, Congolese defense minister General Raymond Damase N'Gollo, acting as mediator on behalf of the Congolese government, issued an appeal for international assistance. With the leadership of the Organization of African Unity (OAU) and the government of France, an international committee was appointed to oversee new elections, and an international arbitration jury was formed to examine possible election fraud. Completion of these measures restored stability to the situation and allowed the Republic of Congo's democratic transition to move forward. See I. William Zartman and Katharina R. Vogeli, "Prevention Gained and Prevention Lost: Collapse, Competition, and Coup in Congo," in *Opportunities Missed, Opportunities Seized: Preventive Diplomacy in the Post–Cold War World,* ed. Bruce Jentleson (Lanham, MD: Rowman & Littlefield, forthcoming).

5. A slightly different version of this four-part framework was originally developed by Douglas E. Lute in "Improving National Capacities for Response to Complex Emergencies," a paper prepared for the conference, "Humanitarian Response and Preventing Deadly Conflict," cosponsored by the Carnegie Commission on Preventing Deadly Conflict and the United Nations High Commissioner for Refugees, Geneva, Switzerland, February 16-17, 1997. Recent evaluations of the United Nations Mission in Haiti (UNMIH) have highlighted these factors in accounting for the relative success of the operation to date. See, for example, United States Army War College, *Success in Peace-*

keeping, United Nations Mission in Haiti: The Military Perspective (Carlisle Barracks, PA: U.S. Army Peacekeeping Institute, 1996); Margaret Daly Hays and Gary F. Weatley, eds., *Interagency and Political-Military Dimensions of Peace Operations: Haiti—A Case Study* (Washington, DC: National Defense University Press, February 1996).

6. The United Nations Mission in Haiti (UNMIH) has been marked by a high level of cooperation between the United States, which provided the bulk of the initial troops for the operation, and UN officials. Additionally, a great deal of attention has been paid to working with the Haitian legislature and security forces to promote democratic practices. See Margaret Daly Hays and Gary F. Weatley, eds., *Interagency and Political-Military Dimensions of Peace Operations: Haiti—A Case Study* (Washington, DC: National Defense University Press, February 1996).

7. For one diplomat's reflections on the process of assembling the coalition and holding it together, see James A. Baker, III, *The Politics of Diplomacy: Revolution, War and Peace 1989-1992* (New York: G.P. Putnam's Sons, 1995), especially pp. 275-299, 308-320, 370-378, 396-406.

8. John M. Sanderson, "The Humanitarian Response in Cambodia: The Imperative for a Strategic Alliance," in *After Rwanda: The Coordination of United Nations Humanitarian Assistance*, eds. Jim Whitman and David Pocock, (New York: St. Martin's Press, 1996), pp. 179-193; Jimmy Carter, "Get Tough on Rights," *New York Times*, September 21, 1993, p. A21; Anthony Lewis, "At Home Abroad; Fragments of Hope," *New York Times*, July 30, 1993, p. A27; Paul Lewis, "United Nations Is Finding its Plate Increasingly Full but its Cupboard Is Bare," *New York Times*, September 27, 1993, p. A8; Elizabeth Becker, "A U.N. Success Story," *New York Times*, April 28, 1995, p. A33.

9. John Eriksson et al., *Synthesis Report*, in The International Response to Conflict and Genocide: Lessons from the Rwanda Experience (Copenhagen: Steering Committee of the Joint Evaluation of Emergency Assistance to Rwanda, March 1996), p. 30.

10. For example, Serbian troops blocked humanitarian convoys delivering food, clothing, medical supplies, and winter materials to refugees in Bosnia's war-torn cities. Even after pledges to allow aid convoys through, the Serbs bombed roads traveled by the relief convoys and highjacked UN trucks to prevent the delivery of such relief supplies. Barbara Crossette, "After Weeks of Seeming Inaction, U.S. Decides to Punish Belgrade," *New York Times*, May 23, 1992, p.1; "Serbs Again Block Supplies in Bosnia," *New York Times*, December 8, 1993, p. A6; Stephen Kinzer, "Yugoslavs Celebrate Sports Victory with a Political Echo," *New York Times*, July 4, 1995, p. 5.

11. See John Stremlau, *People in Peril: Human Rights, Humanitarian Action, and Preventing Deadly Conflict* (Washington, DC: Carnegie Commission on Preventing Deadly Conflict, May 1998).

12. Sadako Ogata, "World Order, Internal Conflict and Refugees," address at Harvard University, October 28, 1996.

13. United Nations High Commissioner for Refugees, International Organization for Migration, and Organization for Security and Cooperation in Europe, *Report of the Regional Conference to Address the Problems of Refugees, Displaced Persons, Other Forms of Involuntary Displacement and Returnees in the Countries of the Commonwealth of Independent States and Relevant Neighboring States*, Geneva, May 30-31, 1996, CIS/CONF/1996/6, July 4, 1996.

14. United Nations High Commissioner for Refugees, *The State of the World's Refugees 1995: In Search of Solutions* (New York: Oxford University, 1995), pp. 48, 172-184. This shift has generated some concern that UNHCR has made this move at the expense of fulfilling its protection mission. This issue is elaborated on in chapter 6.

15. CARE, *1996 CARE International Report* (Brussels: CARE International, 1996).

16. "Donor fatigue" is frequently mentioned by those who fear that badly needed foreign assistance will not be available as an instrument of preven-

tive action. In fact, official development assistance from OECD countries has remained fairly constant, fluctuating between $55 and $60 billion during the 1990s. Meanwhile, resource flows from the private sector have grown substantially, almost tripling between 1986 and 1994, from $37 to $105 billion. Of growing concern, however, is the need to divert scarce foreign assistance resources from long-term development work to meet the urgent humanitarian needs of complex emergencies. For example, two years of emergency work in Rwanda cost the United States $750 million, a sum that is equal to the entire USAID African Development Fund for all of sub-Saharan Africa. See *Healing the Wounds: Refugees, Reconstruction and Reconciliation*, Report of the Second Conference Sponsored by the United Nations High Commissioner for Refugees and the International Peace Academy, June 30–July 1, 1996, p. 49. For a more general discussion, see Ian Smillie, *The Alms Bazaar* (Ottawa: International Development Research Centre, 1995); United States Mission to the United Nations, *Global Humanitarian Emergencies, 1996* (United States Mission to the United Nations, ECOSOC Division, 1996), pp. 22-24; James H. Michel, *Development Co-operation*, Development Assistance Committee 1995 Report, Organization for Economic Cooperation and Development, 1996, pp. 8-9.

17. In the United States this reluctance found its way into official policy guidelines with the release of the Clinton administration's Presidential Decision Directive 25 in 1994. Drawing from the U.S. experience in Somalia, the directive outlined the stringent conditions under which U.S. troops would be engaged overseas, chief among them being the need for a clear end-state and "exit strategy." The White House, "The Clinton Administration's Policy on Reforming Multilateral Peace Operations," Presidential Decision Directive 25 (Washington, DC: The White House, 1994).

18. This section draws on a paper prepared for the Commission by Alexander L. George and Jane E. Holl, *The Warning–Response Problem and*

Missed Opportunities in Preventive Diplomacy (Washington, DC: Carnegie Commission on Preventing Deadly Conflict, May 1997).

19. The Bush administration's decision to commit U.S. troops was considered the logical extension of previous policy. As the leading contributor to Operation Provide Hope, the U.S. was concerned that its efforts would be wasted unless provisions were made for the secure distribution of humanitarian assistance. As conditions deteriorated, both the UN and the Bush administration concluded that "only a U.S.-led coalition could move quickly and efficiently enough to make a rapid impact on the humanitarian catastrophe." See Herman J. Cohen, "Intervention in Somalia," *The Diplomatic Record 1992-1993* (Boulder, CO: Westview Press, 1995), pp. 59-67; George Bush, "Address to the Nation on the Situation in Somalia," *Public Papers of the Presidents of the United States: George Bush 1992-1993*, Book I - January 1 to July 31, 1992 (Washington, DC: U.S. Government Printing Office, 1993).

20. The risk of retribution may be particularly high for indigenous NGOs, although international NGOs, to the extent that their in-country presence relies upon permission from host governments or ruling factions, also put their operations at risk. See Robert I. Rotberg, "Conclusions: NGOs, Early Warning, Early Action, and Preventive Diplomacy," in *Vigilance and Vengeance: NGOs Preventing Ethnic Conflict in Divided Societies*, ed. Robert I. Rotberg (Washington, DC: Brookings Institution Press; Cambridge, MA: The World Peace Foundation, 1996), pp. 263-268.

21. Kofi Annan, *Renewing the United Nations: A Programme for Reform,* Report of the Secretary-General (New York: United Nations, 1997), para. 207-216.

22. This discussion draws on lessons learned from three cases of successful post-Cold War preventive diplomacy: the Baltic States, Congo, and Macedonia. These cases were examined during the conference, "Preventive Diplomacy in the Post-Cold War World," cosponsored by the Carnegie Commission on Preventing Deadly

Conflict and the U.S. Department of State, Policy Planning Staff, April 23, 1996.

23. See Cyrus R. Vance and David A. Hamburg, *Pathfinders for Peace: A Report to the UN Secretary-General on the Role of Special Representatives and Personal Envoys* (Washington, DC: Carnegie Commission on Preventing Deadly Conflict, September 1997).

24. Annan, op. cit., *Renewing the United Nations,* para. 60, 111.

25. In addition, world leaders now have many different forums in which to discuss emerging crises and the means at their disposal to manage these crises. The schedule of high-level international meetings also introduces the important element of continuity to crisis management. The following organizations, for instance, will hold cabinet- or head-of-state-level meetings in 1997-98 (meetings held annually unless otherwise noted):

Arab League
Asia-Pacific Economic Cooperation (APEC)
Association of Southeast Asian Nations (ASEAN)
Black Sea Economic Cooperation
Caribbean Community (CARICOM)
The Commonwealth
Commonwealth of Independent States (CIS)
Community for Eastern and Southern Africa (COMESA)
Economic Community of West African States (ECOWAS)
European Council (twice annually)
La Francophonie
Group of Eight (G-8) (Members meet as G-7 for certain macroeconomic regulatory issues)
Group of 77
Gulf Cooperation Council (GCC)
Nordic Council
North Atlantic Treaty Organization (NATO)
Oil Producing and Exporting Countries (OPEC)
Organization of African Unity (OAU)
Organization of American States (OAS)
Organization of Islamic Countries (OIC)
Organization for Security and Cooperation in Europe (OSCE)

South Asian Association for Regional Cooperation (SAARC)
Southern African Development Community (SADC)
Southern Common Market (MERCOSUR)
United Nations General Assembly
United States-European Union (EU) (twice annually)
Western European Union (WEU)
World Trade Organization (WTO) (ministerial-level meeting every two years)

26. Ruth Wedgwood, "Macedonia: A Victory for Quiet Diplomacy," *The Christian Science Monitor*, October 19, 1995, p. 19. For another example of quiet diplomacy, see Brian Urquhart, *Ralph Bunche: An American Life* (New York: W.W. Norton & Company, 1993), p. 429.

27. Two major schools of power sharing have developed: the "consociational" approach, of which Arend Lijphart is the leading proponent, and the "integrative" approach advanced by Donald Horowitz. The consociational approach focuses on accommodation through achievement of elite agreements. Integrative power-sharing arrangements attempt to defuse tensions by providing incentives for moderate behavior among ethnic group leaders and by enhancing minority influence in the decision-making process. For an overview of these two schools and a discussion of the applicability of power sharing to the resolution of ethnic conflicts, see Timothy D. Sisk, *Power Sharing and International Mediation in Ethnic Conflicts* (Washington, DC: United States Institute of Peace Press and Carnegie Commission on Preventing Deadly Conflict, 1996). See also Donald Horowitz, "Comparing Democratic Systems," *Journal of Democracy* 1, No. 4 (Fall 1990), pp. 73-79; Donald Horowitz, "Making Moderation Pay," in *Conflict and Peacemaking in Multiethnic Societies*, ed. Joseph Montville. (Lexington, MA: Lexington Books, 1990), pp. 451-475; Donald Horowitz, "Democracy in Divided Societies," *Journal of Democracy* 4, No. 4 (October 1993), pp. 18-38; Arend Lijphart, *Democracy in Plural Societies*

(New Haven, CT: Yale University Press, 1977), pp. 16-20, 55-60, 142-146; Arend Lijphart, "Self-Determination versus Pre-Determination of Ethnic Minorities in Power-Sharing Systems," in *The Rights of Minority Cultures*, ed. Will Kymlichka (Oxford: Oxford University Press, 1995), pp. 275-287.

28. Diana Chigas, with Elizabeth McClintock and Christophe Kamp, "Preventive Diplomacy and the Organization for Security and Cooperation in Europe: Creating Incentives for Dialogue and Cooperation," in *Preventing Conflict in the Post-Communist World*, eds. Abram Chayes and Antonia Handler Chayes (Washington, DC: The Brookings Institution, 1996), pp. 25-97; Connie Peck, *Sustainable Peace: The Role of the UN and Regional Organizations in Preventing Conflict* (Lanham, MD: Rowman & Littlefield, 1998); Organization for Security and Cooperation in Europe, *Vade Mecum: An Introduction to the OSCE* (Berne: OSCE, May 1996).

29. For definitions and examples of Track Two diplomacy and multitrack diplomacy, as well as a discussion of relationships in a multitrack system, see James Notter and John McDonald, "Track Two Diplomacy: Nongovernmental Strategies For Peace," *American Perspectives on Conflict Resolution*, Electronic Journals of the U.S. Information Agency, Volume 1, No. 19, December 1996, http://www.usia.gov/journals/journals.htm, updated December 1996; James Notter and Louise Diamond, *Building Peace and Transforming Conflict: Multi-Track Diplomacy in Practice* (Washington, DC: Institute for Multi-Track Diplomacy, 1996), pp. 1-17; Louise Diamond and John McDonald, *Multi-Track Diplomacy: A Systems Approach to Peace* (West Hartford, CT: Kumarian Press, Inc., 1996), pp. 37-51; Kumar Rupesinghe, "Multi-Track Diplomacy and the Sustainable Route to Conflict Resolution," *Cultural Survival Quarterly* (Fall 1995), pp. 13-18.

30. The National Research Council's Committee on International Conflict Resolution is conducting substantial research aimed at identifying and examining the major techniques and concepts involved in conflict resolution. Track Two research currently under way focuses primarily on interactive/problem-solving techniques. Numerous papers are being prepared for the committee, which plans to make these papers available during 1998.

31. In the former Yugoslavia, for example, sanctions had very little effect until they were significantly strengthened in April 1993 and successfully forced President Slobodan Milosevic, for the first time, to accept the Vance/Owen peace plan. See David Owen, *Balkan Odyssey* (London: Victor Gollancz, 1995), pp. 134-135.

32. A study by the Commission has suggested that to improve the UN's ability to maintain sanctions, the UN Collective Measures Committee should be revived and its mandate expanded to include possible inducements. A reconstituted Collective Measures Committee might initially address a five-point agenda: 1) improvements within the UN Secretariat to facilitate the imposition, implementation, and suspension of a sanctions regime; 2) recommendations for national capacity building to impose, monitor, and enforce sanctions; 3) ways to improve cooperation with nonstate parties; 4) combining sanctions with other preventive measures; and 5) the value of financial sanctions. See John Stremlau, *Sharpening International Sanctions: Toward a Stronger Role for the United Nations* (Washington, DC: Carnegie Commission on Preventing Deadly Conflict, November 1996), pp. 57-67.

33. Stremlau, op. cit., *Sharpening International Sanctions*, p. 29.

34. Swift, decisive imposition of sanctions was one of five conditions identified by Hufbauer and Elliott as contributing to their effectiveness. Other conditions identified are: a relatively modest goal; a target state much smaller than the country imposing sanctions, and also economically weak and unstable; friendly relations between the sanctioned state and the sanctioning state prior to the imposition of sanctions; and low costs for the sanctioning state. See Kimberly Ann Elliott and Gary Hufbauer, "'New' Approaches to Economic Sanctions," in *U.S. Intervention Policy for the Post-Cold War World*, eds. Arnold Kanter and Linton F. Brooks

(New York: W.W. Norton & Company, 1994), pp. 132-157.

35. Stremlau, op. cit., *Sharpening International Sanctions*, p. 61.

36. For example, USA*Engage, a coalition representing over 600 American businesses, agricultural groups, and trade associations, seeks to advance public and private sector involvement in world affairs by attempting to educate policymakers on the impact of unilateral sanctions in terms of: 1) costs to the U.S. economy, 2) the damage to security, commercial, and human rights objectives, 3) the adverse impact on U.S. ties with its closest allies, and 4) the damage to U.S. global competitiveness and investment policy. Interested readers can get more information on USA*Engage from their website: http://usaengage.org. See also Richard Lawrence, "U.S. Sanctions Spur Outcry; Corporate America Presses Case against Increasing Curbs on Other Nations," *Journal of Commerce*, May 21, 1997, p. 41D.

37. For a discussion of the impact of sanctions on civilian populations, see Lori Fisler Damrosch, "The Civilian Impact of Economic Sanctions," in *Enforcing Restraint: Collective Intervention in Internal Conflicts*, ed. Lori Fisler Damrosch (New York: Council on Foreign Relations Press, 1993), pp. 274-315. Also see Bryan Hehir, *The Uses of Force in the Post-Cold War World* (Washington, DC: The Woodrow Wilson International Center for Scholars, August 1996). Hehir, in considering the moral dilemma posed by sanctions that will harm innocent civilians, suggests implementation of a "principle of consent," i.e., the support of people who will be directly affected. Hehir highlights South Africa as just such a case. Damrosch, while supporting a similar concept of internal expressions of support for sanctions, also illuminates two further complications: 1) cases where an indigenous nongovernmental leadership cannot be identified or, if it exists, is unable to voice its opinion because of government oppression; and 2) cases where the leadership targeted for punishment enjoys broad popular support.

38. The feasibility and effectiveness of targeted financial sanctions is discussed in Stremlau, op. cit., *Sharpening International Sanctions*; Kimberly Ann Elliott and Gary Hufbauer, op. cit., "'New' Approaches to Economic Sanctions," pp. 133-157; Elizabeth S. Rogers, *Using Economic Sanctions to Prevent Deadly Conflict*, Discussion Paper, 90-02 (Cambridge, MA: Center for Science and International Affairs, Harvard University, 1996).

39. This section draws heavily on a Commission-sponsored study headed by David Cortright. See David Cortright, ed., *The Price of Peace: Incentives and International Conflict Prevention* (Lanham, MD: Rowman & Littlefield, 1997).

40. Until very recently, the lone exception was the much quoted 1971 article by David Baldwin, "The Power of Positive Sanctions," *World Politics* 24, No. 1 (October 1971). Although this remains an under-researched topic, three recent studies are William J. Long, *Economic Incentives and Bilateral Cooperation* (Ann Arbor, MI: University of Michigan Press, 1996); Eileen M. Crumm, "The Value of Economic Incentives in International Politics," *Journal of Peace Research* 32, No. 3 (1995), pp. 313- 330; Cortright, op. cit., *The Price of Peace*.

41. Cortright, op. cit., *The Price of Peace*.

42. William Gamson and André Modigliani, *Untangling the Cold War* (Boston, MA: Little, Brown & Company, 1971); Martin Patchen, *Resolving Disputes Between Nations: Coercion or Conciliation?* (Durham, NC: Duke University Press, 1988), p. 262.

43. On November 26, 1991, the World Bank announced in Paris that a Consultative Group of Donors for Kenya would withhold new loans for at least six months. On May 14, 1992, the World Bank announced on behalf of the Paris Consultative Group of Aid Donors for Malawi that it would not approve $74 million in new loans. The World Bank press statement on behalf of the Consultative Group on Malawi expressed "deep disappointment at the [Malawian] Government's lack of responsiveness to [governance] concerns and what they perceive as its continued poor record in ensuring basic respect

for human rights, release or trial of detainees, better conditions in the prisons, respect for the rule of law, and independent judiciary, public sector accountability and transparency, freedom of speech, and open public participation and debate on policy options and freedoms of association." A similar statement was released on Kenya. See David Gillies, "Human Rights, Democracy and Good Governance: Stretching the World Bank's Policy Frontiers," in *The World Bank: Lending on a Global Scale*, eds. J.M. Griesgraber and B.G. Gunter (London: Pluto Press, 1996), pp. 101-141, especially pp.123-126; John Stremlau and Francisco Sagasti, *Preventing Deadly Conflict: Does the World Bank Have a Role?* (Washington, DC: Carnegie Commission on Preventing Deadly Conflict, June 1998).

44. "Charter of the World Trade Organization. Annex 2: Understanding On Rules And Procedures Governing The Settlement Of Disputes," January 1, 1995, 33 I.L.M. 1143-1153, 1224-1247.

45. See, for example, Gareth Evans, "Cooperative Security and Intrastate Conflict," *Foreign Policy*, No. 96 (Fall 1994), pp. 9-10.

46. Three recent examples of this type of action include: 1) the establishment by the United Nations Security Council of no-fly zones over Bosnia in October 1992 to protect civilians from strafing by Serbian aircraft; 2) the dispatching of over 20,000 troops, an aircraft carrier, and maritime prepositioning ships to the Persian Gulf in October 1994 by President Clinton to discourage Iraqi troops from re-invading Kuwait; and 3) the placement of the USS *Independence* battle group and the USS *Nimitz* off the shores of Taiwan in March 1996 to dissuade the Chinese military from further intimidation of Taiwan. See Michael R. Gordon, "Bush Backs a Ban on Combat Flights in Bosnia Airspace," *New York Times*, October 2, 1992, p. A2; Elaine Sciolino, "U.S. May Seek the Use of Force to Stop Serbs' Flights Over Bosnia," *New York Times*, December 4, 1992, p. A1; Michael R. Gordon, "U.S. Sends Force as Iraqi Soldiers Threaten Kuwait,"

New York Times, October 8, 1994, p. 1; Patrick E. Tyler, "China Warns U.S. To Keep Away From Taiwan Strait," *New York Times*, March 18, 1996, p. A3; Nicholas D. Kristof, "Off Taiwan, U.S. Sailors Are Unworried," *New York Times*, March 19, 1996, p. A3.

47. The conflict in the Gulf in 1990-1991 offers a clear example of how such an approach can work. See Department of Public Information, *United Nations and the Iraq-Kuwait Conflict 1990-1996* (New York: United Nations, 1996). To support its examination of the role of force in preventing deadly conflict, the Commission sponsored two studies on the subject: Andrew J. Goodpaster, *When Diplomacy Is Not Enough: Managing Multinational Military Interventions*, (Washington, DC: Carnegie Commission on Preventing Deadly Conflict, July 1996); Daniel J. Kaufman, "The Role of the Military in Preventing Deadly Conflict," in *Preventing Deadly Conflict: Strategies and Institutions,* Proceeddings of a Conference in Moscow, Russian Federation, eds. Gail W. Lapidus with Svetlana Tsalik (Washington, DC: Carnegie Commission on Preventing Deadly Conflict, April 1998). The Kaufman paper is an outgrowth of Senior Conference XXXII, "The Role of the Military in Preventing Deadly Conflict," cosponsored by the Commission and the United States Military Academy at West Point, June 8-10, 1995.

48. United Nations Department of Public Information, *The Blue Helmets: A Review of United Nations Peacekeeping*, 3rd ed. (New York: United Nations Department of Public Information, 1996), pp. 224-227, 476-478.

49. Robert Oakley and Michael Dziedzic, "Policing the New World Disorder," *Strategic Forum*, No. 84 (October 1996), p. 4.

50. One development which may reduce the reluctance to use ground forces is the potential use of nonlethal technologies and weapons. Nonlethal weapons are means to control or coerce people, disable equipment or otherwise impede aggressive action while minimizing death and unnecessary destruction. These technologies may be antipersonnel, antimateriel, or involve electronic and information warfare. The deployment of

nonlethal or less-than-lethal techniques and technologies would allow peacekeepers additional options between using deadly force in self-defense or in defense of the mission or remaining exposed to an unacceptable level of risk. The use of nonlethal technologies is not without its problems, however. Principal concerns surround their actual safety and effectiveness. See Anthony Fainberg and Alan Shaw, *Nonlethal Technologies and the Prevention of Deadly Conflict* (Washington, DC: Carnegie Commission on Preventing Deadly Conflict, forthcoming).

51. See Gareth Evans, *Cooperating for Peace* (Sydney: Allen and Unwin, 1993), pp. 81-85.

52. The notion of "fire brigade" or rapid reaction capabilities within the UN has come under careful consideration in recent years. Among the earliest supporters of the concept was Brian Urquhart, who has written extensively on the subject. See, for example, Brian Urquhart, "Who Can Police the World?," *New York Review of Books*, May 12, 1994, pp. 29-33; Brian Urquhart, "If the United Nations Is for Real, Give It a Police Force," *International Herald Tribune*, May 23, 1994, p. 4; Brian Urquhart, "Peace-Keeping Saves Lives," *Washington Post*, February 16, 1995; Brian Urquhart, "For a UN Volunteer Military Force," *New York Review of Books*, June 10, 1993, p. 3; and Brian Urquhart, "Whose Fight Is It?" *New York Times*, May 22, 1994. For reactions to Urquhart's proposal, see Lee Hamilton, Gareth Evans, Lord Carver, and Stanley Hoffman, "A UN Volunteer Military Force—Four Views," *New York Review of Books*, June 24, 1993, p. 58; Robert Oakley, McGeorge Bundy, Sadruddin Aga Khan, Olusegun Obasanjo, and Marion Dönhoff, "A UN Volunteer Force: The Prospects," *New York Review of Books*, July 15, 1993, pp. 52-56. The governments of Canada and Denmark also conducted studies on the topic; see Government of Canada, *Towards a Rapid Reaction Capability for the United Nations*, Report of the Government of Canada, September 1995; and Dick A. Leurdijk, "The Netherlands Non-paper. A UN Rapid Deployment Brigade: A Preliminary

Study. Revised version, April 1995," in *A UN Rapid Deployment Brigade: Strengthening the Capacity for Quick Response* (The Hague: Netherlands Institute of International Relations *Clingendael*, 1995), pp. 73-92. See also Carl Kaysen and George Rathjens, *Peace Operations by the United Nations: The Case for a Volunteer UN Military Force* (Cambridge, MA: Committee on International Security Studies, American Academy of Arts and Sciences, 1996).

53. Government of Canada, *Towards a Rapid Reaction Capability for the United Nations*, Report of the Government of Canada, September 1995; Leurdijk, op. cit., *A UN Rapid Deployment Brigade: Strengthening the Capacity for Quick Response*, p. 77.

CHAPTER 4

1. The role of international regimes in conflict prevention is further developed in Gareth Evans, *Cooperating for Peace* (Sydney: Allen & Unwin, 1993), pp. 39-51.

2. International organizations and regimes have a long history of peaceful dispute settlement. The United Nations has functioned as a forum for international dispute resolution since its establishment; for example, see the discussion of the case of Bahrain in the prologue. The World Trade Organization (WTO) and European Union (EU) have well-established dispute resolution mechanisms. The WTO's Dispute Resolution Body (DRB) rules continually on a number of trade conflicts between member states, including, for example, a complaint against the United States by Venezuela and Brazil over U.S. gasoline regulations, settled in 1996, and a complaint against Japan by the United States, EU, and Canada over alcoholic beverages, also settled in 1996. The EU has been a force for peaceful resolution of conflict in political as well as economic disputes. The Conference on Stability in Europe, established in May 1994, brought more than 40 European states together to resolve disputes over borders and the treatment of minorities. Only two months later, Hungary renounced territorial claims against Romania and Slovakia. (Nicholas

Denton, "Hungary Acts on Borders," *Financial Times*, July 15, 1994, p. 2; Patrick Worsnip, "Talks on Stability Fan Old Enmities," *The Independent*, May 28, 1994, p. 7.) A number of states with sea-going interests, including those at critical maritime locations with heated disputes such as Yemen, Eritrea, Qatar, and Bahrain, have agreed to have their differences settled according to the United Nations Convention on the Law of the Sea. For instance, in 1995, Guinea-Bissau and Senegal settled their dispute over territorial waters through the International Court of Justice and the Convention on the Law of the Sea. (More information on the dispute settlement mechanisms of the WTO and the Law of the Sea may be found at their websites: http://www.wto.org/wto/dispute/dispute.htm, and http://www.un.org/depts/los)

3. Canberra Commission on the Elimination of Nuclear Weapons, *Report of the Canberra Commission on the Elimination of Nuclear Weapons* (Canberra Commission on the Elimination of Nuclear Weapons, August, 1996), p. 7.

4. Committee on International Security and Arms Control, National Academy of Sciences, *The Future of the U.S. Nuclear Weapons Policy* (Washington, DC: National Academy Press, 1997), pp. 1-10.

5. At the urging of the United Nations General Assembly, the International Court of Justice offered an advisory opinion, issued in 1996, on the question "Is the threat or use of nuclear weapons in any circumstance permitted under international law?" The Court observed that a threat or use of force by means of nuclear weapons that is contrary to Article 2, paragraph 4, of the United Nations Charter and that fails to meet all the requirements of Article 51 is unlawful. Further, the Court found that the threat or use of nuclear weapons must be compatible with the requirements of the international law applicable in armed conflict, particularly those of the principles and rules of international humanitarian law, as well as with specific obligations under treaties and other undertakings which expressly deal with nuclear weapons. Yet the

Court could not reach a definitive conclusion as to the legality or illegality of the use of nuclear weapons by a state in an extreme circumstance of self-defense, in which its very survival would be at stake. The Court suggested that international law and the stability of the international order, which it is intended to govern, will suffer from the continuing difference of views with regard to the legal status of weapons as deadly as nuclear weapons. As a result, it unanimously agreed that an obligation exists to pursue and bring to a conclusion negotiations leading to nuclear disarmament in all aspects under strict and effective international control. "Legality of the Threat or Use of Nuclear Weapons," Advisory Opinion, International Court of Justice, General List No. 95, July 8, 1996.

6. There are five major documents which address chemical and biological weapons identified in international law: 1) "Protocol for the Prohibition of the Use in War of Asphyxiating, Poisonous or Other Gases, and of Bacteriological Methods of Warfare," February 8, 1928, Treaties and Other International Acts Series (T.I.A.S.) no. 9433; 2) "Convention on the Prohibition of the Development, Production, and Stockpiling of Bacterial (Biological) and Toxin Weapons and on Their Destruction," March 26, 1975, T.I.A.S. no. 9433; 3) "Convention on the Prohibition of the Development, Production, Stockpiling and Use of Chemical Weapons and on Their Destruction," April 29, 1997, 32 International Legal Materials (I.L.M.) 932 (1993); 4) "Agreement Between the United States of America and the Union of Soviet Socialist Republics on Destruction and Non-Production of Chemical Weapons and on Measures to Facilitate the Multilateral Convention on Banning Chemical Weapons," 29 I.L.M. 932 (1990); 5) "Declaration on the Prohibition of Chemical Weapons," 28 I.L.M. 1020 (1989).

7. For discussions of some of the issues which have slowed progress on chemical and biological arms control, see Committee on International Arms Control and Security Affairs of The Association of the Bar of the City of New York,

Achieving Effective Arms Control: Recommendations, Background and Analysis, The Association of the Bar of the City of New York, 1985, pp. 115-118; Frederick J. Vogel, *The Chemical Weapons Convention: Strategic Implications for the United States*, Strategic Studies Institute, U.S. Army War College, Carlisle Barracks, PA, 1997, pp. 8-11. For general and up-to-date information on the Chemical Weapons Convention (CWC), implementation and enforcement of the CWC and the Organization for the Prohibition of Chemical Weapons (OPCW), see Organization for the Prohibition of Chemical Weapons, *The OPCW Home Page*, http://www.opcw.nl/

8. For example, Finland, Germany, Norway, the states of the former Soviet Union, and the United States all conduct various training and inspection programs on CWC verification. In the case of the United States and the former Soviet Union, these programs focus on and advance already-existing bilateral chemical and biological weapons agreements. The German, Norwegian, and Finnish programs are made available to outside parties, especially specialists from developing countries. See Janne E. Nolan et al., "The Imperatives for Cooperation," in *Global Engagement: Cooperation and Security in the 21st Century*, ed. Janne E. Nolan (Washington, DC: The Brookings Institution, 1994), pp. 51-52. Other positive examples of confidence-building mechanisms are seen in regional organizations such as the Rio Group, and in bilateral agreements such as the India-Pakistan Agreement on Chemical Weapons. See Roland M. Timerbaev and Meggen M. Watt, *Inventory of International Nonproliferation Organizations and Regimes — 1995 Edition* (Monterey, CA: Center for Nonproliferation Studies, Monterey Institute of International Studies, 1995). Significant to most of these efforts is the conscious decision by states and regional organizations to promote and improve transparency. While transparency is at the heart of many nonproliferation regimes, there are great disparities in their respective verification systems, which is a significant issue. "When applied in tandem, however, the Non-Proliferation and Chemical Weapons Convention systems will create a high degree of transparency, and synergies between them may increase the underlying effectiveness of each." Leonard S. Spector and Jonathan Dean, "Cooperative Security: Assessing the Tools of the Trade," in *Global Engagement: Cooperation and Security in the 21st Century*, ed. Janne E. Nolan (Washington, DC: The Brookings Institution, 1994), pp. 154-155.

9. The United States accounts for 45-55 percent, with China, France, Germany, Russia and the UK accounting for another 35-40 percent. See International Institute for Strategic Studies, *The Military Balance 1996/97* (London: Oxford University Press, October 1996), p. 273. Also see Stockholm International Peace Research Institute, *SIPRI Yearbook 1997: Armaments, Disarmament and International Security* (Oxford: Oxford University Press, 1997), p. 268.

10. Michael Renner, *Small Arms, Big Impact: The Next Challenge of Disarmament* (Washington, DC: Worldwatch Institute, 1997).

11. For critiques of the accuracy, consistency, and applicability of the register, see Arms Control Association, "ACA Register of U.S. Arms Transfers," *The Arms Control Association Fact Sheet*, August 1996; British American Security Information Council, *Chronicling an Absence of Restraint: The 1995 UN Arms Register*, Basic Papers, No. 13, November 3, 1995 (Washington, DC: British American Security Information Council, 1995); Edward Laurance, "The UN Register of Conventional Arms: Rationales and Prospects for Compliance and Effectiveness," *The Washington Quarterly* 16, No. 2 (Spring 1993), pp. 163-172; Frederic Pearson, "The UN and Regional Organizations in the Control of Conventional Arms Transfers," paper presented at the Center for Defense Information conference, "Conventional Arms Transfer Restraint in the 1990's," Washington, DC, November 16, 1994, pp. 68-82.

12. "Wassenaar Members Review Data Exchange," *Arms Control Today*, Vol. 27, No. 3 (May 1997), p. 32.

13. "Treaty on Conventional Armed Forces in Europe," Article XXI; and "Final Document of

the First Conference to Review the Operation of the Treaty on Conventional Armed Forces in Europe and the Concluding Act of the Negotiation on Personnel Strength," Vienna, May 15-31, 1996. For additional information on the treaty and force levels, see Joseph P. Harahan and John C. Kuhn, III, *On-Site Inspections Under the CFE Treaty* (Washington, DC: On-Site Inspection Agency, U.S. Department of Defense, 1996), pp. 2-3, 15-30. For one ambitious proposal to promote more extensive control of conventional forces, see Task Force on Peace and Security, United Nations Association of the USA, National Capital Area, "A Global Treaty for Reducing Conventional Arms and Armed Conflict," Washington, DC, February 28, 1997.

14. Edward J. Laurance, "Surplus Weapons and the Micro-Disarmament Process," paper presented at the United Nations Centre for Disarmament Affairs Workshop on Micro-Disarmament, "A New Agenda for Disarmament and Arms Control," Monterey Institute of International Studies, November 8, 1995; Juanita Darling, "Gun-Swap Project Overwhelmed by Response in War-Weary Land," *Los Angeles Times*, October 5, 1996, p. A6; Juanita Darling, "Salvadoran Gun Swap Nets Quite an Arsenal," *San Jose Mercury News*, October 6, 1996, p. A20.

15. Suzanne Daley, "In Mozambique, Guns for Plowshares and Bicycles," *New York Times*, March 2, 1997, p. A3.

16. Defense spending in East Asia has increased in absolute terms, but has decreased as a percentage of GDP. The opposite is true for most other regions where both absolute defense spending and defense expenditure as a portion of GDP have declined. For evidence of the rise in East Asian defense spending over the past decade in contrast to other regions, see International Institute for Strategic Studies, *The Military Balance 1996/97* (Oxford: Oxford University Press, 1996), pp. 308, 311.

17. Ibid.

18. These 27 participating states are: Albania, Armenia, Austria, Azerbaijan, Belarus, Bulgaria, Czech Republic, Estonia, Finland, Georgia, Hungary, Kazakhstan, Kyrgyz Republic, Latvia, Lithuania, Moldova, Poland, Romania, Russia, Slovakia, Slovenia, Sweden, Switzerland, Turkmenistan, Ukraine, Uzbekistan, and the Former Yugoslav Republic of Macedonia. Contacts among the world's militaries are more extensive than many realize. In particular, with the end of the Cold War, the volume of military-to-military contacts between East and West has grown significantly. In addition to multilateral contacts such as NATO's Partnership for Peace Program (PFP), the militaries of the world engage in a wide range of bilateral activities that include staff visits, exercises, personnel and unit exchanges, training cadres, and student exchanges. Military-to-military programs offer an important avenue for preventing deadly conflict by enhancing transparency, promoting confidence-building measures, improving communications, and increasing the professionalism among military institutions around the world. They offer significant potential to support arms control initiatives, improve multilateral peacekeeping operations by enhancing interoperability, and promote civil-military relations that support democratic institutions.

19. For information on the founding of the ASEAN Regional Forum, see *Chairman's Statement: The First ASEAN Regional Forum*, Association of Southeast Asian Nations, Bangkok, July 25, 1994.

20. While these two nations will still pursue peaceful nuclear technologies, the ABACC will serve to implement the SCCC's ban on testing, storage, and possession of nuclear weapons. Tariq Rauf et al., *Inventory of International Nonproliferation Organizations and Regimes*, 1996-1997 Edition (Monterey: Center for Nonproliferation Studies, Monterey Institute of International Studies, 1997), pp. 61-62.

21. For a theoretical discussion of the requirements for law within states, see Edward W. Lehman, *The Viable Polity* (Philadelphia, PA: Temple University Press, 1992), pp. 23-60, 139-162; Hans Kelsen, *General Theory of Law and the State*, trans. Anders Wedberg, 20th Century Legal Philosophy Series, vol. 1 (Cambridge, MA: Harvard University Press, 1949), pp. 15-

47, 181-267; Robert Oakley and Michael Dziedzic, "Policing the New World Disorder," *Strategic Forum* No. 84 (October 1996), pp. 1-4.

22. For discussions of the successful characteristics of conflict management, negotiations, and settlement, see Michael E. Brown, ed., *The International Dimensions of Internal Conflict* (Cambridge, MA: MIT Press, 1996); Cameron Hume, *Ending Mozambique's War: The Role of Mediation and Good Offices* (Washington, DC: United States Institute of Peace Press, 1994); Donald Rothchild, "Conclusion: Management of Conflict in West Africa," in *Governance as Conflict Management: Politics and Violence in West Africa*, ed. I. William Zartman (Washington, DC: The Brookings Institution, 1997), pp. 197-277; I. William Zartman, ed., *Elusive Peace: Negotiating an End to Civil Wars* (Washington, DC: The Brookings Institution, 1995); I. William Zartman, "Conflict Reduction: Prevention, Management, and Resolution," in *Conflict Resolution in Africa*, eds. Francis M. Deng and I. William Zartman (Washington, DC: The Brookings Institution, 1991), pp. 299-319.

23. For a discussion of the relationship between conflict and economic growth, opportunity, and performance, see Milton J. Esman, "Economic Performance and Ethnic Conflict," in *Conflict and Peacemaking in Multiethnic Societies*, ed. Joseph V. Montville (New York: Lexington Books, 1991), pp. 477-490, especially 484 and 489. For examples of how inequitable access to economic opportunity has prompted conflict, and how economic reforms have helped to resolve those conflicts, see Michael Renner, *Fighting for Survival* (New York: W.W. Norton & Co., 1996), especially pp. 122-131; and Alicia Levine, "Political Accommodation and the Prevention of Secessionist Violence," in *The International Dimensions of Internal Conflict*, ed. Michael E. Brown (Cambridge, MA: The MIT Press, 1996).

24. United Nations Department of Public Information, "Platform for Action," *The Beijing Declaration and the Platform for Action* (New York: United Nations Department of Public Information, 1996), pp. 46-56.

25. Advances in the global and economic and social agendas have resulted from several other world conferences as well, such as the 1992 Rio Conference on the Environment and Development, the 1993 Vienna Conference on Human Rights, the 1994 Cairo Conference on Population and Development, and the 1995 Beijing Conference on Women.

26. United Nations Development Program, *Human Development Report 1997* (New York: Oxford University Press, 1997), pp. 6-10.

27. Sudhir Anand and Amartya K. Sen, *Sustainable Human Development: Concepts and Priorities*, United Nations Development Program, Office of Development Studies Discussion Paper Series (New York, 1996), pp. 4, 27-31.

28. World Bank, *Global Economic Prospects and the Developing Countries* (Washington, DC: World Bank, 1997), p. 92.

29. United Nations, *Universal Declaration of Human Rights*, DPI/876, (New York: United Nations Department of Public Information, 1995).

30. See Frank Newman and David Weissbrodt, *International Human Rights: Law, Policy, and Process*, 2nd ed. (Cincinnati, OH: Anderson Publishing Co, 1996), pp. xxvi, 8, 14.

31. See United Nations, *Universal Declaration of Human Rights*, DPI/876, (New York: United Nations Department of Public Information, 1988); *Helsinki Final Act*, Conference on Security and Cooperation in Europe, August 1, 1975, 14 I.L.M. 1292 (1975).

32. See *Helsinki Final Act*, Conference on Security and Cooperation in Europe, August 1, 1975, 14 I.L.M. 1292 (1975); *Charter of Paris for a New Europe*, Conference on Security and Cooperation in Europe, November 2, 1991, 30 I.L.M. 193 (1991).

33. The United States' annual country reports on human rights practices have stirred controversy since their inception in 1971, but only in recent years have they taken on greater prominence in shaping policy. See U.S. Department of State, *Country Reports on Human Rights Practices for*

1996—Report Submitted to the Committee on Foreign Relations, U.S. Senate and the Committee on International Relations, U.S. House of Representatives (Washington, DC: U.S. Government Printing Office, 1997).

34. United Nations High Commissioner for Refugees, *The State of the World's Refugees 1995: In Search of Solutions* (Oxford: Oxford University Press, 1995), p. 57.

35. Frank Newman and David Weissbrodt, *International Human Rights: Law, Policy and Process*, 2nd ed. (Cincinnati, OH: Anderson Publishing Co., 1996), pp. 19-21.

36. For a theoretical examination of international arbitration and the role of the arbiter, see Gregory A. Raymond, *Conflict Resolution and the Structure of the State System: An Analysis of Arbitrative Settlements* (Montclair, NJ: Allanheld, Osmun & Co. Publishers, Inc., 1980) pp. 1-25; John Burton, *Conflict: Resolution and Prevention* (New York, NY: St. Martin's Press, 1990), pp. 188-201.

37. Connie Peck, *Sustainable Peace: The Role of the UN and Regional Organizations in Preventing Conflict* (Lanham, MD: Rowman & Littlefield, 1998).

38. For a general discussion of mediation, its use, success, failure, and advantages over arbitration, see John Burton, op. cit., pp. 180-193, 220-223; Gareth Evans, *Cooperating for Peace: The Global Agenda for the 1990s and Beyond* (Sydney: Allen & Unwin, 1993), pp. 64-85; I. William Zartman and Saadia Touval, "International Mediation in the Post–Cold War Era," in *Managing Global Chaos: Sources of and Responses to International Conflict,* eds. Chester A. Crocker and Fen Osler Hampson, with Pamela Aall (Washington, DC: United States Institute of Peace Press, 1996), pp. 445-461.

39. Robert A. Dahl, *Democracy and Its Critics* (New Haven: Yale University Press, 1989), pp. 244-245; John Pinder, "Community Against Conflict: The European Community's Contribution to Ethno-National Peace in Europe," in *Preventing Conflict in the Post-Communist World: Mobilizing International and Regional Organizations,* eds. Abram Chayes and Antonia Handler Chayes (Washington, DC: Brookings,

1996), pp. 170-171; Philippe C. Schmitter and Terry Lynn Karl, "What Democracy Is...And Is Not," in *The Global Resurgence of Democracy,* 2nd ed., eds. Larry Diamond and Marc F. Plattner (Baltimore: Johns Hopkins University Press, 1996), p. 55; Pauline H. Baker and John A. Ausink, *Ethnic Conflict as a Pathology of the State: A New Conceptual Approach* (Institute for the Study of Diplomacy, Edmund A. Walsh School of Foreign Service, Georgetown University, and the Fund for Peace, Washington, DC, 1996).

40. In an examination of the preventive value of various power-sharing techniques, Timothy D. Sisk discusses three ways in which such opportunities can be preserved: federalism, to establish clear institutional links between center and regional/local power centers; vote pooling, an outgrowth of electoral systems that "force" majority groups to form coalitions; and presidential systems, to permit the election of a broadly supported leader with the potential to serve a unifying, nation-building role. See Timothy D. Sisk, *Power Sharing and International Mediation in Ethnic Conflicts* (Washington, DC: USIP Press and Carnegie Commission on Preventing Deadly Conflict, 1996), pp. 27-46. Sisk's comments draw heavily upon the work of Donald L. Horowitz. See Donald L. Horowitz, *Ethnic Groups in Conflict* (Berkeley: University of California Press, 1985), pp. 601-652.

41. See, for example, Stuart Bremer, "Dangerous Dyads: Conditions Affecting the Likelihood of Interstate War, 1816-1965," *Journal of Conflict Resolution* 36, No. 2 (June 1992), pp. 309-341; Stuart Bremer "Democracy and Militarized Interstate Conflict, 1816-1965," *International Interactions* 18, No. 3 (1993), pp. 231-249; Bruce Bueno de Mesquita and David Lalman, *War and Reason: Domestic and International Imperatives* (New Haven, CT: Yale University Press, 1992); Michael Doyle, "Kant, Liberal Legacies, and Foreign Affairs," *Philosophy and Public Affairs* 12, No. 3 (Summer 1983), pp. 205-235; James Lee Ray, *Democracy and International Conflict: An Evaluation of the Democratic Peace Proposition* (Columbia, SC: University of South Carolina Press, 1995); R. J.

Rummel, "Libertarianism and International Violence," *Journal of Conflict Resolution* 27, No. 1 (March 1983), pp. 27-72; R. J. Rummel, "Libertarian Propositions on Violence within and between Nations: A Test against Published Results," *Journal of Conflict Resolution* 29, No. 3 (September 1985), pp. 419-455; R. J. Rummel, *Understanding Conflict and War*, 5 vols. (Los Angeles: Sage, 1975-81); Bruce Russett, *Grasping the Democratic Peace: Principles for a Post–Cold War World* (Princeton, NJ: Princeton University Press, 1993). See also note 5 in chapter 2.

42. I. William Zartman, "Putting Things Back Together," in *Collapsed States: The Disintegration and Restoration of Legitimate Authority*, ed. I. William Zartman (Boulder, CO: Lynne Reinner Publishers, 1995), pp. 267-273.

43. For a discussion of the transitions from military to civilian rule in Chile, see Javier Martínez and Alvaro Díaz, *Chile: The Great Transformation* (Washington, DC: The Brookings Institution; and Geneva: The United Nations Research Institute for Social Development, 1996), pp. 8-40. For a similar discussion of the transformation in Argentina, see Felipe A. M. de la Blaze, *Remaking the Argentine Economy* (New York: The Council on Foreign Relations Press, 1995), pp. 65-122.

44. I. William Zartman "Governance as Conflict Management in West Africa," in *Governance as Conflict Management: Politics and Violence in West Africa*, ed. I. William Zartman (Washington, DC: The Brookings Institution, 1997), pp. 9-48, especially pp. 36-43.

45. For a comprehensive examination of truth commissions and other forms of "transitional justice," see Neil J. Kritz, ed., *Transitional Justice*, 3 vols. (Washington, DC: United States Institute of Peace Press, 1995). See also Henry J. Steiner, ed., *Truth Commissions: A Comparative Assessment*, World Press Foundation Report #16 (Cambridge: World Peace Foundation, 1997).

46. Theodore Meron, "Preventing Genocide: The Contribution of War Crimes Tribunals to Peace, Reconciliation and Deterrence," lecture given in the Henkels Series on Humanitarian Intervention: Ethical and Policy Implications. University of Notre Dame, *Report*, The Joan B. Kroc Institute for International Peace Studies, No. 12 (Spring 1997), pp. 23-24.

47. Kofi Annan, *Renewing the United Nations: A Programme for Reform*, Report of the Secretary-General, A/51/168, July 14, 1997, para. 90.

48. For a general discussion of the democratization process, see Mohammed Ayoob, "State Making, State Breaking, and State Failure" in *Managing Global Chaos: Sources of and Responses to International Conflict*, eds. Chester A. Crocker and Fen Osler Hampson, with Pamela Aall (Washington, DC: United States Institute of Peace Press, 1996), pp. 37-51; Gretchen Casper and Michelle M. Taylor, *Negotiating Democracy: Transitions from Authoritarian Rule* (Pittsburgh, PA: University of Pittsburgh Press, 1996); Anthony Lake, *After the Wars: Reconstruction in Afghanistan, Indochina, Central America, Southern Africa, and the Horn of Africa* (New Brunswick, NJ: Transaction Publishers, 1990); I. William Zartman, ed., *Elusive Peace: Negotiating an End to Civil Wars* (Washington, DC: The Brookings Institution, 1995).

49. Colin Nickerson, "In Quebec, Tribes Talk of Leaving; Indians, Inuit Claim Land Rights," *Boston Globe*, October 13, 1995, p. 1. See also David Kleesh, Gislain Becard, Paul Deer, Mathew Coon-Comb, and Ken Deer, interviewed by Scott Simon, *Weekend Edition*, National Public Radio, October 28, 1995.

50. Arthur S. Banks, Alan J. Day, and Thomas C. Muller, eds., *Political Handbook of the World: 1997* (Binghamton, NY: CSA Publications, 1997), pp. 76-77.

51. Central Office of Information, *Britain 1997: An Official Handbook* (London: The Stationery Office, 1996), p. 25.

52. Ted Robert Gurr, *Minorities at Risk: A Global View of Ethnopolitical Conflicts* (Washington, DC: United States Institute of Peace Press, 1993), p. 133.

53. See James Carroll, "The Silence," *The New Yorker*, April 7, 1997, p. 68.

CHAPTER 5

1. Ian Smillie and Ian Filewod, "Norway," in *Non-Governmental Organisations and Governments: Stakeholders for Development*, eds. Ian Smillie and Henny Helmich (Paris: OECD, 1993), pp. 215-232.

2. Swedish Ministry for Foreign Affairs, *Preventing Violent Conflict: A Study* (Stockholm: Ministry of Foreign Affairs, 1997), pp. 44-45. See also a recent article by Sweden's Secretary of State for Foreign Affairs for reflections on enhancing the UN's conflict prevention efforts: Jan Eliasson, "Establishing Trust in the Healer: Preventive Diplomacy and the Future of the United Nations," in *Preventive Diplomacy: Stopping Wars Before They Start*, ed. Kevin M. Cahill (New York: Basic Books and The Center for International Health Cooperation, 1996), pp. 318-343.

3. See Government of Canada, *Towards a Rapid Reaction Capability for the United Nations*, Report of the Government of Canada, September 1995; Dick A. Leurdijk, ed., *A UN Rapid Deployment Brigade: Strengthening the Capacity for Quick Response* (The Hague: Netherlands Institute of International Relations *Clingendael*, 1995).

4. The preventive defense strategy developed by former U.S. Secretary of Defense William J. Perry centers on preventing conflict through U.S. engagement with allies and former enemies. Preventive defense seeks to halt the outbreak of conflict by turning adversaries into partners. Taking the Marshall Plan as its model, preventive defense is based on enhancing alliances and bilateral relationships, regional confidence building, constructive engagement, and nonproliferation of weapons of mass destruction. Initiatives such as the Cooperative Threat Reduction (Nunn-Lugar) program, the US-Russian Commission on Economic and Technological Cooperation (Gore-Chernomyrdin), Partnership for Peace (PFP), the NATO-Russian Charter (the Founding Act), and International Military Education and Training programs with centers in Germany and Hawaii are central to promoting stability and monitoring developments in a number of regions on the brink of conflict. For example, Partnership for Peace's military exercises and civilian meetings have created an expanding network of security relationships in Europe, building confidence, increasing transparency, and reducing tensions. Likewise, maintaining strong ties with partners in Asia and engaging with China, India, Pakistan, and others to increase understanding and avert crises are vital elements of preventive defense. Similar efforts are under way in Africa and the Americas.

   Continuing the focus on prevention, Secretary of Defense William Cohen emphasizes the importance of U.S. global engagement to shape the international security environment. This strategy is based on the view that maintaining order and stability requires strong U.S. leadership to promote peace, prosperity, and democracy, and for this purpose military-to-military cooperation and nonproliferation programs remain a high priority for the Department of Defense. See William S. Cohen, *The Report of the Quadrennial Defense Review* (Washington, DC: U.S. Government Printing Office, 1997); William S. Cohen, *Annual Report to the President and Congress* (Washington, DC: U.S. Government Printing Office, March 1997); William J. Perry, *Annual Report to the President and Congress* (Washington, DC: U.S. Government Printing Office, March 1996); William J. Perry, speech at the Aspen Institute Congressional Program conference, "US Relations with Russia," Dresden, Germany, August 20, 1997.

5. Craig Turner, "Canada's Diplomacy Coup Amazes U.S.; Ottawa's Land Mines Fight Mixed Skill and Determination," *Toronto Star*, August 31, 1997, p. A1; Ved Nanda, "U.S. Wise to Join Land-Mine Ban Talks," *Denver Post*, August 29, 1997, p. B7.

6. Labor organizations have often provided a channel for broad-based constructive political expression. In the 1980s and 1990s, for example, the Congress of South African Trade Unions (COSATU) was instrumental in building a politically engaged nonwhite middle class in South

Africa. COSATU called for peaceful marches, held strikes, and was party to negotiations with government and employers. On a global scale, an organization that has promoted social justice and internationally recognized human and labor rights is the International Labor Organization (ILO), a UN specialized agency. The ILO along with the governments of member states and their employees have created a system of international standards in all work-related areas, such as the abolition of forced labor, freedom of association, and equality of treatment and opportunity. Alan Cowell, "The Struggle: Power and Politics in South Africa's Black Trade Unions," *New York Times*, June 15, 1986, p. 14; Juliette Saunders, "South African Workers to Stage Nationwide Protests," *Reuters European Business Report*, June 18, 1995. For more information on the International Labor Organization, see their Internet site at http://www.ilo.org./.

7. One observer identifies four "crises" and two "revolutions" which account for the dramatic increase in NGO activities. The crisis of the modern welfare state, the development crisis brought on by the rise in oil prices and global recession in the 1970s, global environmental damage, and a crisis of socialism have all limited or delegitimized the role of governments in meeting the needs of their citizens. Increasingly, people are turning to the private sector to fill the void left by the state. The ability for collective private action has been greatly enhanced by the revolutionary growth in communications technology, which has made possible global organization and mobilization. The second revolution was brought about by the growth of the global economy in the 1960s and early 1970s. This in turn spurred the development of a middle class in many parts of the developing world. This social class has been particularly active in developing and supporting the work of NGOs in its communities. Lester M. Salamon, "The Rise of the Nonprofit Sector," *Foreign Affairs* 73, No. 4 (July/August 1994), pp. 109-122; Jessica T. Mathews, "Power Shift," *Foreign Affairs* 76, No. 1 (January/February 1997), pp. 50-66.

As mentioned earlier, NGOs can also provide early warning of deteriorating circumstances and suggestions regarding the best approach to conflict resolution. The London-based *International Alert* is a prominent example of an NGO involved in early warning and monitoring of conflict situations. Formed in 1985, the organization provides training for conflict negotiators, serves as a neutral mediator, and shares information on indicators of conflict and emergency situations. For more information, see *International Alert Annual Report 1994* (London: International Alert, 1995). A more recent example is the Brussels-based International Crisis Group that was formed in 1995 and focuses primarily on trying to mobilize governments and international organizations to take preventive action.

8. See Thomas G. Weiss and Leon Gordenker, eds., *NGOs, the UN, and Global Governance* (Boulder, CO: Lynne Rienner, 1996).

9. See Larry Minear and Thomas G. Weiss, *Mercy Under Fire: War and the Global Humanitarian Community* (Boulder, CO: Westview Press, 1995), pp. 13-56; Thomas G. Weiss and Cindy Collins, "Operational Dilemmas and Challenges," in *Humanitarian Challenges and Intervention,* eds. Larry Minear and Thomas G. Weiss (Boulder, CO: Westview Press, 1996), pp. 130-131.

10. Cyrus R. Vance and Herbert S. Okun, "Creating Healthy Alliances: Leadership and Coordination among NGOs, Governments and the United Nations in Times of Emergency and Conflict," in *Preventive Diplomacy: Stopping Wars Before They Start*, ed. Kevin M. Cahill (New York: Basic Books, 1996), pp. 194-195.

11. A number of international NGOs, including the International Federation of Red Cross and Red Crescent Societies, Oxfam, International Save the Children Alliance, and Lutheran World Relief, have subscribed to a common code of conduct to guide their mutual activities. This code is a voluntary agreement acknowledging the right to humanitarian assistance as a fundamental principle for all citizens of all countries. In addition, InterAction, an umbrella organiza-

tion of 160 U.S. NGOs, established InterAction Private Voluntary Organization Standards to create a common set of values for each member agency to follow and to enhance the public's trust in the ideals and operations of its members. See International Federation of Red Cross and Red Crescent Societies, *Code of Conduct for the International Red Cross and Red Crescent Movement and NGOs in Disaster Relief*, http://www.ifrc.org/; and InterAction, *PVO Standards* (Washington, DC: InterAction, 1995, amended May 1, 1996).

12. Joe Hinds, *A Guide to Peace, Reconciliation and Community Relations Projects in Ireland* (Belfast, Northern Ireland: Community Relations Council, 1994), pp. 36-37; Mustafa Ceric, Vinko Puljic, Nikolaj Mrdja, and Jakob Finci, "Press Release," Inter-Religious Council in Bosnia-Herzegovina, Sarajevo, June 9, 1997.

13. For a detailed analysis of the role of the Community of Sant'Egidio, see Cameron Hume, *Ending Mozambique's War: The Role of Mediation and Good Offices* (Washington, DC: United States Institute of Peace Press, 1994), pp. 3-4, 15-19, 33, 145.

The first direct contact between the leadership of the insurgents (RENAMO) and the FRELIMO government took place at Sant'Egidio in Rome on July 8, 1990. Not long thereafter, two members of Sant'Egidio were enlisted as primary mediators and served in that capacity for the ten rounds of peace talks held at Sant'Egidio headquarters in Rome before the General Peace Accord was signed on October 4, 1992. (Joining Bishop Jaime Goncalves on the mediation team were Sant'Egidio's founder and leader, Andrea Riccardi, and Don Mateo Zuppi, a parish priest in Rome. A fourth team member, Mario Raffaelli, represented the Italian government.) In concert with the Italian government and other governments, Sant'Egidio maintained a momentum for peace among the two parties until the accord was signed.

This diplomatic solution to the conflict, however, was only the beginning. The challenge after 1992 was to maintain the peace so that

postwar reconstruction efforts could begin to rebuild the nation's economic infrastructure. The primary problem was a social one: reconciling old enemies and ministering to a brutalized generation were essential to successful implementation. Nearly all of "the best-informed observers" predicted the breakdown of the accords due to ill will, inefficient bureaucracy, and immobilizable resources. What they failed to predict, however, was the capacity of local people and institutions to create the framework for locally brokered cease-fire and conflict resolution procedures. As the representatives of Sant'Egidio knew, the grassroots churches were well placed to fulfill this role, both to bring RENAMO and FRELIMO together, and to mobilize people around reconciliation and rebuilding communities. After the war, local churches served as mediating institutions, facilitating the reintegration of RENAMO soldiers into Mozambican society. The churches' relief agencies then expanded their operations into areas previously occupied by RENAMO. Representatives of Sant'Egidio helped sponsor the training of "social integrators" to bring the reconciliation process into local communities. Scott Appleby, *The Ambivalence of the Sacred: Religion, Violence and Reconciliation* (Lanham, MD: Rowman & Littlefield, forthcoming).

14. All Africa Council of Churches, "Recommendations of the Conference of Christian Churches of the Democratic Republic of Congo," Kinshasa, July 26, 1997; All Africa Conference of Churches, "Contribution of Christian Women at the Conference of Christian Churches of Congo," Kinshasa, July 25, 1997.

15. In Chicago, in 1993, for only the second time in history, a Parliament of the World's Religions was convened. This gathering passed a "Declaration Toward a Global Ethic." People from very different religious backgrounds for the first time agreed on core guidelines for behavior which they affirm in their own traditions. This statement attempted to clarify what religions all over the world hold in common and formulated a minimal ethic which is essential for human sur-

vival. See Hans Küng, "The Parliament of the World's Religions: Declaration of a Global Ethic," in *Yes to a Global Ethic*, ed. Hans Küng (New York: Continuum, 1996), pp. 2-96.

16. The Pugwash Conferences on Science and World Affairs were founded by physicist Joseph Rotblat to eliminate the role played by nuclear weapons in international politics. The conferences are rooted in the common humanity of all peoples, rather than in national loyalties. Participants are invited in a personal capacity, not as representatives of governments or institutions. Pugwash urges scientists to consider the social, moral, and ethical implications of their work. There have been more than 200 Pugwash conferences, attracting over 10,000 scientists, academics, politicians, and military figures. Among their many contributions, they have laid the groundwork for the Partial Test Ban Treaty of 1963, the Non-Proliferation Treaty of 1968, and the Antiballistic Missile Treaty of 1972. Recently, the conferences have also begun to discuss poverty and environmental issues. Student Pugwash groups, which discuss these same issues in high schools and universities, have been formed in 24 nations; 50 chapters exist in the United States alone. "Pugwash Conferences Wins 1995 Peace Prize," Associated Press, October 13, 1995; "Rotblat: First Nuclear Protester," Reuters Information Service, October 13, 1995.

17. Other experiments demonstrate the power of shared, highly valued, superordinate goals that can *only* be achieved by cooperative effort. Such goals can override the differences that people bring to the situation, and often have a powerful, unifying effect. Classic experiments readily made strangers at a boys' camp into enemies by isolating them from one another and heightening competition. But when powerful superordinate goals were introduced, enemies were transformed into friends.

These experiments have been replicated in work with business executives and other kinds of groups with similar results. So the effect is certainly not limited to children and

youth. Indeed, the findings have pointed to the beneficial effects of working cooperatively under conditions that lead people to formulate a new, inclusive group, going beyond the subgroups with which they entered the situation. Such effects are particularly strong when there are tangibly successful outcomes of cooperation—for example, clear rewards from cooperative learning in school or at work. They have important implications for childrearing and education. Ameliorating the problem of intergroup relations rests upon finding better ways to foster child and adolescent development, as well as utilizing crucial opportunities to educate young people in conflict resolution and in mutual accommodation.

18. See W.D. Hawley and A.W. Jackson, eds., *Toward a Common Destiny: Improving Race and Ethnic Relations in America* (San Francisco, CA: Jossey-Bass Publishers, 1995).

19. See E. Staub, *The Roots of Evil: The Origins of Genocide and Other Group Violence* (Cambridge: Cambridge University Press, 1989), pp. 274-283.

20. For one treatment of this linkage, see Nik Gowing, *Media Coverage: Help or Hindrance in Conflict Prevention?* (Washington, DC: Carnegie Commission on Preventing Deadly Conflict, September 1997).

21. For example, Internews Network, a nonprofit organization dedicated to promoting international understanding through the innovative use of broadcast media, sponsors conflict prevention training programs on free media in the former Soviet Union. It contributes to developing independent media programming to aid public understanding of sustainable market reform and democracy and develops guidelines and codes of ethics to help former Soviet reporters cover conflict objectively without aggravating tensions. Internews has worked closely with local nongovernmental media to provide training, equipment, technical and organizational know-how, and news exchanges to help develop objective journalism at the national, regional, and local levels. Seminars have been initiated to strengthen television journalists' sense of

Table N.2

Field	Agency
Atomic Energy	International Atomic Energy Agency (IAEA)
Children	United Nations Children's Fund (UNICEF)
Civil Aviation	International Civil Aviation Organization (ICAO)
Crime Prevention and Criminal Justice	Economic and Social Council (ECOSOC) Commission on Crime Prevention and Criminal Justice
Disaster Relief	United Nations Department of Humanitarian Affairs (UNDHA)
Education/Science/Culture	United Nations Education, Scientific, and Cultural Organization (UNESCO)
Environment	United Nations Environment Programme(UNEP)
Food/Agriculture	Food and Agriculture Organization(FAO), International Fund for Agricultural Development (IFAD), World Food Council (WFC), World Food Programme (WFP)
Health	World Health Organization (WHO)
Human Settlements	United Nations Centre for Human Settlements (UNCHS)
Industrial Development	United Nations Industrial Development Organization (UNIDO)
Intellectual Property	World Intellectual Property Organization (WIPO)
Labor	International Labor Organization (ILO)
Maritime	International Maritime Organization (IMO)
Meteorology	World Meteorology Organization (WMO)
Monetary Policy	International Monetary Fund (IMF)
Narcotic Drugs	ECOSOC Commission on Narcotic Drugs
Population	United Nations Population Fund (UNFPA)
Postal Regulations	Universal Postal Union (UPU)
Refugees	United Nations High Commissioner for Refugees (UNHCR)
Research/Training	United Nations Institute for Training and Research (UNITAR), United Nations University (UNU)
Telecommunications	International Telecommunication Union (ITU)
Trade/Development	United Nations Conference on Trade and Development (UNCTAD)
Trade/Tariffs	World Trade Organization (WTO)
Women	United Nations Development Fund for Women (UNIFEM), International Research and Training Institute for the Advancement of Women (INSTRAW), ECOSOC Commission on the Status of Women

Source: Chadwick F. Alger, "Thinking About the Future of the UN System," *Global Governance 2,* No. 3 (Sept.-Dec. 1996), pp. 335-360.

responsibility, impartiality, and accuracy in reporting conflicts, and to heighten their awareness of the devastating effects of irresponsible reporting. The program consists of ten week-long seminars on the coverage of ethnic conflict, balanced news reporting, station management, and technical aspects of production.

Also working in the former Soviet Union is the Commission on Radio and Television Policy, cochaired by former U.S. President Jimmy Carter and Eduard Sagalaev, president of the Moscow Independent Broadcasting Corporation. The commission is made up of 50 respected figures from the mass media, academia, and public survey institutions in the former Soviet Union, Europe, and the United States. Commissioners gather annually to debate media issues and adopt recommendations based on analyses of working groups. Prior working groups have dealt with issues such as television coverage of minorities and changing economic relations arising from democratization, privatization, and new technologies. The commission has also published two policy guidebooks which have been translated into more than a dozen languages, and are used by governmental and nongovernmental groups in the former Soviet Union, Eastern and Central Europe, the Middle East, and Ethiopia. See *Television and Elections* (1992) and *Television/Radio News and Minorities* (1994).

22. See Voice of America, *Conflict Resolution Project Annual Report* (Washington, DC: Voice of America, 1997).

23. Trevor Findlay, *Cambodia: The Legacy and Lessons of UNTAC*, SIPRI Research Report No. 9 (New York: Oxford University Press, 1995); James A. Schear, "Riding the Tiger: The UN and Cambodia," in *UN Peacekeeping, American Policy, and the Uncivil Wars of the 1990s*, ed. William J. Durch (New York: St. Martin's Press, 1996), pp. 135-191; John M. Sanderson, "Preparation for Deployment and Conduct of Peacekeeping Operations: A Cambodia Snapshot," in *Peacekeeping at the Crossroads*, eds. Kevin Clements and Christine Wilson (Canberra: Australian National University, 1994). According to James Schear, who served as an assistant to the head of UNTAC, Yasushi Akashi, Radio UNTAC "gained a reputation as the most popular and credible radio station in the country, and was widely listened to in Khmer Rouge areas."

24. The growing importance and influence of an increasingly effective women's rights movement was reflected in the 1995 Fourth World Conference on Women in Beijing, attended by more than 30,000 women representing 189 countries. The significance of this event lies not only in its opportunity for women from around the world to meet and discuss issues of transnational concern, but also to learn ways to facilitate deeper contact. In particular, the conference emphasized electronic networking as a means by which women might gain access to information and share ideas on a worldwide basis, a resource not available a few years ago. See Human Rights Watch, *Human Rights Watch World Report 1996* (Washington, DC: Human Rights Watch, 1996), p. 351; further information can be found at the UN website, *Women, the Information Revolution and the Beijing Conference*, http://www.un.org/dpcsd/daw/.

CHAPTER 6

1. Jesse Helms, "Saving the U.N.," Foreign Affairs 75, No. 5 (September/October 1996), pp. 2-7; James Holtje, *Divided It Stands: Can the United Nations Work?* (Atlanta, GA: Turner Publishing, Inc., 1995); Peter Wilenski, "The Structure of the UN in the Post-Cold War Period," in *United Nations, Divided World: The UN's Roles In International Relations*, eds. Adam Roberts and Benedict Kingsbury (Oxford: Clarendon Press, 1993), pp. 437-467.

2. For an insightful examination of many of the United Nations' early efforts and innovations in peace and security operations, as examined through the life of United Nations diplomat Ralph Bunche, see Brian Urquhart, *Ralph Bunche: An American Life* (New York: W.W. Norton & Company, Inc., 1993). See also William J. Durch, ed., *The Evolution of UN Peacekeeping: Case Studies and Comparative Analysis* (New York: St. Martin's Press, 1993); United Nations, *The Blue Helmets: A Review of United Nations Peace-keeping* (New York: United Nations Department of Public Information, 1996).

3. The United Nations undertakes a number of tasks in addition to its more publicized work in areas such as peace and security, development, and human rights. Table N.2 identifies many of these fields and corresponding United Nations agencies. A Council on Foreign Relations study highlighted many of these roles as they relate to the U.S. national interest in an effective United Nations. See *American National Interest and the United Nations: Statement and Report of an*

Independent Task Force (New York: Council on Foreign Relations, 1996).

4. United Nations Childrens Fund, *State of the World's Children 1996* (New York: Oxford University Press, 1996).

5. United States Mission to the United Nations, "Global Humanitarian Emergencies 1996" (New York: February 1996), pp. 3-4; U.S. Committee for Refugees, *World Refugee Survey 1997* (Washington, DC: Immigration and Refugee Services of America, 1997), pp. 5-6; United Nations High Commissioner for Refugees, *The State of the World's Refugees 1995* (Oxford: Oxford University Press, 1995), p. 255; United Nations High Commissioner for Refugees, "UNHCR by Numbers 1996" (Geneva: UNHCR Public Information Section, July 1996), p. 12.

6. For varying perspectives on the role of the United Nations secretary-general, see Thomas E. Boudreau, *Sheathing the Sword: The U.N. Secretary-General and the Prevention of International Conflict* (New York: Greenwood Press, 1991); Boutros Boutros-Ghali, "Challenges of Preventive Diplomacy: The Role of the United Nations and Its Secretary-General," in *Preventive Diplomacy: Stopping Wars Before They Start*, ed. Kevin M. Cahill (New York: Basic Books, 1996), pp. 16-32; Thomas M. Franck and Georg Nolte, "The Good Offices Function of the UN Secretary-General," in *The UN and International Security after the Cold War: The UN's Roles in International Relations*, eds. A. Roberts and B. Kingsbury (Oxford: Clarendon Press, 1993), pp. 143-182; James Holtje, *Divided It Stands: Can the United Nations Work?* (Atlanta: Turner Publishing, Inc., 1995), pp. 97-124; Giandomenico Picco, "The UN and the Use of Force: Leave the Secretary-General Out of It," *Foreign Affairs* 73, No. 5 (September/October 1994), pp. 14-18; Brian Urquhart, "The Role of the Secretary-General," in *U.S. Foreign Policy and the United Nations System*, eds. Charles William Maynes and Richard S. Williamson (New York: W.W. Norton & Company, 1996), pp. 212-228.

7. David Owen, *Balkan Odyssey* (London: Victor Gollancz, 1995), see especially pp. 354-355; Peter James Spielmann, "U.N. Chief Considers Reconvening Peace Talks on Bosnia," Associated Press, May 28, 1993.

8. See Olara Otunnu, "The Peace-and-Security Agenda of the United Nations: From a Crossroads into the Next Century," in *Peacemaking and Peacekeeping for the Next Century,* report of the 25th Vienna Seminar cosponsored by the Government of Austria and the International Peace Academy, March 2-4, 1995 (New York: International Peace Academy, 1995), pp. 66-82.

9. Boutros Boutros-Ghali, *An Agenda for Peace*, 2nd ed. (New York: United Nations, 1995), p. 44.

10. Commission on Global Governance, *Our Global Neighborhood* (New York: Oxford University Press, 1995), p. 71.

11. Kofi Annan, *Renewing the United Nations: A Programme for Reform* (New York: United Nations, 1997), para. 110.

12. Ibid., see especially para. 67, 76-79, 111-116, 180-184, 198. Prevention is an element of several other areas of interest in the secretary-general's report, including: drug control, crime prevention, and counterterrorism, para. 143-145; improving UN coordination with civil society, para. 207-216; and general managerial reform to streamline UN operations to eliminate duplication and enhance cooperation and information sharing, Annex.

13. Boutros Boutros-Ghali, *An Agenda for Peace*, 2nd ed. (New York: United Nations, 1995).

14. Boutros Boutros-Ghali, *An Agenda for Development* (New York: United Nations, 1995).

15. Boutros Boutros-Ghali, *An Agenda for Democratization* (New York: United Nations, 1996).

16. See John Stremlau and Francisco Sagasti, *Preventing Deadly Conflict: Does the World Bank Have a Role?* (Washington, DC: Carnegie Commission on Preventing Deadly Conflict, June 1998). The only international financial institution that has a mandate to support the internal political development of borrowing states is the European Bank for Reconstruction and Development. See Melanie H. Stein, "Conflict Preven-

tion in Transition Economies: A Role for the European Bank for Reconstruction and Development?" in *Preventing Conflict in the Post-Communist World: Mobilizing International and Regional Organizations*, eds. Abram Chayes and Antonia Handler Chayes (Washington, DC: The Brookings Institution, 1996), pp. 339-378.

17. In his report to the General Assembly, Secretary-General Kofi Annan has recommended that a commission be established to study the need for fundamental change in the system at large. The Commission supports this call for the reasons outlined herein. Kofi Annan, op. cit., para. 89.

18. This section draws on a study prepared for the Commission by Connie Peck of the United Nations Institute for Training and Research, *Sustainable Peace: The Role of the UN and Regional Organizations in Preventing Conflict* (Lanham, MD: Rowman & Littlefield, 1998). For further discussions on the relative strengths and weaknesses of regional organizations, see Charles Van der Donckt, *Looking Forward by Looking Back: A Pragmatic Look at Conflict and the Regional Option*, Policy Staff Paper No. 95/01, Canadian Department of Foreign Affairs and International Trade, September 1995; Ruth Wedgwood, "Regional and Subregional Organizations in International Conflict Management," in *Managing Global Chaos: Sources of and Responses to International Conflict*, eds. Chester A. Crocker and Fen Osler Hampson, with Pamela Aall (Washington, DC: United States Institute of Peace Press, 1996), pp. 275-285.

19. The charters and treaties of many regional organizations explicitly acknowledge the importance of the United Nations and the primacy of the principles embodied in the UN Charter. The Organization of African Unity Charter (1963) states that one of the group's purposes is "to promote international cooperation, having due regard to the UN Charter and the Universal Declaration of Human Rights." The Association of Southeast Asian Nations (ASEAN) highlights the necessity of "adherence to the principles of the United Nations Charter" in the Bangkok Declaration (1967) and the Singapore Declara-

tion of 1992 affirms ASEAN's "commitment to the centrality of the UN role in the maintenance of international peace and security as well as promoting cooperation for socioeconomic development." The Organization for Security and Cooperation in Europe in the Charter of Paris for a New Europe (1990) reaffirms the "commitment to the principles and purposes of the United Nations as enshrined in the Charter and condemn[s] all violations of these principles. We recognize with satisfaction the growing role of the United Nations in world affairs and its increasing effectiveness...." The European Union's Maastricht Treaty seeks "to preserve peace and strengthen international security, in accordance with the principles of the United Nations Charter." The oldest of the regional organizations, the Organization of American States, resolves "to persevere in the noble undertaking that humanity has conferred upon the United Nations, whose principles and purposes they solemnly reaffirm." Even the Treaty of Washington that led to the formation of the North Atlantic Treaty Organization (NATO) takes full cognizance of the UN Charter and its principles as well as the rights and responsibilities of the Security Council and member states of the UN.

20. Ruth Wedgwood, "Regional and Subregional Organizations in International Conflict Management," in *Managing Global Chaos: Sources of and Responses to International Conflict*, eds. Chester A. Crocker and Fen Osler Hampson, with Pamela Aall (Washington, DC: United States Institute of Peace Press, 1996), pp. 276-278.

21. Richard Feinberg, "The Coup That Wasn't," *Washington Post*, April 30, 1996, p. A13.

CHAPTER 7

1. This section draws upon research into human conflict and education over the past several decades. See, for example, David Hamburg, "An Evolutionary Perspective on Human Aggression," in *The Development and Integration of Behavior: Essays in Honor of Robert Hinds*, ed.

P. Bateson, (Cambridge: Cambridge University Press, 1991); B. Smuts, D. Cheney, et al., *Primate Societies* (Chicago: University of Chicago Press, 1986); M. Brewer and R. Kramer, "The Psychology of Intergroup Attitudes and Behavior," *Annual Review of Psychology* 36 (1985), pp. 219-243; A. Bandura, *Aggression: A Social Learning Analysis* (Englewood Cliffs, NJ: Prentice-Hall, 1973); D. T. Campbell, " Ethnocentric and Other Altruistic Motives," in *Nebraska Symposium on Motivation*, ed. D. T. Campbell (Lincoln: University of Nebraska Press, 1965); G. Allport, *The Nature of Prejudice* (New York: Doubleday, 1958); J. Groebel and R. Hinde, *Aggression and War: Their Biological and Social Bases* (Cambridge: Cambridge University Press, 1989); W. D. Hawley and A. W. Jackson, eds., *Toward a Common Destiny: Improving Race and Ethnic Relations in America* (San Francisco: Jossey-Bass Publishers, 1995); E. Staub, *The Roots of Evil: The Origins of Genocide and Other Group Violence* (Cambridge: Cambridge University Press, 1989); M. Deutsch, *The Resolution of Conflict* (New Haven, CT: Yale University Press, 1973).

2. United Nations Educational, Scientific and Cultural Organization, "A Culture of Peace and Nonviolence within Educational Institutions: Elements for the Launching of an Interregional Project," draft paper prepared November 23, 1995. UNESCO publishes newsletters and other information on the Culture of Peace programs on its website: http://www.unesco.org/cpp/

3. Mikhail Gorbachev, "On Nonviolent Leadership," in *Essays on Leadership* (Washington, DC: Carnegie Commission on Preventing Deadly Conflict, December 1998).

4. Boutros Boutros-Ghali, "Leadership and Conflict," in *Essays on Leadership* (Washington, DC: Carnegie Commission on Preventing Deadly Conflict, December 1998).

5. For a sampling of the literature regarding bureaucratic decision making, primarily in the U.S., see Carnes Lord, *The Presidency and the Management of National Security* (New York: The Free Press, 1988); Robert L. Pfaltzgraff, Jr. and Jacquelyn K. Davis, *National Security Decisions: The Participants Speak* (Lexington, MA: Lexington Books, 1990); D.A. Welch, "The Organizational Process and Bureaucratic Politics Paradigms: Retrospect and Prospect," *International Security* 17 (Fall 1992), pp. 112-146; Scott Sagan, "The Perils of Proliferation," *International Security* 18 (Spring 1994), pp. 66-107; E. Rhodes, "Do Bureaucratic Politics Matter?" *World Politics* 47 (October 1994), pp. 1-41; Irmtraud N. Gallhofer and Willem E. Saris, *Foreign Policy Decision-Making* (Westport, CT: Praeger, 1996); Irving L. Janis, *Crucial Decisions: Leadership in Policymaking and Crisis Management* (New York: The Free Press, 1989), pp. 28-33.

6. Alexander L. George, *Presidential Decision-making in Foreign Policy: The Effective Use of Information and Advice* (Boulder, CO: Westview Press, 1980), pp. 1-12.

7. Steven Kull, "What the Public Knows that Washington Doesn't," *Foreign Policy* 101 (Winter 1995-1996), pp. 102-115.

8. Steven Kull and I.M. Destler, *An Emerging Consensus: A Study of American Public Attitudes on America's Role in the World: Summary of Findings* (College Park, MD: Program on International Policy Attitudes, Center for International and Security Studies at Maryland, 1996), p. 1.

9. Catherine McArdle Kelleher, "Security in the New Order: Presidents, Polls, and the Use of Force," in *Beyond the Beltway: Engaging the Public in U.S. Foreign Policy*, eds. Daniel Yankelovich and I.M. Destler (New York: W.W. Norton & Co., 1994), pp. 238-239.

10. Ibid.

11. Daniel Yankelovich and John Immerwahr, "The Rules of Public Engagement," in *Beyond the Beltway: Engaging the Public in U.S. Foreign Policy*, eds. Daniel Yankelovich and I.M. Destler (New York: W.W. Norton & Co., 1994), pp. 43-77.

APPENDIX 2

1. Connie Peck, *Sustainable Peace: The Role of the UN and Regional Organizations in Preventing Conflict* (Lanham, MD: Rowman & Littlefield, 1998).

2. Gareth Evans, *Cooperating for Peace: The Global Agenda for the 1990s and Beyond* (Sydney: Allen & Unwin, 1993), p. 31.

3. Peter de Costa, "Combining Against Conflict," *Africa Report* 37, No. 5 (September-October 1992), pp. 21-26.

4. "African Charter on Human and People's Rights," O.A.U. Doc CAB/LEG/67/3 Rev. 5.

5. Diana Chigas, with Elizabeth McClintock and Christophe Kamp, "Preventive Diplomacy and the Organization for Security and Cooperation in Europe: Creating Incentives for Dialogue and Cooperation," in *Preventing Conflict in the Post-Communist World*, eds. Abram Chayes and Antonia Handler Chayes (Washington, DC: The Brookings Institution, 1996), pp. 25-97.

6. Reinhardt Rummel, *Common Foreign and Security Policy and Conflict Prevention* (London: International Alert and Saferworld, 1996), p. 16.

7. Reinhardt Rummel, *Common Foreign and Security Policy*, p. 42; European Information Service, "Human Rights: EU Needs To Put Teeth into Policy," *European Report*, December 7, 1996; and European Information Service, "Human Rights: European Parliament Seeks Reform of EU Policy," *European Report*, December 14, 1996.

SELECTED
BIBLIOGRAPHY

Ackerman, Peter, and Christopher Kruegler. *Strategic Nonviolent Conflict*. Westport, CT: Praeger Publishers, 1994.

Ackermann, Alice, and Antonio Pala. "From Peace-keeping to Preventive Deployment: A Study of the United Nations in the Former Yugoslav Republic of Macedonia." *European Security* 5, No. 1 (Spring 1996).

Africa Conference of Churches. "Contribution of Christian Women at the Conference of Christian Churches of Congo." Kinshasa, July 25, 1997.

Africa Council of Churches. "Recommendations of the Conference of Christian Churches of the Democratic Republic of Congo." Kinshasa, July 26, 1997.

"Agreement Establishing the International Institute for Democracy and Electoral Assistance." Founding Conference, February 27-28, 1995.

Ahlström, Christer. *Casualties of Conflict*. Uppsala: Department of Peace and Conflict Research, 1991.

Ahmad, Makram Muhammad. "Turkey: Demirel on Ties With Syria, Terrorism." *Al-Musawwar,* July 26, 1996.

Alexandratos, Nikos, ed. *World Agriculture: Towards 2010, An FAO Study*. Chichester, England: Food and Agriculture Organization of the United Nations and John Wiley and Sons, 1996.

Alger, Chadwick F. "Thinking About the Future of the UN System." *Global Governance* 2, No. 3 (September-December 1996).

Allport, G. *The Nature of Prejudice*. New York: Doubleday, 1958.

American National Interest and the United Nations: Statement and Report of an Independent Task Force. New York: Council on Foreign Relations, 1996.

Anand, Sudhir, and Amartya K. Sen. "Sustainable Human Development: Concepts and Priorities." United Nations Development Program, Office of Development Studies Discussion Paper Series (1996).

Annan, Kofi. *Renewing the United Nations: A Programme for Reform*. New York: United Nations, 1997.

"Anti-Russian 'Hysteria' Over Abkhazia in Georgia." *Pravda*, July 13, 1995.

Appleby, Scott. *The Ambivalence of the Sacred: Religion, Violence, and Reconciliation*. Lanham, MD: Rowman & Littlefield, forthcoming.

Arias Sánchez, Oscar. "A Precondition for Peace and Prosperity in the 21st Century: A Code of Conduct on Arms Transfers." Speech to the State of the World Plenary Session, San Francisco, October 3, 1996.

———, the Dalai Lama, Donald Gann, Gururaj Mutalik, Jose Ramos Horta, Susan Waltz, Elie Wiesel, and Betty Williams. "The Commission of Nobel Peace Laureates' International Code of Conduct on Arms Transfers: A Joint Statement for Peace and Human Rights." New York, May 29, 1997.

Arms Control and Disarmament Agency. "U.S. Nunn-Lugar Safety, Security, Dismantlement Program." Arms Control and Disarmament Agency Fact Sheet, May 20, 1996.

Arms Control Association. "ACA Register of U.S. Arms Transfers." *The Arms Control Association Fact Sheet*, August 1996.

Axworthy, Lloyd. "The Ottawa Process: Towards a Global Ban on Anti-Personnel Mines." Washington, DC: Embassy of Canada, May 1997.

Ayoob, Mohammed. "State Making, State Breaking, and State Failure." In *Managing Global Chaos: Sources of and Responses to International Conflict*, eds. Chester A. Crocker and Fen Osler Hampson, with Pamela Aall. Washington, DC: United States Institute of Peace Press, 1996.

———. "The New-Old Disorder in the Third World." In *The United Nations and Civil Wars*, ed. Thomas G. Weiss. Boulder, CO: Lynne Rienner, 1995.

Azar, Edward E., and John W. Burton, eds. *International Conflict Resolution: Theory and Practice*. Sussex: Wheatsheaf Books, 1986.

al-Baharna, Husain. "The Fact-Finding Mission of the United Nations Secretary-General and the Settlement of the Bahrain-Iran Dispute, May 1970." *International and Comparative Law Quarterly* 22 (1973).

Baker, James A., III. *The Politics of Diplomacy: Revolution, War and Peace 1989-1992*. New York: G.P. Putnam, 1995.

Baker, Pauline H., and John A. Ausink. "State Collapse and Ethnic Violence: Toward a Predictive Model." *Parameters* 26, No. 1 (Spring 1996).

———. "Ethnic Conflict as a Pathology of the State: A New Conceptual Approach." Institute for the Study of Diplomacy, Edmund A. Walsh School of Foreign Service, Georgetown University, and the Fund for Peace, Washington, DC, 1996.

Baldwin, David. "The Power of Positive Sanctions." *World Politics* 24, No. 1 (October 1971).

Ball, Nicole. "The Challenge of Rebuilding War-Torn Societies." In *Managing Global Chaos: Sources of and Responses to International Conflict*, eds. Chester A. Crocker and Fen Osler Hampson, with Pamela Aall. Washington, DC: United States Institute of Peace Press, 1996.

Bandura, A. *Aggression: A Social Learning Analysis*. Englewood Cliffs, NJ: Prentice-Hall, 1973.

Banks, Arthur S., Alan J. Day, and Thomas C. Muller, eds. *Political Handbook of the World: 1997*. Binghamton, NY: CSA Publications, 1997.

Barkey, Henri, and Graham Fuller. *Turkey's Kurdish Question*. Lanham, MD: Rowman & Littlefield, 1998.

BBC International Press Office. "BBC Brings 'Democracy' to Russians." November 30, 1994.

Becker, Elizabeth. "A U.N. Success Story." *New York Times*, April 28, 1995.

Bedford, Eleanor. "Site Visit to Eastern Congo/Zaire: Analysis of Humanitarian and Political Issues." *USCR Site Visit Notes*. Washington, DC: U.S. Committee for Refugees, 1997.

Berger, Suzanne, and Ronald Dore, eds. *National Diversity and Global Capitalism*. Ithaca, NY: Cornell University Press, 1996.

Beschloss, Michael, and Strobe Talbott. *At the Highest Levels: The Inside Story of the End of the Cold War*. Boston: Little, Brown and Company, 1993.

Bialer, Seweryn. "The Changing Soviet Political System: The Nineteenth Party Conference and After." In *Politics, Society and Nationality Inside Gorbachev's Russia*, ed. Seweryn Bialer. Boulder, CO: Westview Press, 1989.

Bissell, Richard E. "The Resource Dimension of International Conflict." In *Managing Global Chaos: Sources of and Responses to International Conflict*, eds. Chester A. Crocker and Fen Osler Hampson, with Pamela Aall. Washington, DC: United States Institute of Peace Press, 1996.

de la Blaze, Felipe A.M. *Remaking the Argentine Economy*. New York: Council on Foreign Relations Press, 1995.

Blustein, Paul. "A Loan Amid the Ruins." *Washington Post*, February 13, 1996.

Boudreau, Thomas E. *Sheathing the Sword: The U.N. Secretary-General and the Prevention of International Conflict*. New York: Greenwood Press, 1991.

Boutros-Ghali, Boutros. "Leadership and Conflict." In *Essays on Leadership*. Washington, DC: Carnegie Commission on Preventing Deadly Conflict, December 1998.

————. "Challenges of Preventive Diplomacy: The Role of the United Nations and Its Secretary-General." In *Preventive Diplomacy: Stopping Wars Before They Start*, ed. Kevin M. Cahill. New York: Basic Books, 1996.

————. *An Agenda for Development*. New York: United Nations, 1995.

Bremer, Stuart. "Democracy and Militarized Interstate Conflict, 1816-1965." *International Interactions* 18, No. 3 (1993).

————. "Dangerous Dyads: Conditions Affecting the Likelihood of Interstate War, 1816-1965." *Journal of Conflict Resolution* 36, No. 2 (June 1992).

Brewer, M., and R. Kramer. "The Psychology of Intergroup Attitudes and Behavior." *Annual Review of Psychology* 36 (1985).

British American Security Information Council (BASIC). "Chronicling an Absence of Restraint: The 1995 UN Arms Register." *Basic Papers*, No. 13, November 3, 1995.

————, and Arias Foundation for Peace and Human Progress. "The International Code of Conduct on Arms Transfers: Fact Sheet." May 1997.

Brown, Lester R. "The Acceleration of History." In *State of the World 1996*, ed. Linda Starke. New York: W.W. Norton & Company, 1996.

Brown, Michael E., ed. *The International Dimensions of Internal Conflict*. Cambridge, MA: MIT Press, 1996.

Brown, Michael E., Sean M. Lynn-Jones, and Steven E. Miller, eds. *Debating the Democratic Peace*. Cambridge, MA: MIT Press, 1996.

Brown, Michael E., and Richard N. Rosecrance, eds. *The Costs of Conflict: Prevention and Cure in the Global Arena*. Lanham, MD: Roman & Littlefield, 1999.

Burton, John. *Conflict: Resolution and Prevention*. New York, NY: St. Martin's Press, 1990.

Bush, George. "American Leadership and the Prevention of Deadly Conflict." In *Essays on Leadership*. Washington, DC: Carnegie Commission on Preventing Deadly Conflict, December 1998.

————. "Address to the Nation on the Situation In Somalia." *Public Papers of the Presidents of the United States: George Bush 1992-1993*. Washington, DC: U.S. Government Printing Office, 1993.

Byman, Daniel, and Stephen Van Evera. "Contemporary Deadly Conflict: Causes and Future Prospects." Paper prepared for the Carnegie Commission on Preventing Deadly Conflict, Washington, DC.

Campbell, D.T. "Ethnocentric and Other Altruistic Motives." In *Nebraska Symposium on Motivation*, ed. D.T. Campbell. Lincoln: University of Nebraska Press, 1965.

Canberra Commission on the Elimination of Nuclear Weapons. *Report of the Canberra Commission on the Elimination of Nuclear Weapons*. August 1996.
CARE International. *CARE International Report 1995 and 1996*. Brussels: CARE International, 1996.

Carroll, James. "The Silence." *The New Yorker*, April 7, 1997.

Carter, Jimmy. "Searching for Peace." In *Essays on Leadership*. Washington, DC: Carnegie Commission on Preventing Deadly Conflict, December 1998.

———. "Get Tough on Rights." *New York Times*, September 21, 1993.

Carter Center. *State of World Conflict Report, 1994-1995*. Atlanta, GA: The Carter Center, 1995.

Casper, Gretchen, and Michelle M. Taylor. *Negotiating Democracy: Transitions from Authoritarian Rule*. Pittsburgh, PA: University of Pittsburgh Press, 1996.

Center for Human Rights. *National Human Rights Institutions: A Handbook on the Establishment and Strengthening of National Institutions for the Promotion and Protection of Human Rights*, Professional Training Series No. 4. Geneva: United Nations, 1995.

Ceric, Mustafa, Vinko Puljic, Nikolaj Mrdja, and Jakob Finci. "Press Release, Inter-Religious Council in Bosnia-Herzegovina." Sarajevo, June 9, 1997.

Cerniello, Craig. "U.S. Security Assistance to the Former Soviet Union." *Arms Control Today* (September 1996).

Chayes, Abram, and Antonia Handler Chayes, eds. *Preventing Deadly Conflict in the Post-Communist World: Mobilizing International and Regional Organizations*. Washington, DC: The Brookings Institution, 1996.

Chazan, Naomi, and Donald Rothchild. "The Political Repercussions of Economic Malaise." In *Hemmed In: Responses to Africa's Economic Decline*, eds. Thomas M. Callaghy and John Ravenhill. New York: Columbia University Press, 1993.

Chigas, Diana, with Elizabeth McClintock and Christophe Kamp. "Preventive Diplomacy and the Organization for Security and Cooperation in Europe: Creating Incentives for Dialogue and Cooperation." In *Preventing Conflict in the Post-Communist World*, eds. Abram Chayes and Antonia Handler Chayes. Washington, DC: The Brookings Institution, 1996.

"Chile: Decree Establishing the National Commission on Truth and Reconciliation." In *Transitional Justice:*

How Emerging Democracies Reckon with Former Regimes, Vol. 1, ed. Neil J. Kritz. Washington, DC: U.S. Institute of Peace Press, 1995.

Cohen, Herman J. "Intervention In Somalia." *The Diplomatic Record 1992-1993*. Boulder, CO: Westview Press, 1991.

Cohen, William S. *Annual Defense Review*. Washington, DC: U.S. Government Printing Office, 1997.

———. *The Report to the Quadrennial Defense Review*. Washington, DC: U.S. Government Printing Office, 1997.

Collins, Joseph. "World Hunger: A Scarcity of Food or a Scarcity of Democracy." In *World Security: Challenges for a New Century*, eds. Michael T. Klare and Daniel C. Thomas. New York: St. Martin's Press, 1994.

Committee for the 1995 World Conference for Women. "Worldwide Facts and Statistics about the Status of Women." New York: Committee for the 1995 World Conference for Women, 1995.

Commission on Developing Countries and Global Change. *For Earth's Sake*. Ottawa: International Development Research Center, 1992.

Commission on Global Governance. *Our Global Neighborhood*. New York: Oxford University Press, 1995.

Committee on International Arms Control and Security Affairs of the Association of the Bar of the City of New York. *Achieving Effective Arms Control: Recommendations, Background and Analysis*. The Association of the Bar of the City of New York, 1985.

Comprehensive Disclosure of Fissionable Materials: A Suggested Initiative. Washington, DC: Carnegie Commission on Preventing Deadly Conflict, June 1995.

Conference on Security and Cooperation in Europe. "Charter of Paris for a New Europe." Conference on Security and Cooperation In Europe. November 2, 1991. 30 I.L.M. 193 (1991).

Congressional Budget Office. *Enhancing U.S. Security Through Foreign Aid.* Washington, DC: Congressional Budget Office, 1994.

"Convention on the Prohibition of the Development, Production, Stockpiling and Use of Chemical Weapons and on their Destruction." April 29, 1997. 32 I.L.M. 932 (1993).

"Convention on the Prohibition of the Development, Production, and Stockpiling of Bacteriological (Biological) and Toxin Weapons and on Their Destruction." March, 26, 1975. T.I.A.S. no. 9433.

Cortright, David, ed. *The Price of Peace: Incentives and International Conflict Prevention.* Lanham, MD: Rowman & Littlefield, 1997.

de Costa, Peter. "Combining Against Conflict." *Africa Report* 37, No. 5 (September-October 1992).

Country Reports on Human Rights Practices for 1996 — Report Submitted to the Committee on Foreign Relations, U.S. Senate and the Committee on International Relations, U.S. House of Representatives. Washington, DC: U.S. Government Printing Office, 1997.

Cranna, Michael, ed. *The True Cost of Conflict.* New York: The New Press, 1994.

Crossette, Barbara. "Agencies Say U.N. Ignored Pleas on Hutu." *New York Times,* May 28, 1997.

———. "After Weeks of Seeming Inaction, U.S. Decides to Punish Belgrade." *New York Times,* May 23, 1992.

Crumm, Eileen M. "The Value of Economic Incentives in International Politics." *Journal of Peace Research* 32, No. 3 (1995).

Cumming-Bruce, Nick. "Malaysia Buys into Military Build-Up." *The Guardian* (London), October 23, 1996.

Dahl, Robert A. *Democracy and Its Critics.* New Haven, CT: Yale University Press, 1989.

Daley, Suzanne. "In Mozambique, Guns for Plowshares and Bicycles." *New York Times,* March 2, 1997.

Damrosch, Lori Fisler. "The Civilian Impact of Economic Sanctions." In *Enforcing Restraint: Collective Intervention In Internal Conflicts,* ed. Lori Fisler Damrosch. New York: Council on Foreign Relations Press, 1993.

Darling, Juanita. "Salvadoran Gun Swap Nets Quite an Arsenal." *San Jose Mercury News,* October 6, 1996.

———. "Gun-Swap Project Overwhelmed by Response In War-Weary Land." *Los Angeles Times,* October 5, 1996.

"Declaration on the Prohibition of Chemical Weapons." 28 I.L.M. 1020 (1989).

Deng, Francis M. *Protecting the Dispossessed: A Challenge for the International Community.* Washington, DC: The Brookings Institution, 1993.

——— and I. William Zartman, eds. *Conflict Resolution in Africa.* Washington, DC: The Brookings Institution, 1991.

Denton, Nicholas. "Hungary Acts on Borders." *The Financial Times,* July 15, 1994.

Deutsch, M. *The Resolution of Conflict.* New Haven, CT: Yale University Press, 1973.

Diamond, Larry. *Promoting Democracy in the 1990s: Actors and Instruments, Issues and Imperatives.* Washington, DC: Carnegie Commission on Preventing Deadly Conflict, December 1995.

Diamond, Louise, and John McDonald. *Multi-Track Diplomacy: A Systems Approach to Peace.* Hartford, CT: Kumarian Press, Inc., 1996.

Doyle, Michael W. *UN Peacekeeping in Cambodia: UNTAC's Civil Mandate.* Boulder, CO: Lynne Rienner Publishers, 1995.

———. "Kant, Liberal Legacies, and Foreign Affairs." *Philosophy and Public Affairs* 12 (Summer 1983).

Durch, William J., ed. *The Evolution of UN Peacekeeping: Case Studies and Comparative Analysis.* New York: St. Martin's Press, 1993.

Eken, Sena, Paul Cashin, S. Nuri Erbas, Jose Martelino, and Adnan Mazarei. *Economic Dislocation and Recovery in Lebanon*, Occasional Paper 120. International Monetary Fund, Washington, DC, February 1995.

Eliasson, Jan. "Establishing Trust in the Healer: Preventive Diplomacy and the Future of the United Nations." In *Preventive Diplomacy: Stopping Wars Before They Start*, ed. Kevin M. Cahill. New York: Basic Books and The Center for International Health and Cooperation, 1996.

Elliott, Kimberly Ann, and Gary Hufbauer. "'New' Approaches to Economic Sanctions." In *U.S. Intervention Policy for the Post-Cold War World*, eds. Arnold Kanter and Linton F. Brooks. New York: W.W. Norton & Company, 1994.

Energy and Atmosphere Program, Sustainable Energy and Environment Division, Bureau for Policy and Program Support, United Nations Development Program. "UNDP Initiative for Sustainable Energy, 1996." United Nations Development Program, New York, 1996.

Eriksson, John, Howard Adelman, John Borton, Hanne Christensen, Krishna Kumar, Astri Suhrke, David Tardif-Douglin, Stein Villumstad, and Lennart Wohlgemuth. *Synthesis Report.* The International Response to Conflict and Genocide: Lessons from the Rwanda Experience. Copenhagen: Steering Committee of the Joint Evaluation of Emergency Assistance to Rwanda, March 1996.

Esman, Milton J. "Economic Performance and Ethnic Conflict." In *Conflict and Peacemaking in Multiethnic Societies*, ed. Joseph V. Montville. New York: Lexington Books, 1991.

Esty, Daniel C., Jack A. Goldstone, Ted Robert Gurr, Pamela T. Surko, and Alan N. Unger. *Working Papers: State Failure Task Force Report.* November 30, 1995.

European Conference on Conflict Prevention. "From Early Warning to Early Action," A Report on the European Conference on Conflict Prevention. Amsterdam: European Conference on Conflict Prevention, 1996.

European Information Service. "Human Rights: European Parliament Seeks Reform of EU Policy." *European Report*, December 14, 1996.

European Information Service. "Human Rights: EU Needs to Put Teeth into Policy." *European Report*, December 7, 1996.

Evans, Gareth. "The UN at Fifty: Looking Back and Looking Forward." Statement to the Fiftieth General Assembly of the United Nations, New York, October 2, 1995.

———. "Cooperative Security and Intrastate Conflict." *Foreign Policy,* No. 96 (Fall 1994).

———. *Cooperating for Peace: The Global Agenda for the 1990s and Beyond.* Sydney, Australia: Allen & Unwin, 1993.

Fainberg, Anthony, and Alan Shaw. *Nonlethal Technologies and the Prevention of Deadly Conflict.* Washington, DC: Carnegie Commission on Preventing Deadly Conflict, forthcoming.

Federation Internationale des Droits de l'Homme, Africa Watch, Union Interafricaine des Droits de l'Homme et des Peuples, Center International des Droits de la Personne et du Développement Democratique. "Rapport de la Commission Internationale d'Enquete sur les Violations des Droits de l'Homme au Rwanda Depuis le 1er Octobre 1990." New York: Africa Watch, 1993.

Feil, Scott. *Preventing Genocide: How the Early Use of Force Might Have Succeeded in Rwanda.* Washington, DC: Carnegie Commission on Preventing Deadly Conflict, April 1998.

————. "Could 5,000 Peacekeepers Have Saved 500,000 Rwandans? Early Intervention Reconsidered." *ISD Reports* III, No. 2, Institute for the Study of Diplomacy, Georgetown University, Washington, DC, April 1997.

Feinberg, Richard. "The Coup That Wasn't." *Washington Post,* April 30, 1996.

Feldman, Shai, and Abdullah Toukan. *Bridging the Gap: A Future Security Architecture for the Middle East.* Lanham, MD: Rowman & Littlefield, 1997.

"Final Document of the First Conference to Review the Operation of the Treaty on Conventional Armed Forces in Europe and the Concluding Act of the Negotiation on Personnel Strength." Vienna. May 15-31, 1996.

Findlay, Trevor. *Cambodia: The Legacy and Lessons of UNTAC,* SIPRI Research Report No. 9. New York: Oxford University Press, 1995.

Franck, Thomas M., and Georg Nolte. "The Good Offices Function of the UN Secretary-General." In *The UN and International Security after the Cold War: The UN's Roles in International Relations,* eds. A. Roberts and B. Kingsbury. Oxford: Clarendon Press, 1993.

Frederikson, Lee. "The Internet or Infomercial: Which Will Turn Your Audience On?" *Marketing News,* January 20, 1997.

French, Howard W. "A Muscular Nigeria Proves a Flawed Peacekeeper." *New York Times,* June 26, 1997.

————. "Sierra Leone a Triumph of Peacemaking by Africans." *New York Times,* December 2, 1996.

Gallhofer, Irmtraud N., and Willem E. Saris. *Foreign Policy Decision-Making.* Westport, CT: Praeger, 1996.

Gamson, William, and André Modigliani. *Untangling the Cold War.* Boston, MA: Little Brown & Company, 1971.

Gardner, Gary. "Preserving Global Crop Land." In *State of the World 1997,* ed. Linda Starke. Washington: Worldwatch Institute, 1997.

Garten, Jeffrey E. *The Big Ten: The Big Emerging Markets and How They Will Change Our Lives.* New York: Basic Books, 1997.

George, Alexander L. *Presidential Decisionmaking in Foreign Policy: The Effective Use of Information and Advice.* Boulder, CO: Westview Press, 1980.

————, and Jane E. Holl. *The Warning-Response Problem and Missed Opportunities in Preventive Diplomacy.* Washington, DC: Carnegie Commission on Preventing Deadly Conflict, May 1997.

Gjelten, Tom. *Professionalism in War Reporting: A Correspondent's View.* Washington, DC: Carnegie Commission on Preventing Deadly Conflict, June 1998.

Gillies, David. "Human Rights, Democracy and Good Governance: Stretching the World Bank's Policy Frontiers." In *The World Bank: Lending on a Global Scale,* eds. J.M. Griesgraber and B.G. Gunter. London: Pluto Press, 1996.

Gilpin, Robert. *War and Change in World Politics.* New York: Cambridge University Press, 1981.

Goldring, Natalie J. "Bridging the Gap: Light and Major Conventional Weapons in Recent Conflicts." British American Security Information Council (BASIC), Washington, DC, 1997; paper prepared for the annual meeting of the International Studies Association, Toronto, Ontario, March 1997.

Goodpaster, Andrew J. *When Diplomacy Is Not Enough: Managing Multinational Military Interventions.* Washington, DC: Carnegie Commission on Preventing Deadly Conflict, July 1996.

Gorbachev, Mikhail. *Memoirs*. New York: Doubleday, 1996.

————. "On Nonviolent Leadership." In *Essays on Leadership*. Washington, DC: Carnegie Commission on Preventing Deadly Conflict, December 1998.

————. *Perestroika: New Thinking for Our Country and the World*. New York: Harper and Row, 1987.

Gordon, Michael R. "U.S. Sends Forces as Iraqi Soldiers Threaten Kuwait." *New York Times*, October 8, 1994.

————. "Bush Backs a Ban on Combat Flights in Bosnia Airspace." *New York Times*, October 2, 1992.

Government of Canada. "Towards a Rapid Reaction Capability for the United Nations." Report of the Government of Canada, September 1995.

Gowing, Nik. *Media Coverage: Help or Hindrance in Conflict Prevention*. Washington, DC: Carnegie Commission on Preventing Deadly Conflict, September 1997.

Greenberg, Melanie, John H. Barton, and Margaret McGuinness, eds. *Mediation and Arbitration to Prevent Deadly Conflict*. Lanham, MD: Rowman & Littlefield, forthcoming.

Greene, Owen. *Tackling Light Weapons Proliferation: Issues and Priorities for the EU*. London: Saferworld, 1997.

Grimmett, Richard F. "Conventional Arms Transfers to Developing Nations, 1989-1996." Washington, DC: Congressional Research Service, The Library of Congress, August 17, 1997.

Grobel, J., and R. Hinde. *Aggression and War: Their Biological and Social Bases*. Cambridge: Cambridge University Press, 1989.

Gruhn, Isebill V. "Banning Land Mines." In *IGCC Policy Brief*. Institute on Global Conflict and Cooperation, March, 1996.

Gurr, Ted Robert. *Minorities at Risk: A Geopolitical View of Ethnopolitical Conflicts*. Washington, DC: U.S. Institute of Peace Press, 1993.

Hamburg, David A. *Education for Conflict Resolution*. April 1995. New York: Carnegie Corporation of New York, April 1994.

————. *Preventing Contemporary Intergroup Violence*. New York: Carnegie Corporation of New York, April 1994.

————. "An Evolutionary Perspective on Human Aggression." In *The Development and Integration of Behavior: Essays in Honor of Robert Hinds*, ed. P. Bateson. Cambridge: Cambridge University Press, 1991.

Hamilton, Lee, Gareth Evans, Lord Carver, and Stanley Hoffmann. "A UN Volunteer Military Force — Four Views." *New York Review of Books*, June 24, 1993.

Harahan, Joseph P., and John C. Kuhn, III. *On-Site Inspections Under the CFE Treaty*. Washington, DC: On-Site Inspection Agency, U.S. Department of Defense, 1996.

Hawley, W.D., and A.W. Jackson, eds. *Toward a Common Destiny: Improving Race and Ethnic Relations in America*. San Francisco, CA: Jossey-Bass Publishers, 1995.

Hayner, Priscilla B. "Fifteen Truth Commissions— 1974 to 1994: A Comparative Study." In *Transitional Justice: How Emerging Democracies Reckon with Former Regimes,* Vol. 1, ed. Neil J. Kritz. Washington, DC: U.S. Institute of Peace Press, 1995.

Hays, Margaret Daly, and Gary F. Weatley, eds. *Interagency and Political-Military Dimensions of Peace Operations: Haiti—A Case Study*. Washington, DC: National Defense University Press, February 1996.

Hehir, Bryan. "The Uses of Force in the Post-Cold War World." Washington, DC: Woodrow Wilson International Center for Scholars, August 1996.

Heininger, Janet E. *Peacekeeping in Transition: The United Nations in Cambodia.* New York: Twentieth Century Fund Press, 1994.

Helms, Jesse. "Saving the U.N." *Foreign Affairs* 75, No. 5 (September/October 1996).

"Helsinki Final Act." Conference on Security and Cooperation in Europe. August 1, 1975. 14 I.L.M. 1292 (1975).

Henkin, Louis, Righard Crawford Pugh, Oscar Schachter, and Hans Smit. *International Law: Cases and Materials,* 3rd ed. St. Paul, MN: West Publishing Company, 1993.

Hinds, Joe. *A Guide to Peace, Reconciliation and Community Relations Projects in Ireland.* Belfast, Northern Ireland: Community Relations Council, 1994.

Hoffman, Bruce, and Paul Wilkinson. *A Violent Trajectory: How Terrorist Campaigns Evolve into Insurgencies and Their Implications.* Washington, DC: Carnegie Commission on Preventing Deadly Conflict, forthcoming.

Holtje, James. *Divided It Stands: Can the United Nations Work?* Atlanta, GA: Turner Publishing, Inc., 1995.

Homer-Dixon, Thomas F. "Environmental Scarcities and Violent Conflict: Evidence from Cases." *International Security* 19, No. 1 (Summer 1994).

———, and Valerie Percival. *Environmental Scarcity and Violent Conflict: Briefing Book.* Toronto: University of Toronto Press, 1996.

Horowitz, Donald. "Democracy In Divided Societies." *Journal of Democracy* 4, No. 4. (1993).

———. "Comparing Democratic Systems." *Journal of Democracy* 1, No. 4 (1990).

———. "Making Moderation Pay." In *Conflict and Peacemaking in Multiethnic Societies,* ed. Joseph V. Montville. Lexington, MA: Lexington Books, 1990.

———. *Ethnic Groups in Conflict.* Berkeley: University of California Press, 1985.

Humanitarian Aid and Effects. The International Response to Conflict and Genocide: Lessons from the Rwanda Experience, Study 3. Copenhagen: Steering Committee on the Joint Evaluation of Emergency Assistance to Rwanda, March 1996.

Human Rights Watch. *Human Rights Watch World Report 1996.* Washington, DC: Human Rights Watch, 1996.

Hume, Mark. "U.S. Advantage in Salmon Wars." *Montreal Gazette,* May 29, 1997.

Hume, Cameron. *Ending Mozambique's War: The Role of Mediation and Good Offices.* Washington, DC: U.S. Institute of Peace Press, 1994.

InterAction. *PVO Standards.* Washington, DC: InterAction, 1995, amended May 1, 1996.

International Alert Annual Report 1994. London: International Alert, 1995.

International Committee of the Red Cross. *The Fundamental Principles of the Red Cross and Red Crescent Movement.* http://www.icrc.org.

International Federation of the Red Cross. *About the International Federation.* http://www.ifrc.org.

International Federation of Red Cross and Red Crescent Societies. *Code of Conduct for The International Red Cross and Red Crescent Movement and NGOs in Disaster Relief.* http://www.ifrc.org.

International Institute for Strategic Studies. *The Military Balance 1996/97.* London: Oxford University Press, October 1996.

International Monetary Fund. *International Financial Statistics Yearbook.* Washington, DC: International Monetary Fund, 1997.

Ismail, Razali. "Paper by the Chairman of the Open-Ended Working Group on the Question of Equitable Representation on and Increase in the Membership of the Security Council and Other Matters Related to the Security Council." Submitted to the UN General Assembly by the Malaysian ambassador to the United Nations as President of the UN General Assembly, New York, March 20, 1997.

Janis, Irving L. *Crucial Decisions: Leadership in Policymaking and Crisis Management.* New York: The Free Press, 1989.

Jean, Francois, ed. *Populations in Danger 1995.* London: Médecins Sans Frontières, 1995.

Jentleson, Bruce, ed. *Opportunities Missed, Opportunities Seized: Preventive Diplomacy in the Post–Cold War World.* Lanham, MD: Rowman & Littlefield, forthcoming.

Jongman, Berto. "War and Political Violence." In *Jaarboek Vrede en Veilegheid* (Yearbook Peace and Security). Nijmegen: Dutch Peace Research Center, 1996.

Kaplan, Roger. *Freedom in the World.* New York: Freedom House, 1996.

Katz, Mark. "Collapsed Empires." In *Managing Global Chaos,* ed. Chester A. Crocker and Fen Osler Hampson, with Pamela Aall. Washington, DC: U.S. Institute of Peace Press, 1996.

Kaufman, Daniel J. "The Role of the Military in Preventing Deadly Conflict." In *Preventing Deadly Conflict: Strategies and Institutions,* Proceedings of a Conference in Moscow, Russian Federation, eds. Gail W. Lapidus with Svetlana Tsalik. Washington, DC: Carnegie Commission on Preventing Deadly Conflict, April 1998.

Kaysen, Carl, and George Rathjens. *Peace Operations by the United Nations: The Case for a Volunteer UN Military Force.* Cambridge, MA: Committee on International Security Studies, American Academy of Arts and Sciences, 1996.

Kelleher, Catherine McArdle. "Security in the New Order: Presidents, Polls, and the Use of Force." In *Beyond the Beltway: Engaging the Public in U.S. Foreign Policy,* eds. Daniel Yankelovich and I.M. Destler. New York: W.W. Norton & Company, 1994.

Kelsen, Hans. *Vol. I. General Theory of Law and State.* 20th Century Legal Philosophy Series, Vol. 1. trans. Anders Wedberg. Cambridge, MA: Harvard University Press, 1949.

Kennan, George F. *Realities of American Foreign Policy.* Princeton, NJ: Princeton University Press, 1954.

Kennedy, Donald M. *Environmental Quality and Regional Conflict.* Washington, DC: Carnegie Commission on Preventing Deadly Conflict, December 1998.

Kissinger, Henry A. *A World Restored.* New York: Grosset and Dunlap, 1964.

Krasno, Jean. "The Group of Friends of the Secretary-General: A Useful Diplomatic Tool." Paper prepared for the Carnegie Commission on Preventing Deadly Conflict, Washington, DC, December 1996 (available at www.ccpdc.org).

Kritz, Neil J., ed. *Transitional Justice.* Washington, DC: U.S. Institute of Peace Press, 1995.

Kull, Steven. "What the Public Knows That Washington Doesn't." *Foreign Policy* 101 (Winter 1995-1996).

———, and I.M. Destler. *An Emerging Consensus: A Study of American Public Attitudes on America's Role in the World: Summary of Findings.* College Park, MD: Program on International Policy Attitudes, Center for International and Security Studies at Maryland, 1996.

Küng, Hans, ed. *Yes to a Global Ethic.* New York: Continuum, 1996.

Lake, Anthony. *After The Wars: Reconstruction in Afghanistan, Indochina, Central America, Southern Africa, and the Horn of Africa.* New Brunswick, NJ: Transaction Publishers, 1990.

Lake, David A., and Donald Rothchild. "Ethnic Fears and Global Engagement: The International Spread and Management of Ethnic Conflict," Policy Paper #20. Institute on Global Conflict and Cooperation, San Diego, CA, January 1996.

Lapidus, Gail W., with Svetlana Tsalik, eds. *Preventing Deadly Conflict: Strategies and Institutions*. Proceedings of a Conference in Moscow, Russian Federation. Washington, DC: Carnegie Commission on Preventing Deadly Conflict, April 1998.

Laurance, Edward J. *Light Weapons and Intrastate Conflict: Early Warning Factors and Preventive Action*. Washington, DC: Carnegie Commission on Preventing Deadly Conflict, July 1998.

———. "The UN Register of Conventional Arms: Rationales and Prospects for Compliance and Effectiveness." *Washington Quarterly* 16, No. 2 (Spring 1993).

———. "Surplus Weapons and the Disarmament Process." Presented at the United Nations Centre for Disarmament Affairs Workshop on Micro-Disarmament "A New Agenda for Disarmament and Arms Control," Monterey Institute of International Studies, November 8, 1995.

———. "U.S. Sanctions Spur Outcry; Corporate America Presses Case Against Increasing Curbs on Other Nations." *Journal of Commerce*, May 21, 1997.

"Legality of the Threat or Use of Nuclear Weapons." Advisory Opinion, International Court of Justice, General List No. 95. July 8, 1996.

Lehman, Edward W. *The Viable Polity*. Philadelphia, PA: Temple University Press, 1992.

de León, Francisco Villagrán. "Thwarting the Guatemalan Coup." *Journal of Democracy* 4, No. 4, October 1993.

Leurdijk, Dick A., ed. *A UN Rapid Deployment Brigade: Strengthening the Capacity for Quick*

Response. The Hague: Netherlands Institute of International Relations *Clingendael*, 1995.

———, ed. "The Netherlands Non-Paper. A UN Rapid Deployment Brigade: A Preliminary Study. Revised April 1995." In *A UN Rapid Deployment Brigade: Strengthening the Capacity for Quick Response*. The Hague: Netherlands Institute of International Relations *Clingendael*, 1995.

Levine, Alicia. "Political Accommodation and the Prevention of Secessionist Violence." In *The International Dimensions of International Conflict*, ed. Michael E. Brown. Cambridge, MA: MIT Press, 1996.

Levy, Jack S. "Prospect Theory and International Relations: Theoretical Applications and Analytical Problems." In *Avoiding Losses/Taking Risks: Prospect Theory and International Conflict*, ed. Barbara Farnham. Ann Arbor, MI: University of Michigan Press, 1994.

Lewis, Paul. "United Nations Is Finding its Plate Increasingly Full But its Cupboard Is Bare." *New York Times*, September 27, 1993.

Lijphart, Arend. *Democracy in Plural Societies*. New Haven, CT: Yale University Press, 1977.

———. *Power-Sharing in South Africa*, Policy Papers in International Affairs 24. Berkeley, CA: Institute of International Studies, University of California-Berkeley, 1985.

Livingstone, Neil C., and Joseph D. Douglass, Jr. *CBW: The Poor Man's Atomic Bomb*. Cambridge, MA: Institute for Foreign Policy Analysis, 1984.

Lockwood, Dunbar. "The Nunn-Lugar Program: No Time to Pull the Plug." *Arms Control Today* (June 1995).

Long, William J. *Economic Incentives and Bilateral Cooperation*. Ann Arbor, MI: University of Michigan Press, 1996.

Lord, Carnes. *The Presidency and the Management of National Security.* New York: Free Press, 1988.

Lund, Michael. *Preventing Violent Conflicts: A Strategy for Preventive Diplomacy.* Washington, DC: U.S. Institute of Peace Press, 1996.

Lute, Douglas E. *Improving National Capacity to Respond to Complex Emergencies: The U.S. Experience.* Washington, DC: Carnegie Commission on Preventing Deadly Conflict, April 1998.

Machel, Graça. *Impact of Armed Conflict on Children.* New York: UN Department of Public Information, 1996.

Mansfield, Edward D. "Democratization and the Danger of War." *International Security* 20, No. 1 (Summer 1995).

Maresca, John J. "The International Community and the Conflict over Nagorno-Karabakh." In *Opportunities Missed, Opportunities Seized: Preventive Diplomacy in the Post–Cold War World*, ed. Bruce Jentleson. Lanham, MD: Rowman & Littlefield, forthcoming.

Martin, William F., Ryukichi Imai, and Helga Steeg. *Maintaining Energy Security in a Global Context,* The Triangle Papers 48. New York: The Trilateral Commission, September 1996.

Martínez, Javier, and Alvaro Díaz. *Chile: The Great Transformation.* Washington, DC: The Brookings Institution; and Geneva: United Nations Research Institute for Social Development, 1996.

Mathews, Jessica T. "Power Shift." *Foreign Affairs* 76, No. 1 (January/February 1997).

Matlock, Jack F., Jr. *Autopsy on an Empire: The American Ambassador's Account of the Collapse of the Soviet Union.* New York: Random House, 1995.

Matthews, Robert O., Arthur G. Rubinoff, and Janice Gross Stein, eds. *International Conflict and Conflict Management: Readings in World Politics.* Scarborough, Ontario: Prentice-Hall Canada, 1989.

McCleary, Rachel M. "Guatemala's Postwar Prospects." *Journal of Democracy* 8, No. 2, April 1997.

McDonald, John W., Jr., and Diane B. Bendahmane, eds. *Conflict Resolution: Track Two Diplomacy.* Washington, DC: U.S. Government Printing Office, 1987.

Médecins Sans Frontières. *Médecins Sans Frontières Activity Report, July 95-July 96.* Brussels, 1996.

de Mesquita, Bruce Bueno, and David Lalman. *War and Reason: Domestic and International Imperatives.* New Haven, CT: Yale University Press, 1992.

Michel, James H. *Development Co-operation.* Development Assistance Committee 1995 Report, Organization for Economic Cooperation and Development (OECD), 1996.

Minear, Larry, and Thomas G. Weiss. *Mercy Under Fire: War and the Global Humanitarian Community.* Boulder, CO: Westview, 1995.

Ministry of Foreign Affairs. *Free and Fair Elections and Beyond.* Stockholm, 1994.

Monga, Vipal. "Daley Expresses Doubts on a Quick Resolution of Pacific Salmon Dispute." *Journal of Commerce*, August 7, 1997.

Montville, Joseph V., ed. *Conflict and Peacemaking in Multiethnic Societies.* Lexington, MA: Lexington Books, 1990.

Moodie, Michael L. "Chemical and Biological Weapons: The Unfinished Agenda." Chemical and Biological Arms Control Institute, May 27, 1997.

Morgenthau, Hans J. *Politics Among Nations.* New York: Knopf, 1948.

Muscat, Robert J. "Conflict and Reconstruction: Roles for the World Bank." Draft manuscript, Washington, DC, 1995.

Nanda, Ved. "U.S. Wise to Join Land-Mine Ban Talks." *Denver Post*, August 29, 1997.

"Nerve Gas Attack on Tokyo Subway Kills 10; Police Raid Religious Sect's Offices, Seize Chemicals." *Facts on File: World News Digest with Index* 55, No. 2834. March 23, 1995.

Newman, Frank, and David Weissbrodt. *International Human Rights: Law, Policy and Process*, 2nd ed. Cincinnati, OH: Anderson Publishing Co., 1996.

Nickerson, Colin. "In Quebec, Tribes Talk of Leaving; Indians, Inuit Claim Land Rights." *Boston Globe*, October 13, 1995.

Nolan, Janne E., John D. Steinbruner, Kenneth Flamm, Steven E. Miller, David Mussington, William J. Perry, and Ashton B. Carter. "The Imperatives for Cooperation." In *Global Engagement: Cooperation and Security in the 21st Century*, ed. Janne E. Nolan. Washington, DC: The Brookings Institution, 1994.

Notter, James, and Louise Diamond. *Building Peace and Transforming Conflict: Multi-Track Diplomacy in Practice*. Washington, DC: Institute for Multi-Track Diplomacy, 1996.

Notter, James, and John McDonald. "Track Two Diplomacy: Nongovernmental Strategies for Peace." In *American Perspectives on Conflict Resolution*, Electronic Journals of the U.S. Information Agency, Vol. 1, No. 19, December 1996. http://www.usia.gov/journals/journals.htm.

Oakley, Robert B., Michael J. Dziedzic, and Eliot M. Goldberg, eds. *Policing the New World Disorder*. Washington, DC: National Defense University, 1998.

Oakley, Robert B., and Michael J. Dziedzic. "Policing the New World Disorder," *Strategic Forum*, No. 84 (October 1996).

Oakley, Robert B., McGeorge Bundy, Sadruddin Aga Khan, Olusegun Obasanjo, and Marion Dönhoff. "A UN Volunteer Force: The Prospects." *New York Review of Books*, July 15, 1993.

"OAS Starts Probe of Guatemala Leader's Use of Emergency Rule." *Chicago Tribune*, May 31, 1993.

Office for Democratic Institutions and Human Rights, Organization for Security and Cooperation in Europe. *OSCE ODIHR Annual Report for 1996*. Warsaw: OSCE, 1996.

Ogata, Sadako. "World Order, Internal Conflict and Refugees." Address at Harvard University, October 28, 1996.

Ohlsson, Leif, ed. *Case Studies of Regional Conflicts and Conflict Resolution*. Gothenburg, Sweden: Padrigu Papers, 1989.

"Open Wounds in Rwanda." *New York Times*, April 25, 1995.

Organization for the Prohibition of Chemical Weapons. *The OPCW Home Page*. http://www.opcw.nl/.

Organization for Security and Cooperation in Europe. *Vade Mecum: An Introduction to the OSCE*. Berne: Organization for Security and Cooperation in Europe, May 1996.

———. *OSCE Provisions Related to the Office for Democratic Institutions and Human Rights (ODIHR)*. Warsaw: Organization for Security and Cooperation in Europe, 1995.

Organization of African Unity. "African Charter on Human and Peoples' Rights." Organization of African Unity Doc. CAB/LEG/67/3 Rev. 5.

Ottaway, Marina. *South Africa*. Washington, DC: The Brookings Institution, 1993.

Ottaway, David. *Chained Together: Mandela, de Klerk, and the Struggle to Remake South Africa*. New York: Times Books, 1993.

Otunnu, Olara. "The Peace-and-Security Agenda of the United Nations: From a Crossroads into the Next Century." In *Peacemaking and Peacekeeping for the Next Century*, report of the 25th Vienna Seminar cosponsored by the Government of Austria and International Peace Academy, March 2-4, 1995. New York: International Peace Academy, 1995.

Owen, David. *Balkan Odyssey*. London: Victor Gollancz, 1995.

Patchen, Martin. *Resolving Disputes between Nations: Coercion or Conciliation?* Durham, NC: Duke University Press, 1988.

"Peace-Keeping Saves Lives." *Washington Post*, February 16, 1995.

Pearson, Frederic. "The UN and Regional Organizations in the Control of Conventional Arms Transfers." Paper presented at the Center for Defense Information conference, "Conventional Arms Transfer Restraint in the 1990's," Washington, DC, November 16, 1994.

Peck, Connie. *Sustainable Peace: The Role of the UN and Regional Organizations in Preventing Conflict*. Lanham, MD: Rowman & Littlefield, 1998.

Perry, William J. Speech at the Aspen Institute Congressional Program conference, "US Relations with Russia," Dresden, Germany, August 20, 1997.

————. *Report of the Secretary of Defense to the President and the Congress*. Washington, DC: U.S. Government Printing Office, 1996.

Pfaltzgraff, Robert L., Jr., and Jacquelyn K. Davis. *National Security Decisions: The Participants Speak*. Lexington, MA: Lexington Books, 1990.

Picco, Giandomenico. "The UN and the Use of Force: Leave the Secretary General Out of It." *Foreign Affairs* 73, No. 5 (September/October 1994).

Pinder, John. "Community against Conflict: The European Community's Contribution to Ethno-National Peace in Europe." In *Preventing Conflict in the Post-Communist World: Mobilizing International and Regional Organizations*, eds. Abram Chayes and Antonia Handler Chayes. Washington, DC: The Brookings Institution, 1996.

Porter, Jack Nusan. *Conflict and Conflict Resolution: A Historical Bibliography*. New York: Garland Publishing, 1982.

Porter, Gareth. "Environmental Security as a National Security Issue." *Current History* 94, No. 592 (May 1995).

"'Prime Evil' de Kock Names Ex-President Botha, Cabinet Ministers, Police Generals in 'Dirty War.'" *Southern Africa Report* 14, No. 38 (September 20, 1996).

"Protocol for the Prohibition of the Use in War of Asphyxiating, Poisonous or Other Gases, and of Bacteriological Methods of Warfare." February 8, 1928. T.I.A.S. no. 9433.

Pruitt, Dean G., and Jeffrey Z. Rubin. *Social Conflict: Escalation, Stalemate, and Settlement*. New York: Random House, 1986.

"Pugwash Conferences Win 1995 Peace Prize." Associated Press, October 13, 1995.

Purver, Ron. "The Threat of Chemical and Biological Terrorism." *The Monitor 3*, No. 2 (Spring 1997).

Quinn, Gregory. "The Iraq Conflict." In *The True Cost of Conflict*, ed. Michael Cranna. New York: New Press, 1994.

Ramazani, R.K. *International Straits of the World: The Persian Gulf and the Strait of Hormuz*. Alphen aan den Rijn, The Netherlands: 1979.

Ramphele, Mamphela, and Francis Wilson. *Uprooting Poverty: The South African Challenge*. Report for the

Second Carnegie Inquiry into Poverty and Development in Southern Africa. New York: W.W. Norton and Co., 1989.

Rauf, Tariq, James Lamson, Shawna McCartney, and Sarah Meek. *Inventory of International Nonproliferation Organizations and Regimes*, 1996-1997 ed. Monterey: Center for Nonproliferation Studies, Monterey Institute of International Studies, 1997.

Ray, James Lee. *Democracy and International Conflict: An Evaluation of the Democratic Peace Proposition.* Columbia, SC: University of South Carolina Press, 1995.

Raymond, Gregory A. *Conflict Resolution and the Structure of the State System: An Analysis of Arbitrative Settlements.* Montclair, NJ: Allanheld, Osmun & Co., 1980.

"Rebels Told to Give Up In West Africa." *New York Times*, June 5, 1997.

Rebuilding Post-War Rwanda. The International Response to Conflict and Genocide: Lessons from the Rwanda Experience, Study 4. Copenhagen: Steering Committee of the Joint Evaluation of Emergency Assistance to Rwanda, March 1996.

Reed, Jack. "De Klerk Lifts ANC Ban, Says Mandela Will be Freed Soon." United Press International, February 2, 1990.

Renner, Michael. *Fighting for Survival.* New York: W.W. Norton & Co., 1996.

Rhodes, E. "Do Bureaucratic Politics Matter?" *World Politics* 47 (October 1994).

Roberts, Adam. *Civil Resistance in the East European and Soviet Revolutions.* The Albert Einstein Institution, Monograph Series Number 4. Cambridge, MA: The Albert Einstein Institution, 1991.

Rogers, Elizabeth. *Using Economic Sanctions to Prevent Deadly Conflict.* Discussion Paper 96-02. Center for Science and International Affairs, Harvard University, 1996.

Rotberg, Robert I. "Conclusions: NGOs, Early Warning, Early Action, and Preventive Diplomacy." In *Vigilance and Vengeance: NGOs Preventing Ethnic Conflict in Divided Societies*, ed. Robert I. Rotberg. Washington, DC: The Brookings Institution; Cambridge, MA: World Peace Foundation, 1996.

"Rotblat: First Nuclear Protester." Reuters Information Service, October 13, 1995.

Rothchild, Donald. "Conclusion: Management of Conflict in West Africa." In *Governance as Conflict Management: Politics and Violence in West Africa*, ed. I. William Zartman. Washington, DC: The Brookings Institution, 1997.

Rummel, Reinhardt. "Common Foreign and Security Policy and Conflict Prevention." London: International Alert and Saferworld, May 1996.

Rummel, R. J. *Death by Government.* New Brunswick, NJ: Transaction Publishers, 1994.

———. "Libertarian Propositions on Violence within and between Nations: A Test against Published Results." *Journal of Conflict Resolution* 29, No. 3 (September 1985).

———. "Libertarianism and Interstate Violence." *Journal of Conflict Resolution* 27, No. 1 (March 1983).

———. *Understanding Conflict and War: Vols. 1-5.* Los Angeles: Sage, 1975-81.

Rupesinghe, Kumar. "Multi-Track Diplomacy and the Sustainable Route to Conflict Resolution." *Cultural Survival Quarterly* (Fall 1995).

Russett, Bruce. *Grasping the Democratic Peace: Principles for a Post–Cold War World.* Princeton: Princeton University Press, 1993.

"Rwanda: UN Commander Says More Troops May Have Saved Lives." Inter Press Service, September 7, 1994.

Sagan, Scott. "The Perils of Proliferation." *International Security* 18 (Spring 1994).

Sagasti, Francisco. *Promoting Development for Prevention.* Washington, DC: Carnegie Commission on Preventing Deadly Conflict, forthcoming.

Salamon, Lester M. "The Rise of the Nonprofit Sector." *Foreign Affairs* 73, No. 4 (July/August 1994).

Sanderson, John M. "The Humanitarian Response in Cambodia: The Imperative for a Strategic Alliance." In *After Rwanda: The Coordination of United Nations Humanitarian Assistance*, eds. Jim Whitman and David Pocock. New York: St. Martin's Press, 1996.

———. "Preparation for Deployment and Conduct of Peacekeeping Operations: A Cambodia Snapshot." In *Peacekeeping at the Crossroads*, eds. Kevin Clements and Christine Wilson. Canberra: Australian National University, 1994.

Schear, James A. "Riding the Tiger: The UN and Cambodia." In *UN Peacekeeping, American Policy, and the Uncivil Wars of the 1990s*, ed. William J. Durch. New York: St. Martin's Press, 1996.

Schmitter, Philippe C., and Terry Lynn Karl. "What Democracy Is...And Is Not." In *The Global Resurgence of Democracy*, 2nd ed., eds. Larry Diamond and Marc F. Plattner. Baltimore: Johns Hopkins University Press, 1996.

Sciolino, Elaine. "U.S. May Seek the Use of Force to Stop Serbs' Flights Over Bosnia." *New York Times*, December 2, 1992.

"Self-Determination versus Pre-Determination of Ethnic Minorities in Power-Sharing Systems." In *The Rights of Minority Cultures*, ed. Will Kymlichka. Oxford: Oxford University Press, 1995.

Sen, Amartya. "Freedoms and Needs: An Argument for the Primacy of Political Rights." *New Republic*, January 10 -17, 1994.

"Serbs Again Block Supplies in Bosnia." *New York Times*, December 8, 1993.

Sierra Leone Web. *Sierra Leone Web—Sierra Leone Archives.* http://www.sierra-leone.org.

"Sierra Leone: Peace, perhaps." *The Economist* December 7, 1996.

"Sierra Leone Signs Pact to End 5-year Civil War." *Baltimore Sun*, December 1, 1996.

Sisk, Timothy D. *Power Sharing and International Mediation in Ethnic Conflicts.* Washington, DC: U.S. Institute of Peace Press and Carnegie Commission on Preventing Deadly Conflict, 1996.

———. *Democratization in South Africa: The Elusive Social Contract.* Princeton, NJ: Princeton University Press, 1995.

Sivard, Ruth Leger. *World Military and Social Expenditures 1996.* Washington, DC: World Priorities, 1996.

Smillie, Ian. *The Alms Bazaar.* Ottawa: International Development Research Centre, 1995.

———, and Ian Filewod. "Norway." In *Non-Governmental Organisations and Governments: Stakeholders for Development*, eds. Ian Smillie and Henny Helmich. Paris: Organization for Security and Cooperation in Europe, 1994.

Smuts, B., D. Cheney, et al. *Primate Societies.* Chicago: University of Chicago Press, 1986.

Snyder, Scott. "North Korea's Nuclear Program: The Role of Incentives in Preventing Deadly Conflict." In *The Price of Peace: Incentives and International Conflict Prevention*, ed. David Cortright. Lanham, MD: Rowman & Littlefield, 1997.

Sparks, Allister. *Tomorrow Is Another Country.* New York: Hill and Wang, 1995.

Spector, Leonard S., and Jonathan Dean. "Cooperative Security: Assessing the Tools of the Trade." In *Global*

Engagement: Cooperation and Security in the 21st Century, ed. Janne E. Nolan. Washington, DC: The Brookings Institution, 1994.

Spielmann, Peter James. "U.N. Chief Considers Reconvening Peace Talks on Bosnia." Associated Press, May 28, 1993.

Stalker, Peter, ed. *States of Disarray: The Social Effects of Globalization*. London: United Nations Research Institute for Social Development, 1995.

Staub, E. *The Roots of Evil: The Origins of Genocide and Other Group Violence*. Cambridge: Cambridge University Press, 1989.

Steele, David. "East Germany's Churches Give Sanctuary and Succor to the Purveyors of Change." In *Religion, The Missing Dimension of Statecraft*, eds. Douglas Johnston and Cynthia Sampson. New York: Oxford University Press, 1994.

Stein, Melanie H. "Conflict Prevention in Transition Economies: A Role for the European Bank for Reconstruction and Development?" In *Preventing Conflict in the Post-Communist World: Mobilizing International and Regional Organizations*, eds. Abram Chayes and Antonia Handler Chayes. Washington, DC: The Brookings Institution, 1996.

Steinbruner, John D. "Reluctant Strategic Realignment: The Need for a New View of National Security." *The Brookings Review* (Winter 1995).

Steiner, Henry J., ed. *Truth Commissions: A Comparative Assessment*, World Peace Foundation Report #16. Cambridge: World Peace Foundation, 1997.

Stockholm International Peace Research Institute. *SIPRI Yearbook 1991-1997: Armaments, Disarmament and International Security*. New York: Oxford University Press, 1991-1997.

Stremlau, John. *People in Peril: Human Rights, Humanitarian Action, and Preventing Deadly Conflict*. Washington, DC: Carnegie Commission on Preventing Deadly Conflict, May 1998.

————. *Sharpening International Sanctions: Toward a Stronger Role for the United Nations*. Washington, DC: Carnegie Commission on Preventing Deadly Conflict, November 1996.

————. "Dateline Bangalore: Third World Technopolis." *Foreign Policy*, No. 102 (Spring 1996).

————, and Francisco Sagasti. *Preventing Deadly Conflict: Does the World Bank Have a Role?* Washington, DC: Carnegie Commission on Preventing Deadly Conflict, June 1998.

————, with Helen Zille. *A House No Longer Divided: Progress and Prospects for Democratic Peace in South Africa*. Washington, DC: Carnegie Commission on Preventing Deadly Conflict, July 1997.

Suhrke, Astri, and Bruce Jones. "Preventive Diplomacy in Rwanda: Failure to Act, or Failure of Actions?" In *Opportunities Missed, Opportunities Seized: Preventive Diplomacy in the Post–Cold War World*, ed. Bruce Jentleson. Lanham, MD: Rowman & Littlefield, forthcoming.

Swedish Ministry for Foreign Affairs. *Preventing Violent Conflict: A Study*. Stockholm: Ministry of Foreign Affairs, 1997.

Task Force on Peace and Security, United Nations Association of the USA, National Capital Area. "A Global Treaty for Reducing Conventional Arms and Armed Conflict." Washington, DC, February 28, 1997.

Thakur, Ramesh, ed. *International Conflict Resolution*. Boulder, CO: Westview Press, 1988.

"The Future of U.S. Nuclear Weapons Policy." Committee on International Security and Arms Control, National Academy of Sciences. Washington, DC: National Academy Press, 1997.

The Newsletter of the International IDEA, No. 7, April 1997, No. 2, October 1995, and No. 1, March 1995.

"The Philanthropy 400." *The Chronicle of Philanthropy 4*, No. 2 (October 31, 1996).

The United Nations and Nuclear Non-Proliferation. New York: United Nations, 1995.

Timberbaev, Roland M., and Meggen M. Watt. *Inventory of International Nonproliferation Organizations and Regimes—1995 Edition.* Monterey, CA: Center for Nonproliferation Studies, Monterey Institute of International Studies, 1995.

"Treaty on Conventional Armed Forces in Europe." Article XXI.

Turner, Craig. "Canada's Diplomacy Coup Amazes U.S.; Ottawa's Land Mines Fight Mixed Skill and Determination." *Toronto Star*, August 31, 1997.

Tutu, Desmond. "Building a Democracy in South Africa." *Washington Post*, August 19, 1996.

———. "Leadership." In *Essays on Leadership.* Washington, DC: Carnegie Commission on Preventing Deadly Conflict, December 1998.

Tyler, Patrick E. "China Warns U.S. to Keep Away from Taiwan Strait." *New York Times*, March 18, 1996.

United Nations. *Questions & Answers about the United Nations — Chapter Six/Who Works at the UN and What They Do There.* http://www.un.org/geninfo/ir/toc_fr.

———. "Setting the Record Straight: Some Facts About the United Nations." United Nations, March 1997 Update, DPI/1753/Rev.12.

———. *The United Nations and the Iraq-Kuwait Conflict 1990-1996.* New York: United Nations, 1996.

———. *The Blue Helmets: A Review of United Nations Peace-keeping.* New York: United Nations Department of Public Information, 1990 and 1996.

———. "Platform for Action." *The Beijing Declaration and the Platform for Action.* New York: United Nations Department of Public Information, 1996.

———. *Universal Declaration of Human Rights*, DPI/876. New York: United Nations Department of Public Information, 1988, 1995.

———. *Assistance in Mine Clearance: Report of the Secretary-General*, Document A/49/357. United Nations, New York, September 6, 1994 .

———. "General and Complete Disarmament, Part L: Transparency in Armaments." A/RES/46/36L, December 6, 1991, in *General Assembly Official Records: 46th Session, Supplement No. 49* (A/46/49).

———. *Women, the Information Revolution and the Beijing Conference.* http://www.un.org/dpcsd/daw/.

United Nations Children's Fund. *State of the World's Children 1996.* New York: Oxford University Press, 1996.

United Nations Conference on Straddling Fish Stocks and Highly Migratory Fish Stocks. "Agreement for the Implementation of the Provisions of the United Nations Convention on the Law of the Sea of 10 December 1982 Relating to the Conservation and Management of Straddling Fish Stocks and Highly Migratory Fish Stocks." United Nations, September 8, 1995, A/CONF.164/37 (1995).

United Nations Department for Economic and Social Information and Policy Analysis. *World Population Prospects: The 1996 Revision.* New York: United Nations Department for Economic and Social Information and Policy Analysis, Population Division, 1997.

United Nations Department of Humanitarian Affairs. Donor Humanitarian Assistance Database—*Total Humanitarian Assistance in 1996 (Global) as of 1 January 1997.* http://www.reliefweb.int.

United Nations Development Programme. *Human Development Report.* New York: Oxford University Press, 1995, 1996, and 1997.

United Nations Division for Ocean Affairs and the Law of the Sea. *Oceans and Law of the Sea.* http://www.un.org/depts/los/.

———. *Oceans and Law of the Sea—Convention on the Law of the Sea.* http://www.un.org/depts/los/.

United Nations Educational, Scientific and Cultural Organization. *Towards a Culture of Peace.* http://www.unesco.org/cpp/uk/leaflet/unesco.

———. "A Culture of Peace and Nonviolence within Educational Institutions: Elements for the Launching of an Interregional Project." Draft paper prepared November 23, 1995.

United Nations Food and Agriculture Organization. *FAOSTAT Statistics Database: Agriculture Data — Production: Crops Primary.* http://www.fao.org.

United Nations High Commissioner for Refugees. "Report of the United Nations High Commissioner for Refugees." Economic and Social Council, E/1996/52, United Nations, New York, May 13, 1996.

———. *The State of the World's Refugees 1995: In Search of Solutions.* Oxford: Oxford University Press, 1995.

United Nations High Commissioner for Refugees and International Peace Academy. *Healing the Wounds: Refugees, Reconstruction, and Reconciliation.* Report of the Second Conference Sponsored Jointly by the United Nations High Commissioner for Refugees and the International Peace Academy, June 30-July 1, 1996.

United Nations High Commissioner for Refugees, International Organization for Migration, and Organization for Security and Cooperation in Europe. *Report of the Regional Conference to Address the Problems of Refugees, Displaced Persons, Other Forms of Involuntary Displacement and Returnees in the Countries of the Commonwealth of Independent States and Relevant Neighboring States.* Geneva, May 30-31, 1996.

United Nations Security Council Resolution 795 (1992) adopted on December 11, 1992 (authorizes the secretary-general to establish a presence of UNPROFOR in the Former Yugoslav Republic of Macedonia).

United States Army War College. *Success in Peacekeeping, United Nations Mission in Haiti: The Military Perspective.* Carlisle Barracks, PA: U.S. Army Peacekeeping Institute, 1996.

United States Committee for Refugees. *World Refugee Survey 1997.* Washington, DC: Immigration and Refugee Services of America, 1997.

United States Department of Defense. *Cooperative Threat Reduction.* Washington, DC, April 1995.

United States Department of State, Bureau of Political-Military Affairs. *Hidden Killers: The Global Landmine Crisis.* Washington, DC: Office of International Security and Peacekeeping Operations, 1994.

United States Government Accounting Office. *Weapons of Mass Destruction, Status of the Cooperative Threat Reduction Program.* Report to Congressional Requestors. September 1996.

United States Mission to the United Nations. *Global Humanitarian Emergencies, 1996.* New York: United States Mission to the United Nations, 1996.

United States Senate Subcommittee on Coalition Defense and Reinforcing Forces. *International Peacekeeping and Peace Enforcement.* 103rd Congress, 1st sess. July 14, 1993.

Urquhart, Brian. "The Role of the Secretary-General." In *U.S. Foreign Policy and the United Nations System,* eds. Charles William Maynes and Richard S. Williamson. New York: W.W. Norton & Co., 1996.

———. "The Higher Education of Ralph Bunche." *Journal of Black Higher Education* (Summer 1994).

———. "If the United Nations Is for Real, Give It a Police Force." *International Herald Tribune,* May 23, 1994.

———. "Whose Fight Is It?" *New York Times,* May 22, 1994.

———. "Who Can Police the World?" *New York Review of Books*, May 12, 1994.

———. "For a UN Volunteer Military Force." *New York Review of Books*, June 10, 1993.

———. *Ralph Bunche: An American Life*. New York: W.W. Norton & Co., 1993.

USA*Engage. *USA*Engage Homepage*. http://usaengage.org. Updated September 18, 1997.

Van der Donckt, Charles. "Looking Forward by Looking Back: A Pragmatic Look at Conflict and the Regional Option." Policy Staff Paper No. 95/01. Canadian Department of Foreign Affairs and International Trade, September 1995.

Vance, Cyrus R., and David A. Hamburg, *Pathfinders for Peace: A Report to the UN Secretary-General on the Role of Special Representatives and Personal Envoys*. Washington, DC: Carnegie Commission on Preventing Deadly Conflict, September 1997.

Vance, Cyrus R., and Herbert Okun. "Creating Healthy Alliances: Leadership and Coordination among NGOs, Governments and the United Nations." In *Preventive Diplomacy: Stopping Wars Before They Start*, ed. Kevin M. Cahill. New York: Basic Books, 1996.

Vogel, Frederick J. *The Chemical Weapons Convention: Strategic Implications for the United States*. Strategic Studies Institute, U.S. Army War College, Washington, DC, 1997.

Voice of America. *Conflict Resolution Project Annual Report*. Washington, DC: Voice of America, 1997.

Waldmeir, Patti. *Anatomy of a Miracle: The End of Apartheid and the Birth of the New South Africa*. New York: W.W. Norton & Co., 1997.

Waltz, Kenneth N. *Theory of International Politics*. Reading, MA: Addison-Wesley, 1979.

"Wassenaar Members Review Data Exchange." *Arms Control Today*, Vol. 27, No. 3 (May 1997).

Watkins, Kevin. *The Oxfam Poverty Report*. Oxford: Oxfam UK & Ireland, 1995.

Wedgwood, Ruth. "Regional and Subregional Organizations in International Conflict Management." In *Managing Global Chaos: Sources of and Responses to International Conflict*, eds. Chester A. Crocker and Fen Osler Hampson, with Pamela Aall. Washington, DC: U.S. Institute of Peace Press, 1996.

———. "Macedonia: A Victory for Quiet Diplomacy." *Christian Science Monitor*, October 19, 1995.

Weiss, Thomas G., and Cindy Collins. "Operational Dilemmas and Challenges." In *Humanitarian Challenges and Intervention*, eds. Thomas G. Weiss and Cindy Collins. Boulder, CO: Westview Press, 1996.

Weiss, Thomas G., and Leon Gordenker, eds. *NGOs, the UN, and Global Governance*. Boulder, CO: Lynne Rienner, 1996.

Welch, D.A. "The Organizational Process and Bureaucratic Politics Paradigms: Retrospect and Prospect." *International Security* 17 (Fall 1992).

White House. *Fact Sheet: Banning Anti-Personnel Landmines*. White House Office of the Press Secretary, May 16, 1997.

———. "The Clinton Administration's Policy on Reforming Multilateral Peace Operations." Presidential Decision Directive 25, Washington, DC, The White House, 1994.

Wilenski, Peter. "The Structure of the UN in the Post-Cold War Period." In *United Nations, Divided World: The UN's Roles in International Relations*, eds. Adam Roberts and Benedict Kingsbury. Oxford: Clarendon Press, 1993.

Wolfensohn, James D. "Address to the Board of Governors of the World Bank Group." Washington, DC, October 1995.

Wooster, Henry. "Faith at the Ramparts: The Philippine Catholic Church and the 1986 Revolution." In *Religion, The Missing Dimension of Statecraft*, eds. Douglas Johnston and Cynthia Sampson. New York: Oxford University Press, 1994.

World Bank. "Bosnia and Herzegovina: Priority Reconstruction Projects Update." World Bank, September 1996.

————. *World Bank Annual Report, 1996*. Washington, DC: World Bank, 1996.

————. *Global Economic Prospects and the Developing Countries*. Washington, DC: World Bank, 1995.

————. *The World Bank Group—Countries and Regions*. http://www.worldbank.org.

World Commission on Environment and Development. *Our Common Future*. Oxford: Oxford University Press, 1987.

World Resources Institute, United Nations Environment Program, United Nations Development Program, and World Bank. *World Resources 1996-97*. New York: Oxford University Press, 1996.

World Trade Organization. "Charter of the World Trade Organization. Annex 2: Understanding On Rules And Procedures Governing The Settlement Of Disputes." January 1, 1995. 33 I.L.M. 1143-53, 1224-47 (1994).

————. *Overview of the State-of-Play of WTO Disputes*. http://www.wto.org/dispute/bulletin.

Worsnip, Patrick. "Talks on Stability Fan Old Enmities." *The Independent*, May 28, 1994.

Yankelovich, Daniel, and John Immerwahr. "The Rules of Public Engagement." In *Beyond the Beltway: Engaging the Public in U.S. Foreign Policy*, eds. Daniel Yankelovich and I.M. Destler. New York: W.W. Norton & Co., 1994.

Zartman, I. William, ed. *Negotiating to Prevent Escalation and Violence*. Lanham, MD: Rowman & Littlefield, forthcoming.

————, ed. *Governance as Conflict Management: Politics and Violence in West Africa*. Washington, DC: The Brookings Institution, 1997.

————, ed. *Collapsed States: The Disintegration and Restoration of Legitimate Authority*. Boulder, CO: Lynne Rienner, 1995.

————, ed. *Elusive Peace: Negotiating an End to Civil Wars*. Washington, DC: The Brookings Institution, 1995.

————, and Saadia Touval. "International Mediation in the Post–Cold War Era." In *Managing Global Chaos: Sources of and Responses to International Conflict*, eds. Chester A. Crocker and Fen Osler Hampson, with Pamela Aall. Washington, DC: U.S. Institute of Peace Press, 1996.

————, and Katharina R. Vogeli. "Prevention Gained and Prevention Lost: Collapse, Competition, and Coup in Congo." In *Opportunities Missed, Opportunities Seized: Preventive Diplomacy in the Post–Cold War World*, ed. Bruce Jentleson. Lanham, MD: Rowman & Littlefield, forthcoming.

Zelikow, Philip, and Condoleezza Rice. *Germany Unified and Europe Transformed: A Study in Statecraft*. Cambridge, MA: Harvard University Press, 1995.

COCOM. *See* Coordinating Committee on
    Multilateral Export Controls
Code of Conduct. *See* International Code of Conduct
    on Arms Transfers
Cold War, xiv, 3, 11, 21, 25-27, 29, 61, 74, 79, 91,
    101, 119, 122, 129, 145, 146, 158, 181, 208
Collective Measures Committee. *See* United Nations
    Collective Measures Committee
collective security, 91, 93, 129, 130, 164, 172
Colombia, 12, 124, 143, 174
COMESCA. *See* Community for Eastern and
    Southern Africa
Commission on Global Governance, 135, 136, 140,
    183, 184
Commission on Radio and Television Policy, 216
Committee on International Security and Arms
    Control. *See* National Academy of Sciences
Common System of Accounting and Control of
    Nuclear Materials. *See* Argentinean-Brazilian
    Agency for Accounting and Control of Nuclear
    Materials
Commonwealth of Independent States (CIS), 41, 42,
    167
Community for Eastern and Southern Africa
    (COMESCA), 201
Community of Sant'Egidio, 116
complacency, xiii, 11, 13, 22, 165
complex emergencies, 21, 109, 112, 113, 139, 180,
    200
Comprehensive Test Ban Treaty (CTBT), 71, 108, 167
conditionality, 52, 57
Conference on Security and Cooperation in Europe
    (CSCE), 90, 148, 167, 168, 170. *See also*
    Organization for Security and Cooperation in
    Europe.
confidence building, 77, 81, 149, 172, 173, 207, 208,
    212
conflict, xi-xiv, 195, 196, 198, 202, 204, 205, 208,
    212-214
    causes of, 11, 25-30, 84, 101, 144
    cost of, 9, 19
    emerging, xiii, xv, 125
    interstate, xiii, 26, 27
    intrastate, 26-28, 60, 81, 84, 92, 93, 106, 136
    management of, 153
    maritime, 60, 61

regional, 89, 139, 171, 172
    resolution of, 25, 51, 93, 106, 113, 119, 120, 122,
        152-155, 170, 180, 202, 205, 213, 214
    role of outsiders, 39, 41, 45, 136
    violent, xiii, 3, 8, 19, 20, 25-30, 35, 43, 62, 63,
        77, 84, 93, 105, 106, 125, 162
conflict resolution. *See* conflict, resolution of
Congo. *See* Republic of Congo, Democratic Republic
    of Congo
Congress of South African Trade Unions, 110, 212
constituency, 163-165
constituency building, 165
constructive engagement, 134, 212
Convention Against Torture and Other Cruel,
    Inhuman, or Degrading Treatment or Punishment,
    132
Convention on Consent to Marriage, Minimum Age
    for Marriage, and Registration of Marriages, 132
Convention on the Elimination of All Forms of
    Discrimination Against Women, 132
Convention on the Nationality of Married Women,
    132
Convention on the Non-Applicability of Statutory
    Limitations to War Crimes and Crimes Against
    Humanity, 132
Convention on the Political Rights of Women, 132
Convention on the Prevention and Punishment of the
    Crime of Genocide, 4, 132
Convention on the Reduction of Statelessness, 132
Convention on the Rights of the Child, 132
Convention on the Rights of Migrant Workers and the
    Members of Their Families, 132
Convention Relating to the Status of Refugees, 132
Convention Relating to the Status of Stateless Persons,
    132
Conventional Armed Forces in Europe Treaty. *See*
    Treaty on Conventional Armed Forces in Europe
conventional weapons. *See* weapons, conventional
cooperation, 11, 22, 36, 37, 54-58, 109, 119, 129, 149,
    155, 194, 202, 212
    government-NGO, 109
    international, 54, 193
    regional, 145, 162
Cooperative for Assistance and Relief Everywhere
    (CARE), xii, 21, 42, 112, 113, 167
cooperative security, 164, 184

Nigeria, 12, 27, 61, 107, 124, 143, 171, 172, 175

Nobel Peace Prize, 33, 119, 169

Non-Proliferation Treaty (NPT), 58, 73, 74, 168, 215

Nonaligned Movement (NAM), 168, 173

nongovernmental organizations (NGOs), 20, 21, 40-42, 45-47, 49, 50, 97, 108, 109, 111-114, 137, 141, 151, 155, 172, 200, 213, 214

nonviolent resistance, 117, 126, 127

NORDEM. *See* Norwegian Resource Bank for Democracy and Human Rights

NOREPS. *See* Norwegian Emergency Preparedness System

norms, xiii, 63, 69, 82, 90, 92, 94, 105, 106, 113, 118, 139, 159, 162, 169

North American Free Trade Agreement (NAFTA), 59, 147, 167

North Atlantic Alliance, 81

North Atlantic Council, 80

North Atlantic Treaty Organization (NATO), 5, 77-81, 147, 164, 167-169, 171, 201, 208, 212, 219
    Coordinating Committee on Multilateral Export Controls (COCOM), 77, 167

North Korea. *See* Democratic People's Republic of Korea

Northern Ireland, 8, 114, 214

Norway, 48, 64, 66, 96, 108, 139, 175, 207

Norwegian Emergency Preparedness System (NOREPS), 109, 168

Norwegian Resource Bank for Democracy and Human Rights (NORDEM), 109, 168

NP. *See* National Party

NPT. *See* Non-Proliferation Treaty

nuclear proliferation, 19, 57, 70

nuclear weapons. *See* weapons, nuclear

Nunn-Lugar program. *See* Soviet Nuclear Threat Reduction Act

OAS. *See* Organization of American States

OAU. *See* Organization of African Unity

ODIHR. *See* Office for Democratic Institutions and Human Rights

OECD. *See* Organization for Economic Cooperation and Development

Office for Democratic Institutions and Human Rights (ODIHR), 148, 168. *See also* Organization for Security and Cooperation in Europe

Ogata, Sadako, 131, 137

OIC. *See* Organization of the Islamic Conference

Oil Producing and Exporting Countries (OPEC), 201

Operation Desert Storm, 20

operational prevention, xv, 37, 39, 40, 43, 64, 161. *See also* prevention.

Organization for Economic Cooperation and Development (OECD), 20, 168, 194, 200

Organization for Security and Cooperation in Europe (OSCE, formerly CSCE), 41, 50, 78, 81, 93, 147-149, 168, 170, 199, 201, 219

Organization of African Unity (OAU), 5, 39, 147, 167, 168, 170, 196, 198, 201, 196, 198, 201, 219
    Mechanism for Conflict Prevention, Management and Resolution (MCPMR), 166, 167, 170

Organization of American States (OAS), 39, 92, 147, 168-170, 198, 201, 219

Organization of the Islamic Conference (OIC), 147, 149, 168, 201

organizations, 21, 32, 33, 35, 51, 108, 110, 113, 114, 119, 130, 153, 163, 169-172, 195, 201, 205, 208, 212, 213
    civic, 110
    dialogue, 37, 53, 69, 78, 129, 130, 172-173
    economic, 94, 147, 171
    intergovernmental, 53, 105, 109, 113, 114
    international, 4, 9, 37, 41, 44, 49, 50, 56, 82, 102, 105, 108, 127, 133
    multilateral, 164
    regional, 47, 50, 59, 62, 81, 90, 137, 146-149, 151, 207, 210
    security, 147, 169

Oslo agreements, 51

Owen, David, 64, 202

Oxford Committee for Famine Relief (Oxfam), 42, 111-113, 168, 213

Pakistan, 22, 26, 27, 124, 143, 152, 174-177, 207, 212

Palestine, 63, 112, 168

Panama, 176

Papua New Guinea, 15

Paraguay, 147, 170, 172

Paris, 203, 219

Parliament of the World's Religions, 214

participatory governance, 90, 94, 95

Partnership for Peace (PFP), 80, 81, 168, 169, 208, 212

peace building, 137, 144

religious institutions. *See* institutions, religious

repression, 29, 31, 95, 97, 115, 127

Republic of Congo, 12, 39, 61, 124, 143, 174, 177, 198, 200

Republic of Korea (ROK), 27, 58

resources, xi, 200, 214

    depletion of, 27, 87

    scarce, 15

response, xiii

    early, 40, 43, 133

    international, 21, 42, 138

    multilateral, 63

responsibility,

    international, 135, 164

    of states, 105

    of the United Nations, 136

    to act, 105

Revolutionary United Front (RUF), 106, 168

Richardson, William, 142

Rio Group, 207

risk factors, xi, xiii

rivalries, 27

rogue states. *See* states, rogue

role of outsiders in exacerbating conflict. *See* conflict, role of outsiders

Roman Catholic Church, 115

Romania, 53, 171, 176, 205, 208

root causes, 69, 137, 151, 170

RPF. *See* Rwandan Patriotic Front

RUF. *See* Revolutionary United Front

rule of law, 37, 65, 90, 94, 100, 105, 116, 172, 196, 204

Russia, 18, 25, 28, 34, 72, 73, 75, 76, 89, 101, 123, 124, 207, 208

Russian Federation, 22, 53, 143, 176

Rwanda, xiv, 3-6, 11, 12, 21, 29, 39, 41, 43, 45, 47, 48, 61, 63, 95, 121, 122, 124, 129, 133, 146, 192, 198, 200

Rwandan Patriotic Front (RPF), 4, 45, 168

SAARC. *See* South Asian Association for Regional Cooperation

SADC. *See* Southern African Development Community

SADCC. *See* Southern African Development Coordination Conference

safe drinking water, 15

safe havens, 28, 131

Sahara, 63, 134, 170

SAM. *See* Sanctions Assistance Monitoring Teams

sanctions, 37, 40, 52-59, 64, 77, 121, 125, 131, 134, 139, 172, 202, 203

    economic, 32, 54-56, 202, 203

    international, 32, 126, 202, 203

    regimes, 52-55

    unilateral, 203

Sanctions Assistance Monitoring Teams (SAM), 53, 168

Santiago Commitment, 169

Saudi Arabia, 22, 75, 143, 176

Save the Children Federation (SCF), 112

SCCC. *See* Common System of Accounting and Control of Nuclear Materials

science and technology, 82, 86, 139, 155, 173

scientific community, xiii, 118, 119, 125

security, 37, 60-65, 69, 70, 74, 78-82, 87, 91, 100, 124, 156, 157, 162, 164, 165, 169-171, 181, 212, 217, 220, 221

    international, 60, 136, 207, 212, 215, 218, 219, 220

    national, 87, 93, 220

    regional, 147, 180

Security Council. *See* United Nations Security Council

Senegal, 61, 170, 176, 206

Serbia, 27, 64, 80

Serrano, Jorge, 39, 198

Sierra Leone, 12, 15, 107, 121, 124, 171, 173, 176

Singapore, 176, 219

Slavery Convention of 1926, 132

Slovakia, 53, 171, 197, 205, 208

small arms, 75, 77, 78

social justice, 83, 98, 115, 123, 165, 213

solidarity, 28, 118, 125, 127

South Africa, 12, 16, 29-33, 78, 81, 95, 96, 98, 110, 111, 117, 124, 126, 143, 158, 172, 197, 212

South Asia. *See* Asia

South Asian Association for Regional Cooperation (SAARC), 168, 173, 201

South China Sea, 60

South Korea. *See* Republic of Korea

Southeast Asia. *See* Asia